The Tate Gallery 1978–80

The Tate Gallery 1978–80

Illustrated Catalogue of Acquisitions

Contents

Cover illustration
Wassily Kandinsky, Swinging, 1925
Acquisition No. T.2344

ISBN 0 905005 82 1
Published by order of the Trustees 1981

Designed and published by the Tate Gallery Publications Department,
Millbank, London SW1P 4RG
Printed and bound in Great Britain by William Clowes (Beccles) Limited, Beccles and London

Foreword

This illustrated catalogue of acquisitions has been published as a supplement to the Biennial Report. Like the Report, it covers the period April 1978–March 1980 and shows once again how much the Gallery owes to the generosity of those who have given works or made funds available.

The Friends of the Tate made substantial contributions towards the purchase of two major modern paintings, "Dynamic Suprematism" by Kasimir Malevich and "Clarinet and Bottle of Rum on a Mantelpiece" by Georges Braque, and an important group of sixteenth and seventeenth century portraits (hitherto on loan to the Gallery), from Mr Loel Guinness. The National Art-Collections Fund and the Pilgrim Trust also made generous contributions towards the latter purchase. During the two-year period, Mr Henry Moore presented a magnificent group of thirty-six of his sculptures to mark his eightieth birthday, and Mr Paul Mellon provided the basis for a representative collection of sporting art by presenting thirty works from his own collection. In April 1978 Gainsborough's "Sir Benjamin Truman" was finally secured for the nation, with the aid of public and private donations.

The British Collection

ABBREVIATION

Egerton, 1978 Judy Egerton, *British Sporting and Animal Paintings 1655–1867: The Paul Mellon Collection,* 1978. By kind permission of Mr Paul Mellon, entries for paintings formerly in his collection and presented by him to the Tate Gallery in 1979 are largely based on this catalogue.

Jacques-Laurent Agasse 1767–1849

T.2350 **Two Hunters with a Groom** *c.*1805

Oil on canvas, $25\frac{1}{16} \times 29\frac{7}{8}$ (63.6 × 75.9)
Presented by Mr Paul Mellon KBE through the British Sporting Art Trust 1979

Prov: . . .; Oscar & Peter Johnson, from whom purchased by Paul Mellon 1968.
Exh: *British Sporting Paintings*, Fermoy Art Gallery, King's Lynn, 1979 (14).
Lit: Egerton, 1978, p.183, no.188, repr. pl.62.

A date *c.*1805 is suggested because the treatment both of horses and landscape is closely similar to that in the painting in the Mellon Collection entitled 'A little bay stallion from Lord Heathfield's stud', two versions of which are listed in the artist's MS. Record Book (coll. Musée d'Art et d'Histoire, Geneva) as having been painted in February 1805 and March 1805. T.2350 may be the picture listed on 3 January 1806 as 'p[t] of two horses a bay hunter & a stallion Evergreen $\frac{3}{4}$ size Hants'. The landscape, a view over rolling countryside to distant blue hills, might well be Hampshire. The two horses are a bay and a chestnut, but the angle at which the chestnut is painted does not reveal its sex, and Agasse usually noted the inclusion of any figure as prominent as the groom is in this picture.

T.2351 **Lord Rivers's Groom Leading a Chestnut Hunter Towards a Coursing Party in Hampshire** 1807

Inscribed 'J.L. Agaſse' lower left
Oil on canvas, $26\frac{3}{4} \times 24\frac{5}{8}$ (67.9 × 52.5)
Presented by Mr Paul Mellon KBE through the British Sporting Art Trust 1979

Prov: George Pitt, 2nd Baron Rivers, by family descent to George Henry Lane Fox Pitt-Rivers; bequeathed by him to Mrs. Stella Edith Maumen, by whom sold through John Baskett to Paul Mellon 1969.
Lit: Recorded in Agasse's MS. Record Book (coll. Musée d'Art et d'Histoire, Geneva): 'September 22 1807 P[ortrait] of a chestnut horse led by a groom – Hant's – s[ize]$\frac{3}{4}$'; Egerton, 1978, no.191, repr. pl.64; *The Tate Gallery 1978–80*, p. 33, repr. in col.

The groom wears Lord Rivers's livery, dark blue greatcoat with yellow collar and cuffs and cockaded hat trimmed with yellow. The group of riders in the background probably includes 2nd Baron Rivers (1751–1828) of Stratfield Saye, Hampshire, Agasse's first, most important and most faithful English patron; and since Agasse records that this scene was painted in Hampshire, it is probably near Stratfield Saye. Lord Rivers bred greyhounds both at Stratfield Saye (where he also had a famous stud) and at his Cambridgeshire estate, Hare Park, aptly named and conveniently situated for coursing meetings at Swaffham and Newmarket.

Agasse reflected Lord Rivers's enthusiasm for coursing in some of his most brilliant canvases. Lord Rivers, shading his eyes from the sun, is the central figure in 'Lord Rivers and his friends coursing' of which there are two versions: (i) ? painted 1815; coll. George Lane Fox, Bramham Park, Yorkshire; exh. Arts Council, *British Sporting Painting 1650–1850*, 1974–5, 126; (ii) ? painted 1818, coll. Musée d'Art et d'Histoire, Geneva. A portrait of Lord Rivers walking in his park with two of his greyhounds (coll. Jockey Club) was engraved in mezzotint by J. Porter, published 1827 (repr. Frank Siltzer, *Newmarket*, 1923, facing p. 130). A larger than life-size portrait of Lord Rivers's greyhounds 'Rolla and Portia', 1805, is in the collection of the Musée d'Art et d'Histoire, Geneva; a group of nine greyhounds, almost certainly painted for Lord Rivers, is in the collection of Mr and Mrs Paul Mellon.

Henry Thomas Alken 1785–1851

T.2352/5 **The Belvoir Hunt:** a set of four *c.*1830–40
T.2352 **1. The Meet**
T.2353 **2. Jumping Into and Out of a Lane**
T.2354 **3. Full Cry**
T.2355 **4. The Death**

Inscribed 'H Alken': (1) and (4) lower left; (2) and (3) lower right
Oil on canvas, each $17\frac{3}{8} \times 25\frac{1}{2}$ (44 × 64.5)
Presented by Mr Paul Mellon KBE through the British Sporting Art Trust 1979

Prov: . . .; Arthur Ackermann & Son Ltd., from whom purchased by Paul Mellon 1964.

Exh: *British Sporting Paintings*, Fermoy Art Gallery, King's Lynn 1979 (24–27).

Lit: Egerton, 1978, p.253, no.275, 1–4.

The Belvoir is one of the oldest and most celebrated hunts; it dates from 1750 and became a foxhound pack in 1762. The kennels throughout the Hunt's history have been at Belvoir Castle. Its country lies in Leicestershire and Lincolnshire, adjoining that of the Quorn and the Cottesmore at Melton Mowbray. Alken's scenes catch something of the qualities, half-dandy, half-daredevil, deliberately cultivated by Meltonian sportsmen; in 'The Meet', one rider nonchalantly smokes a cheroot as he waits, and in 'The Death' one accepts a cigar from another's silver case, but (2) and (3) show most of the field taking fences and ditches with considerable verve and aplomb. The variety of landscape in the four scenes illustrates 'Brooksby's' comments on the Belvoir country (quoted in *Baily's Hunting Directory*, 1966–7, p.10): 'You may ride over small grass meadow, broad grazing land, light heath and heavy plough. It is impossible to sum up its characteristics in a sentence or two'.

If the suggested dating of 1830–40 is correct, the huntsman in Alken's scenes is Thomas Goosey, who had been whipper-in to the Belvoir from 1794 to 1816, and was its huntsman from 1816 to 1842. 'Nimrod' described Goosey as 'being just what a man should be to assist hounds in a flying country like his. He had an eye like a hawk – very quick to his points, and was a more than commonly sportsmanlike-looking person on his horse' (C. J. Apperley, *Nimrod's Hunting Reminiscences*, 1843, ed. 1926, p.129). The Mastership of the Belvoir was held by the Dukes of Rutland until 1896, except between 1830 and 1859; during that period (which almost certainly includes the period of Alken's scenes) the then Duke of Rutland, having retired from the hunting field, gave the Mastership to his nephew, Lord Forester.

James Barenger 1780–1831

T.2356 **Jonathan Griffin, Huntsman to the Earl of Derby's Staghounds** 1813

Inscribed 'J. Barenger. 1813–' lower right
Oil on canvas, $40\frac{1}{16} \times 50$ (101.6 × 127)
Presented by Mr Paul Mellon KBE through the British Sporting Art Trust 1979

Prov: ...; anon. sale, Christie's 17 March 1967 (167 as 'A huntsman in a green coat on a dappled grey hunter'), bt. Betts; Arthur Ackermann & Son Ltd., from whom purchased by Paul Mellon 1967.

Exh: *XVIIIth and XIXth Century Sporting Paintings*, Arthur Ackermann & Son Ltd., 1967 (12, repr.).

Lit: Egerton, 1978, p.233, no.251 (see also cat. no.252).

Jonathan Griffin is portrayed riding a dappled grey horse (probably Spanker), leaning back in his saddle to encourage hounds as they scramble over a hedge in the foreground on the left, while members of the hunt wait in the background on the right. The chief sitter (and probably his mount) can be identified from the portrait by Barenger of 'Jonathan Griffin, Huntsman, on Spanker' in the centre of a group of riders and hounds dated 1819 (coll. Mr and Mrs Paul Mellon; repr. Egerton, *op. cit.*, pl. 84); this picture was engraved by R. Woodman and published in 1823, entitled *The Earl of Derby's Staghounds*, with the names of the principal sitters lettered beneath their portraits. Griffin appears to be riding the same grey, Spanker (for which he reputedly paid eighty guineas, thereafter refusing all offers for him) in the 1813 as well as in the 1819 picture, the dark grey of the horse's coat in 1813 having naturally faded by 1819.

William Blake 1757–1827

T.2387 **Winter** *c.*1821

Tempera on pine, $35\frac{1}{2} \times 11\frac{11}{16}$ (90.2 × 29.7)
Purchased at Sotheby's (Grant-in-Aid) 1979

Prov: Rev. John Johnson; Canon Cowper Johnson; Bertram Vaughan-Johnson; his widow; the Rev. B. Talbot Vaughan Johnson; the Vaughan Johnson Trust, sold Sotheby's 18 July 1979 (58, repr. in colour) bought Agnew's for the Tate Gallery.

Exh: Carfax 1906 (19); Tate Gallery 1913 (55); Burlington Fine Arts Club 1927 (51, repr. pl.38); on loan to the Tate Gallery 1933–4; *The Lyrical Trend in English Painting*, Roland, Browse and Delbanco, March–April 1946 (17, repr. on cover); Paris, Antwerp (repr. pl.23), Zurich and Tate Gallery (repr.) 1947 (33); Port Sunlight 1950 (27); Arts Council 1951 (3, repr. pl.2); Cambridge 1957; on loan to the Tate Gallery 1972 onwards; Tate Gallery 1978 (308, repr.).

Lit: W. Graham Robertson in Alexander Gilchrist, *Life of William Blake*, 1907 ed., p.492 no.4; Thomas Wright, *Life of William Blake*, 1929, I, p.131; Martin Butlin, *The Paintings and Drawings of William Blake*, 1981, I, pp.549, 552 no.808, repr. II, pl.1049.

Repr: Edward Croft-Murray, *Decorative Painting in England 1537–1837*, 1970, pl.150.

'Winter' and the companion painting 'Evening' (now in an American private collection; Butlin, *op. cit.*, no.809, repr. pl.1050) were painted for the Rev. John Johnson for the sides of a fireplace in his rectory at Yaxham, Norfolk. They illustrate his cousin William Cowper's *The Task*, Book IV, lines 120–9 and 243–6 respectively. The lines describing Winter read:

> O Winter! ruler of the inverted year,
> Thy scattered hair with sleet like ashes filled,
> Thy breath congealed upon thy lips, thy cheeks
> Fringed with a beard made white with other snows
> Than those of age, thy forehead wrapt in clouds.
> A leafless branch thy sceptre, and thy throne
> A sliding car, indebted to no wheels,
> But urged by storms along its slippery way;
> I love thee, all unlovely as thou seemest,
> And dreaded as thou art.

A third picture, of 'Olney Bridge', apparently ran across the top of the fireplace but according to family tradition has been destroyed.

That the fireplace was not yet set up, or had already been dismantled, by 1834 is suggested by a shopping-list of wines dated 'March 6 1834' on the back of 'Evening'. Both panels were framed for some time with part of their surfaces covered by mounts, under which the blues remained considerably stronger than elsewhere, suggesting that the pictures have faded and that the paint is closer to watercolour than to Blake's earlier tempera, which tends to have darkened with time. Originally it is likely that there was also considerably more of the gold of which only traces remain on the two pictures.

Although Johnson got to know Blake through William Hayley in the early years of the nineteenth century and had his miniature portrait painted by him in 1802 (Butlin, *ibid.*, no.347, repr. pl.455), 'Winter' and 'Evening' are sylistically, and in their technique, much later. It is likely that they were painted following Johnson's rebuilding of Yaxham Rectory in 1820–1.

British School, Seventeenth Century

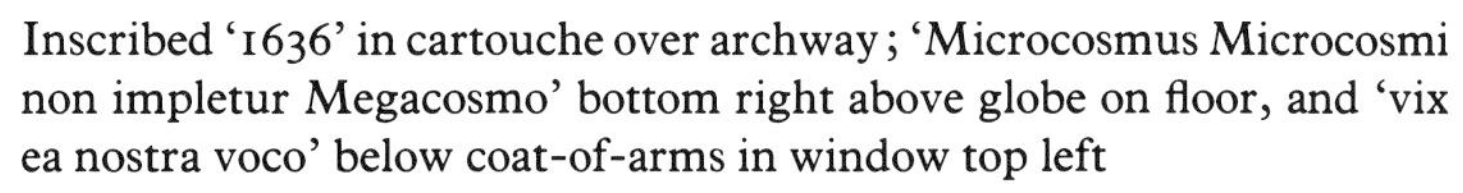

T.2308 **William Style of Langley** 1636

Inscribed '1636' in cartouche over archway; 'Microcosmus Microcosmi non impletur Megacosmo' bottom right above globe on floor, and 'vix ea nostra voco' below coat-of-arms in window top left
Oil on canvas $80\frac{3}{4} \times 53\frac{1}{2}$ (205 × 136)
Purchased (Grant-in-Aid) 1978

Prov: Presumably painted for the sitter and by family descent to Sir Charles Style, 8th Bt., who sold Wateringbury in 1829 and placed some of the family portraits with his relative James Whatman of Vinters, near Maidstone, Kent; recorded there in a watercolour by Charlotte Bosanquet in 1843; on Sir Charles' death in 1879 inherited by his cousin Sir William Style, 9th Bt., who in 1890 sold the family portraits to his brother Albert F. Style of Boxley House, near Maidstone; thence by descent to David Style, who re-purchased Wateringbury 1946; Wateringbury sale, Christie's, 1 June 1978 (329, repr. in col.), bt. by Leggatt Bros. on behalf of the Tate Gallery.

Lit: Joseph Foster, *Alumni Oxonienses*, 1891, for Style; J. M. Rigg, article on William Style in *Dictionary of National Biography*, 1909; Robert Borrowman, *Beckenham Past and Present*, 1910, pp.21, 125, 128, 198, 206, 208; Horatio F. Brown, 'Inglesi e Scozzesi all' Università di Padova 1618–1765' in *Monografie ... del R. Instituto Veneto*, Venice, 1922, p.145;

B. F. Davis, *Transcripts of PCC Wills mainly concerning Bromley, Kent*, typescript, 1934, p.88a, in Bromley and Beckenham Central Library, for transcript of W. Style's will; Style family genealogy, MSS in possession of Lt.-Cdr. Sir Godfrey Style, CBE, DSC, RN; James P. Cunningham, *Dancing in the Inns of Court*, Jordan publications, 1965; John Cornforth, *English Interiors 1790–1848*, 1978, p.58, fig. 52 for repr. of watercolour by Charlotte Bosanquet (original in Ashmolean Museum, Oxford); *The Tate Gallery 1978–80*, p.31, repr. in col.

William Style (1599/1600 or 1603–1679) was the son of William Style of Langley, Kent, and his second wife Mary, daughter of Sir Robert Clarke, Baron of the Exchequer. He matriculated from Queen's College, Oxford, in 1618, aged 15 (hence the uncertainty about his date of birth, since his memorial plaque in Beckenham parish church describes him as having died on 7 December 1679, in his 80th year), and became a student at the Inner Temple that same year, being called to the bar in 1628. He may have travelled abroad, as the register of English visitors at Padua University recorded a 'Mattia Styles Inglese' on 6 July 1625. No Matthew has as yet been found in the Style genealogy for that period, so that in view of the extremely fanciful spelling of English names on this list, 'Mattia' could conceivably be a mistake for William. If William travelled, he would have been then a suitable age at which to have done so; his relative 'Thomas Style Cantianus of Watringbury' was there in December 1669. During his legal career Style published some minor works on law, and in 1640 a translation from the Latin of a devotional handbook by the Nuremberg humanist and theologian Johann Michael Dilherr, entitled *Contemplations, Sighes and Groanes of a Christian*, the original of which was first published in Jena in 1634.

Many features in this portrait closely echo Dilherr's text, and it may have even been painted while Style was working on his translation – his preface is dated 'From my chamber in the Inner Temple August 20 1639', and the date '1636' over the archway could commemorate Style's entering into some kind of new understanding of religious life at that time, which led him to embark upon the translation. The text is basically a simple exhortation, in very flowery language and using the garden as an analogue for the church, to abandon worldly vanities for a more Christian life. It is clearly summed up in the simple and anonymous frontispiece of the book, which shows a man clutching a volume of the *Contemplations* seated on a rock above a formal, hedge-encompassed garden, beside a table covered with objects representing the senses, i.e. flowers for smell, bread and wine for taste, lute for hearing etc. He looks up to heaven and utters a quotation from Ovid, *Metamorphoses* 7.21: 'I see better (things), but follow (the) worse' (the compiler is indebted to Dr David Rogers of the Bodleian Library, Oxford, for his kind help in interpreting the quotations and the imagery of the frontispiece and the painting).

In accord with these sentiments, Style turns his back on his worldly possessions, starting with his coat-of-arms set in the window, reinforced with the motto 'vix ea nostra voco' ('I scarcely call these things my own'), and on worldly music in the shape of a kit, or dancing-master's violin. This is not an empty symbol, as Style left in his will 'to my friend Butler Buggin of the Inner Temple Esq. all my flagaletts, Recorders & Kitts & my small violyn'. The Inns of Court were at this time important musical centres, with elaborate dance entertainments at Christmas and other feasts, which Buggin, who was a younger colleague of Style and more than once Master of the Revels, had a hand in organising (the compiler is indebted to Wallace W. S. Breem, Librarian and Keeper of Manuscripts of the Inner Temple, for this information). The rest of the programme also echoes Dilherr's text: Style turns away from his books and writing ('I will therefore rest from the too much desire of knowledge'), his outer garments ('O vaine mantles,

O lamentable coverings! . . . nothing can hide me from God's judgement, but thy coat, O heavenly Lambe'), and a chair ('I aske not to sit, but to stand and observe thy commandments'). He turns towards an archway which makes no architectural sense but presumably represents the way into the garden of the Church, a common image particularly in Catholic and counter-reformation literature, although it might be fanciful to suggest that the discordant pattern of what should be regular and formal beds is meant to be emblematic of the evils which happen 'even within the Orchyard of the Church', according to Dilherr's preface. The emblematic use of the garden was particularly popular at this time, partly through the publication of Henry Hawkins' *Partheneia Sacra* in 1633, with its discourse on the garden as a marian *hortus conclusus* and a place for 'heavenlie Contemplations'. The garden is, however, protected by a green hedge from the mountainous wilderness beyond, which is dominated by the ruins of pagan antiquity. The object and motto at his feet to which Style so purposefully points with his cane would have been easily understood by his contemporaries: 'The microcosm (or heart) of the microcosm (or man) is not filled (even) by the megacosm (or world)' – that is to say that the human heart is not sated with the whole created world, but only with its Creator. This image of a globe within a burning heart could have been inspired by Peter Heylyn's *Microcosmus. A little description of the Great World.*, 1621, as Heylyn and Style overlapped at Oxford (Heylyn matriculated in 1617) and the former was a high-churchman and divine with counter-reformation sympathies. From the arrangement of the lines, however, it is likely that the artist did not use a globe, but a current circular world map such as that of the Mercator/Hondius world atlas of 1633, where the down-curving ecliptic and position of ships and cartouche correspond with the lines on the painted globe. (The compiler is indebted to Helen Wallis of the British Library and Christopher Terrell of the National Maritime Museum for these suggestions.)

In spite of the considerable quality of this work, it has so far proved impossible to attribute it to any particular artist. It shows a marked Flemish influence, combined with certain archaic qualities and a flatness of modelling that have come to be associated with the provincial British school: on the one hand the sensitive head seems to show something of the influence of Cornelius Johnson, and there is a certain sophistication in placing the figure between two sources of light; on the other, details like the rough painting of the middle distance, the uncertain understanding of perspective and light, as well as the deliberate use of script as part of the composition – a very old-fashioned device by this time and never employed by contemporary fashionable court painters like Van Dyck – hark back to the Jacobean mode of Gheeraedts and Peake. It is very likely that the painter will turn out to be a member of the complex community of expatriate Flemish artists residing in London, so ably charted by Mary Edmond (see her 'Limners and Picturemakers', *Walpole Society*, 1978–80, vol. XLVII, p.60ff.) but examples of whose works are as yet rarely identified. There is, for instance, Cornelius De Neve, a painter associated with the De Critz family of painters, whose few known works (e.g. the 'Richard Sackville, Lord Buckhurst and the Hon. Edward Sackville', signed and dated 1637, at Knole) would seem to fall well within the competence of the Style portrait. Other comparisons remain to be made (The compiler wishes to thank David Style and Jonathan Vickers for their help in tracing the history of T.2308).

T.3029 **Sir Thomas Pope, Later 3rd Earl of Downe** *c.*1635

Inscribed 'Thos Earl of Down/II^d Son of Willm first/Earl of Down', in later hand, top left

Oil on canvas, 79¾ × 47 (202.5 × 119.5)

Purchased (Grant-in-Aid), with contributions from the Friends of the Tate Gallery, the National Art-Collections Fund and the Pilgrim Trust 1980

Prov: ?Wroxton Abbey sale, 24 May 1933 (679); sold by H. Freeman & Sons, 8 Rose and Crown Yard, SW1 at Christie's 16 Feb 1934 (97), bt. Francis Howard; Loel Guinness, by whom lent to the Tate Gallery from 1953 until purchased 1980.

Lit: *The Tate Gallery 1978–80*, p.30, repr. in col.

The sitter, dressed in sober black, stands on a curiously ruckled oriental carpet, against a red-curtained background. He holds a white glove with scalloped edges in his left hand, and rests his right on a chair upholstered in red velvet, on which is also his hat displaying a red-blue ribbon. The gilded hilt of his rapier is a common English type of the 1630s.

Stylistically this portrait belongs to the early or middle 1630s, and there is no reason to doubt the correctness of the inscription, even though it must have been added considerably later, certainly after 1660, the year in which Sir Thomas inherited the earldom from his hononymous nephew. The apparent age of the sitter would also fit that of the 3rd Earl, who was born in 1598 and died in 1668. Inscriptions very similar to this are found on several portraits of the Pope family, particularly ones sold from Wroxton Abbey, Oxfordshire in 1933, but it has not been possible to trace this portrait to that collection (although it is just possible that lot 679 at the Wroxton Abbey sale, 24 May 1933, of 'Thomas, 3rd Earl of Downe, in black court dress with lace collar, sword and embroidered glove in left hand, by Marcus Gheeraedts, 3 ft 9½ ins by 4 ft 9 ins' is the same as T.3029, with incorrect measurements).

In style the portrait is very archaic for its period, and its former attribution to the court painter Marcus Gheeraedts the younger is not tenable. In handling it is very similar to the portrait thought to be of Countess Downe, wife of the 3rd Earl, and her children (now at Cowdray Park), which was formerly at Wroxton. Many 'Gheeraedts'-type portraits of members of the Pope family have now been reattributed to Robert Peake (d. 1619) and it is not inconceivable that the family may have kept up its connections with the Peake workshop. This was inherited by Robert's son William, who died in 1639, and under whom William Dobson is known to have served his apprenticeship (see Mary Edmond, 'Limners and Picturemakers', *Walpole Society*, XLVII, 1978–1980, p.129). The only portrait reasonably attributable to him on the basis of inscriptions – 'A Howard Boy Aged 5' of 1627 (J. Jacob and J. Simon, *The Suffolk Collection at Ranger's House, Blackheath*, GLC 1974, no.20, repr.) – is quite compatible in style with this, especially in the distinctive treatment of the hands. Further comparisons must, however, await the restoration and cleaning of the Tate portrait.

T.3031 **A Lady in Masque Dress, called Lady Tanfield** 1615

Inscribed '1615' on masonry ledge near sitter's left elbow
Oil on canvas, 87½ × 53¾ (221.2 × 136.5)
Purchased (Grant-in-Aid), with contributions from the Friends of the Tate Gallery, the National Art-Collections Fund and the Pilgrim Trust 1980

Prov: Recorded in the possession of Lord Litchfield at Ditchley by Vertue in 1726; by descent to Viscount Dillon; his sale Sotheby's 24 May 1933 (85, repr.), bt. Francis Howard; Loel Guinness, by whom lent to the Tate Gallery from 1953 until purchased 1980.

Exh: *Art Treasures*, Manchester, 1857 (21); *National Portrait Exhibition*, South Kensington, 1868 (669) as 'A Lady of the Time of Queen

Elizabeth'; *Old Masters*, R.A. 1902 (161) as 'Lady Tanfield'; period display, Metropolitan Museum, New York, 1966 (no catalogue).

Lit: Horace Walpole, *Andecdotes of Painting in England*, 1782, iii, p.6; Vct. Dillon, *Catalogue of Paintings in the possession of the Rt. Honble. Vct. Dillon at Ditchley, Spelsbury, Oxfordshire*, 1908, p.39, cat. no.66, pl. XLI; C. H. Collins Baker, *Lely and the Stuart Portrait Painters*, 1912, i, p.28, repr. (as by Van Somer); L. Cust, 'Gheeraerts', in *Walpole Society*, III, 1913–14, p.43, pl.XXX (b) (as by Gheeraedts); C. H. Collins Baker and W. G. Constable, *English Painting of the 16th and 17th Centuries*, 1930, p.41, pl.36; 'Vertue Notebooks II', in *Walpole Society*, XX, 1931–2, pp.14, 76; Ditchley Catalogue (shortened edition) 1933, p.25, cat. 76; Eric Mercer, *English Art 1553–1625*, 1962, pp.180, 184, pl.57a; *The Tate Gallery 1978–80*, p.27, repr. in col.

The lady wears a deep-cut green dress embroidered with silver and trimmed with yellow lace, a dark red cloak, also embroidered with silver, draped over her left shoulder, and a transparent scarf, known as an Irish mantle, which she lifts with her right as if to shield herself from the sun. Her hair falls loosely over her shoulders and she wears a wreath of heart's-ease or pansies. She stands in a landscape between an architectural feature on the right and a peach tree on the left. The rich apparel, allegorical setting and her shorter than usual skirt indicates that she is a lady of the court, dressed for a masque performance, a form of entertainment to which Queen Anne was known to have been addicted. The allegory remains obscure, but there are close parallels between this picture and another anonymous full-length of a lady shielding herself from the sun at the Bristol Art Gallery (R. Strong, *The Elizabethan Icon*, 1969, p.31, repr. p.33). Both pictures belong to the same period and appear to be by the same hand.

The identification of the sitter as Lady Tanfield is fairly recent and does not seem to pre-date the R.A. exhibition of 1902. The suggestion is that this could represent Elizabeth Tanfield (1585 or 6–1639), a grand-niece of Sir Henry Lee. She married in 1602 Henry Cary, later Lord Falkland, also a relative by marriage of the Lees, and the kinship on both sides would seem sufficient reason for there to be a portrait of her at Ditchley, the seat of the Lee family. She was a noted linguist at an early age, and would have been around 30 when this portrait was painted. There is, however, no documentary evidence to substantiate this identification. When Vertue saw the picture at Ditchley in about 1726 (Notebooks II, p.14) he described it as '8. Lady with yellow lace about her neck and ruffles a gauze scarfe' and thought that it represented one of 'Lady Manchester's sisters'. He was thinking here of Elinor Wortley (d. 1667), wife of the Sir Henry Lee who inherited Ditchley in 1611, and who in 1659 married, as her fourth husband, Edward Montague, Earl of Manchester. T.3033 probably represents her sister Anne, and she is known to have had two other sisters. In 1730 Vertue again saw some of the Ditchley portraits 'here in Town to Clean' (Notebooks, II, p.76) and described this portrait once more, this time noting the date: '8. Lady at lenght yellow lace ruff, gauze vail. good action well painted – dated 1615 . . . I guesse to be of the hand of Paul Vansomer'. It is interesting to note that the three pictures he describes as 'Lady Manchester's sisters' – 'Lady Morton' (T.3033), this picture, and 'A Lady Widow in black' for which he also notes the date 1615 (this last was reproduced in Cust, 1913–14, pl.XXIX (b) and later sold in the Ditchley sale as 'Elinor Wortley, Lady Lee, later Lady Manchester', and no date was noted on it) – are all of about the same date and looked sufficiently alike to Vertue for him to ascribe them as a group to Van Somer. From then on the date on this painting went unnoticed until the picture was cleaned in 1964; this led to it being regarded for a time as an Elizabethan rather than a Jacobean painting and to its attribution to Gheeraedts. At present it is not possible to attribute the painting to either of the artists mentioned.

British School, Seventeenth or Eighteenth Century

T.3032 **George Talbot, 6th Earl of Shrewsbury**

Inscribed 'GEORGE/ER: OF SHREWSBWRY' top left
Oil on canvas 90 × 57½ (228.5 × 146)
Purchased (Grant-in-Aid), with contributions from the Friends of the Tate Gallery and the Pilgrim Trust 1980

Prov: At Rufford by 1797; Rufford Abbey sale, Christie's 18 November 1938 (43), bt. Francis Howard; Loel Guinness, by whom lent to the Tate Gallery from 1953 until purchased 1980.

Exh: Fine Art Exhibition, Leeds 1868 (3273).

Lit: Musgrave's *Lists*, c. 1797, British Library Add. MSS 6391, f. 147; E. Hailstone, *Portraits of Yorkshire Worthies*, 1869, no pagination, reproduced.

The 6th Earl of Shrewsbury (1528?–1590), one of the wealthiest nobles of his time, held the office of Earl Marshal of England from 1572, and was Queen Elizabeth's appointed custodian of Mary, Queen of Scots, at whose execution in 1587 he was asked to preside. He is shown standing against a green curtain, wearing a short fur-lined cloak and the Garter insignia, holding gloves in his right hand and his left resting on a sword. The crude execution of this portrait suggests that it is either a late copy of a lost original, or even a complete fake, based on an authentic bust portrait of 1580, versions of which are at Hardwick Hall, Welbeck Abbey, and elsewhere. The latter is more likely in view of such faults of detail as the sword, where the pommel seems to have been copied from a sound original, but the rest of the hilt is fanciful and misaligned (information kindly supplied by the Master of the Armories, Tower of London, A. V. B. Norman). Such antiquarian pastiches were not unknown in the eighteenth century, being ordered to fill a gap in a series of historic personages or eminent ancestors. In this light the picture should not be seen so much as a fake, but as part of a trend that favoured historic revivals and as a fascinating example of contemporary taste and fashion.

Rufford Abbey, whence this portrait was sold in 1938, was granted to the sitter's grandfather, the fourth Earl of Shrewsbury, by Henry VIII in 1537. Although the estate was of little importance among the family's immense possessions, the sixth Earl did build a sizeable house around the ruins of the old abbey. Rufford passed by inheritance to the Savile family in 1626, and became its principal seat after 1680, when the house was rebuilt and a new long gallery added. The house underwent several alterations and extensions in the next two centuries, and any of these might have led to efforts to complete sets of historic ancestral portraits.

Henry Bernard Chalon 1770–1849

T.2357 **A Representation of the Persians in the Costume of Their Country, Attending at Carlton Palace, with Portraits of the Horses Presented to His Majesty by His Excellency The Ambassador from the Emperor of Persia** ?1819

Oil on canvas, 39¾ × 56¾ (101 × 144)
Presented by Mr. Paul Mellon KBE through the British Sporting Art Trust 1979

Prov: . . .; Rutland Gallery until 1963, when sold to Mrs. John West,

Unionville, Chester County, Pennsylvania; sold 1977 to Essex Gallery of Sport, Far Hills, New Jersey, from whom purchased by Paul Mellon, 1977.

Chalon exhibited a picture with this title at the British Institution in 1820 (315). The exhibited picture is likely to have been the more highly-finished version signed and dated 1819, reputedly commissioned by George IV (then Prince Regent) but not paid for, and subsequently purchased by Major Bower, by whose descendant it was sold at Sotheby's 17 November 1976 (155, repr., bt. Richard Green, now in a private collection overseas). T.2357 may be either a preliminary version or a replica painted for an unknown admirer of the exhibited picture.

The Shah of Persia sent an Ambassador to London in 1819 primarily to discuss with Lord Castlereagh certain aspects of the Anglo-Persian treaty concluded by Sir Gore Ouseley in Tehran in 1812, and more recently revised by English plenipotentiaries in Tehran. That treaty had established an Anglo-Persian alliance against a possible Franco-Russian one; the Shah now hoped for positive assurance that England would protect Persia in the event of Russian invasion.

The Persian Ambassador left Tehran in October 1818, laden with presents from the Shah to George III. The Shah had also selected eighteen magnificent Arabian horses to be presented to the Prince Regent. The British government was reluctant to defray any of the cost of the embassy itself, especially as the Persian Ambassador stayed for some weeks in Vienna and Paris en route; however reports that he had been splendidly treated in Paris persuaded Castlereagh that it would be expedient to provide at least a rent-free house and a carriage in London.

Transport of the train of Arabian horses and their Persian grooms posed a different sort of problem. It was agreed that they would travel with the Persian Ambassador as far as Constantinople, that they would then proceed independently to London and that the British government would organize and pay for their transport from Constantinople. A Mr. George Willcox volunteered his services, and was given credit for £1,500, a sum quickly exceeded. Transport from Constantinople to Marseilles, in a specially-chartered merchant freighter, alone cost £1,470, and travel expenses from Marseilles to Paris (presumably overland, riding in stages: but only occasional details of the journey survive in Castlereagh's published correspondence) came to a further £400. By 19 March 1819, the horses and their grooms had arrived in London under Willcox's escort.

On 29 April 1819 *The Times* reported the arrival of the Persian Ambassador in London. He was attended by 'ten or a dozen persons inhabited in silks and turbans, with daggers and long beards', and accompanied by his wife, always referred to as 'the Fair Circassian': she was said to be guarded by two black eunuchs with sabres at their sides, and was throughout kept from the curious eyes of 'loungers and dandies'. The public appearances of the Persian Ambassador and his exotic retinue remained news for the next few months. On several occasions the Ambassador rode in Hyde Park, with Sir Gore Ouseley or the diplomat James Morier, on some of the Arabian horses. *The Times* reported on 3 May that the Persian Ambassador had the previous day ridden a grey horse, 'a beautiful Arab of large size, said to be the favourite charger of the Shah, a present to the Prince Regent, as a mark of his particular esteem'; the horse's trappings were 'studded with diamonds and emeralds, with a gold chain of considerable value', and the Persian Ambassador's dress was 'magnificent, entirely of the finest Cashmere shawl'.

Mental illness had long since incapacitated George III from receiving state visitors; accordingly the presentation of the Shah's gifts (fully listed in *The Times* of 24 May) took place at the Prince Regent's London residence, Carlton House. 'The Arabian horses, brought by His Excellency to England as a present to the Prince Regent, were drawn up in the court-yard'. For George III there was 'a gold-enamelled looking-glass opening with a portrait of his Persian Majesty', a magnificent sword 'celebrated in Persia for the exquisite temper of its blade' and an abundance of pearls, carpets and Cashmere shawls. At a fancy-dress ball at Carlton House in July, the Persian Ambassador was 'presented by HRH the Prince Regent with his portrait set in diamonds, which he placed with his own hand round the Arab's neck, suspended by a dark blue riband'. The Persian Ambassador was taken to Epsom races, to the Tower and to Greenwich. Meanwhile Lord Castlereagh appears to have remained cordial but non-committal over the object of the embassy.

The wording 'A Representation . . .' in the title of the work exhibited at the British Institution in 1820 (the same title, given in full in the heading above, is also used for T.2357, its replica) suggests that Chalon was not an eye-witness of the presentation of the Arabian horses at Carlton House; and certainly he has allowed himself considerable artistic licence in depicting rolling countryside, far removed from the urbanity of St. James's Park, behind the royal stable-block. Chalon depicts seven Arabian horses. Eighteen had left Constantinople; how many in fact survived the long journey to enter the Prince Regent's stables is not known. It should perhaps be pointed out that as George III died on 29 January 1820, the former Prince Regent, now George IV, is properly styled 'His Majesty' in the title of the picture exhibited in the spring of 1820 (ed. Marquess of Londonderry, *Correspondence, Despatches and other Papers, of Viscount Castlereagh*, XII, 1853, pp.112–9; *The Times* 27 April–20 July 1819, *passim*).

Charles Allston Collins 1828–73

T.3025 **May, in the Regent's Park** 1851

Inscribed 'CACollins/1851' bottom right (CAC in monogram) and 'No.3/May in the Regents Park/Charles Collins/17 Hanover Terrace/R[egent's] Park' on a label on the back
Oil on panel, $17\frac{1}{2} \times 27\frac{5}{16}$ (44.5 × 69.4)
Purchased from Richard Green (Grant-in-Aid) 1980

Prov: Said to have been bought at the 1852 R.A. exhibition by a Mr Crooke of Cumberland Terrace, in whose family it remained until the 1940s, when acquired by a private collector who sold it at Sotheby's Belgravia, 1 October 1979 (2, repr. in colour), bt. Richard Green.

Exh: R.A. 1852 (55).

Lit: Allen Staley, *The Pre-Raphaelite Landscape*, 1973, pp.83, 91, 150.

The Collins family moved from Blandford Square to 17 Hanover Terrace, Regent's Park in August 1850. 'May, in the Regent's Park' was presumably painted from a window at this address, looking eastwards across the park, though a critic in *The Athenæum*, reviewing the 1852 R.A. exhibition, thought the view was taken from a window in nearby Sussex Place. Collins' title can be taken to refer both to the month of May and to the large bush of pink May or Hawthorn seen in the left foreground.

One of the first Pre-Raphaelite landscapes to be exhibited, 'May, in the Regent's Park' was adversely criticised for its emphasis on minutiæ and for its bald design. *The Art Journal* (1852, p.166) commented on its 'useless and absurd rules of composition', noting the presence of 'all kinds of inexorable straight lines'. *The Illustrated London News* (22 May 1852, p.407) suggested that 'a tea-tray, not a picture-frame' would be a more appropriate vehicle for it. *The Athenæum* (22 May 1852, p.582) declared that 'The botanical predominates altogether over the artistical, – and to a vicious and mistaken extreme. In nature there is air as well as earth, – she masses and generalizes where these fac-simile makers split hairs and particularize'. Nevertheless, Collins appears to have sold the painting. According to the anonymous vendor of the work at Sotheby's Belgravia in 1979, 'a Mr Crooke who lived in Cumberland Terrace, bought the picture from Burlington House [i.e. The Royal Academy, not then in fact at Burlington House] for £100 in 1851 [i.e. 1852], and it stayed in that family until the 1940's'. Nothing further has been discovered about Mr Crooke.

Collins gave up painting to concentrate on writing in about 1860, the year he married Charles Dickens' daughter Kate. No other landscapes of this kind are known to survive from his brief career as an artist. Until its reappearance at auction in 1979, 'May, in the Regent's Park' was itself known only from description.

John Singleton Copley 1738–1815

T.2386 **Mrs Gill** *c.* 1770–1

Oil on canvas $50\frac{3}{8} \times 40\frac{1}{4}$ (128 × 102.2)
Presented by Mr and Mrs H. J. Heinz II 1979

Prov: Said to have descended from the sitter, whenever possible from mother to daughter; earliest documented owner Mary Pratt (*née* White) of Boston, born *c.* 1808; her son Robert M. Pratt (1836/7–1916/7) bequeathed it, in the absence of any children of his own, to his cousin Louise Dumaresq Blake, who in 1888 married Dr. Charles F. Coxwell, an Englishman; Mrs Coxwell brought the portrait to England in 1919, when it was placed on loan to the Tate Gallery, where it has remained ever since; in November that year she gave the portrait to her daughter Mrs Leonard G. Pinnell (d. 1976), who bequeathed it to her granddaughter Miss Alison F. B. Pinnell, from whom it was bought, through Agnew's, by the donors for presentation to the Tate Gallery.

Exh: On loan to the Museum of Fine Art, Boston, 1917–1919.

Lit: Barbara N. Parker and Anne B. Wheeler, *John Singleton Copley; American Portraits*, Boston, 1938, p.82, repr. pl.17; Jules D. Prown, *J. S. Copley in America 1738–1774*, 1966, pp.76, 215, repr. fig. 276; *The Tate Gallery 1978–80*, p. 18, repr. in col.

This portrait of a plainly dressed old lady seated in a blue armchair is a fine example of Copley's forthright style at the height of his American period, before his departure for Europe in 1774. Variants of this pose and simple setting were favoured by the artist for elderly sitters from the early 1760s onwards, allowing him to produce austere and dignified studies of old age and strong character of considerable power. Notably absent here are any of the modish pretensions – usually heavily dependent on engravings of earlier and contemporary British artists – with which he frequently animated the portraits of more style-conscious Bostonians. Here Copley's affectionate rendering, in bold and unfussed brushstrokes, of wrinkled age and gnarled hands as if in contrast to the smooth plain silks and muslins of the sitter's dress, is further reinforced by his predilection at this period for particularly strong contrasts of light and shade.

A strong family tradition identifies the sitter as Relief Dowse of Salem, Mass. (1676–1759), wife of Col. Michael Gill. Copley experts, however, agree that the painting is executed in Copley's late, mature American style of *c.*1770. It has therefore been suggested that it could represent Mrs. John Gill, daughter-in-law of the above-mentioned Relief. Mrs John Gill was mother of Moses Gill, whose portrait by Copley, dated 1764, hangs in the Museum of the Rhode Island School of Design, Providence, together with portraits of his first and second wives, the latter dated *c.*1773, both also by Copley (Prown 1966, repr. figs. 128, 129, 326).

George Cruikshank 1792–1878 and **Charles Mottram** 1807–76

T.2268 **The Worship of Bacchus** published 1864

Inscribed 'First Proof' b.l. and signed 'George Cruikshank' b.r.
Engraving, $21\frac{7}{8} \times 38\frac{3}{4}$ (55.7 × 98.4), on paper $25\frac{1}{2} \times 41\frac{3}{8}$ (64.7 × 105)
Purchased from Miss F. Egerton (Grant-in-Aid) 1978

Prov: . . .; Miss F. Egerton.

Lit: *The Worship of Bacchus, A Critique ... by John Stewart, A Descriptive Lecture by George Cruikshank and Opinions of the Press*, 1862, pp.7, 8–17; *Art Journal*, 1865, p.117; B. Jerrold, *The Life of George Cruikshank*, new ed., 1898, pp.286–301; A. M. Cohn, *George Cruikshank: a Catalogue Raisonne*, 1974, cat. no.2110; exhibition catalogue, *The Inimitable George Cruikshank ...*, University of Louisville Libraries, Kentucky, USA, 1968, no.105; exhibition catalogue, *George Cruikshank*, Victoria and Albert Museum, 1973–4, nos.392–4.

T.2268 is a proof before letters, on india paper, pulled from the steel engraving of Cruikshank's large oil painting 'The Worship of Bacchus', No.795 in the collection. When the print was finally published in 1864 with the full title, 'The Worship of Bacchus, or The Drinking Customs of Society', the following details were added beneath the bottom edge of the engraved image: 'The Figures outlined on the Steel Plate by George Cruikshank & the Engraving finished by Charles Mottram – Printed by R. Holdgate and Published June 20th 1864 by William Tweedie, 337 Strand, London'.

'The Worship of Bacchus' was intended to be Cruikshank's magnum opus for the cause of temperance which he had espoused since the 1840s. In 1847 he produced 'The Bottle', a Hogarthian series of eight engraved plates showing the disastrous consequences of 'the frequent use of the bottle'. After this date, Cruikshank practised total abstinence and he became a frequent lecturer for the National Temperance League.

In a draft letter (undated, but probably *c.*1867) to the Chairman and Committee of the National Temperance League (private collection, U.S.A.), Cruikshank states that it was late in 1859 when he suggested to the League the idea of painting a large oil (approximately seven by thirteen feet) of 'The Worship of Bacchus' to be engraved as propaganda for the cause. He began sketches of the subject in November 1859 and one of these, inscribed by Cruikshank 'A First Sketch ...', is now in the Victoria and Albert Museum. Cruikshank then made a large oil sketch (present whereabouts unknown) and the idea and the design were approved, though the League requested him to make a large watercolour design (now in the Victoria and Albert Museum, no.71–1880) to be engraved instead of the large oil he had proposed. The watercolour is inscribed 'Designed and Drawn by George Cruikshank. Teetotaller 1860' and is given the full title: 'The Worship of Bacchus – or – The Drinking Customs of Society, showing how the Intoxicating Liquors are used upon every occasion in life, from the Cradle to the Grave'. The engraving was begun; Cruikshank was to draw the outlines on the plate and Charles Mottram was to execute the details. Cruikshank's draft letter to the League reveals that in November 1860 the League sent John Stewart (an art critic who wrote for the *Art Journal*) to say that they had decided, after all, to commission the large oil. The engraving work stopped until this was finished; according to Cruikshank's letter, the painting took about a year and eight months to complete.

The painting was on exhibition by August 1862 in a small gallery at 21 Wellington Street, Strand, when it was noticed by the *Art Journal* (p.195). A pamphlet written by Cruikshank and Stewart was also published in 1862 and this contained the full text of the artist's first lecture on the picture, given on 28 August, in which he gave a detailed description of the numerous incidents depicted on the canvas. John Stewart in his introductory comments rightly pointed out the importance that the engraving had in Cruikshank's scheme: '... the print is the true completion of the work; while the picture is only a portion of the preparatory means to the nobler and more enduring end and aim'. Cruikshank himself felt the painting 'a mighty instrument in aid of the Temperance cause ... that will be increased a hundred fold when the engraving ... is completed'.

George Cumberland 1754–1848

T.2304 **Inside the Peak Cavern, Castleton, Derbyshire** *c.*1820

Inscribed '2d view of the Choir as it is called, on turning a/point beyond – GC' in pencil verso
Watercolour, $5\frac{13}{16} \times 8\frac{11}{16}$ (14.9 × 22.2)
Presented by William Drummond 1978

Prov: From one of two albums of English and Welsh views assembled by Cumberland's daughter Eliza from the artist's sketchbooks of *c.*1815–28; by family descent, sold as 'The Property of a Lady', Sotheby's, 15 July 1976 (15, four repr.), bt. William Drummond, Covent Garden Gallery.

Exh: *George Cumberland*, Covent Garden Gallery, 1977 (30).

'A combination of more horrid ideas is rarely found, than this place affords', remarked the Rev. William Gilpin after visiting 'that celebrated chasm, near Castleton, called the *Devil's cave*' (*Observations, relative chiefly to Picturesque Beauty, made in the year 1772*, 1786, pp.213–4). The Devil's cave, sometimes called Peak's Hole (and now generally known as the Peak Cavern), had been 'celebrated' for at least six centuries before the eighteenth, and continues to attract visitors to the present day. Cumberland might have read, besides Gilpin's remarks, the more detailed accounts given by James Pilkington in *A View of the Present State of Derbyshire*, 1789 and by Stephen Glover in *The Peak Guide*, 1830.

Besides T.2304, the 1977 *George Cumberland* exhibition included seven other drawings of the Peak Cavern. No.24 (still with the Covent Garden Gallery), inscribed 'View of the castle of Castleton and the Cave below', shows the approach to the cavern, via a path which wound down from the ruined castle of Castleton to a deep recess formed by two high limestone cliffs bisected by the emergent River Styx. No.25 (repr. pl.1, now in the collection of Mr. and Mrs. Paul Mellon) focusses on the cavern's vast arched entrance, some twelve yards high, forty yards wide and nearly a hundred yards long. Gilpin had commented that 'So vast a canopy of *unpillared* rock stretching over your head, gives you an involuntary shudder' (*op. cit.*, p.215); but Cumberland, while effectively conveying the mass of the limestone arch, concentrates on actualities, and in particular on the ancient colony of pack-thread spinners established in the cave. No.26 ('Figure of one of the old women who live under the cave in a cottage that never sees the sun', now in a private collection, England), no.27, showing a spinner at work (still with the Covent Garden Gallery) and no.28, inscribed 'appearance and Colour at Coming out from Peaks hole ...' (private collection, England) are views within the first 'great cave'. No.29 (private collection, America) depicts the entrance to an inner cave, 'to which you are conveyed in a flat bottomed oval boat laying on your back on straw and pushed forward by a guide who wades about 2 foot deep in water, and stooping, guides the vessel into this cavern'. Cumberland's inscription on this drawing continues: 'The light above proceeds from Candles already placed there'.

T.2304 is a view within this inner cavern. Pilkington (*op. cit.*, pp.64–65) reported the dimensions of this cavern as seventy yards wide and forty high: 'but not a ray of light can enter it, excepting that which proceeds from a single candle, which he carries with him, and the faint glimmering of this tends only to render him sensible of the extreme darkness and horror of the place'. Candlelight, flickering and fitful, provides the only source of illumination in T.2304. A single minute figure is glimpsed standing high on the steep ascent leading to a high rock sometimes known as 'the Choir' (as in Cumberland's inscription) or 'the Chancel': 'here is sometimes placed, in order to surprise the visitors, a choir of the High Peak singers... under the direction of the parish clerk of Castleton. The sharp and nasal tones of these choristers are not always in unison with each other, but they are far from being out of tune with what may be supposed the ideas of visitors in "these lower regions, where darkness holds an everlasting reign"' (Glover, *op. cit.*, p.67). Another view inside the inner cavern, No.31 in the *Cumberland* exhibition, is now in the collection of the Fitzwilliam Museum, Cambridge.

Gilpin's description of the Peak Cavern was larded with currently fashionable romantic words such as 'horrid', 'tremendous', 'terror' and 'shudder', though he, an arbiter of the picturesque, concluded that he 'never found any picturesque beauty' in such infernal regions (*op. cit.*, pp.214–5). Pilkington and Glover echo, though more faintly, the same attitude to 'awfulness'. Cumberland by contrast observed the natural phenomena of Derbyshire, as he observed landscape in general, with an eye for whatever he found interesting in its own right. Unaffected by current notions of the picturesque, his watercolours are chiefly based on detached and rational observation.

William Daniell 1769–1837

T.2415–2720 **Engraved copper-plates for 'A Voyage Round Great Britain'** 1814–25

Engraved with titles and publication lines
306 copper-plates, various sizes, each approximately 9 × 12 (22.9 × 30.5)
Presented by the Tate Gallery Publications Department 1979

Prov: Longman & Co. and William Daniell, the original publishers; ...; Henry G. Bohn *c*.1850–64; probably one of Bohn's successors, either George Bell & Co. or Chatto & Windus; ...; Armand Maurice, whose business was taken over by Putnam's 1931 and renamed Nattali & Maurice; The Bodley Head, who acquired Putnam's and Nattali & Maurice 1962; purchased from The Bodley Head by the Tate Gallery Publications Department 1972.

Exh: *William Daniell R.A., A Voyage Round Great Britain 1814–1825, An Exhibition of new impressions ...*, The British Council 1980 onwards (three touring exhibitions, each including two of the copper-plates).

Lit: Iain Bain, *William Daniell's A Voyage Round Great Britain ... a note on its production ...*, 1966; [Iain Bain], *William Daniell R.A. A Voyage Round Great Britain ... A prospectus for a new issue ...*, 1977; Iain Bain, *William Daniell's A Voyage Round Great Britain ... A note on its production ...*, 1978.

T.2721–3024 and 3239–40 **Impressions from T.2415–2720** printed 1978–9

With engraved titles and publication lines
306 aquatints, various sizes, images approximately $6\frac{3}{8} \times 9\frac{7}{16}$ (16.3 × 24)
Presented by the Tate Gallery Publications Department 1979

Prov: published by the Tate Gallery Publications Department 1978–9.
Lit: as for T.2415–2720; see also Thomas Sutton, *The Daniells, Artists and Travellers*, 1954, pp.119–36, 165–72.

In the following list of the individual subjects, the acquisition number of the copper-plate precedes that of the print. Titles are as engraved on the plates.

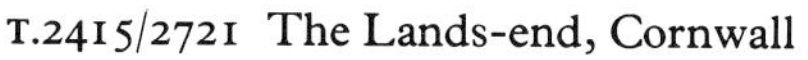

T.2726

T.2739

T.2744

T.2765

T.2415/2721 The Lands-end, Cornwall
T.2416/2722 The long-ships light house, off the landsend, Cornwall
T.2417/2723 The entrance to Portreath, Cornwall
T.2418/2724 Boscastle Pier on the coast of Cornwall
T.2419/2725 Hartland pier, North Devon
T.2420/2726 Clovelly, on the Coast of North Devon
T.2421/2727 Ilfracomb, on the coast of North Devon
T.2422/2728 View of Ilfracombe, from Hilsborough
T.2423/2729 Near Combmartin, on the coast of North Devon
T.2424/2730 Lynmouth, on the coast of North Devon
T.2425/2731 St. Donats, Glamorganshire
T.2426/2732 Britton Ferry, Glamorganshire
T.2427/2733 The Mumbles light-house, in Swansea bay
T.2428/2734 The Worms-head, in Tenby bay
T.2429/2735 Tenby, Pembrokeshire
T.2430/2736 The Eligug-stack, near St. Gowans-head, Pembrokeshire
T.2431/2737 Solva, near St. Davids, Pembrokeshire
T.2432/2738 View of the entrance to Fishguard, from Goodwych sands
T.2433/2739 Goodwych Pier, near Fishguard, Pembrokeshire
T.2434/2740 View near Aberystwith, Cardiganshire
T.2435/2741 Barmouth, Merionethshire
T.2436/2742 View of Caernarvon Castle, from Anglesea
T.2437/2743 The Harbour light-house, Holyhead
T.2438/2744 Light-house on the South Stack, Holyhead
T.2439/2745 Part of the South Stack, Holyhead
T.2440/2746 The Rope bridge, near the Light-house, Holyhead
T.2441/2747 Black marble Quarry, near red wharf bay, Anglesea
T.2442/2748 The entrance to Amlwch harbour, Anglesea
T.2443/2749 Red Wharf Bay, Anglesea
T.2444/2750 Beaumaris Castle, Anglesea
T.2445/2751 View on Puffin Island, near Anglesea
T.2446/2752 The Bath, built by Lord Penryn, near Bangor, N. Wales
T.2447/2753 Penman-maur, taken from near Aber, N. Wales
T.2448/2754 View of Conway Castle, Caernavonshire
T.2449/2755 The Light-house on Point of Air, Flintshire
T.2450/2756 View near Hoyle-lake, Cheshire
T.2451/2757 The Towns-end Mill, Liverpool
T.2452/2758 Seacombe Ferry, Liverpool
T.2453/2759 Liverpool, taken from the opposite side of the River
T.2454/2760 Lancaster Castle
T.2455/2761 View near Lower Heysham, Lancashire
T.2456/2762 Distant View of Whitbarrow Scar, Westmoreland
T.2457/2763 Castle-head, Westmoreland
T.2458/2764 Peel Castle, Lancashire
T.2459/2765 Whitehaven, Cumberland
T.2460/2766 Harrington near Whitehaven Cumberland
T.2461/2767 Mary Port, Cumberland
T.2462/2768 Carlaverock Castle, Dumfrieshire
T.2463/2769 Kirkudbright

T.2777

T.2783

T.2820

T.2464/2770 The Mull of Galloway, Wigtonshire
T.2465/2771 Port Patrick, Wigtonshire
T.2466/2772 Cardness Castle, near Gatehouse, Kirkcudbrightshire
T.2467/2773 Near Carsleith, Galloway
T.2468/2774 Wigton, Galloway
T.2469/2775 Cree-town Kirkudbrightshire
T.2470/2776 The Crag of Ailsa
T.2471/2777 Culzean Castle, Ayrshire
T.2472/2778 Distant View of Ayr
T.2473/2779 Pier at Ardrossan, Ayrshire
T.2474/2780 The Isle of Arran, taken near Ardrossan
T.2475/2781 Ardgowan, Renfrewshire
T.2476/2782 Greenock, on the Clyde
T.2477/2783 Steam boat on the Clyde near Dumbarton
T.2478/2784 Mount Stuart, Isle of Bute
T.2479/2785 Loch Ranza – Isle of Arran
T.2480/2786 Duntrune Castle, Loch Crenan, Argylshire
T.2481/2787 Loch Swene, Argylshire
T.2482/2788 Rassella near Kilmartin Loch Crenan, Argylshire
T.2483/2789 On the Isle of Jura
T.2484/2790 Inverary Castle, Argylshire
T.2485/2791 Dunolly Castle, near Oban, Argylshire
T.2486/2792 Dunstaffnage Castle, Argylshire
T.2487/2793 Clam-shell Cave, Staffa, Iona in the distance
T.2488/2794 Exterior of Fingal's Cave, Staffa
T.2489/2795 Entrance to Fingals Cave, Staffa
T.2490/2796 In Fingals Cave, Staffa
T.2491/2797 Staffa near Fingals Cave
T.2492/2798 The Cormorants Cave, Staffa
T.2493/2799 View from the Island of Staffa
T.2494/2800 The Island of Staffa from the East
T.2495/2801 The Island of Staffa, from the South West
T.2496/2802 View of Iona, from the N. East
T.2497/2803 The Cathedral at Iona
T.2498/2804 View of Ben-more, from near Ulva house
T.2499/2805 Remains of the Chapel &c. on Inch Kenneth
T.2500/2806 Gribune-head in Mull
T.2501/2807 Loch-na-gael, near Knock on Mull
T.2502/2808 Distant view of Cruachan-ben, taken near Arros bridge, Isle of Mull
T.2503/2809 Arros Castle, Isle of Mull
T.2504/2810 Tobermory, on the Isle of Mull
T.2505/2811 Mingarry Castle, Argylshire
T.2506/2812 Ardnamurchan point, Argylshire
T.2507/2813 Scoor Eig, on the Isle of Eig
T.2508/2814 Part of the Isle of Rum
T.2509/2815 Armidal, the Seat of Lord Macdonald, Isle of Skye
T.2510/2816 Iloransay, Isle of Skye
T.2511/2817 Balmacarro-house, Loch-alsh, Roshire
T.2512/2818 Castle Ellen-Donan
T.2513/2819 Loch-Duich, Ross-shire
T.2514/2820 Ilan-dreoch-Glenbeg, Invernesshire
T.2515/2821 The bay of Barrisdale, in Loch Hourne
T.2516/2822 Loch Hourne head
T.2517/2823 Glen-coe taken near Ballachulish
T.2518/2824 Near Kylakin, Skye

T.2519/2825 Liveras, near Broadford, Skye
T.2520/2826 Portree on the Isle of Skye
T.2521/2827 Glenvargle bridge, near Portree, Skye
T.2522/2828 Duntulm, Isle of Skye
T.2523/2829 Dunvegan Castle, Isle of Skye
T.2524/2830 Dunvegan Castle
T.2525/2831 Little Brieshmeal, near Talisker, Skye
T.2526/2832 Loch Scavig, Skye
T.2527/2833 Loch Coruisq near Loch Scavig
T.2528/2834 The Coolin, taken from Loch Slapin
T.2529/2835 From the Isle of Rasay, looking Westward
T.2530/2836 Castle Broichin on the Isle of Raasay
T.2531/2837 Rowadill in Harris
T.2532/2838 Light House on the Isle of Scalpa, Harris
T.2533/2839 Part of the Northern face of one of the Shiant Isles
T.2534/2840 Near view of one of the Shiant Isles
T.2535/2841 Stornaway, on the Isle of Lewis
T.2536/2842 Remains of a Temple at Galston, Isle of Lewis
T.2537/2843 Druidical stone at Strather, near Barvas, Isle of Lewis
T.2538/2844 The Gair-loch, Ross-shire
T.2539/2845 Gair-loch head, Ross-shire
T.2540/2846 Creen-stone rock, Loch Broom
T.2541/2847 Pier at Tanera, Loch Broom
T.2542/2848 Ben Sulvhein, from Loch-Inver
T.2543/2849 View of Cuniag, from Loch Inver
T.2544/2850 Unapool in Kyles-cu Assynt
T.2545/2851 Rispand, Durness
T.2546/2852 Entrance to the Cave of Smowe
T.2547/2853 Whiten-head, Loch Eribol
T.2548/2854 Bay of Tongue
T.2549/2855 Strath-naver, Sutherlandshire
T.2550/2856 The Clett-rock, Holborn-head
T.2551/2857 Thurso, from near Holborn head
T.2552/2858 Castle Sinclair, Thurso
T.2553/2859 Castle Hill near Thurso
T.2554/2860 Mey Castle, Caithness
T.2555/2861 The Ferry at Scarskerry, Caithness
T.2556/2862 Near the Berry-head, Hoy, Orkney
T.2557/2863 The Snook, Hoy, Orkney
T.2558/2864 The Old Man of Hoy
T.2559/2865 Stromness, Orkney
T.2560/2866 Stones of Stennis, Orkney
T.2561/2867 The Cathedral of St. Magnus, Kirkwall, Orkney
T.2562/2868 S.E. view of the Cathedral & Palace, at Kirkwall, Orkney
T.2563/2869 Kirkwall, Orkney, from the Bay
T.2564/2870 N. West View of the Cathedral, Kirkwall
T.2565/2871 Tower of the Bishops Palace, Kirkwall
T.2566/2872 Remains of the Earls Palace, Kirkwall
T.2567/2873 Light House on the Start, Isle of Sandy, Orkney
T.2568/2874 John O'Groats, Caithness
T.2569/2875 Duncansby stacks, Caithness
T.2570/2876 Keiss Castle, Caithness
T.2571/2877 Ackergill Tower, Caithnesshire
T.2572/2878 Castles Sinclair & Girnigo, Caithness
T.2573/2879 Wick, Caithness

T.2832

T.2839

T.2574/2880 Old Wick Castle, Caithness
T.2575/2881 The Stack of Hempriggs, Caithness
T.2576/2882 Scene at Hempriggs, Caithness
T.2577/2883 Forse Castle, Sutherland
T.2578/2884 Dunbeath Castle, Caithness
T.2579/2885 Berrydale, Caithness
T.2580/2886 Castle of Berrydale
T.2581/2887 Helmsdale, Sutherlandshire
T.2582/2888 Dunrobin Castle, Sutherlandshire
T.2583/2889 Dunrobin Castle, from the N.E. Sutherlandshire
T.2584/2890 Dornoch, Sutherlandshire
T.2585/2891 Bonar Bridge
T.2586/2892 Cromarty
T.2587/2893 Pier at Fortrose, Ross-shire
T.2588/2894 Inverness
T.2589/2895 Nairn
T.2590/2896 Obelisk at Forres
T.2591/2897 Nelson's Tower, Forres
T.2592/2898 Brugh-head, Murrayshire
T.2593/2899 Coxtown Tower, near Elgin
T.2594/2900 Finlater Castle, Banffshire
T.2595/2901 Boyne Castle, Banffshire
T.2596/2902 Duff-house, Banff
T.2597/2903 Banff
T.2598/2904 Frazerburgh, Aberdeenshire
T.2599/2905 Kinnaird Head, Aberdeenshire
T.2600/2906 Peterhead, Aberdeenshire
T.2601/2907 Slanes Castle, Aberdeenshire
T.2602/2908 Bridge of Don, Old Aberdeen
T.2603/2909 Aberdeen
T.2604/2910 Dunotter Castle, Kincardineshire
T.2605/2911 Montrose, Forfarshire
T.2606/2912 Inverbernie Bridge
T.2607/2913 Broughty Castle, Forfarshire
T.2608/2914 Dundee, Forfarshire
T.2609/2915 St. Andrews, Fifeshire
T.2610/2916 Wemys Castle, Fifeshire
T.2611/2917 Distant view of Edinburgh, with Wemys Castle
T.2612/2918 Edinburgh, from the Castle
T.2613/2919 Edinburgh, with part of the North Bridge & Castle
T.2614/2920 Edinburgh, from the Calton hill
T.2615/2921 Leith
T.2616/2922 Tantallon Castle, Haddingtonshire
T.2617/2923 The Bass Rock
T.2618/2924 Dunbar, Haddingtonshire
T.2619/2925 Berwick upon Tweed
T.2620/2926 Castle on Holy Island, Northumberland
T.2621/2927 Bamborough Castle, Northumberland
T.2622/2928 North Shields, Northumberland
T.2623/2929 Tynemouth, Northumberland
T.2624/2930 Sunderland Pier, Durham
T.2625/2931 Whitby, Yorkshire
T.2626/2932 Whitby Abbey, Yorkshire
T.2627/2933 Scarborough, Yorkshire
T.2628/2934 Light-house on Flambro'-head, Yorkshire

T.2901

T.2924

T.2629/2935 Boston, Lincolnshire
T.2630/2936 Yarmouth from Gorlstone
T.2631/2937 Lowestoff, Suffolk
T.2632/2938 Southwold, Suffolk
T.2633/2939 The Orford Ness Light houses, Suffolk
T.2634/2940 Harwich, Essex
T.2635/2941 Mistley near Harwich, Essex
T.2636/2942 South End, Essex
T.2637/2943 Sheerness
T.2638/2944 The Reculvers
T.2639/2945 Pier at Margate
T.2640/2946 North Foreland Light House
T.2641/2947 Broadstairs
T.2642/2948 Ramsgate
T.2643/2949 Deal Castle
T.2644/2950 Walmer Castle
T.2645/2951 Dover Castle
T.2646/2952 Dover, from Shakespears Cliff
T.2647/2953 Shakespears Cliff
T.2648/2954 Folkestone, Kent
T.2649/3239 Hythe
T.2650/2955 Dungeness Light House
T.2651/2956 Rye, Sussex
T.2652/2957 Winchelsea
T.2653/2958 Hastings, from near the White Rock
T.2654/2959 Hastings, from the East Cliff
T.2655/2960 Near Beachy-head
T.2656/3240 Brighton
T.2657/2961 Near Regents Square, Brighton
T.2658/2962 Ovington near Brighton
T.2659/2963 Shoreham
T.2660/2964 Pier at Little Hampton
T.2661/2965 View from the Park, Arundel
T.2662/2966 Bognor
T.2663/2967 View from Portsdown Hill
T.2664/2968 West Cowes
T.2665/2969 Lord Henry Seymours Castle
T.2666/2970 Mr. Nash's Castle
T.2667/2971 Ryde
T.2668/2972 Brading Harbour
T.2669/2973 Shanklin Chine
T.2670/2974 Freshwater Bay, Isle of Wight
T.2671/2975 Needles Cliff, & Needles, Isle of Wight
T.2672/2976 Distant view of the Needles & Hurst Castle
T.2673/2977 Christchurch
T.2674/2978 Poole, Dorsetshire
T.2675/2979 Corfe Castle
T.2676/2980 Swanage
T.2677/2981 Lulworth Cove
T.2678/2982 Weymouth
T.2679/2983 Light-house, Isle of Portland
T.2680/2984 St. Catherine's Chapel, Dorset
T.2681/2985 Bridport Harbour, Dorset
T.2682/2986 Lyme Regis, from Charmouth, Dorset
T.2683/2987 Sidmouth, Devon

T.2960

T.2684/2988 Exmouth, Devon
T.2685/2989 Teignmouth, Devon
T.2686/2990 Babicombe, Devon
T.2687/2991 Torbay, Devon
T.2688/2992 Tor-abbey, Devon
T.2689/2993 Tor-quay, Devon
T.2690/2994 Brixham, Torbay, Devon
T.2691/2995 Entrance to Dartmouth, Devon
T.2692/2996 The Junction of the Dart with the Sea
T.2693/2997 Near Kingswear, on the Dart, Devon
T.2694/2998 Kingswear, Devon
T.2695/2999 Salcombe, Devon
T.2696/3000 Bovisand, near Plymouth
T.2697/3001 Quay at Straddon point, near Plymouth
T.2698/3002 The Citadel, Plymouth
T.2699/3003 Catwater, Plymouth, from the Citadel
T.2700/3004 Mount Edgecumbe, from the Citadel, Plymouth
T.2701/3005 View from Mount Edgecumbe
T.2702/3006 Hamoaze, from Mount Edgecumbe
T.2703/3007 Port wrinkle, Cornwall
T.2704/3008 East Looe, Cornwall
T.2705/3009 Polperro, Cornwall
T.2706/3010 Fowey, from Bodenick, Cornwall
T.2707/3011 Fowey Castle, Cornwall
T.2708/3012 Polkerris, Cornwall
T.2709/3013 Mevagissy, Cornwall
T.2710/3014 Mevagissy, Cornwall
T.2711/3015 Gorran haven, Cornwall
T.2712/3016 Port-looe, Cornwall
T.2713/3017 Falmouth, Cornwall
T.2714/3018 The Lizard Light-houses, Cornwall
T.2715/3019 Mullyan Cove, Cornwall
T.2716/3020 Near Mullyan Cove, Cornwall
T.2717/3021 St. Michaels mount, Cornwall
T.2718/3022 St. Michaels Mount, Cornwall
T.2719/3023 Penzance, Cornwall
T.2720/3024 The Land's end, Cornwall

William Daniell's *A Voyage Round Great Britain* was the most ambitious of the many topographical publications produced in England during the early nineteenth century and its plates are a highpoint in the history of aquatint engraving. The work comprised a lengthy descriptive text and 308 aquatints, engraved by Daniell himself and hand-coloured through the agency of William Timms. The first half of the whole work, i.e. volumes I–IV, was issued both in parts (two prints to a part) and in volumes between 1814 and 1820. Volumes V–VIII appeared in volume form only between 1821 and 1825. Daniell made the original pencil drawings on a series of tours between 1813 and 1823, the first two in company with Richard Ayton, who wrote the text for volumes I–II. The remaining six volumes have text by the artist himself. Daniell's route took him clockwise round the coast, commencing and finishing at Lands End. For the first four volumes the firm of Longman shared the risk of publication with him. The retail price of parts was originally 10s. 6d. and of volumes 7 guineas. The last four volumes were published by Daniell alone. Much information about the production and financing of the *Voyage* survives in the Longman account books (see Iain Bain's publications of 1966 and 1978 cited above).

Some of the plates were reissued after Daniell's death, for example by Bohn in the 1850s. In the present century, Thomas Ross & Son held a contract from Nattali & Maurice from 1948 onwards for printing and publishing the *Voyage*. At an unknown date two of the copper-plates ('Dunsky Castle' and 'Hull') were lost. A final edition of the surviving 306 plates was published in 1978–9 by the Tate Gallery Publications Department in association with Editions Alecto. This edition, limited to 90 sets, was printed by Tisiphone Etching Ltd and the Islington Studios, under the supervision of Charles Newington and Frank Tinsley. The impressions were left uncoloured, thus displaying the delicate tones of Daniell's aquatinting. Ayton's and Daniell's 900 page text was also reprinted on this occasion and published in two volumes in 1978 by the Tate Gallery Publications Department and the Scolar Press. These volumes also include small monochrome reproductions of all the plates.

Thomas Gainsborough 1727–88

T.2261 **Sir Benjamin Truman** *c*.1770–4

Oil on canvas, $93\frac{5}{8} \times 59\frac{9}{16}$ (237.8 × 151.3)
Purchased (Grant-in-Aid), with the aid of contributions from Hugh Leggatt through the National Art-Collections Fund; from several directors of Truman's Brewery led by Geoffrey Dent; from Sir Emmanuel Kaye CBE on behalf of Lansing Bagnall Ltd.; from the Viscount Mackintosh Charitable Trust; and from other members of the public 1978

Prov: Painted for the sitter and tied by him in his will to remain at the premises of Truman's brewery at Spitalfields for as long as any descendant of his was connected with it; by descent to Henry Villebois and bought at his death by Messrs. Truman, Hanbury & Co. in December 1886; acquired with the firm by Maxwell Joseph 1973–4, and sold through Colnaghi's to Paul Mellon 1977; after refusal of export licence bought by the Tate Gallery.

Exh: R.A. 1878 (281), as 'Sir Daniel Truman'; Grosvenor Gallery 1885 (12); 45 Park Lane 1936 (32, repr. p.45 in album of illustrations); *British Painting*, Louvre, Paris 1938 (55, repr. in album of illustrations); Tate Gallery 1953 (37, repr. pl.viii); *British Portraits*, R.A. 1956–7 (328, repr. p.24 in album of illustrations).

Lit: G. W. Fulcher, *Life of Thomas Gainsborough RA*, 1856, p.105 (for Miss Read's portrait); Sir Walter Armstrong, *Gainsborough and his Place in British Art*, 1904, p.280 (wrongly catalogued twice); Mary Woodall, *Thomas Gainsborough*, 1949, p.61, repr. f.p.46; E. K. Waterhouse, *Gainsborough*, 1958, pp.21, 93, no.674, repr. pl.117, and f.p.16 in col.; Mary Woodall (ed.), *The Letters of Thomas Gainsborough*, 1961 & 1963, p.85, no.39; *Trumans: The Brewers*, published privately 1966, p.10ff., repr. p.17; John Hayes, *Gainsborough*, 1975, p.216, note 79, repr. pl.76; and in catalogue of *Gainsborough* exhibition, Paris 1981, p.49, repr.; Jack Lindsay, *Thomas Gainsborough*, 1981, last para. of Preface and pp.137–8; *The Tate Gallery 1978–80*, repr. in col. on cover.

The family of Sir Benjamin Truman (1711–80) had been connected with brewing since the seventeenth century; under him the firm became one of the largest commercial enterprises of the period, chiefly through its famed black stout or porter. By 1760 it ranked third among the great London porter firms, and in the following year, on the accession of George III, Truman was knighted in recognition of his extensive investments in the public loans raised to finance the wars of George II. His wealth enabled him to build a fine new residence near the brewery in Brick Lane, Spitalfields, and to rent 'Popes', a country estate at Hertingfordbury in Hertfordshire. At the height of his success he furnished these residences with full length portraits of himself and his family by Gainsborough and later Romney (a fine three-quarter length of Sir Benjamin, seated and about ten years older, by Romney was on the U.S. art market in 1968; a photograph of this picture is in the National Portrait Gallery). Truman seems to have banked with Child's whose mid-eighteenth to early nineteenth-century ledgers have been destroyed, so that it is not possible to establish the exact dates of the commissions, but judging from the age of the sitter and the style of the painting this portrait must have been painted either during Gainsborough's last years in Bath, or immediately on his settling in London in 1774. There appears to have been no portrait of Truman's wife Frances, who died in 1766 (as did his only son), but by September 1777 he had commissioned the artist to paint a full-length of his grand-daughter Frances Read, later Mrs Villebois (now in the collection of Viscount Cowdray; Waterhouse, 1958, repr. pl.164). Gainsborough refers to Miss Read's sittings in a letter of 12 September 1777 to his sister Mrs Gibbon, and in a letter dated 22 September 1777 (partly quoted in Lindsay, 1981, p.137) he writes that her grandfather had paid him fifty pounds as the half price of the portrait, which gives us some indication of what the portrait of Sir Benjamin himself had probably also cost. Later Gainsborough was to paint Truman's other grand-daughter Henrietta, Mrs Mears (Huntington Art Gallery, San Marino, Calif., repr. in the Museum's *Handbook*, 1970, no.17; also C. H. Collins Baker, *Catalogue of Pictures in the Huntington Collection*, 1936, p.49, pl.XIII) and a double portrait of his Villebois great-grandsons, Henry and John (private collection; at the time of writing on loan to Leicester Art Gallery, repr. Waterhouse, 1958, pl.222). Stylistically, however, these last two belong to the early 1780s, and may have been commissioned after Sir Benjamin's death. A strong dynastic sense made him want to keep the business in the family, and his descendants were not to go without firm advice on this matter, written in the Rest Book of 1775 (quoted in *Trumans: The Brewers*, 1966, p.16): '... there can be no other way of raising a great Fortune than by carrying on an Extensive trade. I must tell you Young Man, this is not to be obtained without Spirrit and great Application'. He clearly saw his life-style, which included the family portraits, and the trade on which his wealth was based as an integrated whole, for his will, dated 7 May 1779, directed that his Spitalfields house be maintained 'thoroughly clean' until either of his great-grandsons whom he had designated as his heirs attained the age of twenty-one, and 'that all my paintings at Popes shall be removed from thence to my Dwelling house in Spitalfields and there remain so long as any of my family have a connection or concern in the Trade now carrying on there by me'. His descendants, however, remained sleeping partners, and the drawing room in the Spitalfields house became the firm's board room, with the paintings *in situ*. There Sir Benjamin's portrait exerted a noticeable influence on his successors, so that at least two of them, Sampson Hanbury and Arthur Pryor, who raised the firm to new heights of success in the nineteenth century, had themselves painted in almost identical or related poses and settings (repr. in *Truman's: The Brewers*, 1966).

After the death of Henry Villebois in 1886, his son, also Henry, reclaimed his rights of ownership to the Gainsborough portraits, and they were sold out of the family, with the firm securing the retention of the portrait of Sir Benjamin through purchase (the compiler is grateful to Miss J. Coburn, Head Archivist of the Greater London Record Office, for supplying details from the Truman archives about the picture's history during the 19th century, and to Messrs Truman Ltd. for permission to quote them).

Although Gainsborough's contemporaries considered his remarkably fluent and painterly technique particularly suitable for painting sensitive portraits of women, this portrait, which is in pristine condition, displays to the full his ability to convey by the same means a forceful and virile personality, subtly enhancing it by the use of sober but warm colours, and by placing the figure in an open setting which underlines the sitter's gravity and self-reliant isolation.

George Garrard 1760–1826

T.2358 **A Bay Hunter by a Lake** *c.*1790

Oil on canvas, $22\frac{1}{2} \times 32$ (57.2 × 81.2)
Presented by Mr Paul Mellon KBE through the British Sporting Art Trust 1979

Prov: ...; anon. sale Sotheby's 3 April 1968 (158), bt. Arthur Ackermann & Sons Ltd. for Paul Mellon.

Lit: Egerton, 1978, p.164, no.161.

The hunter, unsaddled, is portrayed in what are probably the grounds of a gentleman's country estate; there is a lake on the left, and a glimpse of a brick wall (perhaps of a stable) on the right. A date *c.*1790 is suggested by comparison with other works by Garrard in the Mellon Collection.

Marcus Gheeraedts the Younger *c.*1561–1635

T.3028 **Captain Thomas Lee** 1594

Inscribed 'Ætatis suae 43/An° D°1594', upper right centre, above lake, and 'Facere et pati Fortia' upper left, above arm. Also 'S! Henry Lee of Ireland' bottom left, in later script
Oil on canvas, $90\frac{3}{4} \times 59\frac{5}{16}$ (230.5 × 151), considerably enlarged on all sides with strips $2\frac{1}{2}$–$8\frac{1}{4}$ (6–21) wide at some later date
Purchased (Grant-in-Aid), with contributions from the Friends of the Tate Gallery, the National Art-Collections Fund and the Pilgrim Trust 1980

Prov: Presumably painted for Sir Henry Lee and always in the Lee-Dillon collections; first recorded at Ditchley by Vertue in 1725; Dillon sale, Sotheby's 24 May 1933 (46, repr.), bt. Francis Howard; Loel Guinness, by whom lent to the Tate Gallery from 1953 until purchased 1980.

Exh: *National Portrait Exhibition*, South Kensington 1868 (631) as 'Sir Henry Lee'; *British Art*, R.A., 1934 (23, repr. pl.XIII); *The Age of Shakespeare*, Gemeentemuseum, The Hague, 1958 (73); *Between Renaissance and Baroque*, Manchester, 1965 (114); period display, Metropolitan Museum, New York 1966 (no catalogue); *The Elizabethan Image*, Tate Gallery, 1969–70 (155, repr.).

Lit: Vct. Dillon, *Catalogue of Paintings... at Ditchley, Spelsbury, Oxfordshire*, 1908, p.23 (31), repr. pl.XVI; *Dictionary of National Biography*, 1909 (on Thomas Lee); L. Cust 'Marcus Gheerarts' in *Walpole Society*, III, 1914, p.35, repr. pl.XII(b); Vertue Notebooks, I, in *Walpole Society*, XVIII, 1930, p.115; C. H. Collins Baker and W. G. Constable, *English Painting in the Sixteenth and Seventeenth Centuries*, 1930, p.44, pl.35A; *Catalogue of Paintings... at Ditchley* (shorter version), 1933, no.30; Note on Dillon sale, *Apollo*, XVII, June 1933, p.292, repr.; E. K. Chambers,

Sir Henry Lee, 1936, pp.31, 185–203, 218, 230–1, repr. pl.IV; Eric Mercer, *English Art 1553–1625*, 1962, pp.165 and 118; Roy Strong, 'Elizabethan Painting: an approach through inscriptions: Marcus Gheeraerts the Younger' in *Burlington Magazine*, CV, 1963, p.149ff., repr. fig.17; Roy Strong, *The English Icon*, 1969, p.279, repr. no.267, and reprint of above article pp.350–1; B. d. Breffny (ed.), *The Irish World*, 1977, p.105, repr. in col.; *The Tate Gallery 1978–80*, p.24, repr. in col.

Thomas Lee (1552 or 3–1601) was the son of Benedict Lee of Bigging and Margaret, daughter of Sir Robert Pakington, and was thus a relative (their fathers were half-brothers) of the influential courtier Sir Henry Lee, KG, the Queen's Champion of the Tilt, from whose family collection at Ditchley this portrait comes. Thomas served in Ireland, already under the first Earl of Essex, in the ruthless campaign to colonise Ulster, captaining a troop of twenty-four horsemen, being alternatively commended by his superiors for good service and bravery, or cautioned and punished for disorderly behaviour and banditry. Reports describe him as a man of 'rash speech and other unadvisedness' and possessed of 'both good merits and evil infirmities'. He had been familiar from childhood with Hugh O'Neill, 2nd Earl of Tyrone, and when the latter became titular native chief of Ulster in 1593, clearly heading for rebellion against the Crown, Lee was employed, as he was on later occasions, as a preliminary agent to arrange parleys between Tyrone and the official commissioners. As a result an open breach was avoided until 1595, when Tyrone was proclaimed a traitor. Lee's uneven military career ended with his involvement in the disastrous campaign of his patron the 2nd Earl of Essex in Ireland in 1599. At its conclusion the Earl took Lee back with him to England, telling him to lie low with Sir Henry Lee until the troubles blew over. Although by all accounts Sir Henry found his cousin a great trial, he was loyal to him, took him to the court, supported his innumerable petitions to Lord Burghley, and stood security for him on the occasions when Thomas was placed under restraint. However, after his near-manic behaviour during Essex's attempted *coup* in February 1601, Thomas was beyond saving: first he appears to have made an offer to Lord Burghley to assassinate Essex, but after the Earl's arrest he declared his devotion to him and suggested to some influential nobles at court that they should kidnap the Queen in order to force her to release Essex. He was immediately arrested at Whitehall, tried for high treason and executed at Tyburn on 17th February.

Thomas was in England for the greater part of 1594, which is when this portrait must have been painted. It is a highly political picture. Although Lee's gentlemanly status is demonstrated by the lace and exquisite embroidery on his rolled-up shirt, by the finely inlaid snap-haunce pistol and 'Spanish'-type helmet, probably of North Italian make (A. V. B. Norman, Master of the Armories of the Tower of London, kindly helped to identify the above; see also B. E. Sargeaunt in *The Times*, 8 October 1934), he is dressed as an Irish kerne, or common foot-soldier – in Elizabethan terms the poorest of the poor – who had to travel lightly armed and bare-legged through the bogs. (That this was standard practice is shown by the bare-legged outfit of the *Hybernus Miles* by J. J. Boissard in *Habitus Variarum orbis gentium*, Antwerp, 1581. Apart from this one detail, however, the costume bears no resemblance to that worn by Lee.) Its use here could be an embittered reference to the more than one occasion when his troop of horsemen was temporarily disbanded, notably in 1583 for marauding in Kilkenny. More probably, it could be a visual underscoring of the views expressed in his *Brief Declaration of the Government in Ireland*, written for Queen Elizabeth during the months he spent in England in 1594 and which he presented to her that November. In it he deplores the deprivations suffered by royal officers in Ireland (he is known to have complained that he would die the poorest man that ever served Her Majesty), and urges the Crown to establish good relations with Tyrone and the northern lords.

The landscape in which Lee stands presumably represents Ireland, open bog-land to the left, and a wood behind him where a small group of armed men just visible above a stretch of open water may be a reference to his part in a campaign the previous year when his commanders, including the apparently still-loyal Earl of Tyrone, commended him for his bravery in entering the deep ford of Golune during an action.

Bearing in mind the punning wit of the Elizabethans, it may be worth noting that Thomas stands in the lee of an oak, which could refer both to the protection of his eminent relative Sir Henry, in whose house and under whose instructions the portrait is likely to have been painted (although the Earl of Essex also had a reputation as a good deviser of allegorical programmes), as well as to its more general meaning as a symbol of reliability and constancy (*Fide et Constantia* was Sir Henry's motto), or even to its notorious quality of attracting lightning. The aspen or linden tree on the sitter's right is also likely to have similar connotations.

The quotation from Livy in the tree beside him (Hist. II, 12; D. Spillan's translation of 1866 is used here) shows that Lee meant his portrait to be both a monument and an *apologia*. 'Both to act and to suffer with fortitude is a Roman's part' were the words uttered by Caius Mucius Scaevola when captured in the enemy camp of the Etrurians who were besieging Rome, having penetrated into it in disguise and made an unsuccessful attempt to assassinate the rebel leader Porsena. At his trial, to show his disdain for personal suffering, he thrust his right hand into the sacrificial fire – a convenient reminder of the fact that a short while before Lee had sustained great personal loss through a disastrous fire caused, he maintained, by enemy arson. Previously to this, not only does Mucius explain his intentions to the Senate in order to avoid being taken for a deserter should he be apprehended by Roman soldiers while wearing Etrurian disguise (because of his contacts with certain Irish chiefs Lee's loyalty had been repeatedly in doubt), but parts of Mucius' speech sound like an attempt to repel accusations of cattle rustling and raids into neighbouring territories which had been levelled at Lee: Mucius wants to 'enter the enemy's camp . . . not as a plunderer or as an avenger in our turn of their devastations. A greater deed is in my mind . . .'. Impressed by Mucius' fortitude, Porsena concludes a peace treaty with the Romans which is nobly adhered to by both sides – exactly what Lee hoped his talks with Tyrone would achieve. Last but not least, Mucius is rewarded by the Senate with a grant of land 'on the far side of the Tiber' – precisely what Lee had been petitioning the Government to do for himself in Ireland.

The picture fits well into the *oeuvre* ascribed to Gheeraedts both on the grounds of style and the characteristic lettering which has come to be known as a 'Gheeraedts script', and as such can be considered as one of his masterpieces. Sir Henry must have been one of the artist's earliest patrons, as the Ditchley collection had several portraits which can be ascribed to him, including the famous full-length of Queen Elizabeth standing on a map of England (National Portrait Gallery), a full-length of Sir Henry in Garter robes (the City of London Hall of Armourers and Brasiers), and a full-length of the 2nd Earl of Essex in Garter robes (National Portrait Gallery). In its technique and design, particularly in the placing of the figure in a naturalistic but politically relevant landscape, Lee's portrait is in harmony with that of the 2nd Earl of Essex standing on a sea-shore with the burning of Cadiz in the background, painted *c.*1596, the best version of which is at Woburn.

The portrait was first recorded at Ditchley by Vertue who in 1725 noted there a portrait of 'Lee in Highlanders Habit leggs naked a target & head peice on his left hand his right a spear or pike. Ætatis suae.43.an^{o} D^{ni} 1594'.

Attributed to **Marcus Gheeraedts, the Younger**
c. 1561–1635

T.3030 **Lady Aston** *c.*1620–3

Oil on canvas, 89½ × 52½ (227 × 133)
Purchased (Grant-in-Aid), with contributions from the Friends of the Tate Gallery, the National Art-Collections Fund and the Pilgrim Trust 1980

Prov: ...; according to a letter to the compiler from R. G. Williams, purchased by Williams & Son of Grafton Street at the sale of Brig.-Gen. Hervey Talbot of Aston Lodge, Warrington, Brown & Co., Chester, 27 April 1927 (but it is not possible to identify it in the catalogue); Leggatt Bros. by May 1931, from whom probably bought by Capt. Loel Guinness; lent by him to the Tate Gallery from 1953 until purchased 1980.

Lit: R. Strong, *The English Icon*, 1969, p.303, no.312 for repr. of version at Adelaide; *The Tate Gallery 1978–80*, p.29, repr. in col.

This full-length of a lady wearing a silver brocade dress, standing on a 'turkey' carpet beside a table covered with red velvet, in a niche of hangings of the same material, conforms very much to the Jacobean pattern for formal full-length portraits as displayed in works ascribed to Larkin, Van Somer, Gheeraedts and others. Her deep *décolletage*, high waist and falling ruff belong to the early 1620s, as does the black twist decoration in her ears, around her wrists and on her bosom which had became fashionable at court under Queen Anne.

A slightly more elaborate version of this portrait, where a leaded window with two broken panes of glass replaces the curtain in the background and a chair the table beside her, is in the National Gallery of South Australia, Adelaide. Its provenance goes back no further than its sale by Mrs Otto Khan at Christie's, 27 May 1938 (Strong, *op. cit.*, misprints the year as 1935), so that a confusion with the Tate version before this date cannot be ruled out.

Strong accepts the traditional identification of the sitter as Gertrude Sadler, wife of Sir Walter Aston, Lord Forfar (1584–1639), James I's ambassador to Spain in 1620–5, and later also under Charles I. The ambassadorial appointment and court connections could well account for the production of more than one formal full-length at about this time. However, the suggestion that this could be Lady Magdalena Aston (d.1635), wife of Sir Thomas Aston (1600–45) of Aston Hall, Cheshire, cannot be ruled out in view of the picture's apparent provenance, even though both families were connected, and the presence of portraits of distant but prominent members of the family would not be unusual.

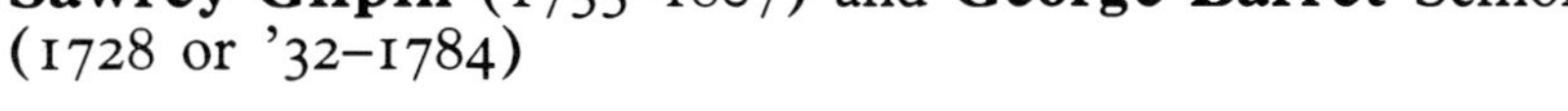

Sawrey Gilpin (1733–1807) and **George Barret** Senior (1728 or '32–1784)

T.2359 **Brood Mares and Colts in a Landscape** ?exh. 1783

Oil on canvas, 24¾ × 29½ (62.8 × 74.8)
Presented by Mr Paul Mellon KBE through the British Sporting Art Trust 1979.

Prov: Anon. sale, Christie's 5 February 1791 (62, as 'Brood Mares and Foals by Gilpin and Landscape by Barrett'); ...; J. S. Mansford by 1868; ...; anon. sale, Christie's 14 July 1961 (140, as 'Gilpin. A string of horses and foals in a woodland clearing'), bt. Betts; Leggatt Brothers, from whom purchased by Paul Mellon 1961.

Exh: ?Society of Artists, 1783 (100, as 'Brood Mares and Colts in a Landscape' by Gilpin); *National Exhibition of Works of Art*, Leeds General Infirmary, 1868 (1104); *Painting in England 1700–1850: Collection of Mr & Mrs Paul Mellon*, Virginia Museum of Fine Arts, Richmond Virginia 1963 (338, pl.96).
Lit: Egerton, 1978, p.120, no.118, repr. pl.44.

The horses are by Gilpin, and the landscape by Barret. Gilpin had little confidence in his own ability to provide realistic settings for his paintings of horses. In 1804 Farington reported a conversation between Gilpin and Francis Bourgeois RA on the 'extraordinary ability' of 'Marshall, a Horsepainter', during which 'Gilpin had said that in managing His backgrounds He [Benjamin Marshall] had done that which Stubbs and Himself never could venture upon' (ed. Kenneth Garlick and Angus Macintyre, *The Diary of Joseph Farington*, VI, p.2282; entry for 28 March 1804). Gilpin's own landscape backgrounds, though pleasantly coloured (usually in bluish-green), lack both originality and definition.

For his more ambitious compositions, Gilpin often invited other artists to add landscape backgrounds (and occasionally figures). Other examples of his collaboration with George Barret include 'Colonel Thornton with his Pointers', 1770 (coll. Winchester House Property Co. Ltd., exh. Arts Council, *British Sporting Painting 1650–1850*, 1974–5, 62) and 'Anglers landing a catch on Lake Windermere' (Mellon Collection). Gilpin's collaboration with William Marlow produced the splendid picture of 'The Duke of Cumberland visiting his Stud', *c.*1764, Gilpin painting the numerous horses and Marlow the landscape with a view of Windsor Castle (coll. Her Majesty the Queen; Millar, 1969, cat.no.826, pl.21). In 'William Coates of Pasture House, Northallerton' (private coll., exh. Arts Council, 1974–5, 64), Gilpin collaborated with Johan Zoffany; in 'Henry Styleman and his first wife', a double portrait with horses and grooms *c.*1783 (coll. Lady Thompson, repr. David Coombs, *Sport and the Countryside*, 1978, p.108), the figures were painted by Zoffany, the landscape by Farington and the horses by Gilpin.

Attributed to **James Hamilton** 1640–1720

T.2266 **Two Hounds Chasing a Hare** *c.*1700

Inscribed 'P ∴ T [?PinxiT] /(?)De/Hamilton' on stone bottom left of centre
Oil on canvas, $43\frac{1}{2} \times 61\frac{7}{8}$ (110.5 × 157)
Bequeathed by Miss Agnes Clarke, 1978
Prov: ...; according to a typescript label on the back of the frame, 'Formerly the property of James T. Talman. Sold by him to his son Edward Watson Talman October 1, 1839 (see receipted bill in Talman Archives)', unverified; ...; according to Miss Clarke's solicitors, probably purchased in England in the 1950s by Miss Clarke and/or her brother John Semple Clarke (formerly citizens of USA), who settled after World War II at Killagorden House, Idless, Truro, Cornwall.

This seems to show mingled influences from Francis Barlow and from the Flemish tradition of such painters as Jan Fyt. The signature is not easily legible, but appears to read 'De Hamilton', a pointer to a family of artists whose work is little known. T.2266 is here attributed to James Hamilton, a Scottish-born artist who during Cromwell's Protectorate went into exile at Brussels, where he and his family were evidently styled 'de Hamilton', and where he died; but it may rather be the work of one of his sons, Ferdinand Philip (1664–1750), Charles William

(1668–1754) or John George de Hamilton (1672–1737), who painted scenes of the chase.

Charles Cooper Henderson 1803–77

T.2360 **Changing Horses to a Post-Chaise outside the 'George' Posting House** ?*c.*1830–40

Oil on canvas, 21 × 30 (53.5 × 76)
Presented by Mr Paul Mellon KBE through the British Sporting Art Trust 1979

Prov: ...; anon. sale, Phillips Son & Neal, 15 May 1972 (27, as 'English 19th Century School: Coaching scene ...') bt. Sabin Galleries, from whom purchased by Paul Mellon 1963.

Lit: Egerton, 1978, p.330, no.364, repr. pl.115b.

Post-chaises were owned by inn-keepers who hired them out, with horses and post-boys, to people who wished to travel privately rather than by stage-coach; they were usually second-hand gentlemen's carriages, painted yellow. The post-boys (usually in fact men) customarily wore yellow or blue jackets, leather breeches, top boots 'and beaver hats in which they kept all their possessions' (Marilyn Watney, *The Elegant Carriage*, 1961, pp.75–6).

An inn sign, painted with a representation of St. George and the Dragon and lettered 'Posting House', spans the road on a gallows. Cooper Henderson may have had the George Inn at Crawley in mind for this scene. Certainly it had (and still has) such a gallows sign, but early nineteenth-century engravings of the inn show it as a different and considerably older building.

John Frederick Herring 1795–1865

T.2361 **Birmingham, with Patrick Conolly up, and his Owner John Beardsworth** 1830

Inscribed 'J. F. Herring. 1830' lower right
Oil on canvas, 21 × 29 (53.2 × 73.7)
Presented by Mr Paul Mellon KBE through the British Sporting Art Trust 1979

Prov: Beaufort Hunt, the son of Birmingham's veterinary surgeon, by descent to Miss Mary C. Marsh; Richard Green, from whom purchased by Paul Mellon 1970.

Exh: Richard Green, *Sporting Paintings*, 1970 (13, repr.).

Lit: Egerton, 1978, pp.298–9, no.322; Christopher Neve, 'Gift from a Galloping Anglophile', in *Country Life*, CLXVI, 30 August 1979, p.584, repr. in colour, fig.1.

Engr: in aquatint by R. G. Reeve, published by S. & J. Fuller, March 21st 1831.

Birmingham, a dark brown colt by Filho da Puta out of Miss Craigie, foaled in 1827 and bred by Mr Lacey, was purchased for 55 guineas by John Beardsworth, and named after his new owner's native city. T.2361 commemorates Birmingham's only Classic win, the 1830 St. Leger at Doncaster, in which Patrick Conolly rode him to victory against the favourite, William Chifney's 1000-guinea Priam. The fork of lightning in the background on the left is not artist's licence, but a record of the fact that a violent thunderstorm raged during the race (J. S. Fletcher, *The History of the St. Leger Stakes, 1776–1901*, 1902, pp. 228–31).

Owner, horse and jockey share the stage with equal honours in this picture (the version noted below, a smaller picture, echoes the composition of T.2361 but lacks its high finish and what Christopher Neve, *op. cit.*, perceptively calls its 'steely veracity'). John Beardsworth, the owner, here portrayed in almost dandified dress of top hat, cut-away coat and nankeen trousers, was a self-made man who established a vast Repository and Carriage Mart described by Pierce Egan as 'the Tattersall's of Birmingham'. The building accommodated 500 vehicles, with stabling for 140 horses; sales were held every Thursday. Beardsworth himself lived in considerable style, remarking that having won the gold, he considered himself entitled to wear it (Pierce Egan, *Book of Sports*, 1831, pp.113–20).

Patrick Conolly went on to win the Derby twice: in 1834 on Plenipotentiary, and in 1841 on Coronation. There is however little to record of Birmingham's subsequent career; Fletcher (*op. cit.*) relates that 'his greatest accomplishment, next to having won the St. Leger, appears to have lain in his trick of following Mrs Beardsworth around her dining-table as if he had been a lap-dog or a tame cat'.

A version of T.2361 measuring $13\frac{1}{2} \times 18\frac{1}{2}$ inches was sold from the collection of Mr and Mrs Jack R. Dick at Sotheby's on 26 June 1974 (68, repr. in colour, bt. S. Lane; subsequently offered at Sotheby's, 21 March 1979, lot 149, bt.in).

T.2362 **Manuella at Richard Watt's Stud Farm, Bishop Burton, Yorkshire** 1825

Inscribed 'MANUELLA' bottom centre and 'J. F. Herring/1825' bottom right in red
Oil on canvas, 40 × 50 (101.5 × 127)
Presented by Mr Paul Mellon KBE through the British Sporting Art Trust 1979

Prov: Painted for Richard Watt, Bishop Burton, near Beverley, Yorkshire, thence by family descent until 1976; Arthur Ackermann & Son Ltd., from whom purchased by Paul Mellon 1976.

Lit: Egerton, 1978, pp.294–5 no.316A.

Manuella, by Dick Andrews out of Mandane, was a bay filly foaled in 1809. She had never raced in public until her then owner, W. N. W. Hewitt, entered her for both the Derby and the Oaks in 1812. Her training performance was however sufficiently spectacular to make her second favourite for the Derby; but her chances were deliberately spoilt by her jockey Sam Chifney junior. He pulled Manuella up in the Derby (which she lost) in order to lengthen the odds and thus enhance the value of his own substantial bet on her for the Oaks the following day (which she won).

Manuella was sold to Lord Sackville in 1812, and soon after that became one of the brood mares at the stud farm of Richard Watt, a noted owner and breeder of racehorses. One of her successful sons was Memnon, winner of the St. Leger in 1825. Herring's portrait of 'Memnon with William Scott up', showing the winner in Doncaster racecourse, with Scott up in Richard Watt's distinctive harlequin colours, was engraved and published in 1826 (versions of this painting include [1] $26\frac{1}{2} \times 33\frac{1}{4}$in., coll. Mr and Mrs Paul Mellon; Egerton, 1978, cat.no.316, colour pl.38; [2] 30 × 40 in., with Ackermann, 1978; repr. Stella A. Walker, *Sporting Art: England 1700–1900*, 1972, pl.54). Richard Watt must have commissioned the portrait of Manuella in the same year as her son Memnon's St. Leger victory: a graceful tribute to a mare who, though evidently no longer in prime racing shape, is still of remarkably elegant conformation.

The pastoral background, remote from the racecourse, is unusually finely handled for Herring, and is convincingly rural in an unstudied manner not found in his later rather overcrowded agricultural scenes. Certain elements in T.2362, particularly the treatment of the heavily gnarled tree and the receding view, suggest that in this instance Herring deliberately attempted to emulate James Ward.

George Henry Laporte 1799–1873

T.2363 **Arab Mare and Foal, with Attendant, by a Ruined Temple** *c.*1835

Oil on canvas, $19\frac{1}{8} \times 26\frac{1}{2}$ (48.5 × 67.5)
Presented by Mr Paul Mellon KBE through the British Sporting Art Trust 1979

Prov: ...; L. F. McCardle, Sheffield Park, Sussex; Richard Green, from whom purchased by Mr Mellon 1971.

Exh: *Annual Exhibition of Sporting Paintings*, Richard Green 1971 (15, repr.).

Lit: Egerton, 1978, p.319, no.348.

Like several other artists who painted Arabian bloodstock, Laporte sometimes added imaginary 'eastern' backgrounds to suggest the 'Arabia' from which the Arab horse was originally imported into England. Here the young attendant's costume and the ruins, tent and palm trees in the background are only moderately fanciful; in other paintings, Laporte introduces the sphinx, pyramids and camels.

Two similar paintings by Laporte remain in the Mellon Collection: 'A Mameluke purchasing an Arab Stallion from a Horse Dealer' and 'Grey Arab Mare and Foal with an Arabian Peasant Family' (Egerton, 1978, p.318, nos. 246–7). A date *c.*1835 is suggested for all three as Laporte was at that time painting Arab horses presented to William IV (died 1837); three such subjects were engraved and published in the *Sporting Magazine*, CXXIII, July 1840.

Frederic, Lord Leighton 1830–96

T.3053 **Lieder ohne Worte** 1860–61

Oil on canvas, $40 \times 24\frac{3}{4}$ (101.7 × 63.0)
Purchased at Christie's (Grant-in-aid) 1980

Prov: Painted for James Stuart Hodgson, sold Christie's 3 June 1893 (26), bt. Sir Charles Cavendish Clifford, 4th Bart; his sister, Miss Augusta Caroline Clifford; given by her to her second cousin, Mme Ernest Mallet of Paris *c.*1930; by descent until sold anonymously, Christie's 29 February 1980 (208, repr. in colour), bt. Roy Miles Fine Paintings for the Tate Gallery.

Exh: R.A. 1861 (550); *Brighton Art Loan Exhibition*, Brighton 1884 (124).

Lit: *Athenaeum*, 4 May 1861, pp.600–1, 25 May 1861, p.698; *The Times*, 4 May 1861, p.12; *The Critic*, 11 May 1861, pp.606–7, 25 May 1861, p.671; *Macmillan's Magazine*, IV, 1861, pp.206–7; *Art Journal*, 1 June 1861, p.172; Henry Stacy Marks, *Pen and Pencil Sketches*, 1894, II, pp.2–3; Mrs. Russell Barrington, 'Lord Leighton's Sketches', *National Review*, December 1896, p.514; Mrs Russell Barrington, *The Life, Letters and Work of Frederic Leighton*, 1906, I, p.251, II, pp.57–65; *Letters of Dante Gabriel Rossetti*, ed. Oswald Doughty and J. R. Wahl, II, 1965, p.399; Leonée and Richard Ormond, *Lord Leighton*, 1975, pp.49, 60, 153; *The Tate Gallery 1978–80*, p. 19, repr. in col.

'Lieder ohne Worte' was probably begun in the second half of 1860. It was produced in the immediate aftermath of Leighton's return to England from his studies and travels on the Continent when, in the summer of 1859, he finally established permanent residence in London. The picture was the largest and the most important of Leighton's exhibits at the Royal Academy in 1861 – being shown at a time when he was acutely aware of opposition to him and his art from the Academic establishment, when many of his pictures were unsold and when he was particularly keen to score a notable public success.

If, in its poetical qualities, 'Lieder ohne Worte' has a precedent in Leighton's *oeuvre* it is to be found in the series of portrait studies of Italian women – notably of the model La Nanna – which were painted during his stay in Rome in 1859 and exhibited at the Royal Academy the same year. In fact, the image of a girl at a fountain seems in many ways to be a recollection of those months in Italy which had brought Leighton's years abroad to a close and perhaps the initial idea for the picture might have owed something to his familiarity with what was a common sight in Italian towns and villages.

Another source for the idea, hinted at in one review of the picture when it was exhibited, might have been the work of the French artist Ernest Hébert (1817–1908) with whom Leighton had become friendly during his time in Paris in 1855. It seems quite likely that Leighton would have been aware of a characteristic picture by Hébert, 'Les Cervarolles (États romain)' which had been exhibited at the Salon of 1859 and is now in the Louvre. The similarities between this painting and 'Lieder ohne Worte' are striking, both in subject matter and in the way the actual paint is handled. Hébert's picture also shows two women water-carriers – one, accompanied by a small girl, coming down a flight of steps towards the spectator, whilst another, holding a water jar on her head, is returning up the steps behind her. However, Leighton makes no acknowledgement of any such direct influence; it is also quite obvious, from all that he said about it, that his intention in painting 'Lieder ohne Worte' was very far removed from the evocation of a specific time or place or particular incident of the kind portrayed by Hébert.

After the picture was completed, Leighton wrote to his father: 'I remember, it is true, telling you *before* I began to paint "Lieder ohne Worte" that I intended to make it *realistic*, but from the first moment I began I felt the mistake, and made it professedly and pointedly the reverse.' In a letter written at about the same time to his teacher Edward von Steinle, he enlarged on this idea: '... I have endeavoured, both by colour and by flowing delicate forms, to translate to the eye of the spectator something of the pleasure which the child receives through her ears. This idea lies at the base of the whole thing, and is conveyed to the best of my ability in every detail ...'.

Leighton's close friend and his first biographer, Mrs Russell Barrington, affirmed on at least two occasions that the artist used a portrait of a boy as a study for the head of the girl in 'Lieder'. The claim has to be treated with caution, but she does offer some evidence to support it for, in an article in the *National Review* of December 1896, she noted that 'Lord Leighton first showed me some of his sketches more than thirty years ago when a friend took me to his studio in Orme Square. One sketch was of a boy's head with a heavy shock of curly hair from under which large almond-shaped eyes looked dreamily at you. As he held it up I exclaimed "Lieder ohne Worte". This was the name of a picture by Leighton which I had seen and which had fascinated me when I was very young. I remember his quick look of surprise ... I did not see the picture entitled "Lieder ohne Worte" for which the sketch of the boy's head was drawn, again till a few years ago, when it appeared on view in Messrs Christie's rooms ...'

Later, in her biography published in 1906, Mrs Barrington illustrated this drawing (vol. I, pl.54) and identified it as a portrait of John Hanson Walker; the drawing is now in the Leighton House collection (no.959). Inscribed and dated

'[18]60/Bath', the carefully executed portrait undoubtedly shows the features of the sixteen or seventeen year old Walker, as a comparison with two slightly later oil portraits of him by Leighton – 'Rustic Music' (Sotheby's, 9 April 1980, 48 repr.) and 'Duett' (coll. H.M. Queen Elizabeth, repr. Ormond pl.68), both of 1861 – proves. The similarities between the admittedly androgynous looks of Walker, as shown in the 1860 drawing, and those of the girl portrayed in 'Lieder ohne Worte' are too close to ignore the probability that one did indeed provide the prototype for the other. Taking into consideration Leighton's evident attraction to the boy and even, perhaps, bearing in mind the seeming ambiguity of the 'quick look of surprise' he gave Mrs Barrington when she drew attention to the resemblance between the two faces, it would be easy to misconstrue the artist's motives in thus capturing Walker's face. It is, however, a transposition which, if anything, serves to highlight Leighton's own sexual ambivalence; more to the point in this instance is the fact that the artist probably found in Walker's looks an ideal beauty which exactly fulfilled the conditions for creating the aesthetic effect he sought.

Two of the three surviving preliminary drawings for the painting emphasize both the characteristically meticulous preparation that went into Leighton's pictures and also, here, his particular preoccupation with the effect that line and form – especially in relation to the pose of the principal figure – would have on the viewer. A sheet of five studies for the girl's hands, undoubtedly taken from life (British Museum, Department of Prints and Drawings 1897.5.12.16) shows Leighton noting the slightest variations in the placing of the fingers in poses which remain essentially the same. A second drawing, in chalk and pencil on blue paper just over half the size of the finished painting (Leighton House Collection no.834; repr. Ormond, pl.82) shows the completed composition ready for transfer to the canvas. The architectural elements and their perspective are precise enough to have been drawn with the aid of a T-square and set-square on a drawing board; similarly, the relief moulding on the well-head looks as though it was drawn with a pair of compasses. This same precision can be seen in the under-drawing on the canvas. A grid of thirty-two rectangles, each $2\frac{7}{8} \times 3\frac{1}{2}$ in. (7.35 × 9 cm.) was superimposed on the design in order to facilitate its enlargement onto the canvas; its presence, with the junction of the vertical and horizontal axes at the exact centre of the girl's trunk, and her limbs subtly placed along these horizontals and verticals, reinforces the devices Leighton used to enhance a sense of repose. This effect was clearly in Leighton's mind when, in referring to the receding figure in the background, he wrote that 'the *tallness* of said figure was inseparable from the sentiment of it in my mind'.

Leighton's first, tentative, title for the painting seems to have been 'The Listener' and it was probably still known as this when he held a private view in his studio at the end of March and the beginning of April 1861 – that is, just before sending-in days at the Academy on 8 and 9 April. One result of this private showing – attended by friends and critics – was that the picture was given a new title, perhaps with some prompting from the artist, proposed by the wife of his friend Ralph Benson who visited the studio on 31 March. The following day Benson wrote to Leighton: 'For the beauty at the fountain I once thought the best title might be some couplet like the following:—

> "So tranced and still half-dreamed she, and half-heard
> The splash of fountain and the song of bird."

But my wife, from my description of the picture suggested a name better suited to the "suggestiveness" of the work: "Lieder ohne Worte": don't you think it rather pretty?' Coinciding exactly as it did with his original conception, Leighton adopted the new title immediately. He was also undoubtedly aware that his audience would inevitably at first see some association between the picture and

Felix Mendelssohn's forty-eight short piano pieces, composed between 1829 and 1845 and also called *Lieder ohne Worte*. Well-known in England under the title of *Songs without Words*, these graceful and thoughtful miniatures had a considerable popularity during the nineteenth century and particularly, it would seem, during the 1860s. It must have been Mendelssohn's music which inspired Mrs Benson's choice and Leighton must have known that it could only help the picture's chance of being noticed when it was hung in the Academy exhibition. The specifically musical connotations must also have appealed to the music-loving artist – he had already dealt with a musical theme in his earlier 'Triumph of Music' (R.A. 1856) and both 'Rustic Music' and 'Duett' can be seen as directly related to 'Lieder' in this sense apart from their common link with John Hanson Walker. Specific comparisons with the work of Whistler at this time are also obvious and his exploration of similar ideas in, for example, 'At the Piano' (R.A. 1860), 'Harmony in Green and Rose: The Music Room' of *c.*1860–1 – part of which Whistler had altered at Leighton's suggestion – or 'Symphony in White No.1' (1862) runs parallel with Leighton's.

Leighton regarded his private view as a great success, with his 'little girl at the fountain', as he described it, proving the most popular of the six works intended for the Royal Academy exhibition. He obviously used the private showing as an opportunity to explain what his intentions were – in this and other pictures – to a sympathetic audience. Evidence of this is to be found in his complaint about what one critic later wrote, that 'what he says in *interpretation* . . . is so verbatim what I said myself to those who visited my studio, that I suspect he must have been of that number'. The anonymous critic to whom Leighton was referring praised 'Lieder' in his review of the exhibition in *Macmillan's Magazine*, as one which 'must carry off the crown of praise from those who look for the noble faculty of poetic imagination' and continued in terms which are, in part at least, unmistakably Leighton's: 'he has not encumbered his representations with anything that is definite or positive in costume or accessories; . . . There is nothing to tell that the fair young girl who sits before us, lost in a dream, is of Roman, Egyptian, Grecian, or Mediaeval time or country. As her fancies are proper to girlhood, so her costume, her beauty, and the architecture with which she is surrounded are indefinite and only beautiful. We might as well attempt to analyze her thoughts as to decide where was her birthplace, what her name. There she is – fair, soft-eyed, graceful as a fawn, self abandoned, sweet, seated by the bright-running fountain that, with a murmurous gurgle, slowly fills the watervessel she has set down – lost in a blissful dream, while the shrill voice of the bird above cleaves the sleeping air of the sunny afternoon, and the delicate shadows widen over the pavement of marble, the rosy light lies softly upon the alabaster walls, and the tall woman, saffron-vested, bearing the vase upon her head, ascends the steps behind, noiseless, with bare feet, her robe's edge upon the marble stair, passing without a sound to break the reverie of youth and love . . . Several red, blue and grey vases stand upon the floor, and concentrate with their deep tints the delicacy of the alabaster that forms the background.'

With one exception, all Leighton's pictures were badly hung, above the line, in the Academy exhibition of 1861. It was a great disappointment to the artist because it was a repetition of the treatment he had received in previous years and also because, as he wrote to his mother, it made it 'impossible to see the finish or delicacy of execution which is an important feature in them.' The affront was felt keenly by Leighton, and by his friends and some critics, particularly in the case of 'Lieder ohne Worte' which seems to have attracted most attention – as it had done earlier in the artist's studio. The writer of the exhibition review in the *Art Journal* made a point of referring to the 'considerable talk in artistic and literary circles . . . because of some vague and floating ideas about these pictures having been sacrificed by the hanging committee'. That there was a considerable amount of gossip about this is certain: D. G. Rossetti, writing to William Allingham on 10 May 1861, complained that 'Leighton might ... have made a burst, had his pictures not been very ill-placed mostly – indeed one of them (the only very good one, *Lieder ohne Worte*) is the only instance of a very striking unfairness in the place ...'. The young painter Henry Stacy Marks, writing in *The Spectator*, repeated this sentiment: 'the hangers have not been guilty of a crueller act this year than that of placing this beautiful picture at a height where its merits can be only partially seen' and the reviewer in *The Critic* of 11 May, whilst complimenting the Academy on the way in which the exhibition had been hung, singled out the treatment given to Leighton as evidently arising from '*malice prepense* and in obvious defiance of the artist's reputation and high intrinsic claims'.

In view of the Academy's bias at this period toward subject painting, it is not surprising that the aesthetic and decorative qualities of 'Lieder ohne Worte' were ignored and the picture denied a good place. Despite these unfavourable circumstances, the work did receive favourable reviews, with only the *Art Journal* outspoken in its condemnation of the 'mere decorative ornamentation' of what was described as 'the well-laboured study for some extensive piece of mural decoration, whose exhibition is wholly out of place in the Royal Academy ...' At least two critics were mentioned by Leighton as having visited his private view and it was probably these two – Tom Taylor and F. G. Stephens – who, with their close knowledge of the painting, and writing, respectively, in *The Times* and *The Athenaeum*, were able to offer Leighton some public encouragement. *The Times* thought that 'the picture is one that wins more and more upon the eye and the imagination the more it is studied. It is Mr Leighton's best work this year'. *The Athenaeum* concluded a long and sympathetic description of the painting with the statement that 'the exquisite and ineffable ideality of indolent lotus-eating was never more perfectly expressed than in this work'.

Stacy Marks, writing in *The Spectator*, was the only critic who commented on the frame of 'Lieder ohne Worte', noting that 'the pure taste and inventiveness which it displays would almost imply that the painter had a hand in its design'. This would indeed seem to be the case. On the frame's inner margin, a series of arch-like semi-circles, modelled in relief with a slight concave section, each with a roundel, or boss, at its centre, echoes the decorative parapet on the wall of the courtyard in which the girl is sitting. The leaf-like pattern which occupies the middle of the frame's width – its dark blue perhaps stencilled on the gilded gesso – seems to recall the pattern of intertwined herons and song-birds which decorate the well-head. It was entirely in keeping with Leighton's thoughts about the overall impact the picture should have, that he clearly considered its frame as directly complementing the image on the canvas.

Frederick Mackenzie 1787–1854

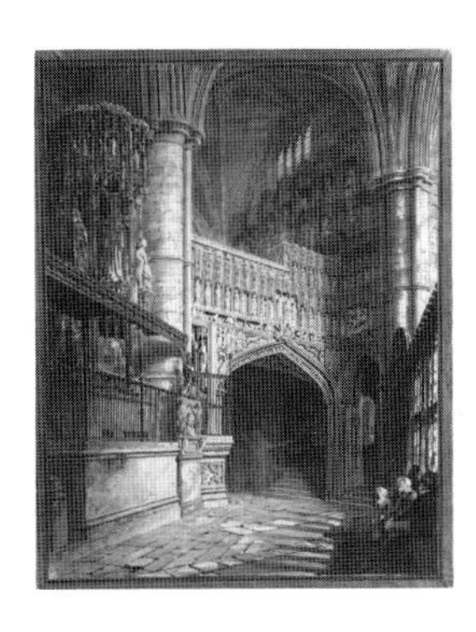

T.3034 The South Ambulatory, Westminster Abbey 1811

Inscribed 'Fred^{k} Mackenzie – 1811' bottom right
Watercolour on paper, image size $30\frac{13}{16} \times 24\frac{1}{4}$ (78.3 × 61.5), extended at edges and laid on linen canvas, $32\frac{13}{16} \times 26\frac{1}{8}$ (83.3 × 66.2)
Bequeathed by Leonard James Penna, 1980

Prov: ...; according to a note on the back of the old frame, 'from the Holne Park sale 1932 of Lord Farnborough's collection' (untraced); Leonard James Penna, Torquay, d.1979.

This view looks towards the Chantry Chapel of Henry V, d.1422, showing the two spiral staircases leading to the altar loft which crosses the ambulatory like a bridge above the King's tomb (for a detailed description of Henry V's Chapel, with plan and illustrations, see *Royal Commission on Historical Monuments. Inventory of the Historical Monuments in London. I. Westminster Abbey*, 1924, pp.71–3, pls.129–40). In the foreground on the left is the canopied tomb-chest of Queen Philippa of Hainault, d.1369 (the railings shown here were removed in the 1820s, and a thirteenth-century retable has subsequently been placed below the tomb), and beyond it the monument to Sir Robert Aiton, d.1638, its bronze bust flanked by the figures of Apollo and Athene. The screen of the Chapel of St. Nicholas is obliquely shown rising behind the figures in the foreground on the right.

Dated 1811, T.3034 is almost certainly related to the series of drawings made by Mackenzie, Augustus Pugin (with whom Mackenzie occasionally collaborated) and others for Ackermann's *History of the Abbey Church of St. Peter's Westminster, Its Antiquities and Monuments*, 1812; thirty-three of its plates were engraved, by Bluck and others, after Mackenzie. T.3034 was not engraved, probably because it included the figures of two female visitors standing in front of the chapel, drawn on a larger scale than was appropriate for such a work, since their presence obscured architectural detail. Mackenzie evidently tried to wash these figures out, but they remain in apparently ghostly form. Another view of Henry V's Chapel by Mackenzie, from a different viewpoint, was engraved for the 1812 publication with the title *North East Area*.

Benjamin Marshall 1768–1835

T.2364 **Emilius** ?1824

Inscribed 'B. Marshall pin . . .' inside upturned top hat bottom left and 'Emilius' bottom right
Oil on canvas, $39\frac{3}{4} \times 49\frac{3}{4}$ (101 × 126.5)
Presented by Mr Paul Mellon KBE through the British Sporting Art Trust 1979

Prov: Painted for Thomas Thornhill, Riddlesworth Hall, Norfolk; by descent to Sir Anthony Thornhill; Major Dermot McCalmont, Cheveley Park, Newmarket; Marshall Field, New York; Thos. Agnew & Sons, from whom purchased by Paul Mellon 1960.

Exh: *Painting in England 1700–1850: Collection of Mr & Mrs Paul Mellon*, Virginia Museum of Fine Arts, Richmond, Virginia 1963 (346, repr. pl.126); *Painting in England 1700–1850 from the Collection of Mr and Mrs Paul Mellon*, Royal Academy, 1964–5 (288), and Yale University Art Gallery, New Haven, Connecticut, 1965 (127); *Derby Day 200*, Royal Academy, 1979 (7.3, repr. p.68); *British Sporting Paintings*, Fermoy Art Gallery, Kings Lynn 1979 (17).

Lit: Egerton, 1978, p.203, no.216.

Emilius was a bay colt by Orville out of Emily, foaled in 1820, bred by John Udney of Aberdeen. 'The Druid' describes Emilius as 'Orville's best son . . . a muscular, compact horse, with great chest and arms, short legs and peculiarly straight hind ones. Add to this a great middle piece and good back ribs, with a muscular neck not too long and rather inclined to arch. He looked, in fact, quite as much a hunter as a blood horse' (quoted in Roger Mortimer, *The History of the Derby Stakes*, 1961, ed. 1973, p.80). Emilius's racing career was short but successful. He did not run as a two-year-old, but as a three-year-old he was undefeated. His greatest success was winning the Derby of 1823, with Frank Buckle up.

In 1824 John Udney sold Emilius for 1,800 guineas to a fellow-member of the

Jockey Club, Thomas Thornhill, squire of Riddlesworth, Norfolk. Emilius won only one match for his new owner, and after several defeats was retired to stud at Riddlesworth. His most famous progeny were Priam and Plenipotentiary, winners of the Derby in (respectively) 1830 and 1834, and the filly Crucifix, winner of the Two Thousand Guineas, the One Thousand Guineas and The Oaks in 1840. Emilius died in 1847.

The setting in T.2364 is evidently Newmarket, with one if its distinctive rubbing-down houses in the background; the picture, presumably painted soon after Thornhill's purchase of the horse in 1824, was Marshall's third major commission from Thornhill, for whom he had already painted portraits of Thornhill's two Derby winners Sam (1820) and Sailor (1823). In T.2364 Marshall employs one of his favourite motifs, a quietly jubilant stable-lad who waits at the side with checked rug and sweat-cover held out for the victorious racehorse, his hat upturned on the ground until he has completed this little ceremonial (also used, for instance, in his portraits of Marmeduke, Antegallican and Emilius's son Priam). Another portrait by Marshall of Emilius with a groom was engraved by J. Webb and published in the *Sporting Magazine*, July 1824.

T.2365 **Sir Charles Bunbury with Cox, his Trainer, and a Stable-lad: a Study for 'Surprise and Eleanor'** ?1801

Oil on canvas, $18\frac{1}{2} \times 14\frac{1}{4}$ (47×36.2)
Presented by Mr Paul Mellon KBE through the British Sporting Art Trust 1979

Prov: ...; Arthur Ackermann & Son, from whom purchased by Paul Mellon, 1966.
Exh: *Derby Day 200*, Royal Academy, 1979 (3.4, repr. p.46); *British Sporting Paintings*, Fermoy Art Gallery, Kings Lynn 1979 (18).
Lit: Egerton, 1978, no.204, pp.193–4.
Repr: Roger Longrigg, *The History of Horse Racing*, 1972, p.72, in colour (the central figure wrongly identified as Cox instead of Bunbury).

A study for 'Surprise and Eleanor', 1801 ($43\frac{1}{2} \times 60$ ins, coll. Stephen C. Clark Jr., Virginia, USA, repr. Basil Taylor, *Animal Painting in England*, 1955, pl.44). The finished picture depicts a moment before the start of a race whose runners include Bunbury's bay filly Eleanor, portrayed with jockey up in the centre, and Mr Mellish's Surprise, shown on the left. The three figures in T.2365 form a group on the right in the finished picture, which shows them assessing Eleanor's chances of success. The study was probably painted early in 1801, since Cox the trainer died in the spring of that year, just before the start of the Epsom meeting in which Eleanor won the Derby on 21 May 1801 (the first filly to win in the history of the race) and the Oaks the next day. Cox's last words were reputedly 'Depend on it, that Eleanor is the hell of a mare' (Roger Mortimer, *The History of the Derby Stakes*, 1961, ed. 1973, p.37). Since just that sort of reassuring opinion is what he (on the left in the study) seems to be conveying to Eleanor's somewhat apprehensive owner Bunbury (in the centre), Marshall may of course be commemorating the trainer and his legendary phrase in a posthumous portrait.

Sir Charles Bunbury (1740–1821), 6th Bart., M.P. for Suffolk 1761–84 and 1790–1812, was more prominent as a racing man than as a politician. He played an important part in extending the authority of the Jockey Club, of which he was regarded as 'the Perpetual President'. With his friend the 12th Earl of Derby, he was co-founder of the Derby, a toss of the coin deciding whether it should be called the Derby or the Bunbury Stakes. Bunbury himself won the first Derby in 1780, with Diomed, and won the Derby twice more, with Eleanor in 1801 and with Smolensko in 1813.

Bunbury was a friend of Charles James Fox and a member of the Literary Club, acting as one of the pall-bearers at Samuel Johnson's funeral. Reynolds's portrait of him at the age of twenty-seven, engraved by James Watson, shows the good looks and shrewd eyes which Bunbury retained when he posed for Marshall some thirty-five years later.

James Pollard 1792–1867

T.2366 The Royal Mail Coaches for the North Leaving The Angel, Islington 1827

Inscribed 'J. Pollard 1827' bottom right of centre
Oil on canvas, 40⅝ × 57⅝ (103 × 146.5)
Presented by Mr Paul Mellon KBE through the British Sporting Art Trust 1979

Prov: ...; Colonel Wetherly, sold Christie's 26 July 1902 (38); Sir Walter Gilbey, sold Christie's 12 March 1910 (125), bt. Agnew; W. Lockett Agnew; ...; anon. sale, Christie's 20 June 1975 (56, repr., and as frontispiece in colour), bt. John Baskett for Paul Mellon.

Lit: N. C. Selway, *James Pollard*, 1965, no.24, repr.; N. C. Selway, *The Golden Age of Coaching and Sport*, 1972, no.32; Egerton, 1978, p.272 no.296, repr. col. pl.35.

The mail coaches for the north, having started early in the evening from inns in the City of London, are seen making their first halt on the journey along the Great North Road at Islington to pick up more passengers.

The Angel Inn in Islington High Street is now at least three centuries old. Its name traditionally derives from a former sign depicting the angel of the annunciation with the Virgin Mary, the latter figure being removed as 'popish' during the seventeenth century. The neat Georgian building which Pollard depicts replaced the original inn early in the nineteenth century, when development of this formerly rural outpost of London was rapid. Pevsner (*London except the Cities of London and Westminster*, 1952, p.237) quotes some 'Suburban Sonnets' published in Hone's *Table Book*, 1827:

> 'Thy fields, fair Islington, begin to bear
> Unwelcome buildings and unseemly piles;
> The streets are spreading and the Lord knows where
> Improvement's hand will spare the neighbouring stiles ...'

Building was rapid over the next decade. In *Oliver Twist*, the first monthly instalment of which appeared in February 1837, Dickens describes Noah Claypole and Charlotte trudging into London by the Great North Road; arriving at The Angel at Islington, Noah 'wisely judged, from the crowd of passengers and number of coaches, that London began in earnest' (Oxford edition, 1949, p.319).

Richard Roper *c.*1730–*c.*1775

T.2367 The Match Between Aaron and Driver at Maidenhead, August 1754: Driver Winning the Third Heat ?1754

Inscribed 'DRIVER and AARON Running the third Heat at Maidenhead, August 1754. / Driver was Rode by Thos. Arnold who won. Aaron was Rod by Sam Tate' across bottom of canvas
Oil on canvas, 34¾ × 47⅞ (88.1 × 121.6)
Presented by Mr Paul Mellon KBE through the British Sporting Art Trust 1979

Prov.: ...; as one of a set of three, anon. sale Sotheby's 25 July 1928 (99), bt.

Lambert; Arthur Ackermann & Son Ltd., 1929; . . .; Jack Gilbey-Ellis, from whom purchased by Paul Mellon 1970.

Exh: *British Sporting Artists*, Arthur Ackermann & Son Ltd., 1929 (106); *British Sporting Painting*, Fermoy Art Gallery, Kings Lynn 1979 (7).

Lit: W. Shaw Sparrow, *A Book of Sporting Painters*, 1931, p.54; Egerton, 1978, p.110, no.105, pl.40.

This is the third in a set of three paintings depicting the three heats run in a match between Mr Lamego's chestnut, Driver, and Mr Roger's bay, Aaron. Driver won the first heat, Aaron the second, and the match was decided by Driver's win of the third heat. The other two paintings remain in Mr Mellon's collection; that depicting the first heat is inscribed *R: Roper pinx*t. (details of the legends inscribed on both are given in Egerton, 1978). In each of the three pictures, the two horses gallop towards a finishing-post on the left, whipped-on by their jockeys. Race meetings were held at Maidenhead until *c.*1815.

John Nost Sartorius 1759–1828

T.2368 The Earl of Darlington Foxhunting with the Raby Pack: Drawing Cover 1805

Inscribed 'J N Sartorius pinxt 1805' bottom left
Oil on canvas, $27\frac{3}{4} \times 35\frac{3}{4}$ (70.5 × 91)
Presented by Mr Paul Mellon KBE through the British Sporting Art Trust 1979

Prov: . . .; Gilpin Brown, Sedbury Hall, Yorkshire; Arthur Ackermann & Son Ltd., from whom purchased by Paul Mellon 1963.

Exh: *XVIIIth and XIXth century Sporting Paintings*, Arthur Ackermann & Son Ltd., 1963 (5); *Painting in England 1700–1850 from the Collection of Mr and Mrs Paul Mellon,* R.A., 1964–5 (285 and 281).

Lit: Egerton, 1978, pp.156–7, no.152, pl.56.

T.2369 The Earl of Darlington Foxhunting with the Raby Pack: Going to Cover 1805

Inscribed 'J N Sartorius pinxit 1805' bottom right
Oil on canvas, $28\frac{1}{8} \times 36$ (71.5 × 91.5)
Presented by Mr. Paul Mellon KBE through the British Sporting Art Trust 1979
Prov., Exh. and *Lit:* as for T.2368.

T2370 The Earl of Darlington Foxhunting with the Raby Pack: Full Cry 1804

Inscribed 'J N Sartorius pinxit 1804' bottom left
Oil on canvas, $27\frac{5}{8} \times 35\frac{7}{8}$ (70.3 × 91)
Presented by Mr Paul Mellon KBE through the British Sporting Art Trust 1979
Prov., Exh. and *Lit:* as for T.2368.

T2371 The Earl of Darlington Foxhunting with the Raby Pack: The Death ?1804–5

Oil on canvas, 28 × 36 (71.2 × 91.5)
Presented by Mr Paul Mellon KBE through the British Sporting Art Trust 1979
Prov., Exh. and *Lit:* as for T.2368.

In each of these four scenes, the Earl of Darlington is the most prominent figure. William Harry Vane, 3rd Earl of Darlington, and from 1827 1st Duke of Cleveland (1766–1842), was passionately devoted to hunting. For nearly fifty years he kept hounds at Raby Castle, acting as his own huntsman and hunting a vast stretch of land from south Yorkshire to Northumberland. In 1818 he successfully opposed plans for the first Stockton to Darlington railway on the grounds that it would cut across his coverts, withdrawing his opposition only when the line was diverted. 'Nimrod' relates that Lord Darlington hunted six days a week, and 'had a change of clothes kept well aired at all the principal inns within his hunt, to the nearest of which he always repaired when the sport was over; and putting himself into a chaise and four, ready dressed for the evening, a small field-piece at the lodge of his part announced his approach to the Castle; and by the time he arrived, dinner ... was upon the table' (C. J. Apperley ['Nimrod'], *Nimrod's Hunting Tours*, 1835).

At the end of each day's hunt Lord Darlington recorded full details of it in a hunting diary, privately published at the close of each season. Sartorius's paintings are dated 1804–5. *Earl of Darlington's Fox-Hounds: Operations of the Raby Pack in the years 1804–5* records that in this season he began hunting on 17 September and ended on 10 April, hunting ninety-one days in all, killing forty-nine foxes ('23 dogs, 10 bitches, 16 Doubtful') and earthing another twenty-four. The setting for the hunt in T.2368–71 is wooded, hilly country, probably in Teesdale; the conical sandstone-capped hill called Roseberry Topping is visible in the distance in each scene.

At Lord Darlington's invitation, J. M. W. Turner visited Raby Castle in 1817; sketches of huntsmen and hounds occur in the 'Raby' sketchbook (T. B. CLVI). In Turner's oil painting 'Raby Castle, the Seat of the Earl of Darlington' (exhibited R.A. 1818, no.729, now in the collection of the Walters Art Gallery, Baltimore), a foxhunt, culminating at the traditional ceremony of the kill, originally figured prominently in the foreground. The reviewer of the *Literary Chronicle* described the exhibited work as a 'detestable fox hunting picture'. Despite his own unbounded enthusiasm for hunting, Lord Darlington himself seems to have considered that the prominence Turner had given to the hunt diverted attention from the view of the Castle. Turner accordingly repainted the picture after the exhibition, decreasing the prominence of the hunt (Martin Butlin and Evelyn Joll, *The Paintings of J. M. W. Turner*, 1977, pp.90–1, no.36, pl.121).

Copies by F. R. Williams of Sartorius's set of four paintings (three signed by the copyist, and two dated 1811) were sold by Sotheby's 21 November 1980 (50, repr., two of them in error as Lot 17).

James Seymour ?1702–52

T.2265 Chestnut Horse with a Groom Near Newmarket
*c.*1730–40

Oil on canvas, 26 × 41⅛ (66.1 × 10.4)
Bequeathed by Miss Agnes Clarke 1978

Prov: ...; according to Miss Clarke's solicitors, probably purchased in the 1950s in England by Miss Clarke and/or her brother, John Semple Clarke (formerly citizens of USA), who settled after World War II at Killagorden House, Idless, Truro, Cornwall.

Exh: *British Sporting Paintings*, Fermoy Art Gallery, King's Lynn 1979 (4).

A pack of hounds disappearing to the right in the middle distance suggests that the main subject is probably a hunter, held by a groom waiting for his master, rather than a racehorse; the hounds' quarry is likely to be the hare, since coursing near Newmarket was very popular. The horse is a chestnut stallion, with a white star on the forehead and a white marking on the muzzle; the saddlecloth is white edged with blue. The groom's livery jacket is dark green, brass-buttoned, and his topboots are spurred. Without further clues, the horse and his master are impossible to identify.

The picture appears to have been painted from Warren Hill, to the east of Newmarket town. In the centre of the distant view of Newmarket rises the spire of St. Mary's Church. A large two-storied building with projecting wings, deliberately and perhaps disproportionately featured in the distance on the right, may be the stable-block of the horse's owner, but no longer stands and cannot now be identified (information kindly supplied by Canon Peter May, Newmarket, to whom at the suggestion of the Suffolk Record Office the problem of identifying the view was referred).

T.2372 **Mr Russell on his Bay Hunter** *c.*1740

Oil on canvas, $34\frac{1}{2} \times 43\frac{5}{8}$ (87.6 × 110.8)
Presented by Mr Paul Mellon KBE through the British Sporting Art Trust 1979

Prov: ...; C. B. Kidd, sold Sotheby's 23 November 1966 (169, repr.), bt. Ackermann for Paul Mellon.

Exh: *British Sporting Paintings*, Fermoy Art Gallery, King's Lynn, 1979 (3, repr. in colour on cover of catalogue).

Lit: Egerton, 1978, p.45, no.48, repr. pl.17; Christopher Neve, 'Gift from a Galloping Anglophile', in *Country Life*, CLXVI, 30 August 1979, p.585, fig.3; *The Tate Gallery 1978–80*, p. 34, repr. in col.

An old label *verso* reads 'Paternal Ancestor (Russell)'. Mr Russell, preceded by a hound, is portrayed in the hunting-field; he turns to face the spectator, revealing individual features and an alert expression which have together stimulated Seymour to one of his ablest and most sympathetic exercises in human portraiture. The sitter, who appears to be in his 40s, has so far eluded precise identification. Given Seymour's continued association with Newmarket, a tentative suggestion is that he may be a junior member of the family of Admiral Russell (created Baron Shingay and Earl of Orford for his victory over the Dutch at La Hogue; d.1729), who acquired the manor of Chippenham Park, just outside Newmarket.

Details of costume, such as the firmly-tied breeches-lacings and the buttoned leather strap above the knee to keep the breeches from riding up, are sharply-observed and painted with Seymour's customary meticulousness.

Attributed to **James Seymour** ?1702–52

T.2264 **Pointer Bitch** *c.*1740

Inscribed 'J:S' bottom left
Oil on canvas, $36\frac{1}{4} \times 45\frac{1}{8}$ (91.7 × 104.6)
Bequeathed by Miss Agnes Clarke 1978

Prov: ...; according to Miss Clarke's solicitors, probably purchased in the 1950s by Miss Clarke and/or her brother, John Semple Clarke (formerly citizens of U S A), who settled after World War II at Killagorden House, Idless, Truro, Cornwall.

Some doubt must attend a positive attribution to Seymour, since the style, particularly in the rather loosely painted background, does not seem crisp enough for this to be Seymour's own work. Similar initials appear on other paintings and drawings which are unlikely to be by Seymour himself, although evidently (like T.2264) contemporary with his work.

The pointer bitch is seen in profile in the foreground, and again (her distinctive markings establishing her identity) in the middle distance, this time in action, with a sportsman and two shooting ponies, one held by a groom. This is evidently a commissioned portrait of a particular animal, perhaps prized both for her skill in the field and for breeding purposes. All clues to her identity are now lost, but the prominent thistle in the foreground on the right may indicate that her proud owner was Scottish.

Manner of **Paul Van Somer** *c.*1576–1621/2

T.3033 **Anne Wortley, Later Lady Morton** *c.*1615–18

Inscribed 'Lady Morton/by Vansomer' above carpet, lower centre right, probably in eighteenth-century hand
Oil on canvas 81 × 50 (206 × 127)
Purchased (Grant-in-Aid), with contributions from the Friends of the Tate Gallery, the National Art-Collections Fund, and the Pilgrim Trust 1980

Prov: First recorded at Ditchley, Oxon in about 1726 by George Vertue; Lord Dillon sale, Ditchley, Sotheby's 24 May 1933 (86), bt. by Francis Howard; Loel Guinness, by whom lent to the Tate Gallery from 1953 until purchased 1980.

Exh: *Art Treasures*, Manchester 1857 (22); *National Portrait Exhibition*, South Kensington, 1868 (673); *Old Masters*, R.A. 1902 (163) as 'Frances Morton, Viscountess Wilmot'; period display, Metropolitan Museum, New York, 1966 (no catalogue).

Lit: Horace Walpole, *Anecdotes of Painting in England*, 1782, vol. iii, p.6, and R. Wornum edition, 1888, vol. ii, p.210; Vct. Dillon, *Catalogue of Paintings . . . at Ditchley, Spelsbury, Oxfordshire*, 1908, p.44, no.81, repr. pl.XXXIX; C. H. Collins Baker, *Lely and The Stuart Portrait Painters*, 1912, vol.i, p.28; L. Cust, 'Marcus Gheeraerts' in *Walpole Society*, III, 1914, p.37, repr. pl.XXIXa; Vertue Notebooks, II, in *Walpole Society*, XX, 1931–2, pp.14 and 76; *Catalogue of Paintings at . . . Ditchley*, 1933, p.30, cat.90; *The Tate Gallery 1978–80*, p.28, repr. in col.

The sitter wears a purplish dress with gold embroidery, and holds a fan in her right hand and a lace handkerchief in her left. Her corsage is covered with multiple strings of pearls; she wears pearl bracelets, a jewelled chain and earrings, and an unusually elaborate head-dress of pearls wired into oak-leaf and other decorative patterns. She stands on rush matting between two green looped-up curtains.

The identification of the sitter as Anne Wortley, Lady Morton can be traced as far back as 1726, when George Vertue saw the portraits at Ditchley (then owned by the Earl of Litchfield) and noted one of 'Lady Morton . . . Seem of . . . the Dutch taste but well' (Notebooks, II, p.14). Later, in 1730, when some of Lord Litchfield's pictures were 'here in Town to Clean', he describes it in recognisable detail: '7. Lady Morton purplish dress a fan in one hand and handkerchief in the other. the silks and ornaments well painted, . . . I guesse to be of the hand of Paul Vansomer' (Notebooks, II, p.76). It is very likely that the inscription on the picture dates from roundabout this time. Anne Wortley was the sister-in-law of Sir Henry Lee (1571–1631/3), cousin of Queen Elizabeth's hononymous Master of the Armoury, from whom he inherited Ditchley in 1611.

There was a not dissimilar full-length identified as Eleanor Wortley, Lady Lee, at Ditchley (Ditchley sale, 24 May 1933 (87), repr. in Cust, 1914, pl.XXIXb) although it is not possible to tell from the reproduction whether it is by the same hand or not.

Anne, the daughter of Sir Richard Wortley of Yorkshire, married firstly Sir Rotheram Willoughby, and later, sometime after 1634, Sir George Morton of Clenson, Dorset. Thus, if one assumes the traditional identification of the sitter as being correct, then the probable dating of the picture on grounds of dress to 1615–18 suggests that Anne is shown here as Lady Willoughby, and that it could be a marriage portrait.

Stylistically the portrait keeps strictly to the 'curtain-and-carpet painters' formula so typical of the Jacobean period, in which the heiratic presence of a full-length figure is enhanced by placing it in a shallow niche between two curtains, the feet planted on matting or an Eastern carpet, with perhaps a chair or a table as the only prop, the latter usually drawn in very uncertain perspective. The hard, flat and brilliantly coloured style of painting which usually goes with it is, however, beginning to give way here to a broader, more shadowed Flemish style associated, as Vertue rightly observed, with Van Somer. The rather unimaginative composition, on the other hand, and manifestly awkward relationship between the figure and the chair, as well as the varying degrees of finish in the handling of the materials (for instance the embroidered bodice and the covering of the chair) suggests the work of several hands. The picture has certain similarities with the portrait, also without a firm attribution, dated circa 1615, of 'Elizabeth Home, Countess of Suffolk' at Rangers House, Blackheath (John Jacob and Jacob Simon, *The Suffolk Collection Catalogue of Paintings*, GLC, 1974, repr. cat. no.17), and it could be that both pictures are a product of the same workshop.

Thomas Spencer fl. 1740–56

T.2373 **A Bay hunter held by a Groom, with a Stag-Hunt in the Background** *c.*1750

Oil on canvas, $45\frac{1}{4} \times 53\frac{3}{8}$ (115 × 135.5)
Presented by Mr Paul Mellon KBE through the British Sporting Art Trust 1979

Prov: ...; anon. sale, Christie's 16 June 1961 (8, as 'A Chestnut Hunter', by John Wootton, repr.) bt. Ackermann, from whom purchased by Paul Mellon 1961.

Exh: *Painting in England 1700–1850: Collection of Mr & Mrs Paul Mellon*, Virginia Museum of Fine Arts, Richmond, Virginia, 1963 (309, pl. 171).

Lit: Egerton, 1978, p.55, no.57.

The bay hunter, with its distinctive markings (white star, and three white socks) is portrayed in profile facing left, bridled but unsaddled; a blue-coated groom holds its reins, as if waiting for his master. In the middle distance a stag-hunt is in progress, and here the hunter is again depicted, now ridden by his master (in a red coat), galloping to the right in a group of riders to hounds in full cry after a stag. Spencer uses a similar device of combining a foreground portrait of a hunter with a background scene showing the horse in action in 'Scipio', which remains ~~in the~~ Mellon Collection (Egerton, 1978, no.56, col. pl.9).

The style is evidently closely mannered on Seymour's, though the handling is more naive and the colouring considerably more garish than Seymour's.

George Stubbs 1724–1806

T.2374 Bay Hunter by a Lake 1787

Inscribed 'Geo: Stubbs pinxit/1787' lower centre
Oil on oak panel, $35\frac{5}{8} \times 54\frac{1}{8}$ (90.7 × 137.4)
Presented by Mr Paul Mellon KBE through the British Sporting Art Trust 1979

Prov: Believed to have been painted for Arthur Annesley, 9th Viscount Valentia (d.1816); by descent to 12th Viscount Valentia, until 1940; Tooth, 1947; Cyril Kleinwort; Leggatt Brothers, from whom purchased by Paul Mellon, 1960.

Exh: *Sport and the Horse*, Virginia Museum of Fine Arts, Richmond, Virginia, 1960 (23, repr.); *Painting in England 1700–1850: Collection of Mr & Mrs Paul Mellon*, Virginia Museum of Fine Arts, Richmond, Virginia, 1963 (324).

Lit: Basil Taylor, *Stubbs*, 1971, p.214, repr. pl.121; Egerton, 1978, p.96, no.94.

The horse has not been identified. Its cropped ears (a current fashion) rob the animal of much of its natural dignity. Taylor (*op. cit.*) notes that the background in this work is characteristic of Stubbs's landscape during the following decade.

T.2375 Otho, with John Larkin up 1768

Inscribed 'Geo: Stubbs pinxit/1768' bottom left and 'Otho' below the horse; 'Otho' also lettered on lintel of door
Oil on canvas, $39\frac{7}{8} \times 50$ (101.2 × 127)
Presented by Mr Paul Mellon KBE through the British Sporting Art Trust 1979

Prov: John Fitzpatrick, 2nd Earl of Upper Ossory (d.1818); ...; probably purchased by the 6th Baron Monson (d.1862); by descent to the 11th Baron Monson, until 1964, when sold to Mallet & Son (Antiques) Ltd.; Leggatt Brothers, from whom purchased by Paul Mellon, 1965.

Exh: *Somerset House Art Treasures Exhibition*, Somerset House, 1979 (L.3, repr. p.15).

Lit: Egerton, 1978, p.80, no.78, repr. pl.30; Christopher Neve, 'A Gift from a Galloping Anglophile', in *Country Life*, CLXVI, 30 August 1979, p.585, repr. fig. 2; *The Tate Gallery 1978–80*, p. 33, repr. in col.

Engr: ?by John Scott, 'from a ... painting ... in the possession of ... the Earl of Upper Ossory', published in the *Sporting Magazine*, 9 October 1796, facing p.64; repr. T. H. Taunton, *Portraits of Celebrated Racehorses ...*, Series I, 1887, facing p.100.

Otho, a bay colt by Moses out of Miss Vernon, foaled in 1760, was bred and first owned by Richard Vernon (1726–1800). Vernon, a founder-member of the Jockey Club, bred and owned a very large number of racehorses, and made a small fortune by astute betting. Under Vernon's ownership, Otho's racing career during the years 1764–6 was moderately successful, and included winning a match for 300 guineas at Newmarket in October 1764 against Lord Bolingbroke's Turf, whose portrait by Stubbs of *c.*1765 is now in the Yale Center for British Art, Paul Mellon Collection (repr. Egerton, 1978, col. pl.12).

Early in 1767 Vernon sold Otho to his stepson, John Fitzpatrick, 2nd Earl of Upper Ossory (1745–1818), who was described by Horace Walpole as a man 'who has all the passions of youth without its ridicules; who loves gaming without making or losing a fortune, and Newmarket without being a dupe or a sharper' (letter of 7 October 1773, ed. W. S. Lewis and others, *Horace Walpole's Correspondence with the Countess of Upper Ossory*, I, 1965, p.154). 1767 was the last but most successful year in Otho's racing career, bringing several victories at Newmarket. T.2375, dated 1768, was presumably commissioned to celebrate these. John Larkin may have ridden Otho on each successful occasion, but Racing Calendars of this period do not record jockeys' names. Certainly Newmarket racecourse provides the setting for T.2375, with one of the rubbing-down houses (see T.2388) shown on the right, and a view of St. Mary's Church and Newmarket town in the middle distance.

Otho was subsequently retired to stud at Ampthill Park, Lord Ossory's seat in Bedfordshire. His services as a stallion were advertised in the *Racing Calendar* from 1773 to 1784; at the height of his renown at stud he commanded the same fees as, for instance, Sweetbriar, Sweetwilliam and Mambrino, three of the stallions painted by Stubbs for his largely unfinished *Turf Review* project. Otho's progeny included Comus, Dorimant, Coxcomb and Saturn.

Neither T.2375 nor any other sporting picture was included in the sale after his death of Lord Ossory's collection of paintings by Old Masters and contemporary British artists (Christie's, 8 April 1819). He had no son, and the picture may have been inherited by one of his daughters. It is not known when it entered the Monson collection; the present Lady Monson suggests that it was probably purchased by the 6th Baron Monson (1796–1862) or, if not by him, by the 3rd or 4th Baron.

T.2388 **Newmarket Heath, with Rubbing-Down House** *c.*1765

Oil on canvas, $11\frac{15}{16} \times 16\frac{1}{2}$ (30.4 × 41.9)
Purchased (Grant-in-Aid) 1979

Prov: The artist's sale, Peter Coxe, 26–27 May 1807, second day (59, one of 'Landscapes with Buildings, &c. a pair, Views on the Race Ground at Newmarket'); . . .; sale of Thomas Garle, deceased, Christie's 24 May 1862 (1, one of 'Two views of the stables at Newcastle', corrected by hand at the time in Christie's copy of the sale catalogue to '. . . Newmarket'), bt. Watson £2.10.0; . . .; anon. sale, Christie's 25 October 1957 (156, one of a pair), bt. Agnew; sold on its own to B. N. Mavroleon, 1958; 'The Property of a Lady', sold Sotheby's 18 July 1979 (140, repr.), bt. Baskett & Day for the Tate Gallery.

Exh: *Landscape in Britain c.1750–1850*, Tate Gallery, 1973–4 (99, repr.; in the first edition of the catalogue, the Mellon study was erroneously repr. instead); *Painting from Nature*, Arts Council, Fitzwilliam Museum, Cambridge, and Royal Academy, 1980–1 (15, repr.).

Lit: Basil Taylor, *Stubbs*, 1971, p.208, repr. pl.34 (erroneously stated to be in the collection of Mr and Mrs Paul Mellon); Egerton, 1978, pp.77–8; *The Tate Gallery 1978–80*, p. 35, repr. in col.

The pair of small landscapes showing different views of one of the rubbing-down houses on Newmarket Heath are the only pure landscape studies by Stubbs to survive. Both were probably originally made for Stubbs's two different portraits of Gimcrack, *c.*1765 (see below). They remained in Stubbs's studio for the rest of his life and were frequently referred to for later compositions. They were kept as a pair until sold separately by Agnew's in 1958; the other study (12 × 16 in.), sold to a private collector but bought back in 1961, was then sold by Agnew's to Mr Paul Mellon, and remains in his collection (Egerton, 1978, pp.77–8, no.76, repr. pl.29).

Both T.2388 and the Mellon study powerfully suggest that the artist had first carefully selected his viewpoint, then intently scrutinised his subject and finally transcribed it as truthfully as possible, making no concessions to picturesque formulae; but the high degree of control and finish in both makes it unlikely that they were actually painted on the spot. They are more likely to have been worked up in the studio from preliminary drawings made on the spot. Stubbs's posthumous sale (cited under *Prov.*) contained many items suggesting a regular practice of preliminary sketching, in chalk, pencil or pen and ink on paper, directly from nature; grouped under the heading 'Drawings, Drawing Books, Studies from Nature, Sketches &c', lots 18–30 in the Second Day's Sale included, for instance, 'Twenty-five sketches in black lead, Landscapes &c.' (lot 20) and, even more tantalising, 'One Book with 200 Landscapes, Views and Sketches' (lot 22). No such items appear to have survived.

The most prominent building in T.2388, in the foreground on the left, is one of four rubbing-down houses which stood on Newmarket Heath in the eighteenth century (one survives, near Running Gap). They were used for 'rubbing down', with wisps of straw, or with rough cloths such as the stable-lad holds in Stubbs's painting of 'Hambletonian' (mentioned below), horses which inevitably sweated profusely after exercise or racing; this one seems to have been reserved for horses belonging to royalty or to members of the Jockey Club. In John Bodger's pictorial map of the racecourses and buildings on Newmarket Heath, published in 1787 (repr. Frank Siltzer, *Newmarket*, 1923, facing p.62), it can be identified as 'the King's Stables'. The two spectators' stands in the background of T.2388 are 'the King's stand', on the left, and 'the Duke's stand', still further distant on the right, with a (moveable) betting-post between them. The railings stretching obliquely away border 'the Duke's course'. Stubbs's viewpoint for this study must have been the south-west (or Suffolk) edge of Newmarket Heath. (Information kindly provided by Canon Peter May, of Newmarket, and Captain Lees, Clerk of the Course at Newmarket.)

Stubbs incorporated most of the details of T.2388, including the foreground weeds, but excluding the betting-post and the more distant spectators' stand on the right, in his large painting 'Gimcrack at Newmarket with a Trainer, Jockey and Stable-lad', *c.*1765 (two versions, one in the collection of the Jockey Club, repr. Taylor, *op. cit.*, pl.32; the other in a private collection). He used the same details again, in 1771, for the background of 'Laura with a Jockey and Stable-lad' (private collection, repr. Taylor *op. cit.* pl.69) and, finally, in 1799, for the very large and extraordinarily powerful 'Hambletonian being rubbed down, with a Trainer and a Stable lad' (private collection, repr. Taylor, *op. cit.*, pl.131), painted at the age of 75.

'Baronet with Sam Chifney up', 1791 (engraved by George Towneley Stubbs in 1794 as Plate XII of the *Turf Review* project) draws on some details of T.2388; but since it shows horse and jockey actually racing, the rubbing-down house is omitted and instead the spectators' stands, their windows now open, are brought into prominence. At least four versions of that painting are known, one in the Royal Collection (Oliver Millar, *The Later Georgian Pictures in the Collection of Her Majesty the Queen*, 1969, p.124, no.1118, noting other versions).

The Mellon study was used for 'Gimcrack with Jockey up', *c.*1765 (collection James Adeane, on loan to the Fitzwilliam Museum), for 'Turf with Jockey up', also *c.*1765 (Yale Center for British Art, Paul Mellon Collection, repr. Egerton, 1978, col. pl.12) and for 'Eclipse with Groom and Jockey', 1770 (in the collection of the Jockey Club, repr. Constance Anne-Parker, *Mr Stubbs the Horse Painter*, 1971, p.143).

'Otho with John Larkin up', 1768 (Tate Gallery, T.2375, q.v.), shows the same rubbing-down house, this time on the right of the picture and observed from the opposite side to that in the Tate study, so that Newmarket town rather than its racecourse appears in the background.

Peter Tillemans 1684–1734

T.2376 **Foxhunting in Wooded Country** *c.*1720–30

Oil on canvas, $40\frac{1}{8} \times 46\frac{1}{16}$ (102 × 117)
Presented by Mr Paul Mellon KBE through the British Sporting Art Trust 1979

Prov: ...; Wheeler Ltd., Ryder Street, 1961; Gooden & Fox, from whom purchased by Paul Mellon 1961.

Exh: Painting in England 1700–1850: Collection of Mr & Mrs Paul Mellon, Virginia Museum of Fine Arts, Richmond, Virginia, 1963 (301).

Lit: Egerton, 1978, p.34, no.35, repr. pl.11; Christopher Neve, 'A Gift from a Galloping Anglophile', in *Country Life*, CLXVI, 30 August 1979, p.585, repr. fig. 4.

The fox in the background centre is not only hotly pursued by hounds running in from the right but is also threatened by hounds from the left; the chase has been through a wood, the pack and its followers have divided and the fox is cornered, for the winding river on the left leaves no way out. The circular movement of this composition may be compared with that of the 'Staghunt in a Forest' by Johannes Hackaert and Nicolaes Berchem, *c.*1650 (no.829 in the collection of the National Gallery, London); the similarity may well reflect one of Tillemans's legacies from the sporting art of his native country. The attribution to Tillemans is therefore retained here, although in a field where Tillemans's style is close to that of John Wootton, and even to that of Wootton's master Jan Wyck, it cannot be entirely certain.

There is a timeless, almost classical air about the landscape which suggests an ideal rather than actual setting for this foxhunt; however, an ancient stone building with a round tower in the middle distance on the left might suggest that the scene was drawn from northern, possibly border country in England.

James Ward 1769–1859

T.2377 **Portraits of Blackthorn, a Brood Mare, with Old Jack, a Favourite Pony, the Property of E. Mundy, Esq.** 1812

Inscribed 'J. Ward. R.A. 1812' bottom left
Oil on panel, $27\frac{3}{4} \times 36\frac{1}{8}$ (70.5 × 91.7)
Presented by Mr Paul Mellon KBE through the British Sporting Art Trust 1979

Prov: Commissioned by Edward Miller Mundy, Shipley Hall, Derbyshire; by descent to Major E. P. G. Miller Mundy, sold Christie's 27 October 1961 (88), bt. Frost & Reed; Edward Speelman Ltd., from whom purchased by Paul Mellon 1966.

Exh: R.A. 1812 (117); B.I. 1825 (16); *Fine Arts*, Derby Museum 1870 (300).

Lit: Recorded in the artist's MS. Account Book (coll. Professor Robert H. Werner), p.67; *Repository of Arts*, June 1812, p.342; *Sporting Magazine*, vol. XIX no. CX, 1826, p.3 no.110; C. Reginald Grundy, *James Ward, R.A., His Life and Works*, 1909, p.369; Egerton, 1978, pp.216–7, no.231.

The artist's MS. Account Book records the purchase by Edward Miller Mundy of two earlier pictures. Both were sold (with T.2377) at Christie's in 1961 (lots 86 and 87). 'Heath Ewe and Lambs', dated 1810 and exhibited that year at the R.A. (75), recorded as a purchase by Mr Mundy in July 1812, is now in the Mellon Collection (Egerton, 1978, cat. no.228, p.214), and a painting of a donkey and foal in a barn with a turkey etc. was recorded as a purchase by Mr Mundy in 1811 (present whereabouts unknown). Unlike Mr Mundy's other two purchases from Ward, T.2377 was evidently a commissioned work, and portrays particular animals which he owned. Presumably with Mr Mundy's permission, Ward exhibited it at the R.A. in 1812 (the year of the picture's date); seeing it in that exhibition, the critic of *The Repository of Arts* commented 'The colouring of these animals is equal to the finest specimens of painting that we remember to have seen, either of Cuyp, Wouvermans, Potter, or any of the best masters of the Flemish or Dutch Schools. The drawing is good, and the penciling masterly'. After the exhibition, Ward evidently helped to arrange for the transport of the picture to Mr Mundy. His Account Book records a copy of a bill delivered to Mr Mundy in September 1812; this bill, totalling £119.6.0, included £7.10.0 for the picture's frame and £1.11.0 for a packing case.

Richard Wilson 1713 or '14–82

T.3026 **Ponte Nomentana** 1754

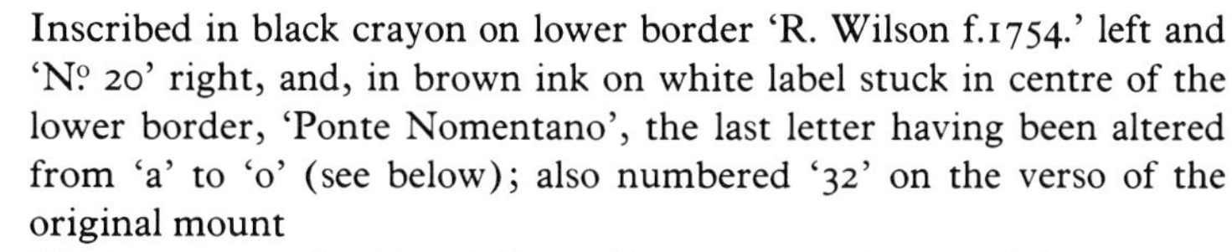

Inscribed in black crayon on lower border 'R. Wilson f.1754.' left and 'N° 20' right, and, in brown ink on white label stuck in centre of the lower border, 'Ponte Nomentano', the last letter having been altered from 'a' to 'o' (see below); also numbered '32' on the verso of the original mount

Black crayon and white chalk on blue paper, $11\frac{5}{16} \times 16\frac{5}{8}$ (28.5 × 42.2), mounted on larger white paper to whose edges four strips of thinner paper, painted with lilac wash, have been stuck to form a border; overall size $14 \times 19\frac{5}{16}$ (35.5 × 49.1)

Purchased (Grant-in-Aid) 1980

Prov: One of a series of twenty 'views of the environs of Rome' commissioned by William Legge, 2nd Earl of Dartmouth (1731–1801); by descent to the 7th Earl of Dartmouth, by whom sold Christie's 29 January 1954 (22), bt. Thos. Agnew & Sons Ltd., by whom sold to F. B. Hart-Jackson, 1960, bought back from him, 1977, and sold to the Tate Gallery 1980.

Exh: *Richard Wilson and his Circle*, City Museum and Art Gallery, Birmingham, 1948–9 (89) and Tate Gallery, 1949 (88); *Il Settecento a Roma*, British Council, Rome, 1959 (669); *105th Annual Exhibition of Watercolours and Drawings*, Agnew's, 1978 (15, repr. pl.1), unsold; *107th Annual Exhibition of Watercolours and Drawings*, Agnew's 1980 (27).

Lit: Brinsley Ford, 'The Dartmouth Collection of Drawings by Richard Wilson', *Burlington Magazine*, XC, 1948, pp.337–345; Brinsley Ford, *The Drawings of Richard Wilson*, 1951, p.61, no.62, repr. pl.62; W. G. Constable, *Richard Wilson*, 1953, p.98.

This is 'N° 20' in a series of twenty 'views of the environs of Rome', commissioned from Wilson, with other drawings, by the 2nd Earl of Dartmouth, and completed in Rome in 1754. As Brinsley Ford (1978, *loc. cit.*) has shown, the commission was negotiated by Wilson's friend Thomas Jenkins, who acted as 'agent in acquiring works of art for rich English cavalieri who passed through Rome'. On 1 June 1754 Jenkins reported from Rome to Lord Dartmouth, who by then was back in England: 'Mr Wilson desires him to say that in this summer he will have finished twenty drawings, views of the environs of Rome, which the writer will send with some of his own drawings ...'. On 25 June 1754 Jenkins sent accounts of sums expended on Lord Dartmouth's behalf, including payments 'to Mr Wilson for twelve drawings views of Rome at three zechins each' (Mr Ford estimates the 'zecchino' at that time to have been worth about half a guinea). Jenkins's letter of 30 March 1755 to Lord Dartmouth refers to the despatch of two groups of drawings by Wilson: 'a portfolio with 30 of Mr Wilson's drawings' was included in a case shipped to England on 28 February 1755, and 'other drawings of Messrs. Pompeo Wilson and myself' were sent 'by the French courier'.

'The drawings made by Wilson at Rome for Lord Dartmouth' are reverently mentioned several times between 1801 and 1811 by Joseph Farington, Wilson's former pupil (relevant passages from his *Diary* are quoted in Ford, 1948, pp.337–9). Farington considered them 'so excellent that it may be justly said they have all the quality of his pictures except the colour'; he also noted that they were much admired by such contemporaries as Hoppner, Sir George Beaumont, Sir Charles Long and William Lock of Norbury. When Farington counted the drawings in 1806, he noted a total of sixty-eight, which presumably included all the twenty 'views of the environs of Rome' and forty-eight other subjects; this total of sixty-eight is supported, Brinsley Ford suggests, by the numbers, ranging from twenty-three to sixty-one, on the verso of the mounts of those drawings which have survived. Farington last mentions the drawings in 1811, after which they were apparently lost sight of for well over a century. One portfolio containing twenty-five drawings was rediscovered in 1948 in a cupboard at Patshull House, Wolverhampton, the Dartmouth seat. These twenty-five drawings (listed by Ford, p.345) include nineteen of the original twenty 'views of the environs of Rome' ('Nº 1' is missing), three separate views, two designs for fountains and one dramatic landscape with figures.

All the twenty-five rediscovered drawings were sold at Christie's by the 7th Earl of Dartmouth in 1954. The present locations of the other eighteen surviving drawings in the 'environs of Rome' series may be thus summarised: four British provincial galleries each own one (Cecil Higgins Museum, Bedford; Whitworth Art Gallery, Manchester; Castle Museum, Norwich; Aberdeen City Art Gallery). There are seven in American public collections (two in the Yale Center for British Art, Paul Mellon Collection; two in the Henry E. Huntington Library and Art Gallery, San Marino; two in the Rhode Island School of Design; and one in the Metropolitan Museum of Art, New York). The remaining seven, so far as is known, are in British or American private collections, two of the finest being in the Loyd Collection.

The Ponte Nomentana, about two miles outside Rome to the north-east, had for centuries carried the old Roman Via Nomentana across the River Anio to the town of Mentana (formerly Nomentum); the bridge shown in T.3026 was rebuilt in mediaeval times. The Alban Hills are seen in the background on the right.

The carefully thought-out composition of T.3026, as of all the surviving Roman views, makes it likely that it was made in the studio; the views may have been based on preliminary drawings made on the spot, but no such studies survive. All the 'environs of Rome' drawings were originally bordered, in the same manner as T.3026, with strips of paper washed with purplish lilac; this was presumably done by Wilson himself, or by an assistant working under his directions. Each drawing was then evidently overmounted to show only about half the width of the lilac border. Since lilac is a particularly fugitive colour, the exposed part of the borders faded drastically, probably within a short time of having been painted, despite the fact that the drawings were apparently preserved at some time or other in an album (Ford, 1948, p.341, note 17). The unexposed part of the border retains the deep colour which may still be seen beneath the new mount of T.3026.

The inscription on the label on the border of T.3026 now reads 'Ponte Nomentano', the last letter evidently having been altered, by a later and rather heavier hand, from the (?surely correct) spelling 'Nomentana', which remains unaltered on the label of the drawing 'Via Nomentana', 'Nº 18' in the 'environs of Rome' series (now in the Yale Center for British Art, Paul Mellon Collection). Altering the final 'a' to 'o' may have been done in the later nineteenth century when 'Ponte Nomentano' was apparently the form chiefly used in England (e.g. by Augustus J. C. Hare, *Walks in Rome*, 13th ed., 1893, and K. Baedeker, *Central Italy and Rome*, 13th ed., 1900).

John Wootton ?1683–1764

T.2378 **?Lady Mary Churchill at the Death of the Hare** 1748

Inscribed 'J. Wootton/Fecit 1748' bottom left
Oil on canvas, $41\frac{3}{4} \times 61\frac{1}{4}$ (106 × 155.5)
Presented by Mr Paul Mellon KBE through the British Sporting Art Trust 1979

Prov: . . .; by descent to the Hon. Rachel de Montmorency, Dewlish House, Dorchester; P. & D. Colnaghi & Co. Ltd., from whom purchased by Paul Mellon, 1962.

Exh: Clandon Park, Surrey, on long loan to the National Trust from the Hon. Rachel de Montmorency until *c.*1961; *Painting in England 1700–1850: Collection of Mr & Mrs Paul Mellon*, Virginia Museum of Fine Arts, Richmond, Virginia, 1963 (308, as 'Lady on Horseback with Huntsmen and Hounds').

Lit: Egerton, 1978, pp.26–8, no.29, pl.10.

The lady was traditionally identified in the de Montmorency family as Lady Mary Churchill (*c.*1735–1801), Horace Walpole's half-sister, the illegitimate daughter of Sir Robert Walpole by his mistress Maria Skerrett, whom he married after his first wife's death. There seems to be little reason to doubt this identification, for although her portrait in T.2378 is hardly a sharply distinguished one, there appears to be a sufficiently credible resemblance to Lady Mary Churchill's features as shown in Arthur Pond's portrait drawing (repr. ed. W. S. Lewis, *Horace Walpole's Correspondence with the Walpole Family*, 1973, facing p.41), in Johann Eckhardt's portrait 'Colonel Charles and Lady Mary Churchill with their eldest son', *c.*1750 (exh. Yale University, Beinecke Rare Book and Manuscript Library, *A Guide to the Life of Horace Walpole*, 1973, 46, repr.) and in Eckhardt's portrait of Lady Mary Churchill with a music book, *c.*1752 (repr. W. S. Lewis, *Horace Walpole*, 1961, pl.11).

Wootton had earlier painted several hunting pictures for Sir Robert Walpole, including the portrait with horses and hounds of 1727 (repr. John Steegman, *The Artist and the Country House*, 1949, pl.34). When Sir Robert Walpole died in 1744, his daughter Mary was still under age. On 23 February 1746 she married Charles Churchill (?1720–1812), the illegitimate son of her father's old friend General Charles Churchill by the actress Ann Oldfield. Charles Churchill served in the Army and succeeded his father as Deputy Ranger of St. James's and Hyde Parks 1745–57. Lady Mary Churchill herself held Court appointments, as Housekeeper first of Kensington Palace and later of Windsor Castle. As her husband's name was never traditionally linked with T.2378, the figure of the man in brown who ceremonially presents the dead hare is presumably that of a hunt servant.

Throughout his life Horace Walpole showed kindness and affection to his half sister; she (in later years with her husband) frequently stayed with him at Strawberry Hill, and Walpole hung Eckhardt's portrait of her in his Great Parlour there. Wilmarth Lewis suggests that the disappearance of Horace Walpole's letters to Lady Mary Churchill is one of the chief losses of his correspondence (*Horace Walpole*, 1961, p.170).

A remote red-brick house with a small turret in the background of T.2378 has not been identified. Lady Mary Churchill and her husband lived first at Farleigh Wallop, near Basingstoke, Hampshire, and later in a 'Gothick' house designed for them by Horace Walpole's friend John Chute.

The frame appears to be contemporary with the painting and may be its original frame.

T.2379 **Muff, a Black and White Dog** ?*c.*1740–50

Inscribed 'J. Wootton' at the base of a stone pillar on the left and, as if carved across the middle of its column, 'MUFF'
Oil on canvas, $49\frac{1}{4} \times 40$ (125×101)
Presented by Mr Paul Mellon KBE through the British Sporting Art Trust 1979

Prov: ?The 2nd Duchess of Portland (d.1785); ...; Mrs W. Duncan, sold Sotheby's 28 November 1962 (86), bt. Oscar & Peter Johnson, from whom purchased by Paul Mellon 1963.

Lit: Egerton, 1978, pp.25–6, no.27.

This is evidently a pet dog of considerable charm but mixed breeding (?spaniel-pointer cross) and indeterminate sex. An old inscription *verso* read (before relining) 'From the Collection of the Duchess of Portland'. That Margaret Cavendish, 2nd Duchess of Portland, should have asked Wootton to paint a pet dog is perfectly credible, particularly as her father, the 2nd Earl of Oxford, had been one of Wootton's earliest and most faithful patrons; but no painting of a dog called Muff is recorded in any of the catalogues of pictures at Welbeck Abbey, nor in the sales of the contents of the Duchess of Portland's Museum in 1786. A portrait by Wootton entitled 'Minx, a little Spaniel Bitch' is listed in a MS. catalogue of paintings at Welbeck in 1747, and it is conceivable that 'Muff' was mis-read or mis-transcribed as 'Minx': last recorded at Welbeck in 1861, that picture must subsequently have left the collection. Two paintings of dogs by Wootton remain in the Duke of Portland's collection: 'The Countess of Oxford's Spaniel Casey', described in the 1747 catalogue as a portrait of the bitch Casey lying on a cushion, with a picture on the wall of Mina and Die, two other dogs; and 'Two Dogs, Gill and Die, and a Dead Hare" (R. W. Goulding & C. K. Adams, *Catalogue of the Pictures belonging to His Grace the Duke of Portland*, 1936, p. x, and nos.485 and 487).

One of Wootton's odder classical buildings in the background on the right offers no clue to the identification of the setting of the dog's portrait; John Harris describes it as a pedimented loggia *in antis*, an improbable construction possibly based on a design by Marot or Le Potre.

Though chiefly known as a painter of horses, Wootton evidently received many commissions for portraits of dogs. Horace Walpole announced to Horace Mann on 25 April 1754 that his favourite dog Patapan 'sits to Wootton tomorrow for his picture'; Walpole hung Patapan's portrait in his bedchamber (ed. W. S. Lewis and others, *Horace Walpole's Correspondence,* XVIII, 1954, pp.220–1). An inventory of pictures belonging to the Dukes of Hamilton, taken in 1759 after the death of the 6th Duke, lists three paintings of dogs by Wootton: 'A dog . . . called Jewell', 'A Dog called Scipio' and 'A Water Dog . . . called Trea' (Hamilton MSS., 13, pp.33 and 35).

The Stern Bequest

The following pictures were bequeathed to the National Gallery by Sir Edward Stern in 1933 but, under the terms of the bequest, remained with Lady Stern until her death in 1979. They were then transferred to the Tate Gallery. The entries which follow are revised versions of those published in Sir Martin Davies' National Gallery catalogue of 1946.

Sir William Beechey 1753–1839

4688 Thomas Law Hodges ?exh. 1795

Inscribed 'Thos Law Hodges/Ætat:suae 18/Painted by Sir Wil^{m} Beechey' in old hand on stretcher

Oil on canvas, $30\frac{1}{8} \times 25\frac{3}{16}$ (76.5 × 64.0)

Bequeathed by Sir Edward Stern to the National Gallery, with life interest to his widow, 1933. Transferred to the Tate Gallery 1979

Prov: ...; Agnew's; with donor by 1902.

Exh: ?R.A. 1795 (214); Burlington Fine Arts Club 1902 (52); *Spring Exhibition*, Whitechapel Gallery, 1907 (78), inexplicably ascribed to J. L. David.

Lit: W. Roberts, *Sir William Beechey R.A.*, 1907, p.48; Martin Davies, *National Gallery Catalogues, The British School*, 1946, p.8.

Thomas Hodges (1776–1857) of Hemsted Place, Cranbrook, Kent, was for many years M.P. for that county. His age of 18 would date the picture to 1794, so that it is probable that the 'Mr Hodges' which Beechey exhibited at the R.A. in 1795 was this picture. (Roberts, *op. cit.*, suggests that the R.A. picture may have been a portrait of William Hodges the painter, but there is no record that Beechey ever painted him). Its good condition, strong likeness and vigorous rendering of youthful vitality makes this one of Beechey's best male portraits.

Francis Cotes 1726–70

4689 Portrait of a Lady 1768

Inscribed 'FCotes R.A. px 1768', with initials in monogram, on tree-trunk, centre right

Oil on canvas, $49\frac{7}{8} \times 40$ (126.7 × 101.6)

Bequeathed by Sir Edward Stern to the National Gallery 1933, with life interest to his widow. Transferred to the Tate Gallery 1979

Prov: The Earl of Hardwicke at Wimpole Hall, Cambs., sold Christie's, 30 June 1888 (52) as 'Kitty Fisher', bt. Murray; with Charles Butler 1889–1891; James Orrock sale, Christie's 4 June 1904 (75, repr.), bt. by Agnew & Son for Sir Edward Stern.

Lit: Byron Webber, *James Orrock*, 1903, i., repr. p.73; Walter Heil 'Portraits by Francis Cotes' in *Art in America*, XX, 1931, pp.2–12; H. Isherwood Kay, 'The Stern Bequest to the National Gallery' in *The Connoisseur*, XCII, 1933, pp.271–4; Tancred Borenius, *La Peinture Anglaise au XVIIIme Siècle*, Paris 1938, pl.44; Martin Davies, *National Gallery Catalogues, The British School*, 1946, p.41; E. K. Waterhouse, *Painting in Britain 1530–1790*, 1953, p.193, pl. 162B; 4th ed., 1978, p.266, fig. 208; Edward Mead Johnson, *Francis Cotes*, 1976, p.94, no.259, fig. 77.

Exh: *Old Masters*, R.A. 1889 (146) as 'A Lady', lent by Charles Butler; *The Royal House of Guelph*, New Gallery 1891 (236) as 'Kitty Fisher', lent by Charles Butler; mixed antiques exhibition, Burlington Fine Arts Club, 1904 (24) as 'Kitty Fisher'.

The persistent identification of the sitter as the courtesan Kitty Fisher is untenable, as she died in 1767, and none of the many known portraits of her resembles this (a fact already pointed out in an anonymous press comment on the Hardwicke sale in 1888, preserved in the Whitley Papers, British Museum, Department of Prints and Drawings). The lady represented is more likely to be a member of the Yorke family (Yorke being the family name of the Earl of Hardwicke, the first recorded owner of this portrait), as Cotes is known to have painted at least one other member of the family, Agneta Yorke, at about the same date (her portrait, now in a British private collection, appears not to be signed, but was engraved by V. Green 1768; see Johnson, 1976, p.88, fig. 85).

The painting must have been completed in December 1768, as the Royal Academy – of which Cotes, as his signature here so prominently stresses, was a founding member – was not established until 10 December 1768.

What could be an oil sketch (possibly a guide for Cotes's drapery painter) for this picture was sold at Christie's, 30–31 July 1981 (271) as 'Reynolds: Portrait of a Lady, said to be Mrs Robinson', 14 × 12 (35.5 × 33.5), bought Gavin Graham Gallery.

Thomas Gainsborough 1727–88

4690 **Admiral Sir Charles Thompson, Bart.** 1774

Oil on canvas, 50 × 40 (127 × 101.8)
Bequeathed by Sir Edward Stern to the National Gallery, with life interest to his widow, 1933. Transferred to the Tate Gallery 1979

Prov: ...; Agnew's; Sir Edward Stern by 1933.

Lit: J. E. Wessely, *Richard Earlom*, Hamburg, 1886, no.53; E. K. Waterhouse, *Gainsborough*, 1958, p.92, no.664, pl.161.

An engraving of 1800 by Richard Earlom states that the picture was painted in 1774, the year Gainsborough moved from Bath to London. The sitter is shown in three-quarter length, leaning against a rock, with sea and ships in the background. He is wearing a captain's uniform and holds a telescope in his left hand. Admiral Thompson (*c.*1740–1799) was promoted Captain in 1772, Rear-Admiral 1794 and Vice-Admiral 1795; he was made a baronet in 1797.

John Hoppner 1758(?)–1810

4692 **Mrs Jordan as Hypolita in 'She Would And She Would Not'** exh. 1791

Oil on canvas, $30\frac{1}{2} \times 25\frac{1}{8}$ (76.5 × 63.9)
Bequeathed by Sir Edward Stern to the National Gallery, with life interest to his widow, 1933. Transferred to the Tate Gallery 1979

Prov: Painted presumably for the sitter, and probably passed into the collection of the Earls of Erroll through Elizabeth, the sitter's natural daughter by the Duke of Clarence, who married the 18th Earl of Erroll in 1820, and died in 1856. Purchased from the Earl of Erroll at an unspecified date by Colnaghi's; with Agnew & Son 1899; purchased by Sir Edward Stern 1900.

Exh: R.A. 1791 (440); Agnew & Son 1899 (6); *International Exhibition*, Paris 1900 (41, illustrated p.89 in I. Spielmann's catalogue of pictures in the British Royal Pavilion); Burlington Fine Arts Club 1902 (50); *Loan Collection of Portraits*, Birmingham 1903 (11, repr. in cat.); *Inaugural Exhibition*, Laing Art Gallery, Newcastle 1904 (52); *Georgian England*, Whitechapel Gallery 1906 (Upper Gallery, no. 139); *Japan – British Exhibition*, White City, 1910 (32); *British Art 1000 – 1860*, R.A. 1934 (434, No.294 in Memorial Catalogue).

Lit: *The Farington Diary* (ed. Greig), 1922, I, p.39 and VIII, p.279; H.P.K. Skipton, *John Hoppner*, 1905, p.57, repr. f. p.36; W. McKay and W. Roberts, *John Hoppner R.A.*, 1909, p.141; W. J. Lawrence, 'Portraits of Mrs Jordan' in *Connoisseur*, XXVI, 1910, p.143 ff., John Jones mezzotint repr. as frontispiece; Freeman O'Donoghue, *Catalogue of Engraved British Portraits*, British Museum, 1910, II, p.662; Martin Davies, *National Gallery Catalogues, The British School*, 1946, p.84.

Dorothea Bland (1762–1816), later known as Mrs Jordan, came from an Irish acting family, and began to make her mark on the London stage from 1785 onwards. She specialised in 'breeches' and comedy parts, performing chiefly at Drury Lane, although she frequently toured the provinces. Her role as Hypolita in Colley Cibber's 'She would and she would not', where the heroine follows her lover to Madrid disguised as a young gentleman of fashion and wears male attire throughout the five acts, was one of her great successes. The performance was so popular in Edinburgh and Glasgow in 1786 that medals were struck in her honour, and she performed the part many times at Drury Lane between 1789 and 1809. In 1790 Mrs Jordan became the mistress of the Duke of Clarence, later William IV, a liaison which lasted until 1811 and produced ten children, all of whom achieved splendid careers and marriages.

Mrs Jordan was painted by most leading portrait painters of the day, including several times by Hoppner. His earliest known portrait of her is as 'The Comic Muse', shown at the R.A. 1786 (now in the Royal Collection). He was also one of the favourite painters of the Royal family from 1785 onwards, and in 1790 – about the date this picture was painted – he spent a week with the Duke of Clarence and Mrs Jordan at Petersham (Farington, *op. cit.*). Whether he painted this portrait at this particular time is not known, but he was presumably working on the state portrait of the Duke which he also exhibited at the R.A. in 1791. Hoppner does not seem to have brought out Mrs Jordan's renowned vivacity, as Farington records that on this occasion Hoppner remarked that 'Mrs Jordan affords very little entertainment in Company. Her thoughts seem to be engaged abt. something not present. Very ignorant as to information, excepting in what relates merely to the stage'. Nevertheless, this is one of the most vivid female portraits from Hoppner's hand. The engraving in mezzotint after it by John Jones was published 1 March 1791.

Sir Henry Raeburn 1756–1823

4693 **Mrs Charles Steuart** (?) *c.*1794

Oil on canvas, $48\frac{7}{8}$ × 39 (124.1 × 99.1)
Bequeathed by Sir Edward Stern to the National Gallery, with life interest to his widow, 1933. Transferred to the Tate Gallery 1979

Prov: Presumably by descent to John Nairne Durrant-Steuart (great-great-grandson of Charles, the 9th laird); his sale, Dowell's, Edinburgh, 19 March 1904 (81), bought by Lawrie; with Agnew's by 1904; Sir Edward Stern by 1909.

Exh: Agnew's, Winter exhibition 1904 (13); *Cent Portraits de Femmes*, Paris, 1909 (34, repr. in cat.)

Lit: Note on the Durrant-Steuart sale in *Connoisseur*, IX, 1904, p.59; Martin Davies, *National Gallery Catalogues, The British School*, 1946, p.110.

The picture is first recorded at the Durrant-Steuart sale in 1904, where the sitter was 'believed to be' the first Mrs Charles Steuart. Charles Steuart, 9th laird of Dalgusie, co.Perth (1756–1821) first married, in 1786, Grace, eldest daughter of Robert Steuart of Ballechin, who died in 1787. He married his second wife, Amelia Anne Sophia (d.1808), second daughter of Laurence Oliphant of Gask, in 1794. As Raeburn returned from Italy in the year of the first Mrs Steuart's death, it is unlikely that he had time to paint her. Stylistically the picture is quite compatible with a later date and is therefore more likely to be a portrait of the second Mrs Steuart, possibly a marriage portrait of *c.*1794. In the absence of any other evidence, however, the possibility cannot be excluded that this could be some other member of the Durrant-Steuart family.

The Modern Collection

Ivor Abrahams b.1935

T.2330 **Winter Sundial** 1971–5

Inscribed 'Ivor Abrahams 75' bottom left
Acrylic over screenprint on board glued to millboard, $27\frac{5}{8} \times 33$ (70.3 × 83.8)
Presented by Mme Andrée Stassart 1979

Prov: Purchased by Mme Stassart from Bernard Jacobson Ltd. at Basel Internationale Kunstmesse 1975

Exh: Bernard Jacobson Ltd., 1975 (no catalogue); Basel Internationale Kunstmesse, June 1975 (no catalogue)

Ivor Abrahams began work on the print 'Summer Sundial' (DP 7384) in 1971, using an illustration from *Amateur Gardening* which he had previously considered for one of the prints in the series 'Privacy Plots' (1970–1). This small and poor quality illustration was rephotographed and enlarged, and used as the basis for five drawings, at least one of which (coll. Bernard Jacobson Ltd.) is dated 1971. Work was postponed during the preparation of the large print 'Open Gate', and resumed in 1974 on a larger scale. After 'Summer Sundial' was completed in 1975, the artist decided to make a second version of the same subject, and made T.2330 as a preparatory study, painting over one of the early proofs. He at first intended that the 'Winter Sundial' print should include an area of flock, as does 'Summer Sundial', where the sundial itself and its base is printed on a separate piece of paper. The background lawn area of T.2330 is cut with a knife, partly to keep the board flat when mounted and partly with reference to the possibility that this area would be cut away. In fact the print was made with few modifications from T.2330, but on a larger scale, 40 × 47 (101.5 × 119.5) to match the 'Summer Sundial'.

The garden subjects of Abrahams, beginning with the four prints 'Garden Emblems' (1967), consist primarily of the repertoire of garden sculpture, whether in the literal sense of statuary or as topiary or shrubbery. A sundial similar to that in T.2330 is part of a 'Garden Model' the artist made in 1969 for the film 'By Leafy Ways' (1971), but the pair of prints and the related drawings are otherwise the only use he has made of one. This particular image is an example of what he calls 'The Gardenesque', the design of a suburban garden using elements – originally from eighteenth century gardens – intended to provoke a prescribed response by rule. Abrahams quotes with approval Bertolt Brecht's description of the artist's need to distance the spectator from the work so that the subjects look exceptional: '... distance and reflection are required ... to produce this disassociation in which the work can be recognised as what it is' (*Ivor Abrahams*, catalogue of exhibition at Kölnischer Kunstverein, 1973, p.23). The recognition of 'The Gardenesque' as a 'recipe or formula' corresponds to Abrahams' stated interest in 'the rules behind the rules' (op. cit. p.18).

The seasonal change of a garden subject is shown in other works by Abrahams, the 'summer' and 'autumn' pair of prints 'For a Time, For a Season' (1971) and, by implication, in the book *Oxford Gardens, a sketchbook* (1977) in which the photographs follow the seasons. There is often in his work a feeling that the garden sculpture is being enveloped by its surrounding shrubbery, and in the pair of sundial prints this relation between the unchanging sculpture and the extreme change of colour of the plants is dramatically emphasised.

Josef Albers 1888–1976

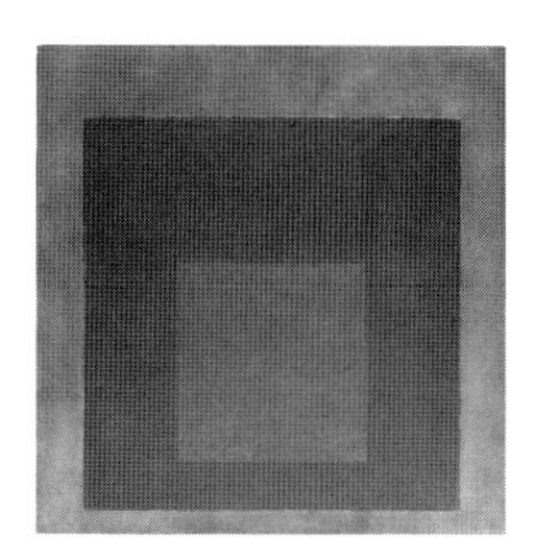

T.2310 **Study for Homage to the Square: Beaming** 1963

Inscribed 'A 63' bottom right, and on back at top '6 × liquit – permt Bright Green (Grumbacher Inc) – Cobalt Green Lt (Lefebvre) – Cerul Blue (W&N) 63'; also on back 'Ground: 6 coats of liquitex (permt pigment)/painting: paints used – from center:/Permanent Bright Green (Grumbacher Inc)/Cobalt Green Light (Lefebvre)/Cerulean Blue (Winsor & Newton)/all in one primary coat/all directly from the tube/Varnish: BUTYL METHACRYLATE Polymer in Xylene/ DANIEL Goldreyer LTD. July 1963'
Oil on masonite panel, 30 × 30 (76.2 × 76.2)
Presented by Anni Albers and the Josef Albers Foundation 1978

Exh: *Josef Albers: Homage to the Square*, Museum of Modern Art, New York, exhibition touring South and Central America, March 1964 – August 1965, and US museums October 1965 – January 1967 (33) as 'Homage to the Square: Beaming'

This and the following two paintings belong to a very large series of square pictures and prints entitled 'Homage to the Square' on which Albers was working from 1949 up to his death in 1976. The works of this series are based on a compositional scheme consisting of four squares nested together, symmetrically set within each other on a vertical axis and asymmetrically placed below centre on the horizontal in accordance with a rigid system of proportions. This can be seen in its complete form (sometimes known as format A) in T.783 'Study for Homage to the Square: Departing in Yellow' acquired in 1965. However because of the need for greater quantities of a particular colour he frequently omitted one or other of the three inner squares. Thus there are some pictures, such as T.2311 and T.2312, in which the largest of these squares is omitted (format B); some such as the present work in which the intermediate square is omitted (format C); and some – though there is no example of this in the Tate – in which the small inner square is omitted (format D). Each area is painted in a single colour, the paint being applied with a palette knife direct from the tube to the panel as thinly and evenly as possible in one primary coat.

Whereas T.783 is inscribed on the back 'Study for Homage to the Square: "Departing in Yellow" ', these three pictures have no titles on the backs, and were presented to the Tate by Anni Albers, the artist's widow, and the Josef Albers Foundation simply as 'Homage to the Square'. However the present work has a Museum of Modern Art, New York, loan label on the back with a number with identifies it as a picture lent to the travelling exhibition *Josef Albers: Homage to the Square* as 'Homage to the Square: Beaming'. The other pictures T.2311 and T.2312 do not seem to have been exhibited and it would appear that Albers never gave them subtitles.

T.2311 **Study for Homage to the Square** 1963

Inscribed 'A 63' bottom right, and on back at top '6 × Liquit – Cobalt Green Lt (Shiva) – Reilly's #4 (Grumb) – Raw Sienna (Shiva)'; also on back 'Ground: 6 coats of liquitex (permt pigment)/painting: paints used – from center:/Cobalt Green Light (Shiva)/Reilly's Gray #4 (Grumbacher)/Raw Sienna (Shiva)/all in one primary coat/all directly from the tube/Varnish: VARNISH WITH BUTYL METHACRYLATE POLYMER IN XYLENE DANIEL GOLDREYER LTD. APRIL 1964 [sic]'

Oil on masonite panel, 30 × 30 (76.2 × 76.2)
Presented by Anni Albers and the Josef Albers Foundation 1978

This picture, like T.2312, is one of the B format, in that the largest square has been omitted. The colours, from the centre out, are Cobalt Green Light (Shiva), Reilly's Gray 4 (Grumbacher), and Raw Sienna (Shiva).

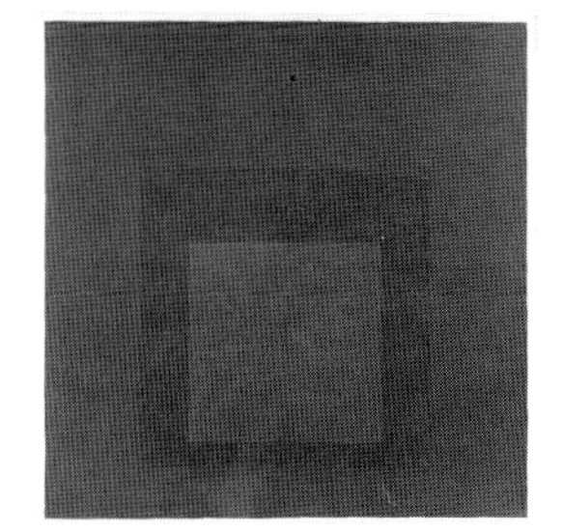

T.2312 **Study for Homage to the Square** 1964

Inscribed 'A 64' bottom right, and on back at top '6 × Liquit – Cobalt Green Lt (Shiva) next [this word has been crossed out, and 'yes' written underneath] Cobalt Green Lt (Rembrandt) – next [this word has again been crossed out and 'yes' written underneath] large permt Bright Green (Grumb. Inc) – I 64'; also on back 'Ground: 6 coats of Liquitex (permt pigment)/painting: paints used – from center:/Cobalt Green Lt. (Shiva)/Cobalt Green Lt. (Rembrandt)/Permt Bright Green (Grumbacher Inc)/all in one primary coat/all directly from the tube/Varnish: VARNISH WITH BUTYL METHACRYLATE/ POLYMER IN XYLENE DANIEL GOLDREYER LTD. APRIL 1964'
Oil on masonite panel, 30 × 30 (76.2 × 76.2)
Presented by Anni Albers and the Josef Albers Foundation 1978

Like T.2311, this is of the B format. The colours, from the centre out, are Cobalt Green Light (Shiva), Cobalt Green Light (Rembrandt), and Permanent Bright Green (Grumbacher).

Ivan Albright b. 1897

T.2316 **Josephine Medill Patterson Albright** 1954

Not inscribed
Bronze, $13\frac{5}{8} \times 8\frac{7}{8} \times 10\frac{9}{16}$ (34.5 × 22.5 × 26.8)
Presented by Mr and Mrs Michael Croydon through the American Federation of Arts 1978

Prov: Mr and Mrs Michael Croydon, Libertyville, Illinois (cast for presentation)
Lit: Michael Croydon, *Ivan Albright*, New York 1978, p.221, repr. pl.113
Repr: exh. catalogue *Ivan Albright*, Art Institute of Chicago, October–December 1964, p.56 (the Art Institute of Chicago cast)

A portrait head of the artist's wife Josephine Medill Patterson Albright, whom he married in 1964. She is the second daughter of Captain Joseph Medill Patterson, founder of the New York *Daily News* and a distinguished First World War officer; her sister Alicia Patterson Guggenheim is the wife of Harry F. Guggenheim. The sculpture was made at the artist's ranch at Dubois, Wyoming, in the summer of 1954 using an oil-based clay and took three and a half months to complete. The first bronze cast of it, made at the Fonderia Marinelli in Florence, was presented by the artist to the Art Institute of Chicago in 1966. The Tate's cast is the first of a later edition of three cast by the Meisner Foundry, New York, early in 1978; the second now belongs to the Centre National d'Art et de Culture Georges Pompidou, Musée National d'Art Moderne in Paris and the third is owned by the artist himself.

Albright studied with two American sculptors, Albin Polasek in Chicago and, later, with Charles Grafley at the Pennsylvania Academy of Fine Arts. However only five different bronzes by him exist: 'Now a Mask' 1930, 'Turn the Other

Cheek' 1931 (modelled from the daughter of Mr and Mrs Art Stanford), 'Head of Marie' 1933, 'Head of Adam Emory Albright' 1935 and the present work. This was therefore the first sculpture he had made since 1935 and he has made no more since (information from Michael Croydon, 24 October 1978).

Michael Andrews b. 1928

T.2334 **Melanie and Me Swimming** 1978–9

Inscribed 'Melanie and Me Swimming 1978–9 Michael Andrews' on stretcher
Acrylic on linen canvas, 72 × 72 (183 × 183)
Purchased from James Kirkman Ltd (Grant-in-Aid) 1979
Exh: *Michael Andrews*, Hayward Gallery, October 1980 – January 1981 (124, repr. in colour) and subsequent tour of the Fruit Market, Edinburgh and Whitworth Art Gallery, Manchester

'Melanie and Me Swimming' is based on a 6 × 4 inch coloured photograph of Michael Andrews and his daughter, then aged 6, taken when they were on holiday at Glenartney Lodge, Near Comrie, Perthshire, in the summer of 1976. The photograph, which was not commissioned, was taken by a friend of Andrews, whom he considers an excellent photographer, Jean Loup Cornet; Andrews liked the photograph so much that he decided to base a painting on it which was executed in his Norfolk studio in 1978 and was finished in February 1979. Andrews first made a careful watercolour study (about 11½ inches square) from the rectangular photograph. The photograph did not include the rocks above the pool which were painted from memory. The large picture was painted on unprimed canvas in acrylic paint applied using a spray gun as well as brushes; in the section depicting rocks strips of cloth saturated in paint were laid on the canvas and pressure applied.

Andrews considered that the scale of the figures in the painting, particularly the heads, was resolved at life size and found that it was important to adhere to this scale so that the figures should feel real to him. He did not stick 'slavishly' to the photograph when executing the watercolour and the larger painting and sees the photograph as a model or substitute object but not as an image to be copied.

Andrews painted a picture of fish, 'School 4', immediately before executing 'Melanie and Me Swimming'; the latter was the first of a *Holiday* series of which five were planned. The second and third of this series, 'Alistair's Day' and 'Peter's Day', respectively, were painted immediately after 'Melanie and Me Swimming'.

Michael Andrews has executed only two other self-portraits, one a drawing when a schoolboy and a painting showing himself frontally, in 1958.

This catalogue entry is approved by the artist and is based on a discussion with him on 19 February 1980.

Francis Bacon b. 1909

T.2414 **Study for Portrait II (after the life mask of William Blake)** 1955

Not inscribed
Oil on canvas, 24 × 20 (61 × 50.8)
Purchased from Lady Caroline Lowell through the Mayor Gallery, London (Grant-in-Aid) 1979

Prov: Hanover Gallery, London; Lady Caroline Lowell, London
Exh: *Bacon, Scott, Sutherland*, Hanover Gallery, June–July 1955 (4); on loan to the Tate Gallery, October 1957 – January 1959; *Francis Bacon*, Tate Gallery, May–July 1962 (44); Kuntsthalle, Mannheim, July–August 1962 (35); Galleria Civica d'Arte Moderna, Turin, September–October 1962 (39, repr.); Kunsthaus, Zurich, October–November 1962 (33); Stedelijk Museum, Amsterdam, January–February 1963 (29); *Francis Bacon*, Guggenheim Museum, New York, October 1963 – January 1964 (31, repr.); *Francis Bacon*, Grand Palais, Paris, October 1971 – January 1972 (22, repr.); Kunsthalle, Düsseldorf, March–May 1972 (22, repr.)
Lit: Ronald Alley and John Rothenstein, *Francis Bacon*, 1964, No. 93, pp.92, 271, repr. p.93 in colour
Repr: *Architectural Review*, CXVIII, 1955, p.189

The idea of painting heads of William Blake was suggested to Bacon by a young composer, Gerard Schurmann, who had set some of Blake's poems to music and who asked him to design a cover for his song cycle. He took Bacon to the National Portrait Gallery to see the plaster cast made after J. S. Deville's famous life mask of William Blake of 1823 and they bought several photographs of it. The pictures were painted from these photographs (showing it isolated against a dark background), though Bacon also revisited the National Portrait Gallery several times to refresh his memory of the head itself. But unfortunately the process of reproduction proved too expensive, so the original project had to be abandoned.

There are altogether five surviving versions of this theme and Bacon destroyed at least two more. The first three paintings were all done in January 1955 in the Imperial Hotel at Henley-on-Thames, the fourth, which is a freer version and shows the head from a different position, was probably executed a few weeks later, and the fifth, which is smaller than the others, was made in 1956.

Though Bacon has a great admiration for Blake's poetry, he dislikes his paintings.

Max Beckmann 1884–1950

T.2395 **Prunier** 1944

Inscribed 'Beckmann A 44.' b.r.
Oil on canvas, $39\frac{1}{2} \times 30\frac{5}{16}$ (100.3 × 77)
Purchased from Richard Feigen & Co. (Grant-in-Aid) 1979

Prov: Dr. Helmuth Lütjens, Amsterdam, 1945; Paul Cassirer & Co., Amsterdam; Mr and Mrs Richard L. Feigen, Bedford, New York, 1958
Exh: *Max Beckmann*, Kunstverein, Düsseldorf, February – April 1950 (90); *Max Beckmann zum Gedächtnis 1884 – 1950*, Haus der Kunst, Munich, June – July 1951 and Schloss Charlottenberg, Berlin, September – October 1951 (152); *Max Beckmann*, Stedelijk Museum, Amsterdam, December 1951 – January 1952 (62) as 'Pruimenboom' (Plum tree); *Max Beckmann 1884–1950*, Kunsthaus, Zurich, November 1955 – January 1956 (119); *Ausstellung Max Beckmann*, Kunsthalle, Basle, January – February 1956 (107); *Max Beckmann*, Gemeentemuseum, The Hague, March – May 1956 (90); *Max Beckmann Paintings and Drawings*, Richard Feigen Gallery, Chicago, August 1961 (no catalogue)
Lit: Erhard Göpel and Barbara Göpel, *Max Beckmann Katalog der Gemälde*, Bern, 1976, vol. I, pp.400–1, repr. vol. II, pl.241; Max Beckmann, *Tagebücher 1940 – 1950*, Munich – Vienna 1979, pp.82, 95
Repr: *Tate Gallery 1978–80*, p.40 in colour

Known also as 'Restaurant Prunier' or 'Café Prunier', this work is no. 667 in the Göpels' catalogue of Max Beckmann's paintings. In the artist's handwritten list of completed work for the year 1944, which is in the possession of his widow, the painting is numbered 12 and given the date 1944 (see Göpel, op. cit., p.p. 38, 400). Reifenberg and Hausenstein, in their pioneering monograph-catalogue of Beckmann's paintings published in Munich in 1949 – which, according to Göpel, tallies more or less with Beckmann's own lists as far as title, date and details of ownership are concerned – entitle the painting 'Pruniers Ponis' (presumably a misprint for 'Paris') and number it 546 out of a total of 660 works.

There are two mentions of the painting in Beckmann's published diaries for the year 1940–1950. On Wednesday, 23 February 1944 he writes that he has started three new sketches, including 'Die Fressenden' (literally 'The Guzzlers' or 'Gobblers' – clearly a reference to the way the two female figures in the finished painting appear to be gorging themselves on lobster) and 'Atelier' (preliminary title for 'Akademie II', Göpel 676). The second, equally brief mention occurs in the entry for Sunday, 13 August 1944, where Beckmann records the painting's completion, this time calling it by its definitive title. As with most of his paintings executed during the Amsterdam years (1937–47), 'Prunier' is inscribed with the letter 'A' between the artist's signature and its date. It was one of several works bought from Beckmann's studio at Rokin 85 in the difficult winter of 1944–5 by Dr Helmuth Lütjens, director of Paul Cassirer's Amsterdam gallery. Lütjens was one of those who befriended and supported Beckmann during his years of seclusion in Amsterdam, where he had gone to avoid Nazi persecution.

In Beckmann's *oeuvre*, 'Prunier' comes midway between the completion of one triptych, 'Carnival' (Göpel 649), and the beginning of another, 'Blind Man's Buff' (Göpel 704), which the artist considered to be his most important pictorial statement. T.2395 shows two ladies eating at Prunier's, the famous seafood restaurant in Paris (9, rue Duphot), the city where Beckmann had spent much of the period 1929–32 and where he had last been in the spring of 1939. According to his widow, Beckmann was fond of seafood and liked to eat at Prunier's with his friends. He returned to Paris in April 1947 and lunched at the restaurant with Stephan Lackner (see Stephan Lackner, *Max Beckmann: Memories of a Friendship*, Miami, 1969, p.102).

One of the ladies in the painting sits beneath a light-shade directly facing the specator, a pose often adopted by women in Beckmann's paintings, especially in the numerous portraits of Quappi, his wife, where she is also on occasion associated with light (holding a burning candle, for example, in Göpel 587). The woman on the left, her head in profile, wears a cloak similar to those worn by certain mythological and theatrical figures in Beckmann's paintings (e.g. Göpel 659 and, most notably, The King in the central panel of the triptychs 'Departure' 1932–3 and 'Actors' 1941–2, Göpel 412 and 604). Both women are observed by a third, bespectacled male presence sitting or standing in shadow behind their table, also chewing a piece of lobster (probably a claw). Outside, the French word *Sorti*(*e*), written back to front, can be seen through the restaurant window, partially concealing the figure of a man and below a directional arrow – a device found elsewhere in Beckmann (e.g. Göpel 526, 677) whose immediate source, according to the artist, was the exit notices in the Paris *métro* (see Lackner, op. cit., p.73). Upside down, this sign could read 'Rokin', the name of the street in which the Beckmanns lived.

Sensual pleasures, especially good food, wine and tobacco, were of considerable significance to Beckmann, and this is reflected in his art. The wartime diary is scattered with descriptions of meals eaten and delicacies procured, and with the names of bars and cabarets frequented. Memories of meals consumed on holiday in the south of France or in Paris provide the starting-point for a number of pictures executed during this period: café-scenes and still-lifes in which food, and particularly fish or sea-food such as herring, mussels and oysters (a reminder possibly that the artist was living close to the North Sea), figure prominently, often with emblematic overtones. Lobster makes its first appearance in 1941, in two still-lifes (Göpel 568 and 577). A painting of 1942 or 1943 (Göpel 652), in which two women eating oysters are watched from behind by male figures, including a silhouetted head framed by the window, is closely related to T.2395. Beckmann returns to the theme of women eating fish in the centre panel of his last, unfinished triptych, 'Ballet Rehearsal' 1950 (Göpel 834). But nowhere are the aggressive qualities of crustacea and the carnivorous instincts of humans made more explicit than in T.2395, where the scarlet colour of the lobster, repeated in the dress of the left-hand figure and also in the central male head, contributes strongly to the impression of sexuality which pervades the ritual. Sharp objects or instruments are a recurrent feature in Beckmann's wartime paintings; in 'Prunier', the dynamic composition is made up of harsh, angular rhythms which reinforce the suggestion of underlying violence.

In a lecture on his painting delivered at the New Burlington Galleries, London, on 21 July 1938, Beckmann spoke about his attitude to form, space and colour, and especially the reasons for his characteristic use of black. 'Many people, I know, would like to see everything white, that is objectively beautiful, or black, that is negative and ugly; but I can only express myself in both together.'

Colour, he said, 'enriches the composition and enables me to penetrate the object more deeply; it has its part in determining my spiritual attitude to the work, but in this it is subordinate to light and especially to the treatment of form . . . Pure local colours and broken tones should be used together, as each needs to be complemented by the other.' (reprinted in catalogue of *Max Beckmann*, Marlborough Fine Art, November 1974, pp.11–21 and also in *Max Beckmann: The Triptychs*, Whitechapel Art Gallery, November 1980 – January 1981, pp.9–12; translation by P. S. Falla).

As the wartime diaries indicate, the period between the end of February and the beginning of August 1944 was a time of surprising productivity for the sixty-year-old Beckmann – he would often work on several paintings at once – despite illness, followed by bouts of depression, and further anxiety caused by uncertainty over his own future and the wartime situation. Especially worrying to him were the prospect of being called up for military service by the Germans (he was finally declared unfit on 31 May), the increasingly frequent Allied air-raids over Amsterdam and the conflicting reports, from June onwards, of the Allied invasion. Beckmann was kept up to date with news by the Posts, a family living in the same house in Amsterdam who owned a radio. Five days after beginning work on T.2395 the artist fell ill with the first stirrings of the heart trouble which was eventually to kill him, and he was unable to paint for a fortnight. The mysterious male head in the centre of the painting, his heavy features largely in shadow but his presence drawn sharply to the viewer's attention by the arrow outside the window (a result of Beckmann's practice of condensing the space of his paintings or, as he put it, reducing a three-dimensional subject to a flat surface), bears a slight resemblance to the artist, though Beckmann never normally portrayed himself wearing spectacles. He was, however, the most autobiographical of painters, appearing throughout his own work in a variety of guises. Diary entries for March 1944 reveal, not unnaturally, a preoccupation with death and it is conceivable that the central dark figure in 'Prunier' was intended, at one level, as a comment on the artist's predicament in Amsterdam that spring.

According to Mrs Beckmann, her husband's sketchbooks which are in her possession throw no further light on the painting. Beckmann's preoccupations at the time are discussed in her forthcoming book on the artist, though there is no mention here of *Prunier*.

The compiler is grateful to Catherine Viviano for forwarding a letter from Mrs Beckmann's secretary and companion containing information supplied by Mrs Beckmann.

Larry Bell b. 1939

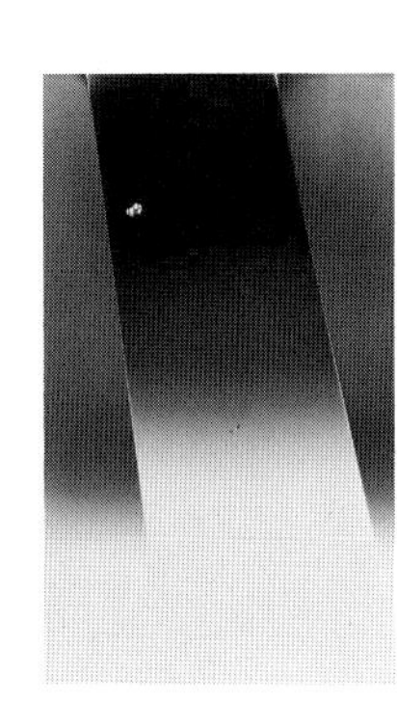

T.2411 **Vapour Drawing LDIF4** 4/16/79 1979

Inscribed 'L. Bell 79' b.c.
Vaporised metal on paper, 60 × 36⅜ (152.6 × 92.4)
Purchased from the artist (Grant-in-Aid) 1979

T.2412 **Vapour Drawing LNVFXI** 7/10/79 1979

Inscribed 'L. Bell 79' b.r.
Vaporised metal on paper, 60⅛ × 42⅜ (152.8 × 107.6)
Purchased from the artist (Grant-in-Aid) 1979

Larry Bell has used the industrial process of vacuum deposition to coat glass surfaces since 1962, when he made the Tate Gallery's mirrored box, 'Untitled' (T.1695). He obtained his first vacuum chamber in 1966 and a larger one in 1969, making it possible to work with large-scale glass surfaces. In March 1978, he made his first 'vapour drawing' on paper, using a modified version of the vacuum coating process.

The material Bell uses to coat both his glass and his paper works is Inconel, a nickel chrome alloy containing iron, magnesium, cobalt and traces of other metals. This is loaded onto filaments (similar to those used for light bulbs), which are then placed in a vacuum chamber. Each filament is approximately six inches long and is made up of stranded tungsten wire around the centre of which is wrapped a twelve inch strip of Inconel wire.

To make a 'vapour drawing', the artist tapes a sheet of 100% rag paper (usually Arches or Rives) to a steel sheet which is then rolled or curved in the vacuum chamber for coating. He controls the coating process by masking the paper with strips of 1 Mill (1/1000 of 1 inch) thick plastic film which he cuts in varying widths and lengths and tapes to the steel sheet. After the initial coating process, the artist may remove the sheet, re-mask the paper and subject it to the vapour source again, until the composition is complete.

Once the paper has been placed in the chamber at an angle so as to catch the Inconel deposit, air is withdrawn from the chamber, creating a vacuum. A small quantity of pure oxygen is then released into the vessel and an electric current is passed through it. The electrical discharge purges the surface of the paper of any extraneous matter, thus preparing it for coating. This process lasts for about four minutes, after which the high voltage discharge is shut off and the pressure inside the vacuum chamber is reduced. A current is then applied to the filaments holding the Inconel material. As a result, the Inconel vaporises and fills the chamber as a gas which is deposited onto the paper as a thin film. The variation in thickness of this coating is determined by the curvature of the steel sheet, in relation to the Inconel-bearing filaments, so that areas closest to the vapour source receive a heavier coating and those curving away from the source, a lighter one. The artist purchases the Inconel material in California and uses a high vacuum coating apparatus which was built for him in 1968 by Edwards High Vacuum of Grand Island, New York. (The parent company is based in Sussex).

The 'vapour drawings' are conceived in series and the artist wrote (21 October 1981) that to date, he had initiated sixty-three series, some comprising as many as seventy works. He has made drawings on both black and white paper, in a variety of sizes and compositional arrangements and has pointed out that the size of these drawings is not determined by their method of fabrication. Some 'vapour drawings' as in the case of T.2411 and T.2412 are designed to be displayed singly but some series were conceived as potentially interlocking, several drawings being hung together to make up a multi-panelled image. A number of these multi-panelled works were recently exhibited in New York (*Larry Bell/Multiples*, Marian Goodman Gallery, January – February 1979)

Asked about the signficance of the titles of T.2411 and T.2412, the artist replied that 'LDIF4' stands for 'Large Diagonal Fade # 4' and 'LNVFXI' for 'Large New Vertical Fade Eccentric # I'. Each drawing is marked with its date of fabrication, following the American convention of preceding day by month.

The 'vapour drawings' resemble in their austerity and beauty the ambiguous, reflective and spatial qualities of Bell's glass works, where, by controlling the density of the metallic coating, he is able to vary degrees of transparency and opacity across a surface.

Asked about the relationship between his drawings and sculpture the artist replied (21 October 1980) 'Inherent in any aspect of an artist's work are the prejudices that make up his rules for that work. The drawings are two dimensional, the sculptures are three dimensional. Both elements contain the traits of my interests, visual and otherwise'.

The above entry is based on information supplied by the artist in two questionnaires which he completed and returned to the Tate in March and October 1980. It has been approved by him.

John Bellany b. 1942

T.2333 **Celtic Marriage** 1978

Inscribed 'J. Bellany' b.l
Oil on hardboard, 96⅛ × 72 (244 × 183)
Purchased from the artist (Knapping Fund) 1979

'Celtic Marriage' is an oblique allusion to John Bellany and his wife Julia at the time of their marriage. The boat in the foreground is based on a model boat in the artist's possession made by his father. The picture was painted quickly, in about a week, at the artist's flat and studio at 43 Linden Gardens', London W11 at about the time of his second marriage.

T.2336 **Star of Bethlehem** 1968

Inscribed 'Bellany' b.r.
Oil on hardboard, 72½ × 96⅝ (184.1 × 255.5)
Presented by the Contemporary Art Society to mark the opening of the Tate Gallery extension 1979

Exh: *John Bellany: Paintings*, Acme Gallery, December 1977 – January 1978 and subsequent tour to Glasgow Print Studio Gallery, Glasgow and the Scottish Arts Council Gallery, Edinburgh (2, repr. and wrongly stated to be in collection of Graham and Aileen Martin)

John Bellany was born and brought up at Port Seton, a fishing village east of Edinburgh. His father and grandfather had been fishermen at Port Seton and Eyemouth. Accounts of the Eyemouth Disaster of 1881 in which almost the whole male population of that village, 150 men, was wiped out in one great storm had a great impact on Bellany, emphasising that fishing can be a dangerous occupation.

Bellany has always painted boats. 'Star of Bethlehem' was the name of an actual fishing boat based in Eyemouth. Many boats had names with Christian connections as religion played a dominant part in the lives of fishermen and their families. According to Bellany there were twelve churches in Port Seton.

While a schoolboy Bellany often worked at gutting fish, a theme of 'Star of Bethlehem' which is also the theme of 'Bethel' 1967 (Coll. Southampton Art Gallery). Both of these pictures were painted at the Royal College of Art where the artist was a postgraduate student from 1965 to 1968 after studying at Edinburgh College of Art from 1960 to 1965.

This catalogue entry and that for 'Celtic Marriage' are based on a discussion with the artist (10 May 1981).

Hans Bellmer 1902–75

T.2305 **La Poupée** (The Doll) *c.*1937–8

Inscribed 'A GERMAINE' and 'Avec les plus jolies [?]/salutations de/ Hans/Bellmer.' on left-hand sheet

Nine photographs tinted with coloured inks, eight $20\frac{7}{8} \times 20\frac{7}{8}$ (53 × 53) and one $28 \times 20\frac{7}{8}$ (71 × 53), plus a sheet of pink paper $31\frac{1}{2} \times 20\frac{1}{2}$ (80 × 52) with a dedication in pencil and a greetings stick-on label with a printed flower; all these mounted together in a horizontal window mount

Presented anonymously through the Friends of the Tate Gallery 1978

Prov: Mme Germaine Hugnet, Paris (gift from the artist); private collector/dealer, Paris; private collector, London

Exh: [? *Exposition Internationale du Surréalisme*, Galerie Beaux-Arts, Paris, January–February 1938 (13) as 'La Poupée (1933–1937), photographies'; Galerie Robert, Amsterdam, spring 1938 (7)]; *Dada and Surrealism Reviewed*, Hayward Gallery, January–March 1978 (12.7, second photograph from left repr.)

Lit: Hans Bellmer, *Les Jeux de la Poupée*, Paris 1949; Alain Jouffroy, *Hans Bellmer*, Chicago n.d., n.p.; Hans Bellmer, *Die Puppe*, Berlin 1962, pp.49–119, 188–9; exh. catalogue *Hans Bellmer*, Centre National d'Art Contemporain, Paris, November 1971 – January 1972, p.92

Bellmer made his first doll in 1933 and took a series of photographs of it in various states of dismemberment and rearrangement, and 'with the necessary background of vice and enchantment', which was first published as a book *Die Puppe* in Karlsruhe in 1934, with a foreword by himself. The photographs were taken by Bellmer, while the settings were constructed by his brother.

His second series of photographs was based on the elements of the central sphere, sometimes with a head and sometimes with two pairs of legs, and was completed in December 1937. Some of the photographs were taken out of doors in the garden of his father's house. Bellmer took the photographs with him when he settled in Paris in 1938 and preparations were made for their publication. The foreword, which was originally written in German; was translated into French in 1938 with the help of George Hugnet, while the idea of hand-colouring the photographs (which had not been done in the case of the first series) was suggested by Paul Eluard. Eluard also wrote fourteen short prose poems in the winter of 1938–9 to accompany the photographs. However in the end the book was not published until after the war, in 1949, when it was brought out by Heinz Berggruen, in a very limited edition, as *Les Jeux de la Poupée*.

The book consists of a foreword by Bellmer followed by fifteen coloured photographs, of which fourteen (numbered from I, II onwards) have texts by Eluard. The set of photographs now owned by the Tate comes from the same series and is closely related but not identical.

Only three of the photographs appear to have been made from the same negatives as those used for the book and even they are slightly different in their colouring; one of the images is not to be found in the book at all; and the others are variants of photographs in the book, evidently taken at the same time but with changes in the arrangement of the forms, different viewpoints and so on. Thus reading from left to right:

1. The photograph on the extreme left contains most of the same elements as pl.I, but differently arranged. It lacks the green bead and the splash of liquid on the floor which appear in the photograph in the book, but includes a further somewhat ear-shaped form.
2. This is very similar to pl.V and seems to be from the same negative. The colouring is almost identical, except that the doll's left breast is greenish instead of orange.
3. From the same negative as pl.II, and similar but not identical in colour.
4. Closely related to pl.XIV, but the lighting and shadows are slightly different. There are also various differences in colour.
5. This image does not appear in the book.
6. This contains the same elements as pl.XIII but differently arranged. The latter also has a carpet beater in the foreground but horizontal (from the left) instead of vertical; the legs are set closer together and the doll is seen more or less from the side; and the setting is also viewed from a different angle.
7. Probably from the same negative as pl.IX, but showing a little more on the right. The colouring of the photograph in the book is similar but bluer.
8. This appears to show the doll in the same pose as pl.VI, but viewed from a completely different angle and without a figure of a man on the left. The colouring bears little relationship.
9. This photograph (the one on the extreme right) is related to pl.VII, which is also a night effect, but shows the doll with the limbs differently arranged, as if she was sitting in the tree instead of standing.

The Tate's set of photographs was hand-coloured by Bellmer and put together specially for Germaine, the first wife of the writer Georges Hugnet, possibly in late 1937 or the very beginning of 1938 as it may have been exhibited at the Galerie Beaux-Arts in January–February 1938. (Georges Hugnet was one of the organisers of the revised version of the exhibition shown at the Galerie Robert in Amsterdam shortly afterwards). Mme Germaine Hugnet writes (letter of 3 August 1979) that she and her husband had various photographs in the late 1930s of Bellmer's doll which Bellmer had given them. One day, Georges Hugnet, who had a framing and book binding workshop at that period, had the idea of choosing some and mounting them together in the way they are now. The selection and arrangement was done by him, and is unique.

Though the book was not officially published until 1949, there are also six or eight copies of a preliminary version made for friends in 1938–9 comprising hand-coloured and black and white photographs by Bellmer and entitled 'La Poupée II'. The photographs, which vary from copy to copy, are mounted like these on pink paper and there is no text.

John Bigge (Sir John Amherst Selby-Bigge, Bt.)
1892–1973

T.3056 **Dieppe** 1931

Inscribed 'J. Bigge' b.r.
Oil on plywood, $17\frac{5}{8} \times 23\frac{7}{8}$ (44.9 × 60.7)
Purchased from Mrs Mary Edwards (Grant-in-Aid) 1980
Prov: Mrs Mary Edwards (the artist's daughter)
Exh: *John Bigge*, Wertheim Gallery, April 1931 (20); *Unit I*, Portsmouth City Museum and Art Gallery, May–July 1978 (JB4)
Lit: C. J. Collier, 'John Bigge', unpublished article

This painting may be dated by its exhibition in 1931 and by its similarity to 'Composition' 1931, illustrated in Herbert Read's *Art Now*, 1933, pl.113. C. J. Collier points out that in paintings of this date Bigge often depicted architecture that looked like tools or parts of machinery, but the object in the foreground of this work seems to be abstract.

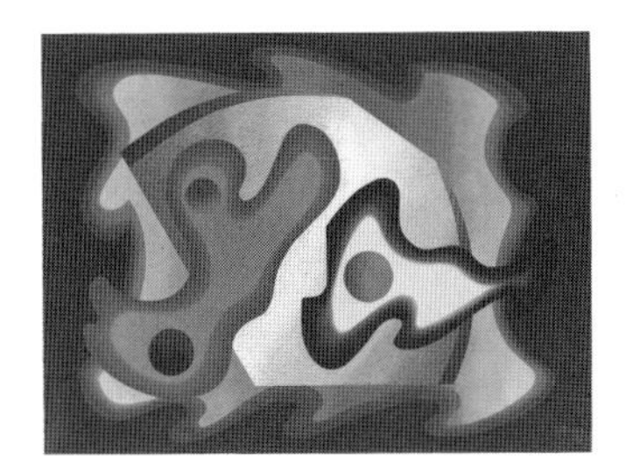

T.3057 **Composition** 1933

Inscribed 'J. Bigge/'33' b.r.
Oil on plywood, $22\frac{5}{8} \times 30\frac{1}{4}$ (58 × 76.9)
Purchased from Mrs Mary Edwards (Grant-in-Aid) 1980
Prov: Mrs Mary Edwards (the artist's daughter)
Exh: *Unit I*, Mayor Gallery, April 1934 (Bigge's four exhibits – 3, 12, 18 and 19 – were all entitled 'Composition'); *Contemporary Art*, Leicester Museum and Art Gallery, May – June 1936 (169); *Unit I*, Portsmouth City Museum and Art Gallery, May – July 1978 (JB2, repr.)
Lit: C. J. Collier, 'John Bigge', unpublished article
Repr: ed. H. Read, *Unit I*, 1934, pl.xxiii (as 'Abstraction', 1933); James Bustard, 'Unit One Today', *Artscribe*, 12, June 1978, p.51

The four paintings by Bigge listed in the catalogue of the 1934 'Unit I' exhibition were all titled 'Composition', and it is not certain that this was one of them. However a label proves that it was at the Mayor Gallery in March 1934, and its selection for reproduction in the book *Unit I* shows its importance. Whereas 'Dieppe' 1939 is Surrealist in character, this picture, painted two years later, illustrates his subsequent shift to abstract art.

'An abstract picture' he declared in *Unit I*, p.51, 'whether it makes use of material or imaginary forms (in any case imaginary forms are derived or distilled from visual experience) must keep its content pure; there must be no association of the forms either with function or symbol. It must be logical in construction, but with its own self-imposed logic. Its forms must appear solid within space (not like cut-out pieces of paper applied to a flat surface), and yet it must dispense with both modelling and perspective, which belong to the world of material experience. Its colour must be integral with its form, colour-form becoming a single concept, and tone-values being merged within colour. It must be illuminated, but have its own internal illumination. It must retain an air of spontaneity and yet have the completeness of inevitability'.

There is a similar abstract painting on the reverse of the panel, painted over.

Peter Blake b. 1932

T.2406 **Self-Portrait with Badges** 1961

Inscribed 'Peter Blake-Self Portrait/with Badges' on back
Oil on hardboard, $68\frac{3}{4} \times 48$ (174.7 × 121.9)
Presented by the Moores Family Charitable Foundation to celebrate the John Moore's Liverpool Exhibitions 1979
Prov: Purchased from the artist through Waddington Galleries by the Moores Charitable Foundation for presentation to the Tate Gallery 1979

Exh: The John Moores Liverpool Exhibition 1961, November 1961 – January 1962 (39, repr. awarded 1st Prize in the Junior Section); *British Self Portraits*, Arts Council exhibition, Laing Art Gallery, Newcastle, February – March 1962 (6) and subsequent tour to Leeds City Art Gallery, Birmingham City Art Gallery, the National Library of Wales, Aberystwyth, Leicester City Art Gallery, Salford Art Gallery, Guildford House, Guildford, and the Bournemouth College of Art; *Peter Blake*, Bristol City Art Gallery, November – December 1969 (25, repr. in colour); *Peter Blake*, Stedelijk Museum, Amsterdam, September – November 1973 (22, repr. in colour) and subsequent tour to Kunstverein Hamburg and Gemeente Museum, The Hague; *Pop Art in England*, Kunstverein, Hamburg, February – March 1976 (4, repr.) and subsequent tour to the Stadt Galerie in Lenbachhaus, Munich, and York City Art Gallery

Lit: Robert Melville, *Motif*, x, 1962/3, p.18; Robert Melville, *New Statesman*, 5 November 1965

Repr: Herbert Read, *Contemporary British Art*, 1964, pl.48; Lucy Lippard, *Pop Art*, *c.*1966, p.45; *Tate Gallery 1978–80*, p.41 in colour

Peter Blake has painted about 11 self-portraits, the first, a head, in about 1949 while a student at the Gravesend College of Art. The second was painted in 1952 during his period of national service in the Royal Air Force and shows the artist wearing an airforce jacket and harlequin trousers. Blake also painted about 8 small heads of himself in 1953–4 during his first year at the Royal College of Art; these were later all thrown away. The last is 'Self-Portrait with Badges' which Blake painted between the end of June and September 1961, working an average of 12 hours a day, at 28 The Avenue, London W4, where at the time he shared a studio with Richard Smith. No studies or photographs were used for the painting and no other versions were made. Blake painted his head, shoes, trousers and shirt using a mirror; the jacket with badges was place on a dummy and painted directly.

Blake has never painted a portrait of himself wearing badges except for this picture, but in 1955 painted two boys wearing badges, 'ABC Minors', a reference to a Saturday morning cinema club for children. He started to collect badges in the mid 1950s; some were bought in shops and some brought back from the USA. Blake first wore denim trousers in 1948 which he made from a boiler suit, and in 1956 obtained his first denim suit which he bought in France. In 'Self Portrait with Badges' he was wearing Levi trousers, a denim jacket which he obtained by exchange for his French denim jacket and a shirt bought from a sports shop. At this time he frequently wore baseball boots, and wide trouser turnups were common in the late 1950s and early 1960s.

The badges in the portrait which can be identified are as follows: on the left (i.e. Blake's right), second row, a First World War medal and below a badge with the head of Yvonne de Carlo and to the right of it one with the head of Max Wall, the English actor. On the right, (Blake's left), first row, is a badge with 'I like Fiorello' (a reference to a show in New York), an American Flag (a reference to 'God Bless America') and 'Diana Crack Shot' (a reference to 'Diana' airguns). Second row, left, a French General, Road Safety and Pepsi Cola badges. In the third row a large Elvis Presley badge, 'Temperance 7' (a pop group) and Red Cross Day (Blake had used this badge in the imagery of 'On the Balcony' 1955–7 (collection Tate Gallery, T.566); beneath them a Lodge Plug badge. In the fifth row an American Boy Scout badge and Adlai Stevenson campaign and Union Jack badges. In the sixth row is a badge with a portrait of an American football player and an Adlai Stevenson campaign badge without words. In the bottom row is a Dan Dare badge. Of the badges in the self-portrait only those of Elvis Presley,

Yvonne de Carlo and Max Wall were of personal interest to Blake and he usually wore only one or two badges at a time.

Blake depicts himself holding an unofficial monthly magazine devoted to Elvis Presley edited by Albert Hand. This magazine was later to reproduce 'Self Portrait with Badges'. At the time the picture was painted denim jackets were rare, not part of a painter's uniform, as they were commonly to become, but Blake liked the idea of himself working in the jacket and wiping his brushes on the sleeve and suggested this in the picture with loose brushtrokes on the sleeve on the left. The scars on the painter's forehead were the result of an accident when he was 17.

The Stars and Stripes at the lower left of the jacket was to indicate Blake's interest in the USA as a phenomenon, though at that time he had not been there; his first visit was in 1963 when he was commissioned by the *Sunday Times* to make drawings in California, where he visited Holywood and Los Angeles.

When Blake painted 'Self Portrait with Badges' he did not see it as relating to other paintings of the time in England, except possibly work of 10 years or so earlier by Lucian Freud, but to paintings by the American artists Ben Shahn and Honoré Sharrer. Blake was conscious that it was idiosyncratic to depict an adult with badges. He saw himself as a realist painter in the realist tradition. He considers that he may have been subconsciously influenced by Watteau's painting 'Gilles' in the Louvre when deciding the pose and situation of 'Self Portrait with Badges'. As he wanted to submit the painting to the John Moores Exhibition, and was short of time, he was unable to include a flower bed in front of the fence in the painting. The background was executed in the garden.

The painting won 1st Prize in the Junior Section of the John Moores Exhibition in 1961. Blake had submitted 'on the Balcony' to the previous John Moores Exhibition in 1959, but it was rejected by the jury.

This catalogue entry is based on a discussion with the artist (19 February 1980).

Mark Boyle b. 1934

T.2413 **Rock and Scree Series** 1977

Not inscribed
Earth etc. on fibreglass, three panels: left, $72\frac{3}{4} \times 72\frac{3}{4} \times 12\frac{1}{2}$ (185 × 185 × 32); centre, $72 \times 72 \times 16\frac{1}{2}$ (183 × 183 × 42.2); right, $72 \times 72\frac{1}{2} \times 11\frac{3}{4}$ (183 × 184 × 30)
Presented by Peter Moores 1979
Exh: *Mark Boyle*, Felicity Samuel Gallery, October–December 1977 (no catalogue); Venice Biennale, 1978 (British Pavilion 17, repr.); *Mark*

Boyles [sic] *und Joan Hills' Reise um der Welt 2*, Kunstmuseum, Lucerne, November–December 1978 (18–20, centre panel repr.); *Art Anglais d' Aujourd'hui, Collection de la Tate Gallery, Londres*, Musée Rath, Geneva, July–September 1980 (1, repr.)

Repr: *Tate Gallery 1978–80*, p.42

Boyle's works are reproductions of randomly chosen areas of the Earth's surface made by a variety of techniques which Boyle prefers to keep secret.

Mark Boyle works with Joan Hills and their three children, Cameron, Georgia and Sebastian when making pieces. This work was begun in the North of Scotland in 1977. Mark Boyle has supplied the following notes:

'Joan and I decided a lot earlier that we were going to make a cliff series of some kind. We were also intrigued by the way in which a randomly selected six foot square of earth surface seems to change when it is separated from its background and to develop an internal coherence that makes it resemble a composition. On the spur of the moment I can't think of any of our pieces that leaves you with a feeling of incompleteness. We had decided we would make some pieces in which in some way we showed what happened outside the random square to see if this feeling of inner coherence was still maintained when you could see the continuation.

'Suddenly the pressures that were lying very heavily on us seemed to part a little in early March 1977 and we thought we had a few days for an expedition. We phoned our pal at the Met Office and got a 3 day forecast for disastrous rain everywhere south of Fort William but very fine farther north. We felt we could complete the initial stages of the work on the site given 72 hrs. good weather. It was important to know, because working on a cliff in driving rain or when the rock surface was wet and slippery could obviously be dangerous. Once we were committed to a fair weather technique the work could be ruined by rain.

'The next day the five of us, Joan and Georgia and Sebastian and Cameron and I loaded the truck and set off at 6 am, in a downpour. We drove in a world of grey and sulphurous yellow mist and spray, through trucks goring and goading one another as they hurtled north. The rain stopped at Crianlarich, and by nightfall we were at Fort William.

'In the morning the weather was glorious. We drove on and on and eventually found a suitable scarp from which we made a selection which was random, except that it was from the scarp exclusively and that the base of the square was horizontal. Then we thought why don't we work in the idea of showing what happens outside the random square, so we started to make pieces on the adjoining 6 foot squares of rock as well.

'We camped at the site, drove crowbars into cracks in the rock and laid planks on the crowbars to act as a kind of scaffolding. Then Joan and Georgia and Sebastian and I started to work. We worked from dawn to dusk in blazing heat each day and the work was desperately hard. As we lowered the pieces and moved them from the scarp to the truck the work was only just started, nothing was fixed and everything was so fragile you could hardly breathe. It was such an agonising hard slog I was terrified that Sebastian and Georgia would never forgive me for getting them into such a scene. As night fell we had everything on the truck. There was still months of work to be done on it but we knew now that the only thing that would spoil it would be our own lack of skill. As we started the long drive back to London it began to rain.'

Georges Braque 1882–1963

T.2318 **Clarinette et Bouteille de Rhum sur une Cheminée**
(Clarinet and Bottle of Rum on a Mantelpiece) 1911

Inscribed 'G. Braque/Ceret' on back of canvas
Oil on canvas, $31\frac{7}{8} \times 23\frac{5}{8}$ (81 × 60)
Purchased from Cofinarte (Grant-in-Aid) with the aid of a special Government Grant and with assistance from the Friends of the Tate Gallery 1978

Prov: With Galerie Kahnweiler, Paris (purchased from the artist); Kahnweiler sale, Drouot, Paris, 7–8 May 1923, lot 137 as 'Nature Morte'; bt. Edouard Jeanneret (Le Corbusier), Paris, 400 frs.; sold by the Le Corbusier Foundation, Palais Galliera, Paris, 10 June 1970, lot 50, repr. in black and white, and in colour, as 'Clarinette et Bouteille de Rhum'; bt. Galerie Beyeler, Basle, 1,260,000 frs.; Jorge de Brito, 1971; sold on his behalf at Sotheby's, London, 4 December 1974, lot 41, repr. in colour as 'Clarinette et Bouteille de Rhum sur une Cheminée'; bt. Cofinarte, Switzerland, £240,000

Exh: *Proposal for a Collection of Contemporary Art*, Cultural Center of the Philippines Museum, Manila, October–November 1976 (9, repr. in colour); *Fundamental Aspects of Modernism*, Fine Arts Gallery, California State University, Northridge, March–April 1977 (8, repr. in colour); *Early Twentieth Century Masterpainters*, Museum of Albuquerque, June–July 1977 (8, repr. in colour)

Lit: George Isarlov, 'Georges Braque', *Orbes*, No.3, Spring 1932, p.83, No.114 as 'La Cheminée' 1911; Marco Valsecchi and Massimo Carrà, *L'Opera Completa di Braque 1908–1929*, Milan 1971, No.81, p.88, repr. p.89 and pl.XIX in colour (colours very inaccurate); Douglas Cooper in exh. catalogue *Braque: The Great Years*, Art Institute of Chicago, October–December 1972, p.49 and repr.

Repr: Ozenfant and Jeanneret, *La Peinture Moderne*, Paris 1925, p.57; Carl Einstein, *Georges Braque*, Paris-London-New York 1934, pl.XII as 'Composition' 1911; Anne Jackson (ed.), *Art at Auction 1974–75*, London 1975, p.122 in colour

This painting is inscribed 'Ceret' on the back, which confirms that it was painted at Céret (Pyrenées-Orientales) in 1911, when Braque was spending the summer there in the company of Picasso. They had gone to Céret at the suggestion of their friend the Catalan sculptor Manolo, who had settled there three years before.

This was Braque's first picture of a still-life group on a mantelpiece, a theme which became the basis for a number of his later works. The objects include a bottle of rum, a clarinet, some sheet music and a pin or nail with its cast shadow. Lower down one can identify a pair of scroll-like corbels, left and right, which support the mantel, and a scallop-shaped motif which is either the handle of a fire-screen or, more probably, a decorative feature on the canopy at the top of the fireplace to prevent smoke escaping.

Though it appears in the Kahnweiler records as 'Clarinet and Bottle of Rum' and is listed by Isarlov as 'The Mantelpiece', there seems some advantage in keeping the more extended title 'Clarinet and Bottle of Rum on a Mantelpiece' under which it has been known in recent years.

Edward Burra 1905–76

T.3051 **The Snack Bar** 1930
Inscribed 'E. Burra 1930' b.l.
Oil on canvas, 30 × 22 (76.2 × 55.9)
Purchased from the Knoedler Gallery (Grant-in-Aid) 1980

Prov: Gerald Corcoran (purchased from the artist); Mrs Helen Grigg, Biot; her husband, Mr T. Grigg; Knoedler Gallery, London
Exh: *Edward Burra*, Tate Gallery, May–July 1973 (23, repr.)
Lit: John Davenport, 'Burra-Burra Land', in *Lilliput*, XXI, No.5, November 1947, pp.376–80 (repr. in colour as 'Snack Counter')
Repr: *Tate Gallery 1978–80*, p.44 in colour

The compiler is grateful to Burra's sister Lady Ritchie, and to his close friends William Chappell, Mrs Barbara Ker-Seymer and Mrs Clover de Pertinez for help in preparing this entry.

Burra is believed to have made very few oil paintings, and to have stopped doing so in the early 1930s. Although writers have stressed that Burra's delicate constitution tended to make him avoid physically demanding techniques, this does not seem to have been the reason why he discontinued painting in oils as early as he did. 'Edward said to me himself at one point "People do not like my oil paintings". I think he enjoyed painting in oils. It would probably later have been more effort. He used to prop the canvas on a chair leaning it against the chair back' (letter from William Chappell to the compiler, 15 November 1980).

The titles of Burra's pictures seem often to have been given by others in the absence of any strong interest by the artist in this matter. The title of the present picture is that given on the only certain occasion of its exhibition in his lifetime. It is perhaps interchangeable with the title 'Snack Counter' given in the 1947 article by Burra's friend John Davenport. There seems a strong likelihood that the Tate's picture was the 'Snack' included in Burra's exhibition at the Leicester Galleries, May–June 1932 (54). The stretcher is inscribed 'Leicester Galleries' and 'Burra (5) Snack'.

Bar interiors, and often the encounters of customers and staff specifically at a bar counter, appear frequently in Burra's work. In a large ink drawing (private collection, London) of a snack bar interior signed and dated 1933 a woman in hat and fur, with a sandwich on a plate and holding a coffee cup in her left hand, sits at a counter facing a barman: a large sausage on a platter lies between them. The type of goods on the shelves and the way they are displayed, the other people in the room, the prominence accorded to ceiling lights, and the inclusion of lighted signs seen across the street all make this drawing exceptionally close to the Tate's picture, but the composition is wholly different.

No documentary evidence has been found of the location of the snack bar in the Tate's picture. America can be ruled out as it seems generally agreed that Burra, though an avid filmgoer, based the details in works of this kind on what he had seen personally, and his first visit to America was after 1930. By 1930 he was, however, familiar with London, Paris and the South of France. Unfortunately none of the incomplete words seen on the signs in the street can be pinned down to either English or French, and no conclusive arguments have been found for either country in the goods on display, the food, the decor or the people. The vehicle seen in the street could be English or French (letter from Science Museum, 20 November 1980). Moreover although in the Tate's picture 'the tart at the counter is typically French . . . as are the feet in the top-left-hand corner, in the street outside', 'Soho tarts were mostly French around 1930 and dressed and made up just like that, I can remember well' (letter from Mrs Clover de Pertinez, 28 October 1980).

William Chappell considers that 'it is more likely to be Soho than anywhere else. One of Ed's favourite parts of London always' (letter, 15 November 1980). Holding the same view, Mrs de Pertinez adds 'Edward went there a lot . . . to buy liver-sausage, salami and other kinds of foreign produce to supplement the superb English country-house cooking at his father's house Springfield before World

War II. The barman's face is of a type Ed called "debased Roman" and particularly admired' (letter, 28 October 1980). While judging the Tate's picture to be most likely an amalgam of people and things seen in different establishments, Mrs Barbara Ker-Seymer records that Burra's 'favourite was called the Continental Snack Bar and was at the bottom of Shaftesbury Avenue next to the London Pavilion . . . It was very handy for the ladies "on the game" to have a sit down and a cup of coffee in their rest periods' (letter, 4 November 1980).

In his 1947 article on Burra cited above, John Davenport describes the scene in the Tate's picture as 'A snack bar in Burra-Burra Land. If you know Hastings really well you may recognise it'. Hastings residents of the period recall that 'There were indeed two or three places of the kind depicted, where one could stand at a high counter and drink coffee or tea and that . . . stayed open until late at night' (reported by Laetitia Yhap in letter, 5 December 1980). However in William Chappell's view the scene is 'certainly not Hastings – you would not get so sophisticated a tart . . . in that depressing resort' (letter, already quoted). Barbara Ker-Seymer is 'in favour now, of it not being in any specific place but being a "Snack Counter in Burra-Burra Land" as described by John Davenport . . . Edward had a photographic eye, everything that interested him registered and was stored away in his head for future use. Not being like Holman Hunt, he didn't have to sit in front of his subject and have everything correct to the most minute detail. If he decided to paint a picture of a snack bar for instance, he called upon his memory of various snack bars he had seen and arranged the pictures from his head to suit the one he was putting on paper. The "Snack Bar" might be anywhere as it was only a background to the two main figures' (letter, 29 November 1980).

Reg Butler 1913–81

T.2332 **Working Model for 'The Unknown Political Prisoner'** 1955–6

Not inscribed
Forged and welded steel, painted black, bronze with plaster base $88\frac{1}{8} \times 34\frac{5}{8} \times 33\frac{5}{8}$ (223.8 × 88 × 85.4)
Presented by Cortina Butler and Creon Butler 1979

Prov: The artist's children

Exh: *50 Ans d'Art Moderne*, Palais des Beaux-Arts, Brussels, April–July 1958 (43, maquette repr. p.215); *Reg Butler: A Retrospective Exhibition*, J. B. Speed Art Museum, Louisville, Kentucky, October–December 1963 (45, repr.)

Lit: *International Sculpture Competition: The Unknown Political Prisoner*, New Burlington Galleries, January 1953, n.p. (British Preliminary Exhibition); Tate Gallery, March–April 1953, n.p. (original prize-winning maquette repr.); Jorge Romero Brest, 'Le Monument au Prisonnier Politique Inconnu', *Art Aujourd'hui* no.5, July 1953 pp.6–11 (prize-winning maquette repr.); Alfred H. Barr Jr. (ed.), *Masters of Modern Art*, New York, 1954, p.159 (maquette repr.); Patrick Heron, *The Changing Forms of Art*, 1955, pp.227–9; Hans Egon Holthusen, *Gutachten der Akademie der Künste zum Entwurf eines Denkmals des unbekannten politischen Gefangenen*, Berlin, 1956, n.p. (maquette repr.); Reg Butler, 'Zum Entwurf für das Denkmal des unbekannten politischen Gefangenen', *Das Kunstwerk*, Heft 2/XI, August 1957, pp.34–5 (maquette repr.); Peter Selz, *New Images of Man*, New York, 1959, pp.41–4 (maquette repr. p.42); 'Did you Hear That? The Artist Speaks' (transcript of BBC T.V. film), *The Listener*, 11 August 1960, pp.213–14 (detail of maquette repr.); 'Reg Butler on his life and work. An interview with Francis Watson' (transcript of BBC radio programme 'People Today'), *The Listener*, 28 March 1963, p.551; A. M. Hammacher, *Modern English Sculpture*, 1967, pp.32–4 (maquette repr. pl.108); Robert Goldwater, *What is Modern Sculpture?* New York, 1969, p.127 (maquette repr. p.124)

Repr: Robert Melville, 'In connection with the sculpture of Reg Butler', *Motif* 6, Spring 1961, p.31, pl.12 (detail), 13 (photomontage showing sculpture on proposed site in Berlin); *Tate Gallery 1978–80*, p.45

This work was made between 1955 and 1956 at the artist's home at Berkhamsted in Hertfordshire. It represents Butler's vision of a monument to *The Unknown Political Prisoner* in its largest and most fully developed form.

The International Sculpture Competition, *The Unknown Political Prisoner*, was announced in January 1952 by the Institute of Contemporary Arts, London. The moving spirit behind the project was Anthony Kloman, a former US cultural attaché in Stockholm who for a brief period became the Institute's Organising Director. Kloman had come to London the previous year with the backing of a number of important but unnamed Americans, one or more of whom put up the £11,500 prize money. The ICA agreed to promote the scheme but the organisational work was carried out by Kloman and his own staff based in a separate office inside the ICA building in Dover Street. At that time Roland Penrose was Vice-Chairman of the ICA and Sir Herbert Read was President. Its Honorary Treasurer was the printer and publisher E. C. Gregory who in 1950 had established the Gregory Fellowships at Leeds University. (Butler was a Gregory Fellow in Sculpture when the competition was announced.)

The chosen theme was intended 'to pay tribute to those individuals who, in many countries and in diverse political situations, had dared to offer their liberty and their lives for the cause of human freedom.' The competition was open to artists of every nationality and it was hoped that 'the sculpture eventually winning the Grand Prize would be installed on some site of international importance, such as a prominent situation in one of the great capitals of the world.' By 1 June 1952, the closing date for applications, some 3,500 entries from fifty-seven countries had been received, the largest number (607) from West Germany. Maquettes were delivered to designated local centres by 30 November 1952. Of the major world nations, only the Soviet Union and its Eastern European satellites regarded the enterprise with suspicion and declined to participate: the sensitive theme and the site eventually proposed for the winning entry, on the border of West and East Berlin, was almost certainly considered by Russia (rightly or wrongly) to be provocative and in furtherance of the Cold War.

Owing to the impracticability of having all the maquettes brought to London, Kloman, assisted by Sir John Rothenstein and H. D. Molesworth, arranged for preliminary contests to take place in the more important of the competing countries in the winter of 1952–3. From these exhibitions national juries selected work to go forward to London for the main competition. Apart from Butler, the twelve winners at the British exhibition, held at the New Burlington Galleries in January 1953, included Chadwick, Frink, Hepworth, McWilliam and Paolozzi. Each winner received a £25 prize, donated by the Arts Council. The International Exhibition of 140 finalists opened to the public at the Tate Gallery on 14 March, the ten-man jury (which included Alfred Barr Jr., Will Grohmann and Herbert Read) having reached its decision shortly before. The Grand Prize of £4,500 was awarded to Butler for his maquette, prizes of £750 were won by Mirko Basaldella, Gabo, Hepworth and Pevsner, and smaller sums were awarded to Adam, Bill,

Calder, Chadwick, Hinder, Lippold and Minguzzi. After the exhibition, the Tate Gallery acquired maquettes by Gilioli, Minguzzi, Pevsner, Roszak, McWilliam and Consagra; the maquette by Gabo (T.2187), together with its earlier version (T.2186), was presented by the artist himself in 1977.

At the time of the competition, it was emphasised by the organisers that the winning maquettes were not finished sculptures but sketches for large-scale works in model form (the maximum height allowed was 18 inches). Final execution of the winning monument on a site 'of world prominence' would be paid for out of competition funds. Much of the confusion surrounding Butler's prize-winning entry resulted from an inability amongst members of the public, not helped by unimaginative display and greatly encouraged by the popular press, to envisage his work as a monument 300–400 feet high. The three figures, or 'watchers', less than an inch tall in the maquette, were not, as was sometimes believed at the time, included merely to indicate scale but were an integral part of the work's formal and emotional impact and would have been considerably greater than life-size in the final monument.

On 15 March, the day after the opening of the exhibition, Butler's prize-winning maquette was severely damaged by a twenty-eight year old Hungarian refugee, Laslo Szilvassy, who was arrested and charged the following day with malicious damage, a charge he admitted. According to a report in *The Times* (24 March 1953), Szilvassy handed a written statement to a Gallery attendant explaining his reasons for breaking the model: '"Those unknown political prisoners have been and still are human beings. To reduce them – the memory of the dead and the suffering of the living – into scrap metal is just as much a crime as it was to reduce them into ashes or scrap. It is an absolute lack of humanism"'. Szilvassy was at pains to point out that his protest was a considered aesthetic response, not a spontaneous, sentimental reaction, and in this sense he was echoing the ill-informed criticisms of the popular press and even of some of the serious art critics: that many of the works on show were too 'abstract' (and therefore 'inhuman'), and private in their symbolism.

Butler made two replicas of the maquette from drawings and measurements of the damaged original taken at Vine Street Police Station. By 2 April the first replica was ready to go on display at the Tate Gallery. In terms of material and technique – brass wire, bent and soldered, with three small bronze figures – it differed little from the original, although the base, intended to suggest an outcrop of rock, was on this occasion the piece of gravestone from which the plaster base of the original had been cast. This first replica remains in the artist's possession; the second, also with a plaster base, was acquired by the Museum of Modern Art, New York, shortly after the Competition; and the damaged original, later restored by the artist, became the joint property of the ICA and the Academy of Fine Art in Berlin, where discussions continued throughout the 1950s as to a suitable site for the monument. (This maquette was later sold by Anthony Kloman to an American private collector.)

The 'Working Model' (T.2332) was made in response to the original wish of certain high-ranking Germans to see the monument built in West Berlin. Chief amongst these were Ernst Reuter, Mayor of the city and spokesman for the West Berlin Senate (who died in September 1953), Hans Scharoun, architect and President of the Academy, the art-historian Will Grohmann, who had been on the International Jury, and the Mayor of Wedding (the district finally selected for the site). Using a more sophisticated technique of welding together pieces of steel already forged by his own hand, the artist this time enlarged his model to over four times the size of the previous maquettes. This enabled him not only to include greater detail – for example, in the ladder-like structure which climbs one of the legs of the tower – but also to demonstrate in miniature exactly how the monument should be constructed, in steel sections welded and bolted together. Photographs in the Grohmann Archive in Stuttgart show the artist enlarging the maquette to the present, working-model size. Butler was an architect by training and the technical problems of building the tower to a height of several hundred feet closely concerned him; he sought additional advice from the engineer Ove Arup. In 1957, he took T.2332 to Berlin for discussions with Scharoun and others, having been informed that the Berlin Senate had voted in favour of erecting the monument. An appeal for public contributions, signed by Will Grohmann, was launched in the German press in 1959. But owing to a series of objections and difficulties, part practical and part political, the monument was not built when the urge to realise it was keenest; and with the death in 1968 of Grohmann, who had been the scheme's most tireless champion, coupled with the reservations of the Bonn Government, hopes of its materialisation soon faded. Attempts to revive the idea were occasionally made but the artist always insisted that these should come from outside and would not be a result of 'any propaganda instigated by me.'

About 1958, at the height of Berlin's interest in the project, the artist wrote a five thousand word account of his entry for the competition which traces the genesis of the work to his ideas after the Second World War for a large-scale tower sculpture standing on the English coast overlooking the sea. Since this account has never been published, and since it contains material directly relevant to an understanding, not only of Butler's work as a whole but of how the particular formal relationships of T.2332 were arrived at, it seems in order to quote from it at some length.

'The story of the monument begins for me as long ago as 1946 . . .

. . . 'As for most people of my age, the immediate post-war years were ones of much introspection. The unbroken English coastline forbidden to holiday crowds for more than six years – apparently as immutable as the sea itself – was populated by the most enigmatical man-made objects to be seen anywhere. The radio and radar towers of Bawdsey [Suffolk] and the rugged inhospitable coastline around St. Merryn and Trevose Head [Cornwall] dominated my thoughts largely because of their setting in bleak and desolate landscape. The influence they may have had on my use of linear forms in sculpture using forged and welded steel between the years 1948–52 is something about which I can only speculate . . . but looking back on my work during those years I think it certain that the forms of my earliest iron sculptures [e.g. 'Woman' 1949, Tate Gallery, 5942] were very much a response to the Bawdsey personages.'

Butler's various projects for 'an enormous iron monument' went back to 1948. 'I am quite sure', he wrote, 'I did not think of it consciously in relation to political imprisonment, but I did see the towers which were its prototype as supra-human creatures born of the war, towers with little that was benign in their personalities, remote inscrutable custodians of a landscape hostile to man. The first of the projects has always been known, rather obliquely as 'The Family Group' [see *Reg Butler: A Retrospective Exhibition*, op. cit., 2, repr.]. It was made in 1948, and was intended as a model for a sculpture to stand on the rocks of Trevose Head. I visualised it some two or three hundred feet high set against the sky on this lonely and forbidding stretch of coast above the estuary to the River Camel.

'If the . . . sculpture is compared with . . . the radio towers at Bawdsey few direct similarities are perhaps noticeable, except the existence of a platform at some distance from the base of the construction. A platform also occurs in a second monument, 'The Box', made in 1951.' (ibid., 16, repr., and see below).

One of the three sculptures which formed Butler's commission for the 1951 Festival of Britain, now at Kenwood, can also be regarded as a prototype or close relation of *The Unknown Political Prisoner* monument, although in appearance it suggests a strange animal or bird rather than a man-made construction. 'Birdcage' (Butler's works are often known by such nicknames, given usually by family, friends or critics as a means of identification, but not always strictly accurate) consists of a similar three-legged iron structure supporting a platform or plate, from which rise a trapezoidal frame and a long thin neck or column. In contrast to the simple linear forms of his earlier iron figures, Butler wrote that both the '*matière*' and the 'total forms' of his sculptures now altered as a result of using oxyacetylene and arc-welding techniques, the former becoming 'more biomorphic, less mechanical' and the latter 'more visual and consequently more complex.'

'The demands of the technique', he continued, 'which I used ironically to describe as steel knitting [see, for example, his 'Reclining Woman' 1951 at Aberdeen Art Gallery, also commissioned by the L.C.C. for the South Bank Exhibition], became altogether too much of a bore, for in the Autumn of 1951 I began once again in my life to make sculptures based on a closed volume. It was at this time that I made 'The Box' – a perverse undertaking since it enclosed two sculptures invisible from outside and seen by no-one other than myself: I remember describing my intention as a way of insisting on my own right to make sculpture now and again purely for myself. The commissions I had carried out during the previous two years had, I know, brought me a lot of publicity which I somehow resented. Anyway, for some reason the sculptures were made and a box was made around them. In the same month as I finished the box, Roland Penrose came to visit me at Hatfield [where Butler was then living] and told me that the Institute of Contemporary Arts was about to launch an international sculpture competition. Roland had planned to stay the night with an American Tony Kloman a few miles away from my home – at Essendon. Talking with Tony on the 'phone and with Roland over supper I learned for the first time that the competition was to be for a monument to those who had died in the concentration camps.

'"The Box" was shown at an ICA exhibition in the spring of the next year, and widely regarded as my entry for the competition. The competition conditions stated that the design should be suitable for erection on a site in a European capital – nothing more. This condition I regarded as an advantage for I have always felt that a good sculpture was capable of creating its own setting provided that it had enough space. Further, since no specific site was given I took it to mean that one would be selected to fit the winning sculpture, and that in consequence my approach to the problem would not be hampered by real or imagined local limitations.

'From the beginning I thought of the monument as being very large. Partly I imagine because of my preoccupation with the coastal monuments, partly because I thought of the project from the start as one which would combine my two major interests, sculpture and architecture; and perhaps most of all because no idea ever occurred to me that the monument would have to be anything other than a very large one! I remember very well at the time I first saw some of the other entries on exhibition, the feeling of surprise when I noticed that hardly anyone had visualised a solution which was monumental in the sense in which I had been thinking of the word. Throughout the many months during which I worked on a number of schemes it never once occurred to me that the solution would be to make a maquette for just another sculpture. All my earlier sketches and models were based on there being a figure or figures situated on a platform, a platform raised on a promontory against the sky or set in the centre of a *place de ville*. [See *Reg Butler: A Retrospective Exhibition*, op. cit., 37–42, repr.] These early sketches and subsequent models caused me much worry and although at the time I could not put my dissatisfaction into words, I think I can see now that they were far too literal, too illustrative. Sometimes, on the one hand, a scheme would irritate me because the figure on the platform seemed somehow inappropriate – too much like an engineer in charge of a technical project; on the other I would be worried because the treatment was too appropriate, too literally a model of a man being hanged, guillotined or crucified.

'By June 1952 I had lived with the idea for six months, and felt that I had arrived precisely nowhere! Since the issue of the competition conditions I had not, of course, worked exclusively on the prisoner scheme; among other things I had made a number of head studies of identical twin boys and had begun to draw and model many projects for heads looking up, and studies for figures looking up – figures whose faces were on the top of their heads. Why, I don't know – one day the idea was just a part of all the other tentative schemes I had around the studio, and the next it had become an obsession. One which in a sense has continued ever since, either in its original form, or in its inversion – the head looking down . . .'

In a BBC television film on his work transmitted in the summer of 1960 (loc. cit.), the artist spoke of his excitement at having seen test flights of de Haviland delta-winged jet aeroplanes over Hatfield in the early 1950s. '. . . I spent much of my time staring up into the sky watching these planes being put through their paces. It may be significant that not so long after that I found that I was modelling heads looking straight up into the sky . . . I think it is reasonable to imagine that one is liable to project into the sculpture feelings that are going on in one's own body.' An analogy may be drawn with Henry Moore's 'Three Standing Women' 1948 in Battersea Park, which is based on the artist's war drawings of figures looking expectantly into the distance.

Butler has, however, consistently warned of the danger of isolating a single motive for a subsequent course of action in his work. 'The whole subject of the monument and the figures looking up has been so discussed, so many theories have been put forward about why I did this or why I did that, that it is impossible for me to know what I might have thought myself, and what I have caught from other people. Of only this can I be certain; at one stage in the early part of the summer of 1952 all the monument schemes consisted of figures standing on scaffold-like platforms, figures impaled on vertical grids or crucified figures, and then overnight the whole direction altered; the tortured figures existed no longer and the towers were empty, while at the foot stood the watchers. The monument and the head-looking-up obsessions had become fused.

'Of the maquettes made during that year [1952–3], only six still exist, three during the period before the fundamental change [all three are in the artist's possession], the maquette submitted to the jury and two copies made later [see above]. The final maquette was, I think, first constructed in July or August, and constantly modified until September or October but of this series of modifications there are no photographic records. Rough studies were made, for a number of later schemes – mostly screens of figures, but of these only sketches now remain.

'. . . The wide publicity which the competition received was not altogether a good thing, for the exhibits were in a sense working diagrams only, certainly in the case of my project, yet they were frequently regarded as the actual monuments. I have very great sympathy for anyone who felt that a little bronze wire sculpture eighteen inches high was, to put it mildly, a slight way of commemorating the ten million victims of the gas chambers and concentration camps . . .

'At the time of submitting the maquette I also made a number of studies for the three watchers [three of these drawings are in the Tate, T.103] and photographs of these as well as eye level views of the maquette were ultimately on view, but not before a general impression had become established that the monument was in fact 18 inches high!

'The way a popular misconception can grow is really remarkable, and an extraordinary example of this occurred in connection with "the cliffs of Dover" rumour. During the original press conference a serious and apparently intelligent reporter asked me how big the monument was intended to be. I replied that it had been designed in such a way that its scale could be varied according to the size of the site chosen. For instance, I said, if the monument were to be put in the centre of Berkeley square, it would need to be about 180 to 200 feet high. If, however, the site selected were the cliffs above Dover, then in that setting it would need to be at least 500 feet high. I cannot think that the reporter completely misunderstood me. It is most probable that some sub-editor was out for a scoop or, for news purposes, chose to print the story as if the scheme were in fact destined for Beachey Head. Other papers all over the country copied the report, Churchill was asked his views as Warden of the Cinque Ports and the completely unfounded rumour became popular belief.' (See, for example, Wyndham Lewis, *The Demon of Progress in the Arts*, 1954, p.36.)

During the competition Butler provided, for the benefit of the public, a full description of his winning maquette. This written explanation was occasionally referred to or quoted in the press, but insufficiently for Butler's own simple reading of the sculpture's symbolic content and his conception of its ultimate scale and presence to be made clear.

'The monument', he wrote, 'is designed to provide interest both as seen from a distance, and close to; and unlike the Cenotaph and other similar monuments to the Unknown Soldier of the 1914–18 war is not a purely abstract architectural solution to the problem.

'It consists of three elements: the *natural rock foundation* which provides a fundamentally "natural" setting even where the monument may be sited in the centre of a city; *the three women* in whose minds the unknown prisoner is remembered and who set the whole dramatic context of the monument; and *the tower* intended as an easily identified symbol which both suggests the tyranny of persecution and the capacity of man to rise beyond it.

'The monument is suitable for erection to a minimum height of 100 ft. When sited in a city square of similar size to that of a typical London Square, its total height would be approximately 120 ft. On a much more open site such as one overlooking a maritime city, a total height of 300 to 400 ft. would be practicable.

'The size of the monument and its simple outline would enable it to be identified from very great distances, and the personal nature of the dramatic scene on the rock surface would avoid that feeling of disappointment so often experienced on reaching similar landmarks first seen from a great way off.

'THE ROCK.

'Ideally, the rock base would be a natural outcrop either used in situ or demounted and reassembled on the selected site. An alternative would be to take casts from a suitable rock and reconstruct the base in concrete from the moulds. In any case its quality would not be that of a work of man but possess those attributes associated with the effects of time and erosion. The public would be admitted to the surface of the rock by means of an internal staircase.

'THE THREE WOMEN: "*The Watchers*"

'These sculptures – from 8 ft. high and upwards according to the total height of the monument – would be of bronze and as may be seen from the maquette, have been placed so as to establish the dramatic significance of the monument. The two outer figures are in a sense spectators, in some ways beyond the reach of the situation. These are an old woman, self-withdrawn yet watchful and a young girl – hers is the partial comprehension of youth. The third woman stands almost immediately beneath and certainly well within the dramatic focus of the tower, she is totally contained by the tension of the occasion, and in full correspondence with the spirit of the monument. The two outer watchers stand as it were midway between the living spectator and the third woman. All three figures are intended both to establish and resolve the situation, and by their reference to human scale to develop in the spectator a sense of participation. The faces of all three women look upwards and the living spectator would – by their presence – be drawn into the same focus by the power and direction of their gaze.

'THE "TOWER".

'This being constructed of steel and suitably painted as a protection, would contrast with the stone of the rock and the bronze of the three women. Although a contemporary structure it follows the main traditions of monumentality, e.g., its scale, relationship with living spectators, its non-illustrative form and its overall quality of "lift".

'Cages, scaffolding, the cross and the guillotine were some of the elements consciously in mind at the time of its evolution. Watch towers, although not consciously thought of, have since been suggested as obvious references. It is hoped that its form is sufficiently ambiguous to allow it to become identified with the Unknown Prisoner idea, a process that would not be possible had its associations been too specific.

'Furthermore a literal untranscribed version of those constructions associated with imprisonment and suffering would not and could not have been justified as a *monument* since a symbol of suffering *alone* would be useless, a mere reminder of defeat.

'For the same reason the presence of the prisoner is implied not stated, his sacrifice being comprehended in the minds of the watchers. As with his physical characteristics the nature of his sacrifice must be universally applicable.

'Seen from a distance then, the monument would afford a powerful, easily identifiable symbol. Close to, a visitor standing on the rock surface in the same dramatic world as that of the three 'watchers', would be drawn by their gaze into contemplation of the upper vastness of the tower. He would hear even on comparatively windless days the constant vibration of the tensioned structure, while at times the air currents passing through the ramifications of the structure would set the whole tower vibrating like a great Aeolian Harp'.

The preoccupation with empty space in T.2332 and other open-work iron sculptures of this period begs mention of the two central influences on Butler's work, both of which he acknowledges: the figurative forged iron sculptures of Picasso and Gonzalez and the surrealist sculptures of Giacometti, who became a close friend of his. T.2332 is reminiscent of Giacometti's 'Palace at 4 a.m.' (Museum of Modern Art, New York) in a number of ways: the cage-like structure, the inclusion in the framework of a female figure and the sense of expectancy and alienation. Two especially hermetic works by Butler, 'The Box' (see above), with its echoes of Duchamp, and 'Boîte de Fetiches' of 1960–61 (see *Reg Butler: A Retrospective Exhibition*, op. cit., 96, repr.) can be regarded as heir to the group of playful but often sinister objects which Giacometti invented between about 1929 and 1932. During the middle and latter part of the 1950s, Butler developed his ideas for tower sculptures in two directions: on the one hand towards vast structures intended to stand in open landscape and, on the other, towards smaller, more compact objects resembling chimneys, like the 'Boîte de Fetiches', which would contain rooms, passages and figures (see Paul Waldo Schwartz, *The Hand and Eye of the Sculptor*, 1969, pp.22–3). In the film 'Five British Sculptors', made in 1964 by Warren Forma, Butler said that the tower sculptures were in a sense a logical development of the boxes. And in the 1960 BBC television film (loc. cit.) he spoke of his interest in Science Fiction and confirmed his commitment to surrealism: 'The whole idea of using art as a means of creating unknown worlds, unknown forms, undiscovered experiences, is the motive power behind the best in surrealism, and something which I continually find exciting ...'

The sculptor told the compiler that, at the time of working on the '*Unknown Political Prisoner* competition, he had no knowledge of Russian Constructivism but feels now that his entry had an affinity with certain ideal architectural projects of the period (e.g. Tatlin's 'Monument to the Third International'). The artist also mentioned his admiration for the Spanish *art nouveau* architect Gaudí.

The source of the work in Butler's personal experience and beliefs has not so far been examined but the sculptor devoted a considerable part of his long unpublished account to an analysis of his state of mind as it was affected by the events of the war.

'I am often asked by people sympathetic to the scheme, how I can account for the fact that not having been a political prisoner myself, I nevertheless managed to produce a monument which although not yet in existence is already beginning to symbolise the idea it represents to different people in many parts of the world. The short answer is of course that one does not have to become a woman before one can attempt a sculpture of Aphrodite: or to be crucified before being able to paint a great crucifixion. However, there is enough genuine concern in this sort of question to deserve my attempting an answer: a sculpture is made out of an artist's awareness, not his knowledge. This is to say that his awareness comes not from the literal experience of being a woman, a political prisoner or for that matter a flower; but from involvement in the substance of the society in which he lives. By this I do not mean self-conscious engagement. As a child will contract emotions such as fear or pleasure from the adults which surround it, without the interposition of anything as overt as verbal communication, an artist is wide open to stimuli which reach him from every sort of source. This receptiveness varies from person to person, in range, scope, intensity and in the kind of personal episodes which act as catalysts sensitising the receptive mechanism of the artist. A man who has undergone long and painful experiences in a concentration camp may well have received such an overdose of experience that to survive at all his creative mechanism has had to develop a film of protective insulation . . .

'I cannot claim any direct contact with the sort of physical and mental horror we associate with concentration camps; all I can claim is, as a pacifist, to have experienced directly the consciousness of being emotionally separated from my country and its convictions.

'Since adolescence I have drawn closer and closer to an absolute pacifist outlook; not on any religious basis, but out of an increasing conviction that through non-agression and that alone can the human race expect to survive the next fifty years. I am convinced that to meet force with force or as a Christian might put it, evil with evil, is to perpetuate the very things the use of force is intended to combat. Those of us in Great Britain with these or similar beliefs during the war, were, if Christians and held to have conscientious objections, directed to agricultural occupations or the driving of ambulances and so on. If unable to convince the examining tribunals of the sincerity of their convictions, or if their opinions were not put forward as an interpretation of Christian dogma, they were imprisoned.

'In my own case, I was neither held to have supported a conscientous objection (all the tribunals which examined me refused to accept my views), nor had I been imprisoned by the end of the war. Why, I suppose I shall never know. I only refer to this personal history because it might be said to have a bearing on my responses to the fundamental social tensions which underlie all political imprisonment. I was neither wounded by the experience to the extent that in self-protection my responses became blunted, nor have I lived a life in which the idea of death or torture for my political ideals was a complete unreality . . .

'The support I had from those with first-hand experience of the concentration camps as well as from British and other European soldiers who suffered imprisonment, completely offset any distress I might have felt at the line taken by the popular English newspapers.'

Between the competition and the decision to erect Butler's winning entry in Berlin, the artist made a number of studies for the 'Three Watchers': 'Much of the sculpture I carried out in the intervening time had a relationship to the idea, but the only work I released from the studio with a direct connection to the monument was a $\frac{1}{3}$ full size study for the head of the "Third Watcher".' (See *Reg Butler: A Retrospective Exhibition*, op. cit., 55, repr.)

Concerning the proposed siting of the monument in West Berlin, Butler wrote that 'Opinion in Berlin at that time was more or less evenly divided between a site in the Tiergarten and one at some distance from the city centre: the Humboldt Höhe in the district of Wedding. The argument for the Tiergarten site was that it was undoubtedly in the central city area and therefore the more important site for an international monument. Against this was the fact that the Tiergarten already contained many monuments – monuments associated with very different feelings from those connected with the idea of the unknown political prisoner, and that to erect the scheme at the proper scale would involve the creation of an artificial promontory. This was not in itself at all impossible, but in so doing the character of the Tiergarten and its buildings and monuments would be completely destroyed.

'The advantages of the Humboldt Höhe were not only that it was in formal terms the perfect natural setting, but that its situation in Wedding, near the borderline between the Eastern and Western sectors of the city, was in an area quite unassociated with tourism.

'The Humboldt Höhe site is, at the time these notes are being written, dominated by the remains of two huge reinforced concrete bunkers which were used as flack towers during the war. After much discussion we felt that the Eastern tower might provide the best siting for the scheme and that the demolition of the Western tower would provide material for the construction of the artificial rock outcrop on which the tower is intended to stand. During this time in Berlin photographs were taken of the site from all aspects, and later on, after I had made the large model known as maquette 2 [T.2332], I made *photomontages* which gave a very specific idea of what the monument would look like when completed.

'The engineering problems connected with the large-scale erection of the monument are very exciting. I have always visualised the main structural elements of the tower as being of welded steel – following closely the sectional forms of the original maquette. These sections, fabricated largely from oxygen-cut steel flats arc-welded together would be prefabricated off site, subsequently being welded and bolted in position on the stone-faced concrete base. With the exception of the design of the central spire no unorthodox techniques are likely to be needed, but the varying stresses which will occur at the base of this member will have to be very carefully allowed for. One possibility here will be to design the central spire as a hollow section through the axis of which, a pretensioned high-tensile member would serve to exert positive compressive stresses on the walls of the tube – in opposition to the tensile stresses set up as a result of wind pressure on the spire.

'Apart from this problem, the consideration requiring the most thought would be that of maintenance: the use of anti-corrosive steels while feasible would be extremely costly, and would by no means result in the structure being safe for any appreciable time without some sort of maintenance. For the most corrosion-resistant steels are not absolutely resistant, particularly where their position makes occasional cleaning impracticable.

'Taking all this into account the most satisfactory solution appears to be the use of normal structural steel, with careful provision in the design to make regular repainting practicable. This would involve the use of special scaffolding easily attached to the structure and capable of carrying maintenance workers. The spire would have to be demountable at the point of connection with the main platform, and by means of specially fitted jacks, this would be lowered into a recess in the base, and maintained, cleaned and painted, section by section, while being re-erected.

'At night warning lights would have to be installed to prevent the tower being a danger to aircraft and I have always hoped these could take the form of apparently continuous columns of red strip-lighting, rather than clusters of individual lights. Seen at night across the skyline of East and West Berlin the whole monument would appear as a floodlit stone promontory on which stood three huge bronze figures, and floating above, a single vertical pencil of red light. It has always been my intention that access to the top of the stone outcrop should be provided, for the character of the scheme should be appreciated in two ways: one by seeing the monument from a long way off as a stark figuration against the sky, and the other by being, not simply close to, but from a position in which the observer could become physically involved. To stand in a crowded street and gaze intently at a nearby building draws other people irresistibly into the experience and I have always felt that to stand on the rock and gaze into the tower would be to become another watcher: to become for a moment a living part of the monument.

'I cannot think of any European capital I would prefer above Berlin, or a site in Berlin I would find more stimulating than the Humboldt Höhe. Here the monument will be seen for miles across the surrounding countryside and would stand, I am certain, the best chance of fulfilling what has always been its purpose; a symbol of a desire to eliminate all the political persecution and racial hatred that has bedevilled man's affairs throughout his history.'

The above entry is based on the following sources: unpublished written material supplied by the artist; the latter's replies in conversation (3 July 1979); press cuttings and a file on the competition kept in the Tate Gallery Library and Archive; and on the unpublished catalogue of the ICA's archives, compiled by John Sharkey. It has been approved by the artist.

George Carline 1855–1920

T.2262 The Gleaners 1887

Inscribed 'Geo. Carline./1887' b.l.
Gouache on paper, $11\frac{3}{8} \times 22\frac{1}{4}$ (28.8 × 56.4)
Presented by Richard Carline 1978
Prov: Dr. Russell, Lincoln (bought 1888); his daughter, by whom given to Richard Carline 1970

The setting of 'The Gleaners' has not been identified. The artist's son, Richard Carline wrote (letter, 14 November 1979) that George Carline 'did not have a country house of his own. He seems to have rented lodgings in a farm house or other. I find he was at Stapleford in Wiltshire in 1886 and stayed on until November ... He may have returned there the next summer.

'It seems to me that the figures may have been based on studies of my mother. She often posed for him – in fact for a great many of his paintings as well as his book illustrations that involved a young woman. The figure standing back view in the centre is wearing a straw hat very like one that appears in other pictures of her and the one on the extreme right side view is wearing a bonnet ... I have an oil sketch of her wearing a green bonnet (which I still possess in our chest of costumes acquired by my father)'. The bonnet of this extreme right hand figure is green. Richard Carline added that although his father took up photography around 1887 and did sometimes use photographs as sources for the backgrounds of paintings, he doubted whether he used them for this purpose as early as 1887, and he could find no photographs related to 'The Gleaners'.

In 1981 Mrs Richard Carline presented to the Tate two impressions of each of two etchings by George Carline of the same composition as 'The Gleaners'. The date of these is not known, but Richard Carline wrote in the letter already quoted that his father sold examples in 1888 and 1889. Both etchings conform in close detail to the imagery of the gouache, with the exception that the position of the child with its back to the viewer who is third from the left in the gouache has been moved sideways so as to stand clear from the figure which it had there slightly obscured. In both etchings, the composition of the gouache is reversed.

One etching, plate size 127 × 254 mm, employs a noticeably coarser and more simplified kind of mark than the other. The Tate's two impressions of this etching are of the same (the only?) state, but on one of them, below the plate, the artist has added in pencil variations of details of some of the figures. The plate size of the more finely-detailed etching is 128 × 258 mm; the Tate's impressions are of two states, of which (though none of the four prints is inscribed) the closeness of the more complete to the gouache suggests that it may be the final version of this etching.

T.2262 is in a gilded frame designed by the artist with ears of wheat in relief on three sides.

T.2263 **Under a Midsummer Sun** 1889

Inscribed 'George Carline/1889' b.r.
Oil on canvas, $10\frac{1}{8} \times 14\frac{3}{16}$ (25.7 × 36)
Presented by Richard Carline 1978

Prov: By descent from the artist

Exh: Fine Arts Section, International Exhibition, Edinburgh [?summer?] 1890 (120); RBA, April 1892 (10); [one-man] *Exhibition of Portraits and other Pictures*, The Exhibition Room, Frewin Court, adjoining 51 Cornmarket Street, Oxford, January 1909 (51), as 'Under the Midsummer Sun'; *Pictures by George Carline*, Hills and Saunders, Oxford, April 1913 (7); *Exhibition of Works of The Corbet and Carline Families*, Shrewsbury Art Gallery, March–April 1958 (61)

Richard Carline wrote of this picture (letter, 14 November 1979): 'My father was very inclined towards experiment in technique, and I think this was the first he painted mainly with the palette-knife. He used this method right on until the year he died . . .

'. . . I think he was spending that summer [1889] at Mersea in Essex . . . I cannot identify the model. If it was not for the short tucked up skirt, the face and hair look very like my mother. I do not know who she [sic.] could have posed for it. My mother would have been 27. The red parasol was a favourite idea, since my father had already painted a large canvas called "In the Garden of Hollyhocks" the previous year. My mother definitely posed for this standing woman sheltered beneath the red parasol. This picture had a considerable success . . .'

'He painted a small oil panel of my mother in a punt under the red parasol'. (This painting was sold Christies, 19 May 1978 (22, repr.).)

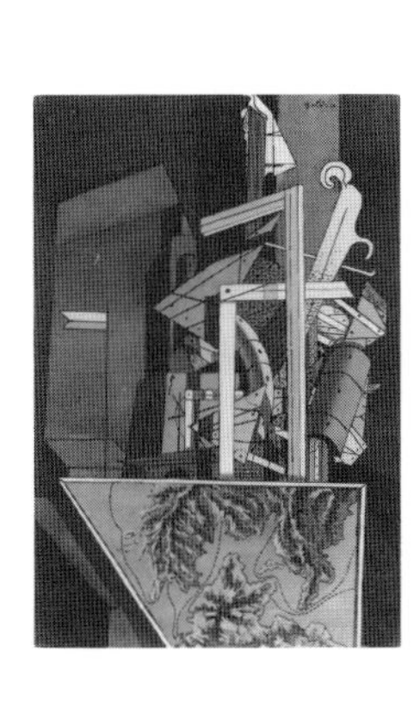

Giorgio de Chirico 1888–1978

T.2309 **The Melancholy of Departure** 1916

Inscribed 'G. de Chirico' t.r.
Oil on canvas, $20\frac{3}{8} \times 14\frac{3}{16}$ (51.8 × 36)
Purchased from Cofinarte (Grant-in-Aid) 1978

Prov: René Gaffé, Brussels; through Zwemmer Gallery, London; Sir Roland Penrose, London, 1937; Cofinarte, Switzerland

Exh: [?*Giorgio de Chirico*, Galerie Paul Guillaume, Paris, June 1926 (13) as 'Mélancolie du Départ']; *Chirico Picasso*, Zwemmer Gallery, June 1937 (5) as 'Mélancolie du Départ' 1915; *Exposition Internationale du Surréalisme*, Galerie Beaux-Arts, Paris, January–February 1938 (not in catalogue); *The Impact of Machines*, London Gallery, July–August 1938 (64); *Giorgio de Chirico (1911–17)*, London Gallery, October–November 1938 (8); *The Early Chirico, 1911–17*, London Gallery, April 1949 (8); *Gloire de la Peinture Moderne: Hommage à James Ensor*, Palais des Thermes, Ostend, July–August 1949 (48, repr.); *Eretentoonstelling James Ensor*, Gemeentemuseum, The Hague, September–October 1949 (48); *Le Muse Inquietanti: Maestri del Surrealismo*, Galleria Civica d'Arte Moderna, Turin, November 1967–January 1968 (54, repr.); *Metafisica di de Chirico*, Galleria Annunciata, Milan, April–May 1968 (works not listed, repr.); *Proposal for a Collection of Contemporary Art*, Cultural Center of the Philippines Museum, Manila, October–November 1976 (11, repr. in colour); *Fundamental Aspects of Modernism*, Fine Arts Gallery, California State University, Northridge, March–April 1977 (10, repr. in colour); *Early Twentieth Century Masterpainters*, Museum of Albuquerque, June–July 1977 (10, repr. in colour); *Du Spatialisme au Futurisme Italien*, Musée Rath, Geneva, October 1977–January 1978 (40, repr. in black and white, and detail in colour); *Dada and Surrealism Reviewed*, Hayward Gallery, January–March 1978 (1.14, repr. in colour

Lit: James Thrall Soby, *Giorgio de Chirico*, New York 1955, pp.112–13, repr. p.222; Claudio Bruni, *Catalogo Generale Giorgio de Chirico. Volume primo: Opere dal 1908 al 1930*, Milan *c.*1971, No.36, repr. as 'Melanconia della Partenza' 1916; Marianne W. Martin, 'Reflections on De Chirico and *Arte Metafisica*', *Art Bulletin*, LX, 1978, pp.351–2, repr. p.351

Repr: Isabella Far, *de Chirico*, New York 1968, pl.27 in colour as 'The Melancholy of Departure' 1916; *Tate Gallery 1978–80*, p.46 in colour

This picture was painted in Ferrara during the war at a time when de Chirico was serving as a clerk in the Italian Army, but was able to resume painting in his spare time partly in barracks, partly in furnished rooms and hotels, and partly in military hospitals. It is one of three still-life paintings made at this period with maps and with a loose 'scaffolding' of forms in the background, the others being 'Politics' and 'Evangelical Still Life', both of which are signed and dated 1916. On style it would seem to be the last or the last but one of the three.

A. Bates has noted that the map in 'Evangelical Still Life' (now in the Museum of Modern Art, New York) is the same as the one in Carlo Carrà's 'Metaphysical Muse' of 1917, and that the latter shows more of the surrounding area which makes it possible to identify the site as the Istrian Peninsula just south of Trieste and containing the towns Fiume and Pola. On the other hand, the maps in 'The Melancholy of Departure' and 'Politics' have not been identified, and it seems very probable that the one in this work (which includes a dotted line indicating the route of a sea or lake voyage) is purely imaginary.

The theme of travelling is recurrent in de Chirico's works of about 1913–16 and there are several earlier paintings of piazzas and colonnades, with trains puffing smoke in the background, which have titles of this kind, such as 'The Anxious Journey' 1913 in the Museum of Modern Art, New York, and 'The Anguish of Departure' 1914 in the Albright-Knox Art Gallery, Buffalo. One of the paintings of this type made in 1914 is also sometimes known as 'The Melancholy of Departure', though more usually nowadays as 'Gare Montparnasse'.

Jean Crotti 1878–1958

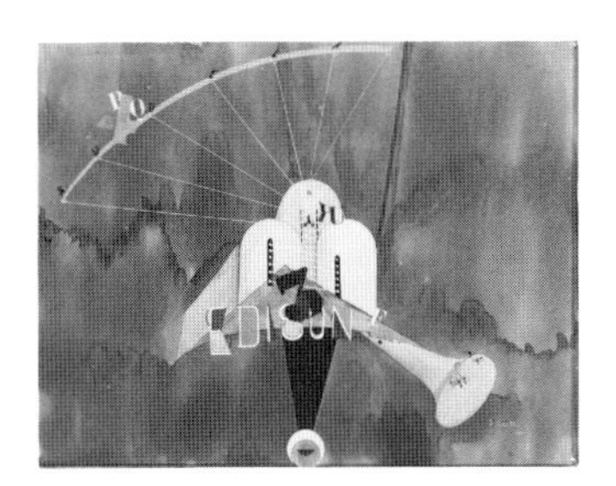

T.2315 **Portrait d'Edison** (Portrait of Edison) 1920

Inscribed 'J. Crotti./1920' b.r.; the composition incorporates the words 'EDISON Inventeur', and 'L'AU DELA', and the letters and numbers '4PO', '3', 'YU' and 'F'
Gouache, watercolour and pencil on paper, $19\frac{1}{4} \times 25\frac{3}{8}$ (48.9 × 64.5)
Purchased from the Brook Street Gallery (Grant-in-Aid) 1978

Prov: Sale of works by Suzanne Duchamp and J. Crotti, Drouot, Paris, 18 February 1970, lot 17 repr.; bt. Brook Street Gallery, London; with B. H. Holland Gallery, Chicago; with Brook Street Gallery, London

Exh: *Rétrospective Jean Crotti*, Musée Galliera, Paris, December 1959–January 1960 (91); *Art of the Dadaists*, Helen Serger, La Boetie, Inc., New York, September–November 1977 (not in catalogue)

Repr: Waldemar George, *Jean Crotti*, Paris 1930, n.p.; Waldemar George, *Jean Crotti et la Primauté du Spirituel*, Geneva 1959, repr. pl.26 and in colour on cover

A work of Crotti's Dada period, painted as a tribute to the famous American inventor Thomas Alva Edison (1847–1931), whose more than one thousand patents included the incandescent electric lamp, the phonograph, the carbon telephone transmitter, and the motion-picture projector. The trumpet-like loudspeaker with the notes issuing from it is clearly an allusion to his phonograph. None of the other forms can be identified precisely, though the bow shape at the top left marked 'L'AU DELA' (The Beyond) appears to be some kind of aerial and the three pale arched forms grouped together in the centre may have been intended to suggest electric lamps.

The background has faded somewhat and was originally a stronger blue, as can be seen round the edges where it has been protected by the mount.

Salvador Dali b. 1904

T.2343 **Métamorphose de Narcisse** (Metamorphosis of Narcissus) 1937

Inscribed 'Gala Salvador Dali 1937' b.r.
Oil on canvas, $20\frac{1}{8} \times 30\frac{3}{4}$ (51 × 78)
Purchased from the Edward James Foundation (Grant-in-Aid) 1979

Prov: Edward James, West Dean (purchased from the artist 1937); Edward James Foundation, West Dean

Exh: *The 1937 International Exhibition of Paintings*, Carnegie Institute, Pittsburgh, October–December 1937 (278, repr.), lent by Edward James; on loan to the Tate Gallery from 1958 until acquired; *Salvador Dali*, Tokyo Prince Hotel Gallery, Tokyo, September–October 1964 (135, repr.); Prefectural Museum of Art, Nagoya, October 1964 (135, repr.); Kyoto Municipal Art Gallery, November 1964 (135, repr.); *Salvador Dali 1910–1965*, Gallery of Modern Art, New York, December 1965–September 1966 (77, repr. in colour); *Dali*, Museum Boymans-van Beuningen, Rotterdam, November 1970–January 1971 (55, repr. and again in colour on dust jacket of catalogue); Staatliche Kunsthalle, Baden-Baden, January–April 1971 (48, repr.); *Dali: Art-in-Jewels Exhibition and Paintings*, Whitechapel Art Gallery, June–July 1971 (13); *Dada and Surrealism Reviewed*, Hayward Gallery, January–March 1978 (12.42, repr.); *Salvador Dali: Rétrospective 1920–1980*, Centre Georges

Pompidou, Musée National d'Art Moderne, Paris, December 1979–April 1980 (218, repr. in colour); *Salvador Dali*, Tate Gallery, May–June 1980 (156, repr. in colour)

Lit: Salvador Dali, *Metamorphosis of Narcissus*, New York 1937, repr. in black and white, and in colour; Salvador Dali, *The Secret Life of Salvador Dali*, New York 1942, pp.24–5, detail repr. facing p.167; A. Reynolds Morse and Michel Tapié, *Dali: a Study of his Life and Work*, Greenwich 1958, p.55, repr. p.48; Fleur Cowles, *The Case of Salvador Dali*, London–Melbourne–Toronto 1959, pp.289–94; Robert Descharnes, *The World of Salvador Dali*, 1962, pp.166, 222–3 and repr. p.166 in colour (dated 1936–7)

Repr: *L'Oeil*, No. 169, January 1969, pp.30–1

The artist said to Robert Descharnes of this picture, when he was preparing a book on his work:

'A painting shown and explained to Dr. Freud.

'Pedagogical presentation of the myth of narcissism, illustrated by a poem written at the same time.

'In this poem and this painting, there is death and fossilization of Narcissus.'

The poem referred to was published in 1937 in a small book by himself entitled *Metamorphosis of Narcissus*, which also contains two explanatory notes. The first of these, printed facing a colour reproduction of the picture, reads as follows:

WAY OF VISUALLY OBSERVING THE COURSE OF THE METAMORPHOSIS OF NARCISSUS REPRESENTED IN THE PRINT ON THE OPPOSITE PAGE:

If one looks for some time, from a slight distance and with a certain "distant fixedness", at the hypnotically immobile figure of Narcissus, it gradually disappears until at last it is completely invisible.

The metamorphosis of the myth takes place at that precise moment, for the image of Narcissus is suddenly transformed into the image of a hand which rises out of his own reflection. At the tips of its fingers the hand is holding an egg, a seed, the bulb from which will be born the new narcissus – the flower. Beside it can be seen the limestone sculpture of the hand – the fossil hand of the water holding the blown flower.

This is followed by a quotation from André Breton's *What is Surrealism?* about Dali's invention of the paranoiac-critical method, and by this further note:

THE FIRST POEM AND THE FIRST PAINTING OBTAINED ENTIRELY THROUGH THE INTEGRAL APPLICATION OF THE PARANOIAC-CRITICAL METHOD:

For the first time, a surrealist painting and poem objectively allow the coherent interpretation of a developed irrational subject. The paranoiac-critical method is beginning to establish the indestructible pudding of the "exact details" that Stendhal demanded for the description of Saint Peter's Church in Rome, and it is doing this in the domain of the most paralysing surrealist poetry.

The lyricism of poetic images is philosophically important only when it has attained, in its operation, the same exactness as mathematics do in their operation.

The poet must, before anyone, prove what he says.

FIRST PORT-LLIGAT FISHERMAN – What's wrong with that chap, glaring at himself all day in his looking-glass?

SECOND FISHERMAN – If you really want to know (*lowering his voice*) he has a bulb in his head.

"A bulb in the head", in catalan, corresponds exactly with the psychoanalytic notion of "complex".
If a man has a bulb in his head, it might break into flower at any moment, Narcissus!

Finally, there is the poem itself:

Under the split in the retreating black cloud
the invisible scale of Spring
is oscillating
in the fresh April sky.
On the highest mountain,
the god of the snow,
his dazzling head bent over the dizzy space of reflections,
starts melting with desire
in the vertical cataracts of the thaw
annihilating himself loudly among the excremental cries of minerals,
or
between the silences of mosses
towards the distant mirror of the lake
in which,
the veils of winter having disappeared,
he has newly discovered
the lightning flash
of his faithful image.
It seems that with the loss of his divinity the whole high plateau
pours itself out,
crashes and crumbles
among the solitude and the incurable silence of iron oxides
while its dead weight
raises the entire swarming and apotheosic
plateau from the plain
from which already thrust towards the sky
the artesian fountains of grass
and from which rise,
erect,
tender,
and hard,
the innumerable floral spears
of the deafening armies of the germination of the narcissi.

Already the heterosexual group, in the renowned poses of preliminary expectation, conscientiously ponders over the threatening libidinous cataclysm, the carniverous blooming of its latent morphological atavisms.

In the heterosexual group,
in that kind date of the year
(but not excessively beloved or mild),
there are
the Hindou
tart, oily, sugared
like an August date,

the Catalan with his grave back
well planted
in a sun-tide,
a whitsuntide of flesh inside his brain,

the blond flesh-eating German,
the brown mists
of mathematics
in the dimples
of his cloudy knees,

there is the English woman,
the Russian,
the Swedish women,
the American
and the tall darkling Andalusian,
hardy with glands and olive with anguish.

Far from the heterosexual group, the shadows of the advanced afternoon draw out across the countryside, and cold lays hold of the adolescent's nakedness as he lingers at the water's edge.

When the clear and divine body of Narcissus
leans
down to the obscure mirror of the lake,

when his white torso folded forward
fixes itself, frozen,
in the silvered and hypnotic curve of his desire,
when the time passes
on the clock of the flowers of the sand of his own flesh,

Narcissus loses his being in the cosmic vertigo
in the deepest depths of which
is singing
the cold and dyonisiac siren of his own image.
The body of Narcissus flows out and loses itself
in the abyss of his reflection,
like the sand glass that will not be turned again.

Narcissus, you are losing your body,
carried away and confounded by the millenary reflection of your disappearance
your body stricken dead
falls to the topaz precipice with yellow wreckage of love,
your white body, swallowed up,
follows the slope of the savagely mineral torrent
of the black precious stones with pungent perfumes,
your body . . .
down to the unglazed mouths of the night
on the edge of which
there sparkles already
all the red silverware
of dawns with veins broken in "the wharves of blood".

Narcissus,
do you understand?
Symmetry, divine hypnosis of the mind's geometry, already fills up your head,
with that incurable sleep, vegetable, atavistic, slow
Which withers up the brain
in the parchment substance
of the kernel of your nearing metamorphosis.

The seed of your head has just fallen into the water.

Man returns to the vegetable state
by fatigue-laden sleep
and the gods
by the transparent hypnosis of their passions.
Narcissus, you are so immobile
one would think you were asleep.
If it were question of Hercules rough and brown,
one would say: he sleeps like a bole
in the posture
of an herculean oak.
But you, Narcissus,
made of perfumed bloomings of transparent adolescence,
you sleep like a water flower.

Now the great mystery draws near,
the great metamorphosis is about to occur.

Narcissus, in his immobility, absorbed by his reflection with the digestive slowness of carnivorous plants, becomes invisible.

There remains of him only
the hallucinatingly white oval of his head,
his head again more tender,
his head, chrysalis of hidden biological designs,
his head held up by the tips of the water's fingers,
at the tips of the fingers
of the insensate hand,
of the terrible hand,
of the excrement-eating hand,
of the mortal hand
of his own reflection.

When that head slits
when that head splits
when that head bursts,
it will be the flower,
the new Narcissus,
Gala –
my narcissus.

When Dali was taken by Stefan Zweig and Edward James to meet Freud in London in July 1938, he brought this one picture with him as an example of his work, as well as a magazine containing an article he had written on paranoia. Though little conversation took place between them, Freud wrote to Zweig on the following day: 'Until now I was inclined to regard the Surrealists – who seem to have me adopted as their patron saint – as 100 per cent fools (or let's rather say, as with alcohol, 95 per cent). This young Spaniard, with his ingenuous fanatical eyes, and his undoubtedly technically perfect mastership has suggested to me a different estimate. In fact, it would be very interesting to explore analytically the growth of a picture like this . . .'

In the book by Descharnes it is dated 1936–7, though the date on the picture itself is 1937. The book *Metamorphosis of Narcissus* in which it is reproduced in colour was 'issued . . . from the presses' in June 1937, so the picture must have been finished in the early part of the year and may have been begun in 1936.

(The compiler is very grateful to the artist for permission to reprint his texts in full.)

John Davies b. 1946

T.2382 **Young Man** 1969–71

Not inscribed
Painted polyester, fibreglass and inert fillers, wool, cotton and leather, 71 × 20 × 11 (180.5 × 51 × 28)
Presented by Mme Andrée Stassart 1979
Prov: Purchased by Barry Miller through the Whitechapel Art Gallery 1972 for Mme Andrée Stassart
Exh: *John Davies*, Whitechapel Art Gallery, June–July 1972 (3, repr.)

'Young Man' is a self-portrait but was deliberately not titled so. It was started in 1969 in Stroud, Gloucestershire, where John Davies had a studio for a year, while teaching at the Cheltenham Art College. An art student made a mould from Davies' head and body and the sculptor himself made a mould from his hands. Davies made the cast in polyester resin in his studio in Faversham, Kent, though he may have started on the head in Stroud.

The jacket of the sculpture had been worn by Davies, but the rest of the clothing was bought in jumble sales and was not worn by him. The hair is a nylon wig and the hands and face were coloured with oil paint.

Davies was 'trying to make a figure, not like a piece of sculpture, but more like a person.' He was interested in what seemed to him to be 'two worlds, the world of art and sculpture, the other the world outside the studio; there was such a disparity between them that I wanted to combine them. I wanted my sculpture to be more like life in the street.' He did not intend his sculptural figures to be 'more extraordinary than people we see around us'.

This catalogue entry is based on a discussion with the artist on 10 August 1979.

Jessica Dismorr 1885–1939

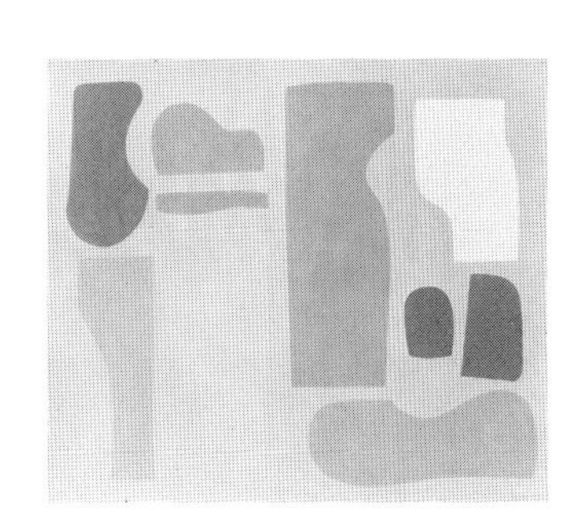

T.2322 **Related Forms** 1937

Inscribed 'J. Dismorr' b.r.
Gouache on millboard, $21\frac{7}{8} \times 25\frac{7}{8}$ (55.5 × 65.7)
Presented by Quentin Stevenson in memory of Catherina Giles and R. H. M. Ody 1978
Prov: Bequeathed by the artist to R. H. M. Ody; Jonathan Ody; Quentin Stevenson
Exh: *Jessica Dismorr*, Mayor Gallery, April–May 1965 (catalogue number unknown, but between 34 & 39); *Jessica Dismorr and her Circle*, Archer Gallery, February 1972 (32); *Thirties*, Hayward Gallery, October 1979–January 1980 (6.31, repr.)
Repr: *Axis*, No. 8, 'Early Winter' 1937, p.25

In 1937, works by Dismorr titled 'Related Forms' were included in the exhibition 'Unity of Artists for Peace, Democracy and Cultural Development', 41 Grosvenor Square, London, April–May (73) and at the London Group in November (306), but it is not known if either of these was the Tate's work. As many as six works with (or given) this title were included in the Dismorr exhibition at the Mayor Gallery, April–May 1965. Neither the extent nor the defining characteristics of the 'Related Forms' series are known. Paintings in private collections inscribed by the artist 'Assembled Forms' and 'Disassociated Forms' are broadly similar in their formal language, though the 'Disassociated' forms are more starkly contrasting than those in the Tate's picture, which employs white, two shades of a putty colour and three of grey in subtly balanced relation. On the reverse of the

Tate's picture is a badly damaged and even more subtly-coloured work painted entirely in greys, in which the edges of the several separate forms are almost or actually straight.

So far as is known, Jessica Dismorr's work was exclusively abstract from 1936 until her death. Her still lifes of 1935 are transitional to abstraction. These and the earliest abstract works bear a strong relation (perhaps still suggested in the Tate's work) to the shapes of vases, curtains and scrolls of music. After the period of the Tate's pictures, Dismorr's painting tended increasingly to the overlapping of forms. As well as by the three adjectives cited above, she variously prefixed the word 'Forms' in the titles of her works from 1936 by 'Stationary', 'Separated' and 'Superposed'.

Frank Dobson 1888–1963

T.2317 **Nude** 1946

Inscribed 'Frank Dobson/46' b.r.
Brown conté crayon on paper, 12 × 18 (30.5 × 45.5)
Presented by S. G. Hand in memory of Mrs I. M. Whitaker 1978

Prov: S. G. Hand (purchased at the RA 1947)

Exh: RA, May–August 1947 (942)

Raymond Duchamp-Villon 1876–1918

T.2307 **Le Grand Cheval** (The Large Horse) 1914

Inscribed on base 'R. DUCHAMP-VILLON/1914' and 'Susse Fondeur Paris'
Bronze, 39⅜ × 38⅞ × 26 (100 × 98.7 × 66)
Purchased at the Louis Carré sale through the Waddington and Tooth Galleries, London (Grant-in-Aid) 1978

Prov: Louis Carré, Paris (purchased from the artist's heirs 1961); Louis Carré sale, Palais d'Orsay, Paris, 27 April 1978, lot 21 repr.

Exh: *Sculptures de Duchamp-Villon*, Galerie Louis Carré, Paris, June–July 1963 (14, repr.); *Apollinaire et le Cubisme*, Palais des Beaux-Arts, Lille, April–May 1965 (23, repr.); *Duchamp-Villon: Le Cheval Majeur*, Galerie Louis Carré, Paris, June–December 1966 (not in catalogue)

Lit: Walter Pach, *Raymond Duchamp-Villon, Sculpteur (1876–1918)*, Paris 1924, pp.12–15; Walter Pach, *The Masters of the Modern Movement*, 1925, pp.86–7, 111–12; Walter Pach, *Queer Thing, Painting*, New York 1938, pp.144–6; George Heard Hamilton and William C. Agee, *Raymond Duchamp-Villon 1876–1918*, New York 1967, pp.22–4, 86–103, repr. figs. 65–8

Repr: *Cahiers d'Art*, 1931, p.227 (the plaster); *Tate Gallery 1978–80*, p.48 in colour

The 'Horse' was Duchamp-Villon's last major sculpture and is said by his American friend Walter Pach to have been begun about a year before the outbreak of the First World War, and to have been finished in the autumn of 1914. The two earliest surviving studies are of the traditional theme of a horse and rider, depicted at the moment of preparing to leap. From then on the rider was eliminated and the horse transformed stage by stage into an expression of dynamic machine power. The development encompassed five distinct stages, as well as at least five additional studies and scores of drawings, of which only two are known from photographs. The sculpture was already nearing completion when he enlisted in

August 1914 as a medical under-officer in the 11th Regiment of Cuirassiers. As an officer in an artillery regiment, he became an expert horseman and was able to use his greater knowledge of horses to make various adjustments to his work, which he finally completed during a period of leave.

The sculpture as left by him in the autumn of 1914, and as it remained at the time of his death, was only 44 cm high and was still slightly sketchy in its handling. According to his brothers Jacques Villon and Marcel Duchamp he had intended to enlarge it, and two enlargements have been carried out since his death under their supervision. The first (this one), 100 cm high, was made in 1930–1 under Villon's direction and was first exhibited in the Duchamp-Villon exhibition at the Galerie Pierre in Paris in June 1931. The second, which is 150 cm high and is usually known as 'Le Cheval Majeur' (The Larger Horse), was executed in 1966 under the supervision of Duchamp.

Mme Diane Foy of Editions Louis Carré et Cie writes (letter of 29 June 1978) that the bronze exhibited at the Galerie Pierre in 1931 was probably the one bought by the Museum of Modern Art, New York, in 1937, and that Jacques Villon had a further plaster made from the original model in 1954 and asked Louis Carré to publish this work in an edition of six, plus one artist's cast. All the bronzes are now in museums as follows:

1/6 Museum of Modern Art, New York
2/6 Museum of Sculpture in the Open Air 'Middelheim', Antwerp
3/6 Centre d'Art et de Culture Georges Pompidou, Musée National d'Art Moderne, Paris
4/6 Walker Art Center, Minneapolis
5/6 Munson Williams Proctor Institute, Utica, NY
6/6 Art Institute of Chicago
artist's proof Tate Gallery

The one now owned by the Tate was cast by Susse for Louis Carré himself in 1961 and remained in his private collection for the rest of his life.

Ian Hamilton Finlay b. 1925

T.2408 **Sea Poppy I** 1968

Not inscribed
Etched (sandblasted) plate glass on wooden plinth, $13\frac{3}{4} \times 12 \times 2\frac{1}{2}$ ($35 \times 30.5 \times 6.4$)
Presented by the Contemporary Art Society 1979

T.2409 **Sea Poppy II** 1968

Not inscribed
Etched (sandblasted) plate glass on wooden plinth, $13\frac{5}{8} \times 11\frac{3}{4} \times 2\frac{1}{2}$ ($34.5 \times 29.9 \times 6.4$)
Presented by the Contemporary Art Society 1979

In 1966 Tarasque Press published a screenprint 'Sea Poppy I' designed by Alistair Cant in collaboration with Ian Hamilton Finlay, in which port letters and fishing numbers of fishing boats were arranged concentrically. In 1968 Wild Hawthorn Press published a screenprint 'Sea Poppy II' in which names of fishing boats were arranged likewise. In addition, Wild Hawthorn Press published postcard versions of both 'Sea Poppy I' and 'Sea Poppy II' in 1968, while a version of 'Sea Poppy I' in calligraphic form designed by Ian Hamilton Finlay and George L. Thomson and executed in glass reinforced concrete was installed in Finlay's garden at

Stonypath in 1978. The names and port letters and fishing numbers of boats were obtained from issues of *Fishing News*, a weekly trade newspaper published in London relating to the sea fishing industry.

Finlay commissioned glass versions of 'Sea Poppy I' and 'Sea Poppy II' from T. and W. Ide, Glasshouse Fields, London E.1 in 1968. Each was made in an edition of six; some were of plain glass and others were blue or amber. They are glass poems which may be placed on a windowsill, or side-lit, and viewed from either side.

Finlay told the compiler (December 1979): 'The works have to be seen in the context of concrete poetry of the time. Just as pure cubism lasted only a short time, so pure concrete poetry lasted only a short time.' 'Sea Poppy I' and 'Sea Poppy II' were amongst his earliest poems made in sandblasted glass form, the first being 'Wave/Rock' of 1967. These were the earliest works of Finlay which in his view 'extended concrete poetry off the page into object form. I had the very deliberate intention of working with the technically-proficient commercial firm so as to produce a work which could not be confused with neo-Dada, and in order to maintain the connection with concrete art.'

Sea Poppy is the name sometimes given to the yellow horned poppy (*Glaucium flavum*, Fam. *Papaveraceae*) a bright yellow poppy which grows on the sea shore in Great Britain and on the Continent.

Barry Flanagan b. 1941

T.3059 **a nose in repose** 1977–9

Not inscribed
Hornton stone and twenty elmwood blocks
Stone $16\frac{1}{2} \times 30\frac{3}{4} \times 10\frac{7}{8}$ (42 × 78 × 26.5), base $35\frac{1}{4} \times 30\frac{3}{4} \times 12$ (90.2 × 178 × 30.5)
Purchased from the Waddington Galleries (Grant-in-Aid) 1980

Exh: *Barry Flanagan: Recent Sculpture*, Waddington Galleries, April–May 1980 (no catalogue)
Lit: *Barry Flanagan: Sculptures in Stone 1973–1978*, Waddington Galleries 1980, p.38, repr. p.30
Repr: *Tate Gallery 1978–80*, p.49 in colour

When studying at the Birmingham College of Art 1955–57 Barry Flanagan worked with several sculptural materials including stone and later made carvings in stone at Beer Quarry, Devon in 1958–59. When studying at St. Martins School of Art in 1964–66 Flanagan says that he 'worked in everything but stone.' He returned to stone carving in 1973 in Italy, at the Pietra Santa quarry, near Carrara, where he carved 'Untitled' 1973 (private collection) using a pneumatic chisel.

Flanagan does not like to cut deeply into a block, so he choses a piece of stone carefully, a shape he can use so that he can respond to the 'geography' of the stone. He describes his approach as 'soliciting stability in the stone'. 'a nose in repose' was made at his studio at Watlington in the Chilterns, from Hornton stone from Edgehill Quarry. He first saw the stone as a pyramidal shape, but 'dubs it a "nose", . . . a civil weaponry at peace'.

The wood supporting the stone part of 'a nose in repose' is composed of planed and sandblasted pit-props made at Brackley, Northamptonshire.

Flanagan has long been fascinated by spirals, suggesting to him, for example, the umbilical cord which symbolises his attachment to the physicality of the material world and for the attachment of man to work. Flanagan is also interested in the spiral in Alfred Jarry's drawings for *Ubu Roi* and in snails and other similarly-shaped molluscs.

This catalogue entry is based on a discussion with Barry Flanagan (19 May 1980) and is approved by him.

Naum Gabo 1890–1977

T.3054 **Construction on a Line** 1937

Inscribed 'N. GABO' low down, at corner
Perspex, $17\frac{3}{4} \times 17 \times 3\frac{1}{2}$ ($45 \times 43 \times 9$)
Purchased from Mrs Lois Ventris (Grant-in-Aid) 1979

Prov: Mrs Dora Ventris, London (purchased from the artist through the London Gallery 1938); Michael Ventris, London; Mrs Lois Ventris, London

Exh: *Constructions by N. Gabo*, London Gallery, January 1938 (10) as 'Construction on a Line in Space' 1937; *Naum Gabo*, Tate Gallery, March–April 1966 (10); *Naum Gabo: The Constructive Process*, Tate Gallery, November 1976–January 1977 (61)

Lit: Herbert Read and Leslie Martin, *Gabo: Constructions, Sculpture, Paintings, Drawings, Engravings*, 1957, p.183, pl.59 (probably a different version)

Repr: *Gabo–Pevsner* (exh. catalogue), Museum of Modern Art, New York 1948, p.30 (probably a different version)

Mrs Gabo remembers Naum Gabo showing her the very first tiny model for this work held up in his small pliers when they were living in London before the war, in Cholmely Gardens, where they moved in the spring of 1937 (he also showed her 'Construction on a Plane' at the same time). This was probably the model 10.8 cm high presented to the Tate in 1977 (T.2178).

This larger work was the first version on a large scale and was included in Gabo's exhibition at the London Gallery in January 1938 as 'Construction on a Line in Space' 1937. It was bought there by Mrs Dora Ventris, who afterwards invited Gabo to come to her flat in Highpoint to advise her on how to display it. He returned after the visit saying what a charming but sad lady she was and that she had introduced him to her talented son, Michael. Gabo was very taken with Michael and tried to guide him in his architectural studies and it was to the Gabos, in Cornwall, that Michael came when his mother committed suicide. Michael Ventris subsequently achieved great distinction as an archaeologist by deciphering the Minoan Linear B script in 1952–3, but was killed in a car accident not long afterwards, in 1956. Gabo then decided to dedicate this sculpture to his memory.

There are further versions on the same scale in the collections of the Wadsworth Atheneum at Hartford, James Johnson Sweeney, New York, and Mrs Gabo herself, while what seems to have been yet another belonged at one time to Mies van der Rohe.

Albert Gleizes 1881–1953

T.2410 **Portrait de Jacques Nayral** (Portrait of Jacques Nayral) 1911

Inscribed 'Albert Gleizes. 1911' b.r.
Oil on canvas, $63\frac{3}{4} \times 44\frac{7}{8}$ (162×114)
Purchased at Sotheby's (Grant-in-Aid) 1979

Prov: Joseph Houot (Jacques Nayral); Mme Joseph Houot; Commandant

Georges Houot, La Flèche; sold by Mme Georges Houot at Sotheby's, London, 5 December 1979, lot 92 repr. in colour

Exh: Salon d'Automne, Paris, October–November 1911 (609); Salon de 'La Section d'Or', Galerie La Boëtie, Paris, October 1912 (38); *Les Maîtres de l'Art Indépendant 1895–1937*, Petit Palais, Paris, June–October 1937 (Room 28, 17); *Le Cubisme (1907–1914)*, Musée National d'Art Moderne, Paris, January–April 1953 (64); II Bienal, São Paulo, December 1953 – February 1954 (Cubist room 16); *Albert Gleizes 1881–1953*, Guggenheim Museum, New York, September–November 1964 (11, repr.); Musée National d'Art Moderne, Paris, December 1964–January 1965 (11, repr.); Museum am Ostwall, Dortmund, March–April 1965 (11, repr.)

Lit: Guillaume Apollinaire in *L'Intransigeant*, 12 October 1911; Albert Gleizes, 'L'Epopée' in *Le Rouge et le Noir*, October 1929, p.64

Repr: Joan A. Speers (ed.), *Art at Auction: The Year at Sotheby Parke Bernet 1979–80*, 1980, p.114 in colour; *Tate Gallery 1978–80*, p.50 in colour

Jacques Nayral (a pseudonym for Joseph Houot) was a young poet and dramatist who was a friend of Gleizes and married his sister Mireille in 1912. Gleizes began work on his portrait in 1910 (the 1964–5 exhibition included a preliminary drawing signed and dated 1910, with an inscription that it was the second of the studies for this work). Nayral, who was a supporter of the social ideas of the Abbaye de Créteil, was editor-in-chief of the publishing house of Figuière. He was directly responsible for the publication of the book *Du Cubisme* by Gleizes and Metzinger, as well as Apollinaire's *Peintres Cubistes*, and for the project to publish a series *Tous les Arts.* The portrait shows him seated out of doors, in the garden of Gleizes's house at Courbevoie.

Reviewing the Cubist room at the Salon d'Automne of 1911 in *L'Intransigeant*, Apollinaire wrote of this portrait: 'It is a very good likeness, yet in this impressive canvas, there is not one form or colour that was not invented by the artist. This portrait has a grandiose appearance that should not escape the notice of connoisseurs.'

Nayral was killed in action in December 1914, at the age of thirty-five, in an attack on a German trench near Arras.

Peter Greenham b. 1909

T.2401 Father d'Arcy 1976

Not inscribed

Oil on canvas, 30 × 20½ (76.2 × 51.2)

Presented by the Trustees of the Chantrey Bequest 1979

Prov: Purchased from the artist by the Trustees of the Chantrey Bequest 1976

Exh: RA, May–August 1976 (369); *British Painting 1952–1977*, RA, September–November 1977 (149, repr.)

Repr: *RA Illustrated*, 1976, p.3

Father Martin d'Arcy S.J. (1888–1976) writer, lecturer and broadcaster both on radio and television was Master of Campion Hall, Oxford from 1933 until 1945. He was painted and drawn by several artists including Augustus John and Wyndham Lewis; the portrait, in oils, by John belongs to Campion Hall.

This portrait by Peter Greenham was not a commission; Mrs Brinsley Ford, who knew the sitter well, suggested to the artist that he might paint a portrait of Father d'Arcy who was living in the Mount Street Jesuit Community adjoining the Farm Street Roman Catholic church, London W.1. The portrait was painted in 4 or 5 sittings, each of $1\frac{1}{2}$ to 2 hours from about 10.30 am to 12.30 pm in May and June 1975 in Father d'Arcy's small bed-sitter where, being rather frail, he spent most of his time. Greenham made a few drawings of the head and the hands, which at one time were clasped together, but as the sitter moved his hands they were omitted from the finished oil.

This catalogue entry is based largely on a discussion with the artist (November 1979) and is approved by him.

Anthony Gross b. 1905

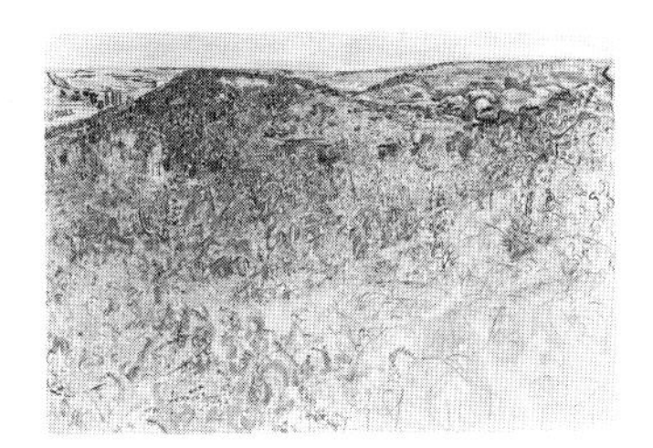

T.2393 **Pech de Murat** 1978

Inscribed 'Anthy Gross/1978' b.r.
Oil on canvas, $35\frac{1}{4} \times 51\frac{1}{2}$ (89.5 × 130.5)
Presented by the Trustees of the Chantrey Bequest 1979
Prov: Purchased from the New Art Centre under the terms of the Chantrey Bequest 1979
Exh: *Anthony Gross*, New Art Centre, February 1979 (no catalogue); RA, May–August 1979 (53) as 'Pech Murat'

The artist has explained that 'Pech de Murat' is the name of the large hill in the centre of the painting, 'Pech' meaning peak. The view is almost identical to that in the watercolour 'Quercy Blanc', 1975–7 (T.2111), and is taken from the top of the hills near the artist's home in this area near Cahors in the Lot, which has been the principal subject of his landscapes for some twenty years. He wrote (18 October 1980) that, as with the water-colour, 'here also I attempt to make the picture glow from within with the light, its own light absorbed from outside.'

Meraud Guevara b. 1904

T.2331 **Seated Woman with Small Dog** *c.* 1937

Not inscribed
Oil on canvas, $35 \times 25\frac{5}{8}$ (89 × 65)
Presented by Salander Galleries, New York, 1979
Prov: Private collection, New York; Salander Galleries
Exh: *Meraud Guevara*, Valentine Gallery, New York, April 1939 (?12, repr.); *Meraud Guevara*, Salander Galleries, New York, October–November 1978 (15, as 'Woman with Hat')
Repr: *Art in America*, LXVI, November–December 1978, p.92, as 'Femme au Chapeau' *c.*1938

The smooth clarity of this picture's technique is characteristic of all Meraud Guevara's works of the late 1930s of which the Gallery has reproductions. Among characteristics of the Tate's picture which are shared by a number of her contemporary works are unusual hats or hair styles and the accompaniment of a human figure by another living creature (bird or animal) or by some kind of picture-within-a-picture (a painting, or a view through window or door).

In a letter of 16 September 1979 the artist explained that this picture was painted in her studio at 30 Rue Dauphine, Paris, of which it represents the interior. It was painted without a model, the view through the window was imaginary, and though she may have had a hat similar to the one shown, both it and the dog were 'mostly imaginative'. In reply to questions about the significance of the picture's imagery, Mrs Guevara wrote 'I give no special significance to the picture other than the composition . . . and balance in a given space'. In reply to a question listing thirteen artists or periods of art with which critics had compared her work of the late 1930's, the artist wrote 'At the time I painted this picture I think the painters I most admired were Goya (specially portraits) also Ingres (portraits) Balthus, early Tal-Coat and my husband [Alvaro] Guevara – Also of course the relationship between a Portrait and a Picture – when the identity of the sitter has no importance'. She made preparatory sketches for the Tate's picture but did not keep them.

In the 1978 Salander Galleries exhibition this painting was shown as 'Woman with Hat', circa 1939, on information from the artist. However although it was reproduced in the catalogue of the 1939 Valentine Gallery exhibition, this reproduction is not correlated by either title or catalogue number to any of the listed works, which include 'Femme assise' (5), 'Femme au chien' (11), 'Femme assise au petit chien' (12), 'Femme au chapeau' (14) and 'Negresse' (19). Mrs Guevara commented on this list in her letter of September 1979 'I think the title was "Femme assise au petit chien"'. In a later letter she confirmed this title emphatically. She also thought that it was painted 'a few years before the war probably around 1937 but I cannot remember the exact year'.

This entry has been approved by the artist.

William Henderson b. 1941

T.2389 **Rougey** 1979

Inscribed 'William Henderson/"Rougey" 1979' on back
Acrylic on cotton duck, 69 × 57¼ (175.2 × 145.4)
Purchased from the artist through the Ian Birksted Gallery (Knapping Fund) 1979
Exh: *Hayward Annual 1979*, Hayward Gallery, July–August 1979 (50)

In 1967 William Henderson started to execute paintings using grids in the imagery, in which the paint was applied relatively thickly, marks being built up on marks. Grids became increasingly important in his work until about 1976 when the verticals and horizontals of the grids began to become less formal and measured and oblique lines were introduced. In these works the paint was applied more thinly, using heightened, even strident colours and there was a return to illusory pictorial space in the paintings. Henderson made parallel bands of different colours by loading the brush with more than one colour. This method was the most direct way the artist could think of for applying bands of several colours at once. Since 1976 the number of parallel bars of colour in each of Henderson's paintings have become fewer and illusory pictorial space has become more dominating. Henderson sees such paintings as being somewhat analogous to non-specific musical improvisations.

'Rougey' was painted in the artist's studio in Brixton in late February and March 1979. The works painted immediately before and after 'Rougey' were, respectively, 'Gjalla' (Coll: Arts Council) and 'Gjalla No. 2' (Coll: Contemporary Art Society).

This catalogue entry is based on a conversation with the artist (18 December 1979) and has been approved by him.

David Hepher b. 1935

T.2404 **Albany Flats** 1977–9

Not inscribed

Oil and sand on canvas, $77\frac{3}{4} \times 110$ (194.4 × 275.2)
Purchased from the Angela Flowers Gallery (Grant-in-Aid) 1979

Exh: *David Hepher*, Angela Flowers Gallery, October–November 1979 (no catalogue, 3 on announcement card, repr.)

Lit: David Hepher, 'Urban Realism', *Artscribe*, No.22, April 1980, pps.46–48

Repr: Angela Flowers postcard 1980; *Artscribe*, No.22, April 1980, p.47; *Architectural Review*, CLXVII, No. 998, April 1980, p.227

At the time of its completion, the artist considered 'Albany Flats' the most successful of a series of paintings of high-rise council blocks which he has worked on since 1974. It was first exhibited at the Angela Flowers Gallery in 1979 (loc. cit.), together with 'Peckham Flats' (1975–6) and 'Walworth Flats' (1976–9); the first two paintings in the series, 'Stockwell Flats I' (1974–5) and 'Stockwell Flats 2' (1975) having been shown together in *New Work*, an Arts Council group exhibition, held at the Hayward Gallery in November–December 1975. Between 1969 and 1974 Hepher made meticulous analytical paintings of suburban house fronts and has described the tower blocks he now paints as 'a kind of inner-city suburbia (which) perhaps house the next generation on from the people who first lived in the pre-war suburban houses I was painting earlier.' (David Hepher, 'Urban Realism', *Artscribe* No.22, April 1980, p.48). The subject of T.2404 is Bradenham Block, a block of flats on the Albany Estate, which is situated between the Walworth Road and the Old Kent Road in the London borough of Southwark and which is one of the largest public housing estates in Europe. Believing that the best work comes out of the familiar experiences of daily life, he deliberately chose to paint a building near his home and place of work, to which he could have regular access.

In his article in *Artscribe*, Hepher denies that his paintings are intended to be seen as overt political or social comments on the way people are forced to live in the inner cities. 'Inevitably, in painting these buildings questions about society that interest me arise, but it is not because of these questions that I paint the flats. I have always painted houses, or housescapes. A house, or more symbolically a home, is one of the earliest images a child paints. In many ways it represents, particularly for the English, the face people present to the world, at the same time providing a refuge from too close a contact with other people. All the owner's personality is revealed in his home. This is why I only paint residential flats – they have a soul that glamorous office architecture doesn't have. In spite of their beauty I don't want to paint the sleek and shiny city blocks. I think there is a danger of that becoming incestuous, too much like art celebrating art. I like best to work from council blocks, preferably stained and eroded by the dirt and the weather, where the facial appearance is continually changed by the people who live there, their comings and goings, and the changing decor. I would like to think that the pictures could make people look differently at the flats around them, to see beauty in objects that they normally dismiss as ugly.' He acknowledges that the hard-edged geometry of such buildings allows him to pursue certain formal interests in his paintings, 'I wouldn't be painting them without abstract art and while drawing them I am constantly reminded of the grid structure of Agnes Martin or Mondrian', but is more concerned with attempting to record as accurately as possible what he sees when confronting a specific building than with exploiting its formal possibilities.

Hepher worked on 'Albany Flats' over a period of about eighteen months in a studio at the Camberwell School of Art where he teaches. He worked from detailed annotated drawings and visited the flats regularly to make notes on the particular section he was concentrating on, or to refresh his memory. He regards his working drawings as means to an end and seven of those made for 'Albany

Flats' which he presented to the Tate Gallery Archive in 1979, contain not only structural information about the architecture of the building and colour notes but also incidental details about specific flats or groups of flats, as he found them on the days he visited the site. The artist feels that one of the dangers inherent in choosing a subject as apparently banal as a tower block is that the resulting painting could be read as a statement about banality. He avoids this by concentrating on the way in which the building's superficially unified facade is broken up or altered by such reflections of the individual lives of its inhabitants as for example, pot plants, ornaments, window boxes, the different patterns and textures of curtains etc. Nevertheless, he is aware that too much anecdotal interest can interfere with the overall idea and sense of mass in his paintings and, in consequence, he sometimes omits certain small human details recorded in the drawings, from the finished work, in order to retain the sense of grandeur and menace which such buildings communicate. For example, on one of the Tate's drawings for T.2404 he has shown a woman leaning on a balcony and recorded 'hot weather – doors open, presence of people implied but not visible' and on another 'pretty woman appeared briefly at window', although no figures appear in the painting.

When he began the painting, Hepher first drew out the basic design on the canvas and blocked it in in an elementary way. Starting with an area in the centre of the canvas, he then painted to a finished state blocks of between four and six units of flats, building up the work section by section so that no area of the painting is more emphasised than any other. It is intended that the viewer's eye should range over the surface of the work, picking up areas of interest and activity, a process which echoes the artist's own close scrutiny of his subject. In order to heighten the sensation of standing directly in front of the block of flats, he has employed natural rather than conventional pictorial perspective, (the horizontals are slightly bowed) so that the building appears to tower above the viewer.

In general, Hepher wishes his paintings to communicate to the spectator his experience of confronting his subject in a direct, tactile sense, (in T.2404 he mixed building sand with oil paint to approximate the concrete texture of the tower block's facade) and, in consequence, prefers not to work from photographs, finding the information they provide too superficial and insubstantial to be of use when he starts to paint.

Unless otherwise stated, this entry is based on a conversation with the artist (22.1.80) a note from the artist (30.11.80) and a statement he contributed to the catalogue for the exhibition *Working Process*, Sunderland Arts Centre, February–March 1978 (n.p.). The entry has been read and approved by him.

Eva Hesse 1936–1970

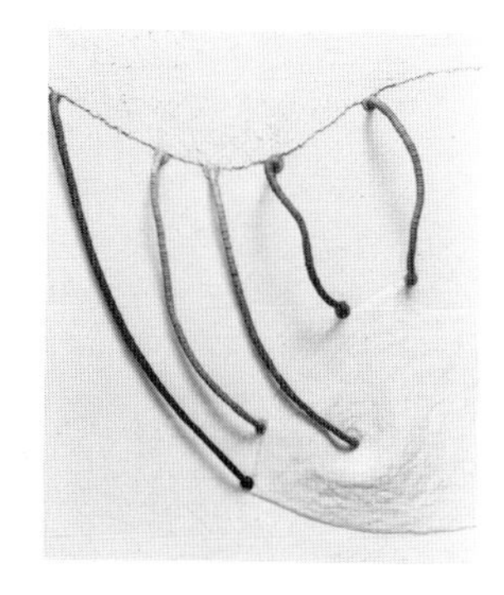

T.2383 **Tomorrow's Apples (5 in White)** 1965

Inscribed 'Eva Hesse 1965' and '5 in WHITE' on reverse
Painted concretion, enamel, gouache, varnish, cord and papier mâché mounted on chipboard, $25\frac{3}{4} \times 21\frac{7}{8} \times 6\frac{1}{4}$ (65.2 × 55.6 × 16)
Purchased through the Whitechapel Art Gallery from Donald Droll, acting for the artist's estate (Grant-in-Aid) 1979

Exh: *Eva Hesse: Materialbilder und Zeichnungen*, Studio für Graphik, Kunstverein für die Rheinlande und Westfalen, Kunsthalle, Düsseldorf, August–October 1965 (6, as 'Tomorrows Apples', repr. catalogue cover); *Eva Hesse: A Memorial Exhibition*, Guggenheim Museum, New York, December 1972–February 1973, Albright-Knox Art Gallery,

Buffalo, March–April 1973, Museum of Contemporary Art, Chicago, May–July 1973, Pasadena Museum of Modern Art, September–November 1973, University Art Museum, Berkeley, December 1973–February 1974 (4, as '5 in White', repr. 4th page, plate 4, n.p.); *Eva Hesse 1936–70*, Mayor Gallery, September–October 1974 (2, as 'Five in White' repr. opp. foreword and fig. 2, n.p.); *Eva Hesse 1936–1970: Sculpture*, Whitechapel Art Gallery, May–June 1979, Rijksmuseum Kröller-Müller, Otterlo, June–August 1979 (2, repr. 14, n.p.); *Eva Hesse 1936–1970 Skulpturen und Zeichnungen*, Kestner-Gesellschaft, Hanover, August–September 1979 (2, repr. p.18)

Lit: Linda Shearer, catalogue foreword to *Eva Hesse*, Mayor Gallery 1974 (op. cit. as '5 in White', n.p.); Lucy Lippard, 'Eva Hesse', New York 1976, pps.38, 42, n. 9, p.215, repr. fig. 45, p.37, fig. 53, p.159, No. 6 in catalogue raisonné of sculpture; Andrea Hill, 'Eva Hesse', *Artscribe*, No. 18, July 1979, p.41; *Tate Gallery 1978–80*, p.51 repr.

This was one of a series of fourteen reliefs included in Eva Hesse's first major exhibition held at the Kunsthalle, Düsseldorf in 1965. In 1964, Hesse and her husband, the sculptor Tom Doyle, were given the chance of working for a time in Germany, under the patronage of the German industrialist and collector, Arnhard Scheidt. In June 1964, the two artists left New York and set up a studio in one of Scheidt's disused factories in Kettwig-am-Ruhr. They remained in Germany until September 1965 and it was during this period that Hesse, who had trained as a painter, began to work in three dimensions. (She had made only one sculpture previously, a soft tube of cloth and wire, used in an artists' performance work, in Woodstock in 1962).

Discussing the German reliefs in an interview with the American critic, Cindy Nemser ('Art Talk', New York 1975, p.207), Hesse admitted that she had always had difficulty in translating her often complex drawings into paint, 'The ... transference to a large scale and in painting was always tedious. It was not natural ... so I started working in relief and with line. I would vary the cord lengths and widths and I would start with three dimensional boards and I would build them out with papier mâché or kinds of soft materials. I varied the materials a lot but the structure would always be built up with cords.' The reliefs were constructed out of a variety of media, plaster and metal were also used; the Kettwig studio had previously been a weaving shed and, at Doyle's suggestion, Hesse began to work with some of the industrial materials that had been abandoned there. On 14 December she wrote to her friend Rosalind Goldman in New York (Lippard, p.28), that she was making a structure involving a mesh screen through which she had pushed and knotted plaster-soaked string. This early relief was either lost, destroyed or remained unfinished but Lippard notes that its structure and method of fabrication (the grid and the compulsive process of winding or wrapping) set the pattern for Hesse's mature work.

The fourteen reliefs shown at Düsseldorf were completed between March and July 1965 and the exhibition opened on 6 August. In a further letter to Rosalind Goldman, 4 May 1965 (repr. Lippard, fig. 44), Hesse sketched the first four reliefs and these, together with T.2383, were reproduced on the cover of the Düsseldorf catalogue. The catalogue appears to list the works chronologically, the order of the first eleven corresponding with the following list in the artist's diary; 'March 1. Ringaround Arosie. April 2. Two Handled Orangekeyed Utensil. April 3. An Ear in a Pond. May 4. Legs of a Walking Ball. May 5. (blank; later named Oomamaboomba.) June 6. Tomorrow's Apples. June 7. 2 in 1. June 8. H + H. July 9. Cool Zone. July 10. Pink' ... 'July. C–Clamp Blues.' The final three pieces were presumably made in July. Lippard suggests that the catalogue illustration shows the first five completed reliefs (although 'Tomorrow's Apples' is listed as 6 in both catalogue and diary). Hesse left all the reliefs in Germany when she returned to New York and where these were unmarked or unavailable for inspection, Lippard and Tom Doyle determined which was which after the artist's death. Their task was made more difficult because the catalogue describes all the works as *materialbild* (mixed media) and gives similar dimensions for each. Despite the fact that T.2383 appears in the catalogue photograph, Lippard notes that it seems to be stylistically later than its placing in the catalogue would indicate. It arrived back from Germany with the title '5 in white' (although Doyle did not remember Hesse using this alternative title) and was exhibited as such until the Whitechapel Retrospective in 1979. In the Whitechapel catalogue, T.2383 is reproduced below an excerpt from the artist's notebook (Kettwig c. December 1964, coll. Allen Art Museum, Oberlin, Ohio), a slightly misleading juxtaposition because the notebook lists the titles of drawings for possible inclusion in an earlier group exhibition, held at the Kunsthalle, Düsseldorf in December 1964. Some of the drawings' titles, including 'Tomorrow's Apples' correspond with the titles of the reliefs Hesse exhibited at the same museum in 1965 but the drawings were not studies for the reliefs.

In her foreword to the Guggenheim catalogue (op. cit. n.p.), the American critic Linda Shearer emphasised the importance of taking into account Hesse's training as a painter and draftsman in any evaluation of her sculpture, pointing out that the German reliefs evolved naturally out of a preference for linear imagery and that the artist literally interpreted line in solid materials, extending two dimensional spatial concepts into three dimensions. Shortly before leaving for Germany, Hesse had been working on a series of collaged ink drawings, employing eccentric semi-organic shapes in deliberately awkward and off-balance compositions which she later compared to the reliefs, referring to both as deliberately absurdist, as 'impossible space', 'impossible machines' (Lippard p.24). In Kettwig her drawings became flatter, more simplified and less concerned with technique, increasingly suggesting sculptural forms. By early 1965 the dominant images had become a series of organic shapes with machine-like appendages isolated against white backgrounds. These drawings were the direct antecedents of the German reliefs but as Lippard points out ('Eva Hesse: The Circle', in *From the Centre*, p.156, New York 1976) the reliefs can also be read as three dimensional manifestations of the eccentric biomorphic shapes with which Hesse had always been obsessed, the '... irregular rectangles, parabolas, trailing linear ends, curving forms, the circles bound or bulged out of symmetry ...' which had appeared in her expressionist drawings from as early as 1960.

'Ringaround Arosie' (Düsseldorf 1) and 'Tomorrow's Apples' are the simplest of the six earliest reliefs but whereas 'Ringaround Arosie', consisting of two pink breast-like cord circles on a grey ground has overt sexual references, (the artist said it reminded her of a breast and penis, Lippard p.38), T.2383 is less obviously anthropomorphic and it is stylistically closer to some of the later more abstract works in the series, e.g. 'Cool Zone' (Düsseldorf 9) and 'Up the Down Road' (Düsseldorf 12). 'Tomorrow's Apples' consists of a contoured white ground, divided by texture into three main areas, in the uppermost section the surface is only slightly raised, the application of what appears to be a piece of plaster-soaked cloth giving an even, grainy texture; the papier mâché process gives the surface of the centre section a fragmented, tortoise-shell appearance and the lower area, an indented mound, is irregularly textured. Five cord-wrapped rods, secured by being knotted through the chipboard support, arch over the flat central channel. These are brightly painted (from left to right, ultramarine, magenta, brick red, cerulean blue and acid green). Each colour is graded by being mixed with white, and intensifies towards the bottom of the cord. The colours act against the monochrome surface of the relief, so that the rods sometimes appear to float above the surface and the shadows they cast give an ambiguous depth to the work.

From 1957–59 Hesse attended the Yale School of Art and Architecture where she studied with Josef Albers. The hybrid German reliefs, described by Linda Shearer writing in the Mayor Gallery catalogue (op. cit.) as 'Hesse's first truly original statements . . . notable for their unusually acid and vibrant colour' have little relation to Albers' theories of colour and design but Shearer suggests that they reveal 'a positive aspect' of the effect of his teaching. Referring to Albers' Bauhaus emphasis on the value of a true understanding of the properties of materials and the principles of construction, she writes, 'I think we must attribute Hesse's initial use of materials such as papier mâché, cord, aluminium and wire to at least a subliminal recall of Albers' classroom.' In July 1964 Hesse wrote in a notebook of her dissatisfaction with the way in which she was using colour, '. . . I end up with red, yellow, blue, green and I hate it' and when she returned to New York in September 1965, she began to work in monochrome, her last coloured piece, 'Untitled' 1965 being completed in October of that year.

T.2394 **Addendum** 1967

Not inscribed
Painted papier mâché, wood and cord, $4\frac{7}{8} \times 119\frac{1}{4} \times 5\frac{7}{8}$ ($8\frac{1}{8}$ at deepest point) (12.5 × 304.5 × 15 (20.5) without cords; length of cords approx. $118\frac{1}{8}$ (300)
Purchased from Victor Ganz (Grant-in-Aid) 1979

Prov: Purchased by Victor Ganz from the Fourcade Droll Gallery, New York 1972

Exh: *Art in Series*, Finch College Museum of Art, Contemporary Wing, New York, November 1967 – January 1968 (no catalogue, tape recording by participating artists); *Eva Hesse A Memorial Exhibition*, Guggenheim Museum, New York, December 1972–February 1973, Albright-Knox Art Gallery, Buffalo, March–April 1973, Museum of Contemporary Art, Chicago, May–July 1973, Pasadena Museum of Modern Art, September–November 1973, University Art Museum, Berkeley, December 1973–February 1974 (18, repr. pl.18); *Eva Hesse 1936–1970: Sculpture*, Whitechapel Art Gallery, May–June 1979, Rijksmuseum Kröller-Müller, Otterlo, June–August 1979 (25, repr. 16, n.p.); *Eva Hesse 1936–1970: Skulpturen und Zeichnungen*, Kestner-Gesellschaft, Hanover, August–September 1979 (25, repr. fig. 25 pp.20 and 48)

Lit: Lucy Lippard, 'Eva Hesse: The Circle', *From the Centre,* New York 1976, p.159 (reprinted from *Art in America*, LIX, no.3, May–June 1971); Lucy Lippard, *Eva Hesse*, New York 1976, statement by the artist p.96, pp.192, 216 (n. 17), 59 in catalogue raisonné of sculpture, repr. fig. 129, pp.94–5; artist's statement reprinted *Eva Hesse 1936–1970: Sculpture,* Whitechapel Art Gallery and *Eva Hesse 1936–1970 Skulpturen und Zeichnungen*, Kestner-Gesellschaft, Hanover (op. cit.); Andrea Hill, 'Eva Hesse', *Artscribe* 18, p.42, repr. p.43

Repr: Mel Bochner 'The Serial Attitude', *Artforum*, VI, December 1967, p.33 (as 'Untitled' 1967); David Lee, 'Serial Rights', *Art News*, LXVI, no.8, December 1967, p.44

This was Hesse's major piece for 1967, a year described by Lucy Lippard as '. . . the most geometric, serial and Minimal' of the artist's career. On her return to New York from Germany in 1965 Hesse began to simplify the forms in her sculpture, placing formalized versions of the elements she had used in the German reliefs within a more geometric framework. She re-adopted her more sombre palette of the early sixties and began to work increasingly in monochrome. This clearer and more structural approach was, in part, a response to the prevailing climate in New York at the time; the new Minimal works of Sol LeWitt, who had been a friend since 1960 and who was to be one of the strongest supporters of her work, were a particular influence. Other artists important to her development at that time were Mel Bochner, Robert Ryman, and Carl Andre.

The earliest piece to incorporate a rectangular support, hemispheres and dangling cords was 'Ishtar' (repr. Lippard fig. 70), completed in December 1965. This is a vertical relief bearing a series of twenty hemispheres, arranged two-by-two. A cord falls from the centre of each dome and these accumulate in two cascades at the bottom of the piece. The idea was further explored in 'Ennead' (repr. Lippard fig. 80), probably completed after March 1966, where the symmetry of a grid of smaller raised hemispheres is again deliberately counteracted by emergent strings, which, this time, drop to the floor in a tangled mass. In the middle of 1966, Hesse's drawings, hitherto more organic, began to reflect her new preoccupation with structure and she applied the grid format to a series of delicate ink and wash drawings of circles or targets. However, these were not working drawings for sculptures and Lippard notes that Hesse was never at ease with mechanical or scale drawings, 'Bochner and Le Witt showed Hesse how to make a 'working drawing', but difficulties with scaling led her to make the one for *Addendum* full scale' (note 17, op. cit.). This drawing executed on plain white paper, is currently on loan from a private collection in New York to the Wadsworth Atheneum, Hartford, Connecticut.

Three further wall pieces directly related to T.2394 are 'Untitled' (1966), 'One More Than One' (1967) and 'Ditto' (1967) (Lippard figs. 114–116). The first consists of a rectangular framework containing a single convex dome which is linked to the floor by a rubber tube issuing from its centre. In 'One More Than One', two plastic cords hang from a pair of roughly textured concave half-circles or inverted 'breasts' and in 'Ditto', which resembles both Hesse's drawings of the period and the earlier 'Ishtar', cords dangle from a series of nine flatter textured circles, arranged in lines of three within a smooth rectangle. The exhibition, *Art in Series*, at Finch College Museum in New York where 'Addendum' was first shown was jointly organized by Elayne Varian and Mel Bochner. All works in the exhibition were based on arithmetical or serial progressions and among other artists who participated were, Donald Judd, Dan Flavin, Sol LeWitt, Robert Smithson, Elsworth Kelly, Jasper Johns and Robert Rauschenberg. Bochner chose T.2394 as one of the illustrations for his key article, The Serial Attitude (loc. cit.) which discussed the theme of the exhibition. However, despite Hesse's interest in serial concepts, her work always veered towards the expressive and 'Addendum', although one of her more 'minimal' works, retains an organic informality which sets it apart from the austere and economic works of some of her co-exhibitors. Reviewing the exhibition in the *Village Voice* ('Repeating Absurdity', December 14, 1967, p.18), John Perreault commented on the restrictions of working within a tight arithmetical format. 'Only one artist in the show, Eva Hesse, in a piece called "Addendum" – a grey structure containing a serial arrangement of semi-spheres out of which hang lengths of grey cord that fall to the floor and get all tangled up in each other – sees, questions, and in a way relishes the absurd implications of this new cliche.'

There was no catalogue for the exhibition but the participating artists made Acoustiguide recordings explaining their work. Hesse stated: 'The title of this work is Addendum, a thing added or to be added. A title is after the fact. It is titled only because that is preferred to untitled. Explanations are also after the fact. The work exists only for itself. The work must contain its own import.' She went on to describe the structure of T.2394, giving basic dimensions and explaining the placement of the seventeen hemispheres, which are based on the following interval progression; $\frac{1}{8}$, $\frac{3}{8}$, $\frac{5}{8}$, $\frac{7}{8}$, $1\frac{1}{8}$, $1\frac{3}{8}$, $1\frac{5}{8}$, $1\frac{7}{8}$, etc. She said that she chose three discrete units, rope, rectangle, hemisphere, ('as different in shape as possible') and set about unifying them through sequential placement, the device of repetition and the unified textured grey of the surface. This reconciliation of opposites is deliberately unbalanced by the artist's specification that the work is to be hung seven feet from the floor, so that the flexible cords start their downward journey in parallel lines but, because of their length, collapse in a random mass at ground level. The artist concluded her statement, 'Series, serial, serial art, is another way of repeating absurdity.' (This sentence repeated several times was originally to have been her only comment on the work.) In one of a series of interviews with Cindy Nemser given towards the end of her life, (Cindy Nemser, 'Art Talk: Conversations with 12 Women Artists', New York 1975, pp.209–10) Hesse commented in reference to 'Ennead', on her earlier use of a circular motif; 'I think the circle is very abstract. I could make up stories of what the circle means to men, but I don't know if it is that conscious. I think it was a form, a vehicle. I don't think I had a sexual, anthropomorphic or geometric meaning: It wasn't a breast and it wasn't a circle representing life and eternity. I think it would be fake – maybe on an unconscious level, but that's so opposed – to say it was an abstract life symbol or a geometric theory ... One memory I have: I remember always working with contradictions and contradictory forms which is my idea also in life. The whole absurdity of life, everything for me has always been opposite ... And I think, I know that, in forms I use in my work, that contradiction is certainly there. When I was younger ... I was always aware that I could combine order and chaos, string and mass, huge and small. I would try to find the most absurd opposites or extreme opposites and I was always aware of their contradiction formally ... within the circle I remember taking this straight perfect form and then putting a hole in the centre and dropping out a very ... flexible surgical hose ... I would make it very ... long and then it would squiggle and wiggle. That was the extreme you could get from that perfect, perfect circle.' Asked about her repetitive use of forms, she replied 'If something is meaningful, maybe it's more meaningful said ten times. It's not just an aesthetic choice. If something is absurd, it's much more greatly exaggerated, absurd, if it's repeated.'

John Hoyland b. 1934

T.2402 Saracen 1977

Inscribed on reverse 'JOHN HOYLAND 1977'
Acrylic on canvas, 96 × 90 (243.8 × 228.6)
Purchased from Theo Waddington & Co. Ltd. (Grant-in-Aid) 1979
Exh: Waddington Galleries, Toronto, March–April 1978; *John Hoyland*, Serpentine Gallery, September–October 1979 (31, repr. in colour)
Lit: John McEwen, 'John Hoyland in mid career', in *Arts Canada,* April–May 1978, pp.36–37, repr. in colour; *Tate Gallery 1978–80*, p.52 and repr. in colour

T.2403 North Sound 1979

Inscribed on reverse 'NORTH SOUND 15.7.79 HOYLAND'
Acrylic on canvas, 90 × 96 (228.6 × 243.8)
Purchased from the Waddington Galleries (Grant-in-Aid) 1979
Exh: *John Hoyland*, Serpentine Gallery, September–October 1979 (ex catalogue)

'North Sound' and 'Saracen' were painted almost two years apart. Yet John Hoyland considers that these works are 'possibly cousins, at least part of the same family of configurations which go back ... to the early sixties.' (Conversation with the artist, 23 Sept. 1980). Hoyland paints families of canvases, that is groups of works that have a similar basic format but whose internal colour and formal relationships are modified. These formats may be similar for a considerable period.

Hoyland used not to give titles to his works, preferring to substitute the date on which he considered the work finished. A friend suggested a number of titles to him and he now creates his own. However, he considers these neither explanatory nor descriptive. Rather he hopes that they will provide some sort of counterpoint which will not limit the possibility for change and will also allow each individual to make multiple readings. He expects there to be some resonance between the title and the work.

Wassily Kandinsky 1866–1944

T.2344 **Swinging** 1925

Inscribed 'K/No 291/1925', '"Schaukeln"' and '50 × 70' on back of millboard
Oil on millboard, $27\frac{3}{4} \times 19\frac{3}{4}$ (70.6 × 50.1)
Purchased from Mme Andrée Stassart (Grant-in-Aid) 1979

Prov: Mme Nina Kandinsky, Paris; with Galerie Maeght, Paris; Mr and Mrs Victor Kiam, New York; with New Gallery, New York; Mr and Mrs Paul M. Hirschland, New York, 1960; Japanese buyer 1973; with Berggruen, Paris; Mme Andrée Stassart, Liège, 1974

Exh: *Kandinsky*, Kunstverein Jena, Prinzessinnenschlösschen, Jena, March–April 1925 (no catalogue traced); *Kunstausstellung Dresden 1925*, Dresden Kunstgenossenschaft exhibition, Brühlsche Terrasse, Dresden, July–October 1925 (350); *Kandinsky*, Braunschweig, May 1926 (no catalogue traced); *Kandinsky*, Stendhal Art Galleries, Los Angeles, February 1936 (15); *Kandinsky*, Galerie Chalette, New York, November–December 1957 (11, repr.) as 'Rocking'; *Wassily Kandinsky*, New Gallery, New York, February 1961 (9, repr.); *Wassily Kandinsky 1866–1944: A Retrospective Exhibition*, Guggenheim Museum, New York, touring exhibition to the Pasadena Art Museum, San Francisco Museum of Art, Portland Art Museum, Marion Koogler McNay Institute, San Antonio, Colorado Springs Fine Arts Center, Baltimore Museum of Art, 1962 (35, repr. in colour); *Proposal for a Collection of Contemporary Art*, Cultural Center of the Philippines Museum, Manila, October–November 1976 (23, repr. in colour): *Fundamental Aspects of Modernism*, Fine Arts Gallery, California State University, Northridge, March–April 1977 (24, repr. in colour); *Early Twentieth Century Masterpainters*, Museum of Albuquerque, June–July 1977 (24, repr. in colour)

Lit: Will Grohmann, *Wassily Kandinsky: Life and Work*, 1959, No.291, pp.195, 335, repr. p.364 (illus. 178) as 'Shaking'

Repr: *Tate Gallery 1978–80*, p.53 in colour

This picture is No.291 in Kandinsky's hand-list, with a note that it was painted in February 1925. It was therefore executed at Weimar, before he moved with the Bauhaus to Dessau in June that year. Its emphasis on regular geometric forms such as circles and triangles is related to the ideas set out in his book *Point and Line to Plane* which he wrote in its final form in the latter part of 1925 and which was published in 1926.

The original German title 'Schaukeln' has sometimes been translated as 'Shaking' or 'Rocking', but the most accurate English equivalent would seem to be 'Swinging'.

There appear to be no drawings or watercolours for this painting.

Phillip King b. 1934

T.2345 **Within** 1978–9

Inscribed 'P. King 1978/9' on wood (not visible when assembled)
Elm wood, slate, oil paint, 87 × 126 × 102 (220 × 320 × 260)
Purchased from the Rowan Gallery (Grant-in-Aid) 1979

Exh: *Phillip King*, Rowan Gallery, March – April 1979 (no catalogue)

Lit: John Glaves-Smith, 'Phillip King/Shelagh Wakeley', *Art Monthly*, May 1979, p.15 repr.; William Feaver, *The Observer*, 1 April 1979; *Arts Review*, XXXI, p.179; Lynne Cooke, 'Phillip King's recent sculpture' *Artscribe*, No.18, July 1979, pp.44–7

Repr: *Art News*, LXXIX, 1980, p.72; *Financial Times*, 3 April 1979; *Art International*, XXIII, September 1979, pp.70–1

King has always been interested in works which employ balancing or leaning and has always attempted to make pieces which appear to have lost their gravitational fixation: they seem to be dematerialised. (He has himself half-seriously suggested a sculptural parody of Archimedes – 'The loss in weight is equal to the gain in quality.')

The use of the cone as a basic sculptural form is found in works such as 'Through' (1965), 'Rosebud' (1962), and 'And the birds began to sing' (1964). In these works King was interested in the object conveying its internal structure from an understanding of the outside. These earlier sculptures are clearly defined objects; the emotional response they evoke, in part triggered off by the colour, is one of simple, often joyful, apprehension of the object.

In the later works which lead up to 'Within' the spaces which the objects inhabit are displayed both on their inside and out. He does not distinguish in importance between inner and outer and from 'Open Bound' (1973) on there is what he refers to as more 'push-and-pull' within the work and a more 'all-over disposition' of interest within it. In these pieces he likens the absence of a major element to modern musical compositions where the work is sustained evenly without emphasis.

This lack of emphasis in part reflects King's working method; he builds from a starting point in a particular direction expecting but not knowing when he might return to the beginning again, whilst expecting to do so. Whilst the process is in a sense additive, King compares it to the carver's methods of making sculpture – revealing something that is already there, like discovering a possible construction from within the material. 'Within' was assembled at Phillip King's Bedfordshire studio. He works by selecting pieces from a pool of material in and around the studio and then altering and reshaping the pieces as he is working. His approach is improvisatory, and he and his assistant try out a number of possibilities for the placement and fixing of each element. Whilst he tries to make the active process as short as possible and the time in between, the time for thinking as long, at no point is it a preconceived process but one that proceeds by trial and error.

King says that he is more interested in the emotional feelings that the sculpture arouses – primitive responses occasioned by their archetypal images.

'Within' is made from thirty-two pieces of slate, steel and elmwood fixed together by bolting, glueing and welding. The form is developed from one large upright elm trunk against which other elements rest or are fixed. A second wooden member leans towards the first with a 'bridge' constructed from glued wooden blocks and steel members dividing them. King recalls that part of his reason for using this was to get the sculpture to 'first-floor level' (to raise part of it from the ground). He began with a simple wooden trunk, but its final form, with slots and fixing points, is very different. He cut and changed the other parts as he worked on the piece not only to fix them together but also for aesthetic reasons. Each element performs a structural function and is used to make up a complex interdependent arrangement. King likens the structure to that of a wall where each part operates in relation to all the others.(He has supplied a set of step-by-step instructions for erecting the piece which reveal a cumulative structural organisation). The steel, for example, has a linear appearance but its function is also to encase other parts and act as support and fixing points for the wood and slate. King used elm in this work because it was cheap and because he liked the natural feel of the material.

R. B. Kitaj b. 1932

T.3055 **The Rise of Fascism** 1975–9

Inscribed 'Kitaj' b.r.
Pastel, charcoal and oil on paper, $33\frac{1}{2} \times 62\frac{5}{16}$ (80.5 × 158.4)
Purchased from Marlborough Fine Art (Grant-in-Aid) 1980

Exh: *R. B. Kitaj: Pastels and Drawings*, Marlborough Fine Art, October–November 1980 (27, repr., and incorrectly dated 1979–80)

Lit: Timothy Hyman, 'Kitaj: A Prodigal, Returning', *Artscribe*, No.25, October 1980, pp.38–9 (repr., and incorrectly dated 1979–80); Sara Selwood in 'Commentary', *Times Literary Supplement*, 24 October 1980, p.1200; *Tate Gallery 1978–80*, p.54 repr. in colour

R. B. Kitaj's first pastels began to appear in 1974 and since 1978 he has worked almost exclusively in that medium, often, as with 'The Rise of Fascism', on a large scale. Apart from the cat in the centre foreground and some other minor areas painted in oil, this work is entirely executed in Roché handmade pastels, with a small amount of charcoal, on Barcham Green 'Porridge' paper. In conversation with the compiler, the artist spoke of his admiration for Degas (and, to a lesser extent, Redon) and of his determination to master the technique of pastel, though there are affinities between Kitaj's use of the medium here and his own characteristic manner of working with thin, dry oil paint on canvas to achieve a grainy surface texture.

Concerning the iconography and genesis of T.3055, Kitaj wrote:

'The central grotesque bather is the fascist. The bather at the left is the beautiful victim. The righthand bather is the ordinary European watching it all happen. A bomber appears in the upper left corner which will cross the English Channel and bring an end to it all one day.

'The three figures were originally drawn on separate sheets of paper from women who posed for me in New York and London. Later, between 1975 and 1979, when I took it into my head to make a composition, I asked a few other women to assume the poses that would represent the bathers in fascist Europe. After the drawings were glued together, the images began to change many times.

'Much of the drawing was ultimately invented but the pose of the righthand figure is based on a picture by the Cordoban painter Romero de Torres (d. 1930).'

The method of fusing together drawings done on separate pieces of paper to produce a single image, which can be seen in several other pastels of this period, (e.g. nos.2, 3, 4, 40 and 41 in the 1980 Marlborough exhibition catalogue, op. cit.), contributes to the ambiguous relationship, both physical and psychological, between the three figures in T.3055. While one effect of this cutting and joining is to emphasise the fragmentary nature of the composition, Kitaj also makes use of the edges of the paper to reinforce contour and volume. When questioned about the extreme anatomical foreshortening in the torso of the left-hand bather the artist replied that it was in fact possible and that a source existed for it in a pornographic magazine. 'The often unlikely joining', Kitaj added, 'of limbs and postures in Cézanne's Bather compositions are also entrenched in one's memory . . . but the pose *was* taken from the *life*.'

Despite the hieratic arrangement of figures in T.3055, the artist denied any obvious symbolic content beyond the simple allegory described above. Asked whether the presence of a black cat in the context of female nudes was deliberately intended to evoke traditional associations of the prostitute or courtesan, Kitaj thought that it suggested instead only a general sense of mystery and evil. He agreed that the picture as a whole could be read as an ironic inversion of the classical bathers subject and said that the brutal elements in its imagery – the fascist with her pistol and the Fortress bomber – were meant to convey an atmosphere of menace and unease, 'unlike the sublime apparatus of those great familiar bathers of 80 years ago in French painting.'

The above entry is based on a conversation with the artist (11 April 1980) and a letter from him (postmarked 21 April 1980). It has been edited and approved by him.

Eileen Lawrence b. 1946

T.2407 **Prayer Stick I** 1977

Inscribed 'Prayer Stick' b.l. and 'Eileen Lawrence' b.r.
Watercolour, cotton tape and paper collage, 96 × 6 (244 × 15.3)
Presented by the Contemporary Art Society 1979

Prov: Purchased by the Contemporary Art Society 1977

Exh: *10th Paris Biennale*, Palais de Tokyo and Musée d'Art Moderne de la Ville de Paris, September – November 1977 (Eileen Lawrence 11); *Eileen Lawrence*, Arnolfini Gallery, Bristol, January – February 1978 (no catalogue); *Eileen Lawrence: Scrolls*, Chapter Gallery, Cardiff, March – April 1978 (no catalogue)

Lit: *Catalogue of 10th Paris Biennale*, 1977 p.144; *Arnolfini Review*, January 1978

Eileen Lawrence began depicting feathers in her paintings in 1971 or 1972 and soon afterwards began to include bird's eggs in her imagery. 'Prayer Stick I' was painted at her studio at 25 Haddington Place, Edinburgh and was one of twenty works based on the lines:

Sitting motionless
Waiting
For winter's long shadows
To stretch into spring
Beneath my window
A bird builds its nest

In December 1977 the artist wrote (published in *Skira Annual 1977*), 'The bird and the shadows were real. Around March 1977, perhaps a week before the shadows, the bird could be seen bringing to a crack in the stonework beneath my window ledge, the fabric that would build its nest. The activity stopped shortly after the shadows, the bird and the nest both disappeared. Strong winds had obviously destroyed what had been built. I do not know what happened to the bird; I hope it chose a more sheltered place to rebuild. I am exploring the way in which my medium, watercolour, fuses with the support, paper. I work with a great many different paper surfaces including paper I make myself. Into these handmade papers I incorporate small fragments of my subject matter, real feathers, eggs and reeds; these are laid alongside painted images of the same subject matter. I am now also incorporatng the painted image directly into the handmade papers. This somewhat illusionistic device involves a partial destruction of the painted image, in some sense a symbolic act, detailed watercolours of feathers, eggs and reeds are painted then torn up, they are introduced into the basic paper pulp and reprocessed into a sheet of handmade paper; this paper also has in it the real fragments of my subject matter.

By tearing up the painted image I do not consider that I am indulging in a negative act, or an emotional activity, but am making a very serious and positive attempt to expand the traditional limitations of my medium, water-colour on paper. I respect the skill which I have aquired over the years but I have no desire to rely totally upon a certain kind of technical facility. Once one is aware of one's limitations one can do something about pushing the boundaries of those limitations. "Decisiveness and energy must take the place of the inertia and indifference that have led to decay in order that the ending may be followed by a new beginning." I CHING, Wilhelm translation, p.76.'

'Prayer Stick I' was painted on English and Japanese papers and on recycled paper discarded in the course of her painting.

This catalogue entry is based on information supplied by the artist and approved by her.

Louis le Brocquy b. 1916

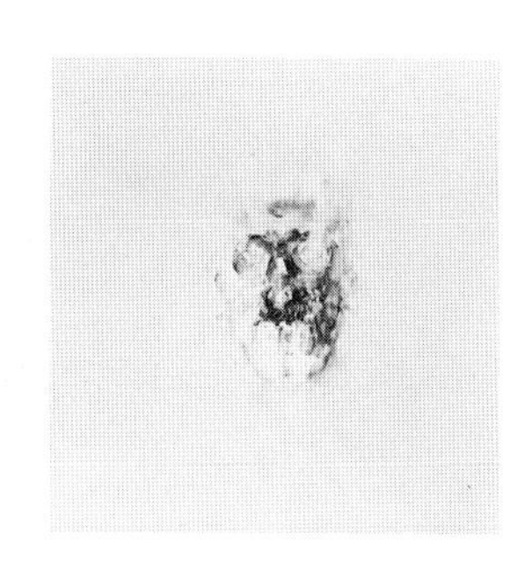

T.2335 **Study towards an Image of James Joyce** 1977

Inscribed 'LE BROCQUY/77' on back of canvas
Oil on canvas, $27\frac{1}{4} \times 27\frac{1}{4}$ (69.2 × 69.2)
Purchased from the artist through Gimpel Fils (Grant-in-Aid) 1979

Exh: *Louis le Brocquy: Studies towards an Image of James Joyce*, Galleria d'Arte San Marco dei Giustiniani, Genoa, November – December 1977 (works not numbered, as 'Study 66', repr.); Gimpel & Hanover Galerie, Zurich, January – February 1978 (works not numbered, repr.); Gimpel Fils, March – April 1978 (works not numbered, repr.); Arts Council Gallery, Belfast, May 1978 (works not numbered, repr.); Hugh Lane Municipal Gallery of Modern Art, Dublin, June – July 1978 (works not numbered, repr.); Gimpel & Weitzenhoffer, New York, September – October 1978 (works not numbered, repr.); Waddington Galleries, Montreal, November 1978 (works not numbered, repr.); Waddington Galleries, Toronto, December 1978 (works not numbered, repr.)

Lit: Michael Peppiatt, 'Interview with Louis le Brocquy', *Art International*, XXIII, No.7, October 1979, pp.60–6

Louis le Brocquy's fascination with heads began in 1963 when he saw the Melanesian–Polynesian images in the Musée de l'Homme in Paris (skulls, partly remodelled in clay, then painted in a decorative way), and he began shortly afterwards to paint disembodied heads, or rather heads seen in complete isolation. This interest was reinforced later by the discovery in 1965 of a further head cult near Aix-en-Provence, this time of Celtic or Celto–Ligurean origin, which he says provided a confirmatory revelation to him of the image of the head as a kind of magic box that holds the spirit prisoner. As he told Michael Peppiatt: 'I'm fascinated by appearances and what they reveal, the way expressions change from instant to instant in some people because of the vitality rising within them and transforming them the whole time. So the head, for me at least, is a paradox, both hiding or masking the spirit and revealing or incarnating it.'

Though most of his early studies had generic titles such as 'Head' or 'Ancestral Head', there were also a few based on the heads of friends or famous writers such as Keats or James Joyce. However it was only in 1975 that he began to make extensive, systematic series of the same person, starting with one of W. B. Yeats, and following with series of Joyce, Federico Garcia Lorca, Samuel Beckett and Francis Bacon, in that order. He deliberately chose individuals of outstanding talent who were also vulnerable and poignant as human beings because of their suffering in life and the originality and breadth of their vision. In each case he steeped himself as deeply as possible in their work before beginning to paint. Though he knew Yeats, Beckett and Bacon, he had never met Joyce or, of course, Lorca. His paintings and drawings were made with reference to numerous photographs of them and in Joyce's case to a bronze cast of his death mask which he owns and has hanging on the wall. These images often gave differing impressions and he made no attempt to resolve them into a final, definitive image. Many of the paintings were made without reference to a photograph while painting, but if he used photographs, he tended to have two or more beside him at the same time.

The catalogue of the touring exhibition *Louis le Brocquy: Studies towards an Image of James Joyce* (which consisted of 24 charcoal drawings of Joyce, 35 watercolours, and 10 oils, all executed in 1977) included the following note by the artist, dated March 1977:

'It is said that no Dubliner can quite escape from the microcosmic world of Dublin, and in this I am certainly no exception. James Joyce is the apotheosis, the archetype of our kind and it seems to me that in him – behind the volatile arrangement of his features – lies his unique evocation of that small city, large as life and therefore poignant everywhere. But to a Dublin man, peering at Joyce, a particular nostalgia is added to the universal "epiphany", and this perhaps enables me to grope for something of my own experience within the ever-changing landscape of his face, within the various and contradictory photographs of his head which surround me, within my bronze death-mask of him and, I suppose, within the recesses of my own mind. Indeed I think that this preoccupation of mine is not altogether unlike that of the Celts of prehistory, with their oracular cult of the human head, the mysterious box which holds the spirit prisoner.

'To attempt today a portrait, a single static image of a great artist such as Joyce, appears to me to be futile as well as impertinent. Long conditioned by photographs, the cinema and psychology, we now perceive the human individual as facetted, kinetic. And so I have tried as objectively as possible to draw from the depths of paper or canvas these changing and even contradictory traces of the man. In this fragmentary search I have seemed at times to encroach on archeological ground. Is there an archaeology of the spirit? Certainly neither my will nor my skill has played any essential part in these studies. For the fact is that many of them emerged entirely under my ignorant left hand – my right hand being for some months immobilised in plaster. So it would appear that no dexterity whatever was involved in forming these images, which tended to emerge automatically, so to speak, jerked into coherence by a series of scrutinised accidents, impelled by my curiosity to discover something of the man and, within him, the inverted mirror-room of my own experience.'

Though the series only began in 1977, he had made several earlier studies in oil of James Joyce, including 'Image of James Joyce as a Boy' 1964 (now in the Hirshhorn Museum, Washington) and four pictures of 1964, 1967, 1969 and 1972 all entitled 'Reconstructed Head of James Joyce'. He told Michael Peppiatt that he must have made altogether something like 120 studies of Joyce, if one counts all the watercolours and charcoal drawings as well as the oils.

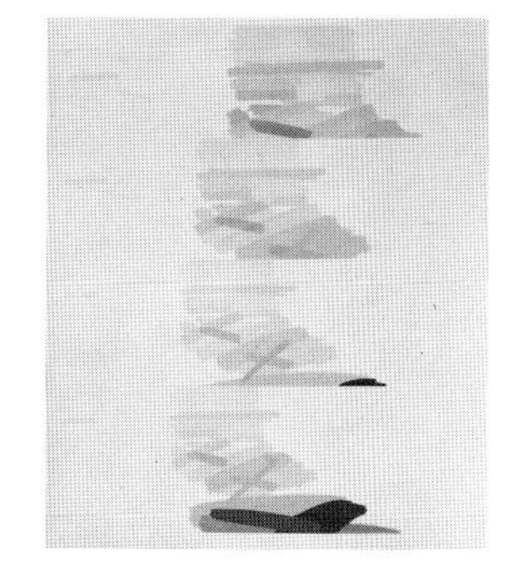

John Loker b. 1938

T.2267 **Four Shifts I** 1977–8

Inscribed on original stretcher '"FOUR SHIFTS I" John Loker'
Acrylic on canvas, 84 × 72 (216.5 × 183)
Purchased from the Angela Flowers Gallery (Knapping Fund) 1978
Exh: John Loker, Paintings and Drawings, Angela Flowers Gallery, March – April 1978 (no catalogue, listed on announcement card)

Since 1972, John Loker's paintings have been based on, or suggested by landscape. The majority have been variations on four principal themes, to which the artist has given the following generic titles, 'Horizons' (1972–4), 'Extracts' (1974–80), 'Shifts' (1977–80) and 'Sections' (1979–). All these groups have formal roots in a series of abstract horizontal fibreglass and resin wall reliefs, composed of two or more adjoining sections, which Loker made between 1968 and 1970, (although, at that time, he had not considered a landscape connection). In 1971, Angela Flowers invited him to submit a work for an exhibition of artists' postcards and he made a collage of six discrete panoramic landscape photographs, butted together in pairs to form three parallel horizontal bars. The blocks of landscape in this work, 'Six Horizons' (1971), resembled the wedge-shaped perspectival planes of Loker's earlier abstract panels, which, because of their width, had to be 'scanned' or read in sections, the joins between panels acting as points of focus. The vertical joins between the paired photographs in the postcard collage accentuated the horizontality of the work, while at the same time calling attention to three artificially created horizon lines. However, the photographs introduced a further dimension by dealing with the illusion of spatial recession in a literal, figurative sense. Reading downwards from the top left panel, the three 'horizons' established a distant view, a middle ground and a foreground, so that the eye was increasingly drawn into the landscape while travelling down the work.

Loker's discovery of a figurative equivalent for his formal concerns led next to a series of paintings based on photographs he took of a Dorset coastline in 1971. In 'Coast 2', (1973) (Coll. Rugby City Art Gallery) three atmospheric views of the same double horizon line created by beach and sea are represented almost filmically by three 'frames' isolated against a unified sprayed background. Running down the centre of the work, three small grey-blue blocks, (a concrete pillbox on the beach) focus the eye and, by their fractionally altered relationship with beach and sea in each 'frame', record the artist's shifting viewpoint, his gradual movement into the landscape when photographing it. By 1974 Loker had stopped working with photographs and in the 'Extracts' & 'Shifts' series gradually moved away from anecdotal references which could lead to identification with features in specific landscapes.

The artist worked on 'Four Shifts I' for a period of approximately three months in tandem with 'Four Shifts Centre I' (1977–8) (coll. Wetering Galerie, Amsterdam), which was also exhibited at Angela Flowers, March – April 1978. These, together with a slightly later painting, 'Four Shifts Centre II' (1978) (coll. the artist) are seen by Loker as an informal group relating to an experience of landscape, rather than to any specific place. The title of T.2267 describes four shifting views of a horizontal slice of 'landscape'. It is composed on a drawn grid which gradually enlarges towards the top of the painting. As the scale of the grid changes in each section, so the blocks of colour are enlarged and intensified as they move up the surface, and, in a process resembling photographic enlargement, certain peripheral areas described in the lower sections are lost, as 'details' are clarified towards the top. The blocks of colour are built up diagonally and horizontally, suggesting fragments of hills and sky and because of their altered scale in each section they recreate the sensation of travelling over and into a landscape, where distant features appear static and the foreground gradually enlarges and slips away. However, the painting does not describe actual topographical features and while it calls up an experience of the external world, an encounter with nature, its strong interior rhythms, in relation to both colour and form, constantly relocate the eye on the surface of the canvas and facilitate an abstract or formal reading. Loker paints from the top of the canvas down and generally works with his canvas on the flat in the early stages. He regards painting as a reductive process; as the colours in T.2267 were built up, he varied their intensity in the lower sections and partially obscured the lines of the grid with layers of sprayed paint. In order to do this, he used a fixative diffuser, which enabled him to exercise a greater degree of control than would have been possible with a spray-gun. When repeating and adjusting a mark, Loker consciously tries to recall the speed or gesture with which the original was made, finding in this intuitive approach a more accurate way of recreating his forms than any attempt to copy their outward appearances. His colours, in this case predominantly pale greys, blues, mauves and pinks against a subtle grey-blue background, are carefully orchestrated in relation to the changing scale of each mark.

Loker regards the process of drawing as independent from, but complementary to his painting. He made eight drawings relating to 'Four Shifts I'. Four of these, 'Four Shifts 1–4' (1 & 2 1977; 3 & 4 1978) were made concurrently with the painting and exhibited at Angela Flowers with it. A further four drawings 'Pennine Shifts 1–4' were worked on subsequently and exhibited at the Park Square Gallery, Leeds and the Wetering Galerie, in 1978. Most of these drawings are in private collections in Holland.

This entry is based on a conversation with the artist (22 August 1980). It has been read and approved by him.

Richard Long b. 1945

T.3027 **Slate Circle** 1979

Not inscribed
Slate, 214 pieces, diameter 260 (660 approx)
Presented by Anthony d'Offay 1980
Exh: *Richard Long*, Museum of Modern Art, Oxford, November – December 1979 (no catalogue)

The Slate Circle is made by laying 214 stones in a haphazard pattern within a circle drawn on the ground in pencil with a diameter of 6.60 metres. None of the stones touch, and they are chosen at random except that there should be a fairly even distribution of sizes and lengths. The Gallery has the certificate of ownership which accompanies the work, giving directions for laying the slate.

Long chose the slate for this piece from a quarry in mid-Wales that he had passed whilst completing part of a piece entitled 'Four Walks: Winter 1977', the specific walk being 'From the source of the River Severn to the summit of Snowdon, 60 miles'. (This is the only connection between the sculpture and the walk).

A similar work using 168 slate pieces from the same quarry was shown in *Un Certain Art Anglais* at ARC, Paris, and the Van Abbemuseum, Eindhoven in 1979.

Conroy Maddox b. 1912

T.3052 **Passage de l'Opéra** 1940

Inscribed 'Conroy Maddox' b.r. and, on back of canvas, 'PASSAGE DE L'OPÉRA/OIL 1940/CONROY MADDOX' and 'CONROY MADDOX/11 HIGHFIELD RD/EDGBASTON/BIRMINGHAM'
Oil on canvas, 54 × 37 (137.2 × 94)
Purchased from the Mayor Gallery (Grant-in-Aid) 1980

Prov: James Kirkman, London (purchased from the artist through the Hamet Gallery 1971); Hamet Gallery, London; Mayor Gallery London
Exh: Mixed exhibition, Birmingham Royal Society of Arts Gallery, *c.*1947; *Britain's Contribution to Surrealism*, Hamet Gallery, November 1971 (54, repr.); *Conroy Maddox*, Hamet Gallery, January - February 1972 (6); *Dada and Surrealism Reviewed,* Hayward Gallery, January - March 1978 (14.19)
Lit: Simon Wilson, *Surrealist Painting*, 1975, p.11, repr. pl.20 in colour
Repr: John Sunderland, *Painting in Britain 1525–1975*, 1976, pl.215 in colour; Richard Shone, *The Century of Change: British Painting since 1900*, 1977, pl.102 in colour

The *Passage de l'Opera*, one of the old arcades of Paris, was the subject of a long essay evoking its poetry and mystery by the Surrealist writer Louis Aragon written in 1924 and published in 1926 as part of a compilation titled *Le Paysan de Paris.* It subsequently became a place of special significance for all the Surrealist group. According to Aragon the Passage de l'Opéra ran from the Rue Chauchat to the Boulevard des Italiens before it was swept away by the extension of the Boulevard Haussmann to its present junction with the Boulevard des Italiens.

In a letter to the compiler of 8 January 1975 (T.G. Archive 7510.13) the artist wrote: 'You asked if I had any comment to make about my painting, Passage de l'Opéra. It was certainly inspired by my reading of Louis Aragon's "Le Paysan de Paris" and seeing, since I cannot now recollect whether the actual passage existed during my visits between 1937 and 1939, the actual place or an old photograph. The street and places had a particular fascination to the Surrealists and the passage was no exception. Aragon points out that his wanderings around the Passage de l'Opéra were without purpose, yet he waited for something to happen, something strange or abnormal so as to permit him a glimpse of a "new order of things". Such experiences, however incongruous and enigmatic were conducive to Surrealism's attraction to the marvellous. The passage was well known as a meeting place among the prostitutes, which by its challenge to the respectability of society was welcomed by the group.

'The picture was not painted until I returned to England, then entirely from memory. Certainly over a year after I had seen, either the place or a photograph. It was not until the Cardinal and Short book "Surrealism, Permanent Revelation" was published in 1970 [London, Studio Vista] that I again saw a photograph of the passage and was able to check the accuracy of my memory. Apart from some architectural discrepancies, the lion in the foreground was certainly not present and obviously never had been in spite of my conviction that such a statue existed near the entrance. Although it is impossible to recall now, I was probably aware of a collage by Max Ernst titled "The Lion of Belfort" which may, subconsciously, have had some influence at that time.

'Since the painting is carried out in tones of grey, it might suggest that it was a photograph, rather than the actual place that influenced the painting.'

The Lion of Belfort is a gigantic stone recumbent lion erected outside the fortified French border city of Belfort to commemorate the 104 day siege of the city during the Franco–Prussian War of 1870–1. There is a smaller bronze version of it, well known to Conroy Maddox, in Paris at the corner of the Cimetière du Sud (dit de Montparnasse) nearest the Place Denfert-Rochereau. The work by the Surrealist artist Max Ernst referred to by Conroy Maddox is volume one of Ernst's five volume collage novel published in 1934, *Une Semaine de Bonté.* Each volume is separately titled, the title of volume one being *Le Lion de Belfort.* It consists of 35 separate untitled collages many of which contain lion imagery. Of the 35 the one which seems most closely to relate to T.3052 is in fact the very first in the volume.

Kasimir Malevich 1878–1935

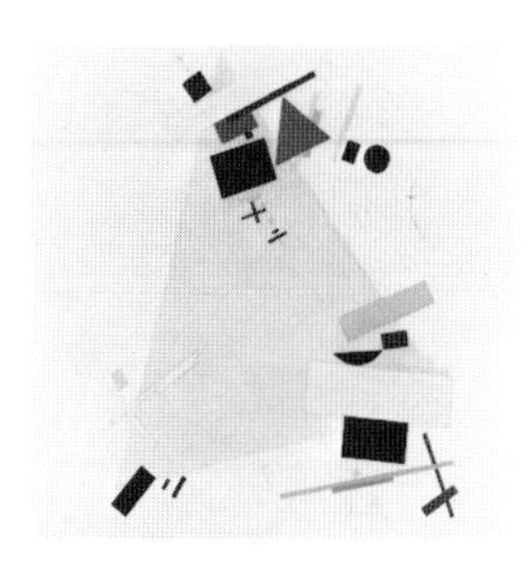

T.2319 **Dynamic Suprematism** *c.*1915–16

Inscribed 'Supremus/N57/Kazimir Malevich/Moskva/1916' on back of canvas (Kazimir Malevich and Moskva in cyrillic old style)
Oil on canvas, $31\frac{5}{8} \times 31\frac{5}{8}$ (80.2 × 80.3)
Purchased from Comvalor Finanz AG through Thomas Gibson Fine Art Ltd. (Grant-in-Aid) with aid from the Friends of the Tate Gallery, the Gytha Trust, the Trustees of the Tate Gallery and Discretionery Funds 1978

Prov: Tretyakov Gallery, Moscow (purchased from the artist 1929); Comvalor Finanz AG, Zug

Exh: *Bubnovy Balet* (Jack of Diamonds), Moscow, November 1916 (among 140–99, all listed as 'Suprematism of Painting'); *Vystavka proizvedenii K.S. Malevicha*, Tretyakov Gallery, Moscow, 1929 (works not listed); *Khudozhniki RSFSR za 15 let*, Russian Museum, Leningrad, November 1932 – May 1933 (1239) as 'Dynamic Colour Composition'; Historical Museum, Moscow, June 1933 (1239)

Lit: Troels Andersen, *Malevich: Catalogue raisonné of the Berlin Exhibition 1927, including the Collection of the Stedelijk Museum Amsterdam*, Amsterdam 1970, p.106 (note on no.91), repr. p.29 as 'Dynamic Suprematism' 1916

Repr: Camilla Gray, *The Great Experiment: Russian Art 1863–1922,* 1962, pl. XVI in colour as 'Dynamic Suprematism' 1916; Kasimir Malewitsch, *Suprematismus – Die gegenstandlose Welt,* Cologne 1962, pl.15; *Tate Gallery 1978–80*, p.55 in colour

This picture belonged for over forty years to the Tretyakov Gallery in Moscow. According to information from I. P. Gorin of the Ministry of Culture of the USSR, it was shown in the three exhibitions listed above and was acquired in 1929 from an exhibition (presumably the Malevich retrospective at the Tretyakov Gallery itself). A certificate from A. G. Khalturin, head of the Department of Visual Arts and the Preservation of Monuments of the Ministry of Culture of the USSR confirms that permission was given in December 1975 for it to be exported from the Soviet Union.

The canvas is inscribed on the back 'Supremus No.57 Kazimir Malevich Moscow 1916'. A painting inscribed 'Supremus No.50' belongs to the Stedelijk Museum, Amsterdam, and two entitled 'Supremus 56' and '58' are kept in the Russian Museum, Leningrad. It is possible that these numbers refer to the exhibition *0.10 Poslandnaya futuristicheskaya vystavka* at the Art Bureau N.E. Dobychina, Moscow, in December 1915 – January 1916 in which nos.48–59 were works by Malevich grouped together as 'Painterly Masses in Movement' (nos. 60–77, in contrast, were works by Malevich listed as 'Painterly Masses in Two Dimensions in a State of Rest'), though the opening date, 19 December 1915, conflicts with the date 1916 on the back of the picture. The painting in the Stedelijk Museum inscribed 'Supremus N 50' is also dated on the back 1916.

The present work bears the stamp of the exhibition *Khudozhniki RSFSR za 15 let* (Artists in the RSFSR through 15 years) on the stretcher and seems to have been listed in the catalogue as 'Dynamic Colour Composition', but has been known in recent years as 'Dynamic Suprematism'. A closely related pencil drawing measuring 34.2 × 33.8 cm was placed on extended loan to the Museum of Modern Art, New York, in 1935 but disappeared by 1938 and is still untraced. It is reproduced by Troels Andersen on p.106 of his book with a note that it is a copy of the present work, then still in the Tretyakov Gallery. The fact that there are various minor differences, such as fewer shapes and slight modifications in the colours and the placing of the forms, suggest that it may equally well have been done as a preliminary study. However X-ray photographs of the painting itself confirm the uniformity of the paint layer and the absence of any lower layers, so the composition seems to have been completely worked out in advance and the forms drawn straight onto the canvas.

Manolo Millares 1926–72

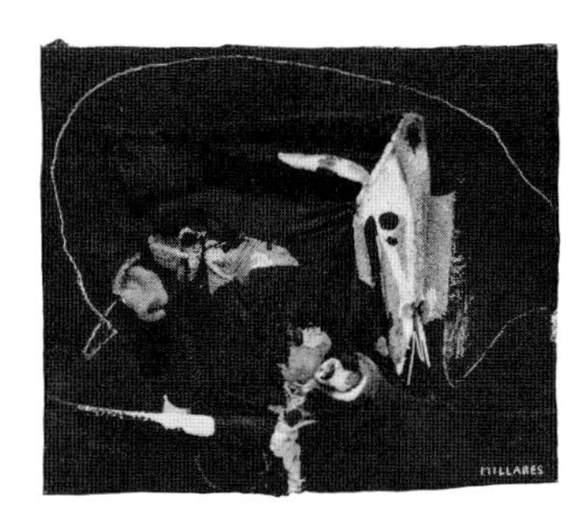

T.2385 **Painting** 1964

Inscribed 'MILLARES' b.r. and 'MILLARES–CUADRO 1964' on stretcher
Acrylic on burlap, $15\frac{3}{8} \times 18\frac{1}{4} \times 4$ (39 × 46.3 × 10)
Presented by Sir George Labouchere through the Friends of the Tate Gallery 1979

Prov: Sir George Labouchere, Madrid and Bridgnorth (purchased from the artist through the Galería Juana Mordó, Madrid, *c.*1964–5)

Exh: *Colección del Excmo. Sr. George Labouchere,* Museo Nacional Arte Contemporánea, Madrid, June 1965 (10)

Repr: *The Friends of the Tate Gallery: Annual Report 1st May 1979 – 30th April 1980*, 1980, p.15

Michael Moon b. 1937

T.2321 **Table** 1978

Not inscribed
Acrylic on cotton duck and calico, $83\frac{1}{2} \times 63 \times 3\frac{3}{4}$ (212.1 × 160.1 × 9.6)
Purchased from the Waddington Galleries (Knapping Fund) 1978

Exh: *Recent Works by Michael Moon.* Waddington Galleries, November – December 1978 (no catalogue)

The technique of casting from objects in his studio, the tools of the trade, had been developed by Moon since 1976. A full description of the process used to make 'Drawing' 1976 (T.2073) can be found in *The Tate Gallery 1976–8*: he used a similar process for 'Table'. This work consists of four superimposed layers of canvas taken from the surfaces of his studio table.

Moon's interest in earlier art, particularly Cézanne, Bonnard and Cubism can be found in this work. He is concerned not only with the method of production and the nature of the objects but also with specific compositional problems. He descibes the largest panel of 'Table' as having the slight perspectival feeling of an up-tilted plane similar to Bonnard. The superimposition of further planes and their compositional arrangement he likens to Cubist works.

In his earlier 'strip paintings' (cf. T.1255, 'Untitled' 1970) Moon had made careful gradations of colour over a surface. He returns to this here in the two uppermost panels where he covered the underside of the table with pigment which ranges from red to orange. He used the underside both because he wanted 'clean' pulls from the surface and because he was interested in the spatial ambiguity which results from upturning the table and applying it to the surface of the painting. (At one time he had planned to indicate the legs of the table projecting from the work). The other panels are cast from the table top and bear the traces of earlier workings and earlier castings: Moon says that this gives them a 'lived-in feeling'. The largest panel is made up of a number of the table panels; they are not joined together in a precise way, but the overall shape is important.

This work was shown alongside a group of similar pieces which Moon feels is mid-way towards a return for him to painting. He found that the strip paintings had become systematic and mechanical and used the casting method as a way to make objects. His increased interventions in this work (by applying colour and superimposing casts), he would like to think might eventually lead him back to facing a blank canvas again. He works entirely from the objects around him, taking a cast and superimposing the results loose on the wall before making stretchers for the work and putting it together. He emphasises that his current work is concerned with objects that are 'charts of an activity', and is happy to incorporate chance occurrences when the canvas is stripped from the object.

This information was drawn from a conversation with the artist on 20 November 1980. The entry has been approved by the artist.

Henry Moore, O.M., C.H. b. 1898

T.2269 **Three Points** 1939–40

Not inscribed
Bronze, 5½ × 7½ × 3¾ (14 × 19 × 9.5)
Presented by the artist 1978

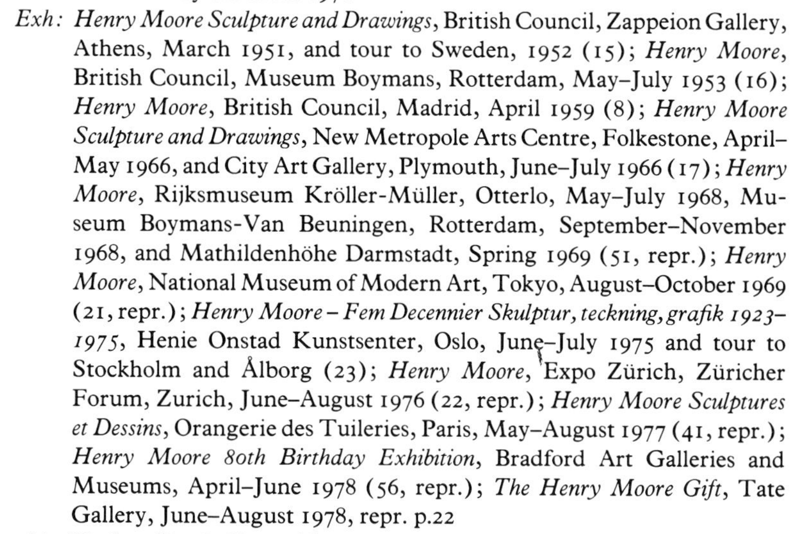

Exh: *Henry Moore Sculpture and Drawings*, British Council, Zappeion Gallery, Athens, March 1951, and tour to Sweden, 1952 (15); *Henry Moore*, British Council, Museum Boymans, Rotterdam, May–July 1953 (16); *Henry Moore*, British Council, Madrid, April 1959 (8); *Henry Moore Sculpture and Drawings*, New Metropole Arts Centre, Folkestone, April–May 1966, and City Art Gallery, Plymouth, June–July 1966 (17); *Henry Moore*, Rijksmuseum Kröller-Müller, Otterlo, May–July 1968, Museum Boymans-Van Beuningen, Rotterdam, September–November 1968, and Mathildenhöhe Darmstadt, Spring 1969 (51, repr.); *Henry Moore*, National Museum of Modern Art, Tokyo, August–October 1969 (21, repr.); *Henry Moore – Fem Decennier Skulptur, teckning, grafik 1923–1975*, Henie Onstad Kunstsenter, Oslo, June–July 1975 and tour to Stockholm and Ålborg (23); *Henry Moore*, Expo Zürich, Züricher Forum, Zurich, June–August 1976 (22, repr.); *Henry Moore Sculptures et Dessins*, Orangerie des Tuileries, Paris, May–August 1977 (41, repr.); *Henry Moore 80th Birthday Exhibition*, Bradford Art Galleries and Museums, April–June 1978 (56, repr.); *The Henry Moore Gift*, Tate Gallery, June–August 1978, repr. p.22

Lit: Herbert Read, *Henry Moore*, 1965, p.125 (original lead version repr. pl. 108); David Sylvester, catalogue of *Henry Moore*, Tate Gallery, 1968, pp.36–7 (repr. pl.37 and on cover); Robert Melville, *Henry Moore Sculpture and Drawings 1921–1969*, 1970, pp.20–21 (repr. pl.210); Alan G. Wilkinson, catalogue of *The Drawings of Henry Moore*, Art Gallery of Ontario, Toronto, November–December 1977, and tour to Japan and at Tate Gallery, June–August 1978, p.99, no.125; Alan G. Wilkinson, *The Moore Collection in the Art Gallery of Ontario*, Toronto, 1979, p.204 (another cast repr. fig.167)

Repr: *London Bulletin*, 18–20, June 1940, p.21 (original lead version); Herbert Read (intro.), *Henry Moore Sculpture and Drawings*, 1944, pl.103b (lead), and David Sylvester, ed., ibid., 4th, completely revised edition, 1957, no.211; Will Grohmann, *The Art of Henry Moore*, 1960, pl.75, as 'Three Peaks'; Elda Fezzi, *Henry Moore*, Florence, 1971, pl.9 in colour

The work is no.211 in the Lund Humphries catalogue of Moore's sculptures. It exists in three different materials: lead, cast iron and bronze. The lead version is the earliest and was first shown at the Leicester Galleries in February 1940 in an exhibition which Moore shared with Anthony Gross and Ivon Hitchens. The Tate's bronze is from the original edition of two, the other being in the collection of the Kunsternes Hus, Oslo. A further edition of eight bronzes was cast from the lead in 1958 and published by Marlborough Fine Art.

The idea for the sculpture came from a sheet of drawings of 'Pointed Forms' 1939 (Albertina, Vienna, repr. Read, op. cit., pl.107). Wilkinson dates Moore's interest in pointed forms to 'a sketch of *c.*1938 . . . inscribed "Do drawings of two forms practically touching"' (op. cit., 1979, fig.165). Considering David Sylvester's suggestion, made in the Tate exhibition catalogue of 1968, that the inspiration for 'Three Points' came from the pinching of Gabrielle d'Estrées' nipple in the famous School of Fontainebleau double portrait, Wilkinson comments: 'he [Moore] said that it was a mistake to try to track down a single source for "Three Points"' (ibid.). In conversation with the compiler (12 December 1980), the artist said that it was important that the points in the sculpture should not touch (in some bronzes, due to a fault in the casting, the points actually meet) because he wanted the work to convey a sense of anticipation and anxiety. He used the analogy of the sparking plug to illustrate this idea. When asked if the spiky forms in T.2269, with their aggressive and perhaps also phallic connotations, were derived from surrealist imagery – for example, the surrealist sculptures of Giacometti – Moore said that this was certainly one possible influence as Surrealism was very much in the air when he made the work.

Sharp, pointed forms occasionally appear in other sculptures by Moore (see, for example, T.2273 below) but it was not until the late 1960s, in such works as 'Spindle Piece' (Lund Humphries 592), 'Oval with Points' (L.H. 596) and 'Pointed Torso' (L.H. 601), that the artist returned to the theme in full and on a much larger scale. For a discussion of the pointing and touching motives in Moore's late work, see Alan Bowness, Introduction to *Henry Moore Sculpture 1964–73* (L.H. Vol. 4), 1977, p.11.

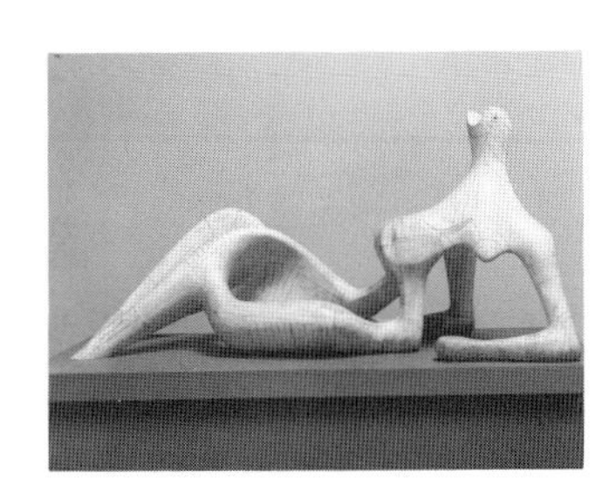

T.2270 **Reclining Figure** 1951

Not inscribed
Plaster, $41\frac{1}{2} \times 89\frac{1}{2} \times 35\frac{1}{8}$ (105.5 × 227 × 89)
Presented by the artist 1978

Exh: *Henry Moore: an exhibition of Sculpture from 1950–1960*, Whitechapel Art Gallery, December 1960–January 1961 (3, bronze cast repr.); *Henry Moore Sculptures et Dessins*, Orangerie des Tuileries, Paris, May–August 1977 (60, repr.); *The Henry Moore Gift*, Tate Gallery, June–August 1978, repr. p.27

Lit: *Sculpture and Drawings by Henry Moore*, Tate Gallery, May–July 1951 (catalogue by David Sylvester) pp.14–15; Erich Neumann, *The Archetypal World of Henry Moore*, 1959, pp.108–9; Will Grohmann, *The Art of Henry Moore*, 1960, p.53; Philip James (ed.), *Henry Moore on Sculpture*, 1966, pp.101, 118 (bronze repr. pl.37, 38); David Sylvester, catalogue of *Henry Moore*, Tate Gallery, July–September 1968, p.53; John Hedgecoe and Henry Moore, *Henry Moore*, 1968, pp.188, 197, 263; John Russell, *Henry Moore*, 1968, pp.125–7; Robert Melville, *Henry Moore Sculpture and Drawings 1921–1969*, 1970, p.167; Mary Banham and Bevis Hillier (ed.), *A Tonic to the Nation*, 1976, pp.83, 182 (a photograph of the artist working on the plaster repr. p.56); Alan G. Wilkinson, catalogue of *The Drawings of Henry Moore*, Art Gallery of Ontario, Toronto, November–December 1977, and tour to Japan and at Tate Gallery, June–August 1978, p.43; Alan G. Wilkinson, *The Moore Collection in the Art Gallery of Ontario*, Toronto, 1979, pp.114–16 (four views of plaster cast repr.)

Repr: Elda Fezzi, *Henry Moore*, Florence, 1971, pl.15 (detail, in colour); Giulio Carlo Argan, *Henry Moore*, Milan, 1971, pl.105

This work is the original plaster from which the bronze (Lund Humphries 293), commissioned by the Arts Council for the Festival of Britain and exhibited on the South Bank in the summer of 1951, was cast. An edition of five bronzes was made; the cast shown on the South Bank was loaned to Leeds City Art Gallery after the Festival and placed in the grounds of Temple Newsam House, where it was vandalised during the night of 3–4 November 1953. In 1956 it was removed from public view and in 1961 lent to the Scottish National Gallery of Modern Art. Its ownership was later transferred to the Scottish Arts Council who presented it to the National Galleries of Scotland in 1969. Another bronze cast is in the Musée National d'Art Moderne, Paris. The Moore Collection, Art Gallery of Ontario, owns a plaster cast taken, with the artist's permission, from the original plaster by one of Moore's assistants for use by the British Council in their exhibitions of Moore's work which toured Europe, Canada, New Zealand and South Africa between 1953 and 1959.

The 'Reclining Figure' is based on sketches (L.H. vol. 2, pl.100) and maquettes executed in 1950 (L.H. 292a, b and 292). The relationship of T.2270 to the earlier 'Four-Piece Composition: Reclining Figure' 1934 (T.2054) is discussed in the Tate Gallery's *Illustrated Catalogue of Acquisitions* for 1976–8, p.120: in particular, the way dismemberment or separation of solid forms leads in Moore's work to the opening out of a single unified form in space such as is realised for the first time in the 1951 'Reclining Figure'. In the 1968 book with John Hedgecoe, op. cit., Moore mentions the sculpture as being one of a group of key works in his *oeuvre*. 'The "Festival Reclining Figure"', he wrote, 'is perhaps my first sculpture where the space and the form are completely dependent on and inseparable from each other. I had reached the stage where I wanted my sculpture to be truly three-dimensional. In my earliest use of holes in sculpture, the holes were features in themselves. Now the space and form are so naturally fused that they are one.' (p.188). In conversation with the compiler (12 December 1980), the artist repeated his stated belief that 'form and space are one and the same thing' and that 'in order to understand form . . . you must understand the space that it would displace if it were taken away.' (ibid., p.118)

T.2270 is remarkable not only for this interpenetration of solid and void but also for the use of thin strings stuck to its surface (in the bronze casts these appear as ridges), which serve to heighten the viewer's perception of volume by drawing his eye across the forms. Neumann, op. cit., pp.98–9, speculates on the meaning of the scooped-out head, which resembles a mouth cavity in T.2270, and other simplified heads in Moore's work. This particular motif goes back at least as far as the 1934 'Four-Piece Composition', T.2054 (see above).

With regard to the siting on the South Bank of the original bronze cast of 'Reclining Figure', the artist told the compiler (12 December 1980) that the sculpture was not made with a specific architectural relationship in mind and that he was not worried about where it would be placed on what was, after all, only a temporary site.

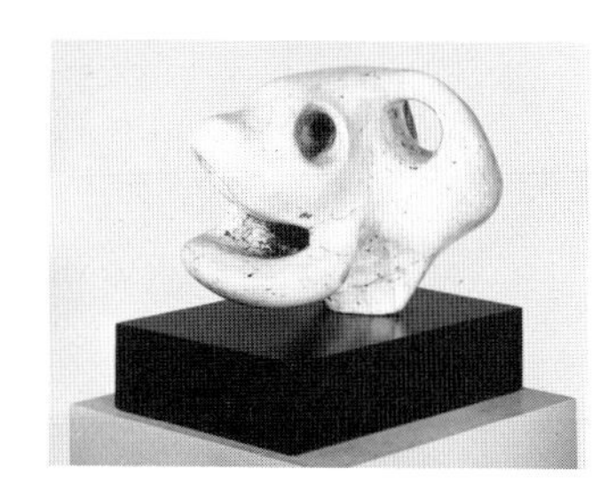

T.2271 **Animal Head** 1951

Not inscribed
Plaster, $7\frac{3}{4} \times 8\frac{1}{2} \times 11\frac{5}{8}$ (19.7 × 21.6 × 29.5)
Presented by the artist 1978

Exh: *Henry Moore: New Bronzes and Drawings*, Leicester Galleries, 1951 (16); *Henry Moore*, Hatton Gallery, Newcastle upon Tyne, November–December 1958 (10, repr.); *Henry Moore*, Musée Rodin, Paris, 1971 (34, repr.); *Mostra di Henry Moore*, Forte di Belvedere, Florence, May–

September 1972 (69, repr. in colour); *Henry Moore Sculptures et Dessins*, Orangerie des Tuileries, Paris, May–August 1977 (63, repr.); *Henry Moore 80th Birthday Exhibition*, Bradford Art Galleries and Museums, April–June 1978 (85, repr.); *The Henry Moore Gift*, Tate Gallery, June–August 1978, repr. p.28

Lit: Erich Neumann, *The Archetypal World of Henry Moore*, 1959, p.120 (bronze repr. pl.96a-c); Will Grohmann, *The Art of Henry Moore*, 1960, p.108; Herbert Read, *Henry Moore*, 1965, p.189

The original plaster for L.H. 301 (repr. volume 2, pl.30, 30a). For Moore's remarks on the interchangeability of form and space, see the note on T.2270 above. Compare also with T.2277 below.

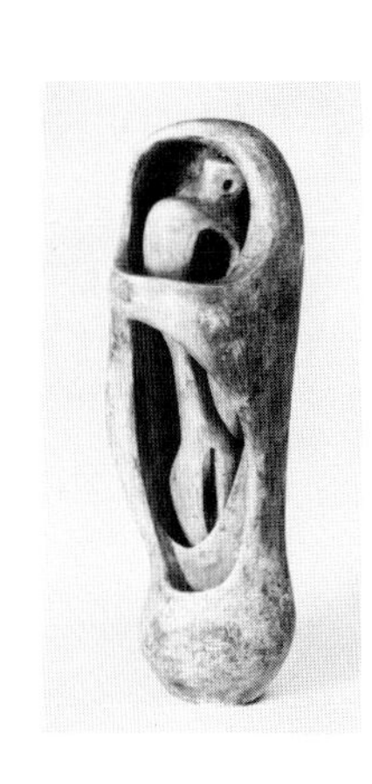

T.2272 **Upright Internal/External Form** 1952–3

Not inscribed
Plaster, 77 × $26\frac{3}{4}$ × $27\frac{1}{4}$ (195.6 × 68 × 69.2)
Presented by the artist 1978

Exh: *Henry Moore Sculptures et Dessins*, Orangerie des Tuileries, Paris, May–August 1977 (61, repr.); *Henry Moore 80th Birthday Exhibition*, Bradford Art Galleries and Museums, April–June 1978 (9); *The Henry Moore Gift*, Tate Gallery, June–August 1978, repr. p.29

Lit: Erich Neumann, *The Archetypal World of Henry Moore*, 1959, pp.126–7 (repr. pl.104); Herbert Read, *Henry Moore*, 1965, pp.182–6; Philip James (ed.), *Henry Moore on Sculpture*, 1966, p.247; John Russell, *Henry Moore*, 1968, p.121; David Sylvester, catalogue of *Henry Moore*, Tate Gallery, July–September 1968, p.85; John Hedgecoe and Henry Moore, *Henry Moore*, 1968, pp.131 (detail repr.), 198; Alan G. Wilkinson, *The Moore Collection in the Art Gallery of Ontario*, Toronto, 1979, pp.116–17

Repr: Herbert Read (intro.), *Henry Moore Sculpture and Drawings 1949–1954*, 1968, pl.25

This is the original plaster for L.H. 296, of which there are three bronze casts, one in the collection of the Kunsthalle, Hamburg. As with T.2270 (see above), the British Council took a plaster cast from the original plaster for showing in their travelling exhibitions in the 1950s; this was afterwards loaned to Leeds City Art Gallery. The sculpture grew out of a maquette (L.H. 294) which was followed by a working model (L.H. 295).

In the book with John Hedgecoe (1968), Moore wrote about this work as follows. 'I have done other sculptures based on this idea of one form being protected by another. These are some of the helmets I did in 1939 in which the interior of the helmet is really a figure and the outside casing of it is like the armour by which it might be protected in battle. I suppose in my mind was also the Mother and Child idea and of birth and the child in embryo. All these things are connected in this interior and exterior idea. There were two versions of this sculpture, one in bronze and one in wood. Wood has a warmer, more human feel to it than bronze, but at the time I was unable to find the right piece of wood for it. I had intended that it should be somewhere around nine or ten feet high, and as I did not want the idea to go stale on me I began it in plaster some six or seven feet high. Eventually after having started the plaster version and nearly finished it, my timber merchant told me he had found a piece of elm wood that was suitable and so I used that for the second version.' (repr. L.H. vol. 2, pl.26, 26a, b). He also compared the outer shell to 'petals which enclose the stamen of a flower. Besides acting as a protection, they provide an attraction.' A related sculpture by Moore is actually entitled 'Upright Internal/External Form (Flower)' (L.H. 293a, b).

In conversation with the compiler (12 December 1980), the artist said that there were three fundamental 'form ideas' in his work, all of them rooted in the human figure: the reclining figure (his favourite), the mother and child (usually seated), and one form enveloping another, which might also include the mother and child motif. There are works which incorporate the first and last themes, such as L.H. 298 and 299, both closely related to T.2272, and those which incorporate all three – for example, 'Reclining Mother and Child' 1960–1 (L.H. 480).

T.2273 **Helmet Head and Shoulders** 1952

Not inscribed
Bronze, $6\frac{1}{2} \times 5\frac{7}{8} \times 3\frac{3}{4}$ (16.5 × 14.9 × 9.5)
Presented by the artist 1978

Exh: *Henry Moore: an exhibition of sculpture from 1950–1960*, Whitechapel Art Gallery, December 1960–January 1961 (15, repr.); *Henry Moore: an exhibition of sculpture and drawings*, Ferens Art Gallery, Kingston upon Hull, October–November 1963 (11); *Henry Moore*, Tate Gallery, July–September 1968 (76); *Henry Moore*, University of York Visual Arts Society, Heslington Hall, March 1969 (6); *Small Bronzes and Drawings by Henry Moore*, the Lefevre Gallery, November–December 1972 (22, repr.); *Henry Moore*, Henie-Onstad Kunstsenter, Oslo, June–July 1975 and tour to Stockholm and Ålborg (40); *Henry Moore*, Expo Zürich, Zürcher Forum, Zurich, June–August 1976 (40); *Henry Moore 80th birthday exhibition*, Bradford Art Galleries and Museums, April–June 1978 (78, repr.); *The Henry Moore Gift*, Tate Gallery, June–August 1978, repr. in colour p.28

Lit: Herbert Read, *Henry Moore*, 1965, p.177 (repr. pl.159); John Russell, *Henry Moore*, 1968, p.118 (repr. pl.115)

Repr: Herbert Read (intro.), *Henry Moore Sculpture and Drawings 1949–1954*, 1968, pl.33

The work is No.304 in the Lund Humphries catalogue of Moore's sculpture; it was cast in an edition of ten.

In conversation with the compiler (12 December 1980), Moore said that the conjunction of sharp points with the helmet form was intended to express the idea of aggression and war, although in this sculpture the shoulders introduce a protective element which relates it to T.2272 above.

T.2274–6

T.2274 **Upright Motive No. 1: Glenkiln Cross** 1955–6

Not inscribed
Bronze, 131 × $38\frac{1}{2}$ × 38 including base (332.8 × 97.8 × 96.5)
Presented by the artist's daughter 1978

Exh: *50 Ans d'Art Moderne*, Palais des Beaux Arts, Brussels, April–July 1958 (234, repr.); *Sculpture in the Open Air*, Battersea Park, May–September 1960 (32, repr.); *Henry Moore: an exhibition of sculpture from 1950–1960*, Whitechapel Art Gallery, December 1960–January 1961 (27, repr.); *Henry Moore at King's Lynn*, King's Lynn Festival, July–August 1964 (2); *Henry Moore*, Arts Council, Tate Gallery, July–September 1968 (95, repr.); *Henry Moore Exhibition in Japan*, National Museum of Modern Art, Tokyo, August–October 1969 (39, repr.); *Mostra di Henry Moore*, Forte di Belvedere, Florence, May–September 1972 (93, repr.); *Henry Moore*, Expo Zürich, Zürcher Forum, Zurich, June–August 1976 (51); *The Henry Moore Gift*, Tate Gallery, June–August 1978, repr. pp.32 and 33

Lit: Will Grohmann, *The Art of Henry Moore*, 1960, pp.197–215 (repr.

pl.155, 156); Herbert Read, *Henry Moore*, 1965, pp.203–8 (repr. pl.191); Henry Moore, John Russell and A. M. Hammacher, *Drie Staande Motieven*, Rijksmuseum Kröller-Müller, Otterlo, 1965, n.p. (repr.); Philip James (ed.), *Henry Moore on Sculpture*, 1966, pp.253–7 (repr. pl.108, 109, 110); John Russell, *Henry Moore*, 1968, pp.141–56 (repr. pl.143, 162); David Sylvester, catalogue of *Henry Moore*, Tate Gallery, 1968, p.127 (repr. pl.118, 130); John Hedgecoe and Henry Moore, *Henry Moore*, 1968, pp.164, 245, 250 (repr. p.244); Alan G. Wilkinson, *The Moore Collection in the Art Gallery of Ontario*, Toronto, 1979, pp.135–9 (first cast repr. fig.116; original plaster repr. pl.106)

Repr: Alan Bowness (ed.), *Henry Moore Sculpture 1955–64*, 1965, pl.19 (detail); Elda Fezzi, *Henry Moore*, Florence, 1971, pl.21 in colour

T.2275 **Upright Motive No.2** 1955–6

Inscribed 'Moore' on side of base
Bronze, 132 × 30¼ × 38¼ including base (335.2 × 76.8 × 97.2)
Presented by the artist 1978

Exh: *Henry Moore: an exhibition of sculpture from 1950–1960*, Whitechapel Art Gallery, December 1960–January 1961 (26, repr.); *Henry Moore*, Arts Council, Tate Gallery, July–September 1968 (96, repr.); *Henry Moore 80th Birthday Exhibition*, Bradford Art Galleries and Museums, April–June 1978 (8, repr.); *The Henry Moore Gift*, Tate Gallery, June–August 1978, repr. p.33

Lit: Will Grohmann, *The Art of Henry Moore*, 1960, pp.197–215; Herbert Read, *Henry Moore*, 1965, pp.203–8 (repr. pl.191); Henry Moore, John Russell and A. M. Hammacher, *Drie Staande Motieven*, Rijksmuseum Kröller-Müller, Otterlo, 1965, n.p. (repr.); Philip James (ed.), *Henry Moore on Sculpture*, 1966, pp.253–7 (repr. pl.110); John Russell, *Henry Moore*, 1968, pp.141–56 (repr. pl.162); David Sylvester, catalogue of *Henry Moore*, Tate Gallery, 1968, p.127 (repr. pl.118, 130); John Hedgecoe and Henry Moore, *Henry Moore*, 1968, pp.245, 250; Alan G. Wilkinson, *The Moore Collection in the Art Gallery of Ontario*, Toronto, 1979, p.139

Repr: Alan Bowness (ed.), *Henry Moore Sculpture 1955–64*, 1965, pl.22

T.2276 **Upright Motive No.7** 1955–6

Inscribed 'Moore' on side of base
Bronze, 134 × 30⅜ × 38¼ including base (345.4 × 77.2 × 97.2)
Presented by the artist 1978

Exh: *Henry Moore: an exhibition of sculpture from 1950–1960*, Whitechapel Art Gallery, December 1960–January 1961 (28, repr.); *Henry Moore*, Arts Council, Tate Gallery, July–September 1968 (97, repr.); *Henry Moore 80th Birthday Exhibition*, Bradford Art Galleries and Museums, April–June 1978 (7, repr.); *The Henry Moore Gift*, Tate Gallery, June–August 1978, repr. p.33

Lit: Will Grohmann, *The Art of Henry Moore*, 1960, pp.197–215; Herbert Read, *Henry Moore*, 1965, pp.203–8 (repr. pl.190, 191); Henry Moore, John Russell and A. M. Hammacher, *Drie Staande Motieven*, Rijksmuseum Kröller-Müller, Otterlo, 1965, n.p. (repr.); Philip James (ed.), *Henry Moore on Sculpture*, 1966, pp.253–7 (repr. pl.110); John Russell, *Henry Moore*, 1968, pp.141–56 (repr. pl.160, 162); David Sylvester, catalogue of *Henry Moore*, Tate Gallery, 1968, p.127 (repr. pl.118, 130); John Hedgecoe and Henry Moore, *Henry Moore*, 1968, pp.245, 250;

Alan G. Wilkinson, *The Moore Collection in the Art Gallery of Ontario*, Toronto, 1979, p.139

Repr: Alan Bowness (ed.), *Henry Moore Sculpture 1955–64*, 1965, pl.21

These three sculptures, catalogued here together, are L.H. 377, 379 and 386 respectively. They are illustrated together as a group in Lund Humphries, volume 3, pl.17, 18, and 20 (three separate views). The Tate's grouping of the sculptures, with the 'Glenkiln Cross' in the middle, follows the format adopted by the Kröller-Müller Museum, Otterlo, where the 'Three Upright Motives' were erected in April 1965, outdoors on a pedestal especially designed by the artist. The booklet which accompanied the unveiling of the sculptures, with a text by John Russell, remains one of the chief sources of information about the group, the other being Moore's own statements collected in James (1966) and Hedgecoe (1968). The three sculptures are also grouped together in the same arrangement at the Amon Carter Museum, Fort Worth, Texas, on a black granite base designed by Philip Johnson, architect of the Museum.

In the book with Hedgecoe, Moore wrote about the origin of the 'Upright Motive' series (thirteen maquettes were made in 1955 of which five, including the three catalogued here, were enlarged). 'The maquettes . . . were triggered off for me by being asked by the architect to do a sculpture for the courtyard of the new Olivetti building in Milan. It is a very low horizontal one-storey building. My immediate thought was that any sculpture that I should do must be in contrast to this horizontal rhythm. It needed some vertical form in front of it. At the time I also wanted to have a change from the Reclining Figure theme that I had returned to so often.' The maquettes were not in the end used for the Olivetti commission but Moore started to work on some of them in full size, for his own interest. 'I started by balancing different forms one above the other – with results rather like the Northwest American totem poles – but as I continued the attempt gained more unity also perhaps became more organic – and then one in particular . . . took on the shape of a crucifix – a kind of worn-down body and a cross merged into one.' (James, op. cit., p.253). The sculpture which developed a primitive cruciform head later became known as the 'Glenkiln Cross' (T.2274), after a farm on a private estate in Scotland where the first cast of the work was sited. The original plaster for this sculpture is in the Moore Collection, Art Gallery of Ontario.

Regarding the symbolism of the sculptures, Moore wrote of his predilection for working in threes when relating things (for example, the 'Three Standing Women' in Battersea Park) and how, when the 'Glenkiln Cross' was placed between two others, the three automatically assumed the appearance of a Crucifixion group. But in conversation with the compiler (12 December 1980) the artist stressed that the religious content was generalised, and elsewhere he has written that he does not necessarily 'expect others to find this symbolism in the group'. However, the incision of a ladder and other Crucifixion symbols on the lower part of 'Glenkiln Cross' suggests that a religious interpretation would not be misplaced.

T.2277 **Animal Head** 1956

Not inscribed

Bronze, $19\frac{7}{8} \times 11\frac{3}{8} \times 22\frac{3}{4}$ including base ($50.5 \times 28.9 \times 57.8$)

Presented by the artist 1978

Exh: *Henry Moore: Sculptures, Dessins, Estampes*, Galerie Gérald Cramer, Geneva, December 1962 – January 1963 (16); *Henry Moore Sculpture and Drawings*, New Metropole Arts Centre, Folkestone, April–May 1966 and City Art Gallery, Plymouth, June–July 1966 (24); *Henry Moore*, Mappin Art Gallery, Sheffield, July–September 1967 (19);

Henry Moore, University of York Visual Arts Society, Heslington Hall, March 1969 (16); *Henry Moore*, Musée Rodin, Paris, 1971 (37, repr.); *Henry Moore 80th Birthday Exhibition*, Bradford Art Galleries and Museums, April–June 1978 (32, repr.); *The Henry Moore Gift*, Tate Gallery, June–August 1978, repr. p.34

Lit: Will Grohmann, *The Art of Henry Moore*, 1960, p.108 (repr. pl.103); Herbert Read, *Henry Moore*, 1965, p.224 (repr. pl.211); Alan G. Wilkinson, *The Moore Collection in the Art Gallery of Ontario*, Toronto, 1979, p.144 (original plaster repr. pl.116)

Repr: Alan Bownesss (ed.), *Henry Moore Sculpture 1955–64*, 1965, pl.79b

Lund Humphries 396. Another cast is in the Kröller-Müller Museum, Otterlo, and the original plaster is in the Moore Collection, Art Gallery of Ontario.

T.2278 **Falling Warrior** 1956–7

Not inscribed
Bronze, 24 × 60 × 32½ including base (61 × 152.4 × 82.5)
Presented by the artist 1978

Exh: *Henry Moore*, British Council, Museum Folkwang, Essen, July–August 1960 and tour to Hamburg, Zürich and Munich (43, repr.); *Henry Moore: an exhibition of sculpture from 1950–1960*, Whitechapel Art Gallery, December 1960–January 1961 (50, repr.); *Henry Moore*, British Council, Stedelijk Museum, Amsterdam, June–July 1961 (37); *Henry Moore*, British Council, Akademie der Künste, Berlin, July–September 1961 (38, repr.); *Henry Moore*, Musée Rodin, Paris, 1961 (37, repr.); *Henry Moore at King's Lynn*, King's Lynn Festival, July–August 1964 (11); *Henry Moore Sculpture and Drawings*, New Metropole Arts Centre, Folkestone, April–May 1966 and City Art Gallery, Plymouth, June–July 1966 (31, repr.); *Henry Moore*, Arts Council, Tate Gallery, July–September 1968 (99, repr.); *Henry Moore Exhibition in Japan*, National Museum of Modern Art, Tokyo, August–October 1969 (41, repr.); *Mostra di Henry Moore*, Forte di Belvedere, Florence, May–September 1972 (98, repr. in colour); *The Henry Moore Gift*, Tate Gallery, June–August 1978, repr. p.34

Lit: Will Grohmann, *The Art of Henry Moore*, 1960, pp.217–8 (detail repr. pl.168); Philip James (ed.), *Henry Moore on Sculpture*, 1966, p.22; David Sylvester in catalogue of *Henry Moore*, Tate Gallery, 1968, pp.127–8 (repr. pl.120; detail repr. pl.122); John Russell, *Henry Moore*, 1968, p.139 (repr. pl.136); John Hedgecoe and Henry Moore, *Henry Moore*, 1968, p.279 (repr. pp.276–9); Alan Bowness, Introduction to *Henry Moore Sculpture 1964–73*, 1977, p.8

Repr: Alan Bowness (ed.), *Henry Moore Sculpture 1955–64*, 1965, pl.27–30; Herbert Read, *Henry Moore*, 1965, pl.192 in colour

This work is Lund Humphries 405; other casts are in various public collections. It is not to be confused with L.H. 404, the nine-inch long 'Maquette for Fallen Warrior' 1956, which was cast in an edition of nine bronzes and later enlarged to similar size as T.2278. Moore was unhappy with the pose of the figure in this sculpture, whose left arm dangles limply and whose right foot appears to rest on a shield. He felt it to be 'dead' and 'so . . . altered it to make the action that of a figure in the act of falling, and the shield became a support for the warrior, emphasising the dramatic moment that precedes death.' (Hedgecoe, op. cit., p.279)

Grohmann, discussing the 'Warrior' sculptures of this period, finds 'Fallen Warrior' to be the more 'helpless' and 'Falling Warrior' to possess greater 'dignity': 'In both, the movement of sprawling, falling, propping himself up and lying on his back is seen from all sides and, as we walk round the figure, the view changes with every step.' (op. cit., p.217). Alan Bowness uses 'Falling Warrior' to illustrate the relationship between the viewer's sense of his own body and his appreciation of figure sculpture: 'The extraordinary impact of the "Falling Warrior" of 1956–7 ... derives from the half-conscious connection we immediately make between his fall and the idea of being ourselves in the same situation.' (op. cit., 1977, p.8). He also proposes a source in Moore's drawings of miners for this work and the earlier 'Warrior with Shield' (L.H. 360).

In conversation with the compiler (12 December 1980), the artist said that photographs showing the plaster for 'Falling Warrior' at an early stage often appeared more directly expressive of his intentions than the finished sculpture. (One of these photographs is reproduced in John Read, *Henry Moore: Portrait of an Artist*, 1979, p.112). There were occasions such as this when he would have liked to have taken a cast of the work in progress.

T.2279 **Seated Woman** 1957

Not inscribed
Plaster, 57 × $54\frac{7}{8}$ × 36 including wooden bench (144.8 × 139.5 × 91.5)
Presented by the artist 1978

Exh: *Henry Moore at King's Lynn*, King's Lynn Festival, July–August 1964 (12); *The Henry Moore Gift*, Tate Gallery, June–August 1978, repr. pp.36 and 37

Lit: Will Grohmann, *The Art of Henry Moore*, 1960, p.230 (bronze repr. pl. 179, 180); Philip James (ed.), *Henry Moore on Sculpture*, 1966, p.131 (bronze repr. pl.43, 44); David Sylvester in catalogue of *Henry Moore*, Tate Gallery, 1968, p.127 (bronze repr. pl.119); John Hedgecoe and Henry Moore, *Henry Moore*, 1968, pp.326, 329 (bronze repr. pp.327, 8)

This is the original plaster for L.H. 435; there are six casts, one of which is in the Hirshhorn Museum, Washington. Moore wrote in 1968 (Hedgecoe, op. cit.) that he had always been 'more interested in the female form than in the male' and that both 'Seated Woman' and 'Woman' (T.2280 below) 'have the big form that I like my women to have.' He told the compiler (12 December 1980) that, while working on the back of 'Seated Woman', he was reminded of his mother whose back he used to massage with oils as a boy of seven or eight because she suffered from rheumatism. This gave him a knowledge of the back's contours, its soft and hard parts – like the features of a landscape – and he said that backs had consequently always been as important to him, and as interesting to sculpt, as fronts. Moore also wrote: '"Seated Woman" is pregnant. The fullness in her pelvis and stomach is all to her right. I don't remember that I consciously did it this way, but I remember Irina telling me, before Mary was born, that sometimes she could feel that the baby was on one side and sometimes on the other' (ibid.).

T.2280 **Woman** 1957–8

Inscribed 'Moore %' on base and stamped with foundry mark 'GUSS: H. NOACK BERLIN' on side of base
Bronze, $56\frac{3}{4}$ × $31\frac{1}{8}$ × $36\frac{1}{4}$ including base (144 × 79.1 × 92.1)
Presented by the artist 1978

Exh: *Henry Moore*, British Council, Salla Dalles, Bucarest, February–March 1966 and tour to Bratislava, Prague and Jerusalem, ending up at the Tel-Aviv Museum, November–December 1966 (23, repr.); *Henry Moore*, Mappin Art Gallery, Sheffield, July–September 1967 (3); *Henry Moore*, Rijksmuseum Kröller-Müller, Otterlo, May–July 1968, Museum Boymans-Van Beuningen, Rotterdam, September–November

1968 and Mathildenhöhe Darmstadt, Spring 1969 (95, repr.); *Henry Moore 80th Birthday Exhibition*, Bradford Art Galleries and Museums, April–June 1978 (5, repr.); *The Henry Moore Gift*, Tate Gallery, June–August 1978, repr. p.38

Lit: Will Grohmann, *The Art of Henry Moore*, 1960, pp.230–1 (repr. pl.181, 182); David Sylvester in catalogue of *Henry Moore*, Tate Gallery, 1968, p.127 (detail repr. pl.121); John Hedgecoe and Henry Moore, *Henry Moore*, 1968, p.326 (repr. pp.322–4); Alan Bowness, Introduction to *Henry Moore Sculpture 1964–73*, 1977, p.8); Alan G. Wilkinson, *The Moore Collection in the Art Gallery of Ontario*, Toronto, 1979, p.158 (original plaster repr. pl.131; another cast repr. pl.132)

Repr: Alan Bowness (ed.), *Henry Moore Sculpture 1955–1964*, 1965, pl.52–5; Herbert Read, *Henry Moore*, 1965, pl.204 in colour

L.H. 439, also known as 'Seated Torso' or 'Parze'. There is an edition of eight bronzes, one of which is in the Moore Collection, Art Gallery of Ontario, together with the original plaster. The Tate's cast was the artist's own, making nine in all. Wilkinson, in the catalogue of the Toronto collection, op. cit., calls the sculpture 'one of the most potent images of fertility produced in the 20th century' and relates it to Moore's early interest in Palaeolithic sculpture – an influence the artist acknowledges in Hedgecoe (p.326). Moore also wrote in Hedgecoe: '"Woman" has that startling fullness of the stomach and the breasts. The smallness of the head is necessary to emphasise the massiveness of the body. If the head had been any larger it would have ruined the whole idea of the sculpture. Instead the face and particularly the neck are more like a hard column than a soft goitred female neck.' (ibid.). Alan Bowness sees the base or pedestal upon which 'Woman' is placed as a device to distance and isolate the figure. (This would apply equally to the previous sculpture, T.2279, which is seated on a bench.) He also finds the seated woman sculptures of this period 'at times ... close to being drained of humanity ... almost too impersonal and withdrawn.' (op. cit., 1977, p.8)

T.2281 **Three Motives against Wall No.2** 1959

Inscribed 'Moore 10/10' on side of base
Bronze, $18\frac{1}{8} \times 42\frac{5}{8} \times 15$ (46 × 108.2 × 38.1)
Presented by the artist 1978

Exh: *Henry Moore: an exhibition of sculpture and drawings*, Ferens Art Gallery, Kingston upon Hull, October–November 1963 (33); *Henry Moore*, Museu de Arte Moderna, Rio de Janeiro, January–February 1965 (21); *Henry Moore*, Art Gallery of Ontario, Toronto, October–November 1967 and tour to Charlottetown (Prince Edward Island) and St Johns (Newfoundland), ending up at the National Gallery of Canada, Ottawa, June–September 1968 (8, repr.); *Henry Moore Exhibition in Japan*, National Museum of Modern Art, Tokyo, August–October 1969 (44, repr.); *Henry Moore Sculpture, Drawings, Graphics*, Turnpike Gallery, Leigh, Lancs., November–December 1971 (6); *The Henry Moore Gift*, Tate Gallery, June–August 1978, repr. p.39

Lit: David Sylvester in catalogue of *Henry Moore*, Tate Gallery, 1968, p.55 (repr. pl.52); John Russell, *Henry Moore*, 1968, p.173 (repr. pl.167); Alan G. Wilkinson, *The Moore Collection in the Art Gallery of Ontario*, Toronto, 1979, pp.152, 159 (original plaster repr. pl.133)

Repr: Alan Bowness (ed.), *Henry Moore Sculpture 1955–64*, 1965, pl.70, 71

This work is no. 442 in the Lund Humphries catalogue of Moore's sculpture. There are ten casts, one of which is in the Hirshhorn Museum, Washington. The original plaster is in the Moore Collection, Art Gallery of Ontario.

Wilkinson, op. cit., traces Moore's placing of sculptural figures against a rectangular slotted wall, or in a cell-like room, to various drawings done in the 1930s, although the first sculpture to realise this theme was not executed until 1957 (L.H. 424). Moore told the compiler (12 December 1980) that his interest in making relief sculpture, which had lain dormant since his work on the London Underground Building in the late Twenties, was reawakened when he was commissioned to design a large wall relief in brick for the façade of the Bouwcentrum in Rotterdam (L.H. 375), unveiled in December 1955. This project led to the idea of releasing the forms from their incorporation in the fabric of the wall so that they become free-standing, as in T.2281; the wall, with its mysterious slits, acts as a background of considerable emotive force.

As Wilkinson notes, the three shapes in T.2281 were based on flint stones in the artist's studio. Each can be turned, thus making possible a multiplicity of different ways in which the work as a whole can be viewed. Moore first thought of the possibility of using a turntable for sculpture which could not otherwise be seen in the round when he was carving his *Screen* for the Time-Life Building in Bond Street in 1952–3, but considerations of safety prevented his scheme from being carried out.

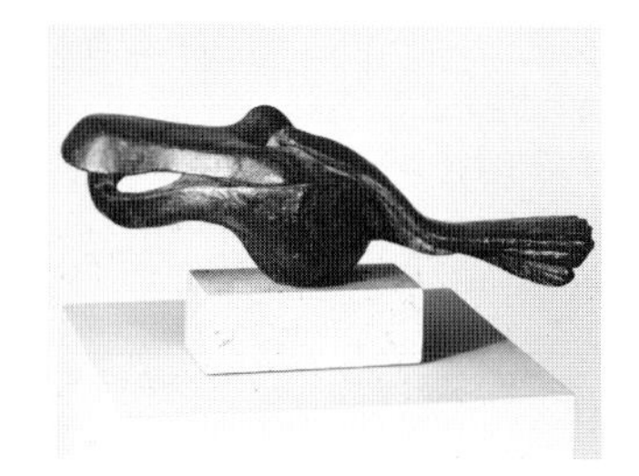

T.2282 **Bird** 1959

Not inscribed
Bronze, $4\frac{3}{4} \times 14\frac{3}{4} \times 5\frac{1}{8}$ (12.1 × 37.5 × 13)
Presented by the artist 1978

Exh: *Henry Moore Sculpture and Drawings*, New Metropole Arts Centre, Folkestone, April–May 1966 and City Art Gallery, Plymouth, June–July 1966 (38); *Mostra di Henry Moore*, Forte di Belvedere, Florence, May–September 1972 (105, repr.); *Henry Moore–Fem Decennier Skulptur, teckning, grafik 1923–1975*, Henie Onstad Kunstsenter, Oslo, June–July 1975 and tour to Stolkholm and Ålborg (57); *Henry Moore*, Expo Zürich, Zürcher Forum, Zurich, June–August 1976 (61); *Henry Moore 80th Birthday Exhibition*, Bradford Art Galleries and Museums, April–June 1978 (81, repr.); *The Henry Moore Gift*, Tate Gallery, June–August 1978, repr. p.41

Lit: John Hedgecoe and Henry Moore, *Henry Moore*, 1968, p.405, repr.

Repr: Alan Bowness (ed.), *Henry Moore Sculpture 1955–64*, 1965, pl.78a, b

L.H. 445, cast in an edition of twelve. In Hedgecoe, op. cit., Moore wrote: 'Ten years ago [i.e. 1958] I made a teracotta bird table. A big, black crow (I particularly like crows) used to come and eat from this table. I think it came because it was old and sick and it was the only way it could get its food. It had something wrong with its beak and it stood almost horizontally. That bird is why I did this sculpture.'

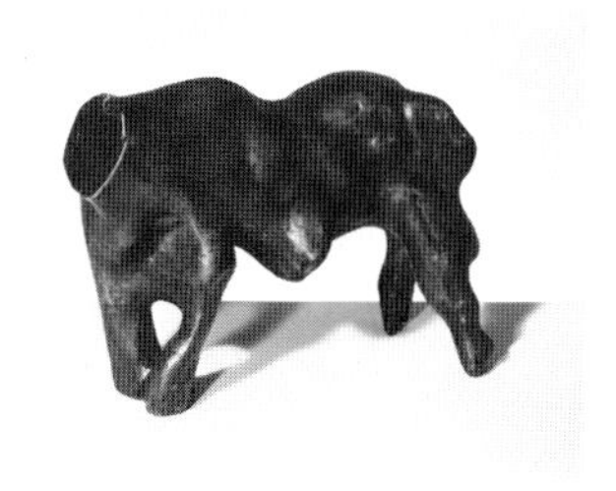

T.2283 **Headless Animal** 1960

Not inscribed
Bronze, $6\frac{1}{4} \times 8\frac{7}{8} \times 3\frac{3}{4}$ (15.8 × 22.4 × 9.4)
Presented by the artist 1978

Exh: *Henry Moore*, Arts Council, Tate Gallery, July–September 1968 (110, repr.) *The Henry Moore Gift*, Tate Gallery, June–August 1978, repr. p.42

Lit: David Sylvester in catalogue of *Henry Moore*, Tate Gallery, 1968, p.127 (repr. pl.115); Alan G. Wilkinson, *The Moore Collection in the Art Gallery of Ontario*, Toronto, 1979, p.160 (another cast repr. pl.136)

Repr: Alan Bowness (ed.), *Henry Moore Sculpture 1955–64*, 1965, p.27, no.449

This work is L.H. 449, of which there are six casts; another is in the Moore

Collection, Art Gallery of Ontario. The artist told the compiler (12 December 1980) that animals had always interested him as a subject for sculpture because they posed entirely different problems from those confronting the sculptor of the human figure. He liked them above all for their energy and vitality. In T.2283 he was concerned primarily with the body and legs of the imaginary creature; the head presented no problem and he thought the sculpture would look better without one.

T.2284 **Relief No. 1** 1959

Inscribed 'Moore 0/6' on drapery near left foot
Bronze, $87\frac{3}{8} \times 49\frac{1}{4} \times 19\frac{5}{8}$ (221.9 × 125.1 × 49.8)
Presented by the artist 1978

Exh: *Henry Moore: an exhibition of sculpture from 1950–1960*, Whitechapel Art Gallery, December 1960–January 1961 (71, repr.); *Henry Moore*, Rijksmuseum Kröller-Müller, Otterlo, May–July 1968, Museum Boymans-Van Beuningen, Rotterdam, September–November 1968 and Mathildenhöhe, Darmstadt, Spring 1969 (100, repr.); *The Henry Moore Gift*, Tate Gallery, June–August 1978, repr. p.40

Lit: Will Grohmann, *The Art of Henry Moore*, 1960, p.232 (original plaster repr. pl.190); Herbert Read, *Henry Moore*, 1965, p.224 (repr. pl.210); Philip James (ed.), *Henry Moore on Sculpture*, 1966, pp.275–7 (repr. pl.126); John Hedgecoe and Henry Moore, *Henry Moore*, 1968, p.391, repr.; John Russell, *Henry Moore*, 1968, p.178 (repr. pl.183); Alan G. Wilkinson, *The Moore Collection in the Art Gallery of Ontario*, Toronto, 1979, p.161 (another cast repr. pl.138)

Repr: Alan Bowness (ed.), *Henry Moore Sculpture 1955–64*, 1965, pl.72, 73

L.H. 450, cast in an edition of six bronzes plus one, the artist's cast, which is now the Tate's work. Another cast is in the Moore Collection, Art Gallery of Ontario. Wilkinson, op. cit., discusses the origins of the work in Moore's maquettes for the Bouwcentrum 'Wall Relief' 1955 (L.H. 375; see note on T.2281 above).

The artist told the compiler (12 December 1980) that his intention in 'Relief No. 1' had been to emphasise the projectional, forceful qualities of relief as opposed to using it pictorially like a narrative frieze, as Renaissance sculptors had done and as he had been taught to do at art college (for a fuller account of Moore's views on relief sculpture, see Philip James, op. cit., pp.275–7). Hence the stylisation and exaggeration of certain protrusions and recessions in the sculpture: the umbilicus and the chest, for example. In Hedgecoe, Moore compared the work to a similar plaster which he had not had cast into bronze because he was dissatisfied with it: 'The projecting parts are too evenly spread and too evenly apportioned throughout the figure. There is no obvious focal point. In the bronze sculpture [T.2284] you know the middle and you know where the shoulders are. It has a centre, a kernel, and an organic logic.' (op. cit.)

T.2285 **Three Part Object** 1960

Inscribed 'Moore 8/9' and stamped with foundry mark 'H. NOACK BERLIN' on base
Bronze, $49\frac{3}{4} \times 28\frac{1}{4} \times 24\frac{1}{8}$ including base (126.4 × 71.8 × 61.3)
Presented by the artist 1978

Exh: *Henry Moore: an exhibition of sculpture from 1950–1960*, Whitechapel Art Gallery, December 1960–January 1961 (67, repr.); *Henry Moore: an exhibition of sculpture and drawings*, Arts Council, Cambridge, York, Nottingham and Southampton, 1962 (46, repr.); *Henry Moore: an exhibition of sculpture and drawings*, Ferens Art Gallery, Kingston upon

Hull, October–November 1963 (36); *Henry Moore Sculptures and Drawings*, New Metropole Arts Centre, Folkestone, April–May 1966 and City Art Gallery, Plymouth, June–July 1966 (41); *Henry Moore*, Rijksmuseum Kröller-Müller, Otterlo, May–July 1968, Museum Boymans-Van Beuningen, Rotterdam, September–November 1968 and Mathildenhöhe Darmstadt, Spring 1969 (106, repr.); *Henry Moore*, Arts Council, Tate Gallery, July–September 1968 (113); *Henry Moore*, University of York Visual Arts Society, Heslington Hall, March 1969 (25); *Henry Moore Drawings and Sculpture*, Arts Council, Supplementary Works lent by Henry Moore, Gordon Maynard Gallery, Welwyn Garden City, July 1969 (HM4); *Henry Moore Exhibition in Japan*, National Museum of Modern Art, Tokyo, August–October 1969 (46, repr.); *Henry Moore: Sculpture, Drawings, Graphics*, Turnpike Gallery, Leigh, Lancs., November–December 1971 (8); *Henry Moore*, Playhouse Gallery, Harlow, March–April 1972 (2); *Mostra di Henry Moore*, Forte di Belvedere, Florence, May–September 1972 (112, repr.); *The Henry Moore Gift*, Tate Gallery, June–August 1978, repr. p.43

Lit: Herbert Read, *Henry Moore*, 1965, p.240 (repr. pl.231); John Russell, *Henry Moore*, 1968, pp.159–161 (repr. pl.171); John Hedgecoe and Henry Moore, *Henry Moore*, 1968, p.351 (repr.); Alan Bowness, Introduction to *Henry Moore Sculpture 1964–73*, 1977, p.13

Repr: Alan Bowness (ed.), *Henry Moore Sculpture 1955–64*, 1965, pl.102, 103

This work is no.470 in the Lund Humphries catalogue of Moore's sculpture; it was cast in an edition of nine bronzes.

In Hedgecoe, op. cit., Moore wrote that '"Three-Part Object" is a strange work, even for me. Three similar forms are balanced at angles to each other. In my mind it has a connection with insect life, possibly centipedes. Each segment has a leg, and there is an element in the sculpture nearer to an animal organism than a human one.' In conversation with the compiler (12 December 1980), the artist pointed to the free invention of forms in this work and thought that they combined to produce a convincing organic whole with a life of its own. Bowness describes the sculpture as ugly and its forms as 'snout-like' and sees it as a reminder that 'Moore has always preferred vitality to beauty.' (op. cit., 1977, p.13)

T.2286 **Seated Woman: Thin Neck** 1961

Not inscribed
Bronze, 67 × 32 × $40\frac{3}{4}$ including base (172 × 81.4 × 103.6)
Presented by the artist 1978

Exh: *Henry Moore: an exhibition of sculpture and drawings*, Ferens Art Gallery, Kingston upon Hull, October–November 1963 (38); *Henry Moore Sculpture and Drawings*, New Metropole Arts Centre, Folkestone, April–May 1966 and City Art Gallery, Plymouth, June–July 1966 (1, repr.); *Henry Moore Exhibition in Japan*, National Museum of Modern Art, Tokyo, August–October 1969 (49, repr.); *Henry Moore*, Staatsgalerie Moderner Kunst, Munich, October–November 1971 (1, repr.); *The Henry Moore Gift*, Tate Gallery, June–August 1978, repr. p.45

Lit: Herbert Read, *Henry Moore*, 1965, p.243 (repr. pl.233); Philip James (ed.), *Henry Moore on Sculpture*, 1966, p.278; Alan G. Wilkinson, *The Moore Collection in the Art Gallery of Ontario*, Toronto, 1979, p.170 (original plaster repr. pl.148)

Repr: *Henry Moore: Recent Work*, Marlborough Fine Art, July–August 1963, no.12 in colour; Alan Bowness (ed.), *Henry Moore Sculpture 1955–64*,

1965, pl.116–19; John Hedgecoe and Henry Moore, *Henry Moore*, 1968, pp.358, 359

This work is L.H. 472; there are seven bronze casts and the original plaster is in the Moore Collection, Art Gallery of Ontario. The sculpture was based on a maquette (L.H. 471), part of which, the 'thin neck' of the title, was inspired by finding the breast bone of a bird.

'Since my student days', Moore has written, 'I have liked the shape of bones, and have drawn them, studied them in the Natural History Museum, found them on seashores and saved them out of the stewpot.

'There are many structural, and sculptural principles to be learnt from bones, e.g. that in spite of their lightness they have great strength. Some bones, such as the breast bones of birds, have the lightweight fineness of a knife-blade. Finding such a bone led to me using this knife-edge thinness in 1961 in a sculpture "Seated Woman" (thin neck). In this figure the thin neck and head, by contrast with the width and bulk of the body, give more monumentality to the work. Later in 1961 I used this knife-edged thinness throughout a whole figure, and produced "Standing Figure."' (quoted in Philip James, op. cit.) The 'Standing Figure' referred to here is the related sculpture 'Standing Figure: Knife-Edge' (L.H. 482) whose clay maquette actually incorporated a bone fragment.

Since the late-1950s Moore has worked mainly from small maquettes, several of which have had as their starting-point a found stone or bone fragment. Among sculptures in the Henry Moore Gift which have originated wholly or partly in this way (according to David Sylvester in the 1968 Tate *Henry Moore* catalogue) are the following: T.2281, T.2286, T.2290, T.2292, T.2293, T.2295, T.2298, T.2303.

A photograph in Hedgecoe (op. cit., p.359) shows the head and shoulders of T.2286 side by side with those of another, more naturalistic female figure sculpture by Moore. 'The contrast of these two heads', the artist comments, 'shows that facial features are not essential for expression. With her long neck, one is distant and proud while the other is more sympathetic.' (ibid., p.358)

T.2287 **Two Piece Reclining Figure No. 3** 1961

Inscribed 'Moore 0/7' and stamped with foundry mark 'H. NOACK BERLIN' on left foot
Bronze, $58 \times 94\frac{3}{4} \times 44\frac{7}{8}$ (147.4 × 240.7 × 114.1)
Presented by the artist 1978

Exh: *Henry Moore*, Mappin Art Gallery, Sheffield, July–September 1967 (6); *Henry Moore: Sculpture, Drawings, Graphics*, Turnpike Gallery, Leigh, Lancs., November–December 1971 (10, repr.); *Henry Moore*, Expo Zürich, Zürcher Forum, Zurich, June–August 1976 (64); *The Henry Moore Gift*, Tate Gallery, June–August 1978, repr. in colour p.46

Lit: Herbert Read, *Henry Moore*, 1965, pp.229–32 (repr. pl.217); Philip James (ed.), *Henry Moore on Sculpture*, 1966, pp.266–74; John Russell, *Henry Moore*, 1968, p.187 (repr. pl.191, 192); John Hedgecoe and Henry Moore, *Henry Moore*, 1968, pp.338, 349; David Sylvester, catalogue of *Henry Moore*, Tate Gallery, 1968, pp.93–4; Alan G. Wilkinson, *The Moore Collection in the Art Gallery of Ontario*, Toronto, 1979, p.172 (original plaster repr. pl.151)

Repr: Alan Bowness (ed.), *Henry Moore Sculpture 1955–64*, 1965, pl.129–134

This, the third in the series of two-piece reclining figures, is no.478 in Lund Humphries; there are in all eight bronze casts, including the Tate's which was the artist's.

Moore's first two-piece reclining figure was made in 1959 but his interest in broken or dismembered figures goes back as far as the early 1930s and can be seen in such semi-abstract works as the Tate's 'Four-Piece Composition: Reclining Figure' of 1934 (T.2054). However, with the large two-piece figures of 1959–61 Moore recognised that he was using the space between forms more sculpturally than before. His remarks about the early two-pieces, collected in James (1966) and in Hedgecoe (1968), are worth quoting at some length as they are also to a certain extent applicable to later two-piece sculptures in the Tate's collection (e.g. T.2294 and T.2295 below).

'... I realised what an advantage a separated two-piece composition could have in relating figures to landscape. Knees and breasts are mountains. Once these two parts become separated you don't expect it to be a naturalistic figure; therefore, you can justifiably make it like a landscape or a rock ...' (James, op. cit., p.266)

'... In the maquette [for 'Two-Piece Reclining Figure No. 1'] the leg and the head end were joined but when I came to enlarge the sculpture there was a stage when the junction between the leg and the head didn't seem necessary. Then I realised that dividing the figure into two parts made many more three-dimensional variations than if it had just been a monolithic piece ...' (Hedgecoe, op. cit., p.338)

'Making a sculpture in two pieces means that, as you walk round it, one form gets in front of the other in ways you cannot foresee ... The space between the two parts has to be exactly right. It's as though one was putting together the fragments of a broken antique sculpture in which you have, say, only the knee, a foot and the head. In the reconstruction the foot would have to be the right distance from the knee, and the knee the right distance from the head, to leave room for the missing parts – otherwise you would get a wrongly proportioned figure. So, in these two-piece and three-piece sculptures [see below, T.2289 and T.2292] the space between the pieces is a vital part of the sculpture.' (ibid., p.349)

In conversation with the compiler (12 December 1980) about both the two- and three-piece reclining figures, Moore was at pains to stress his concern with the interdependence of space and proportion as outlined above, although the figure/landscape analogy is of equal importance when assessing this particular development in his art.

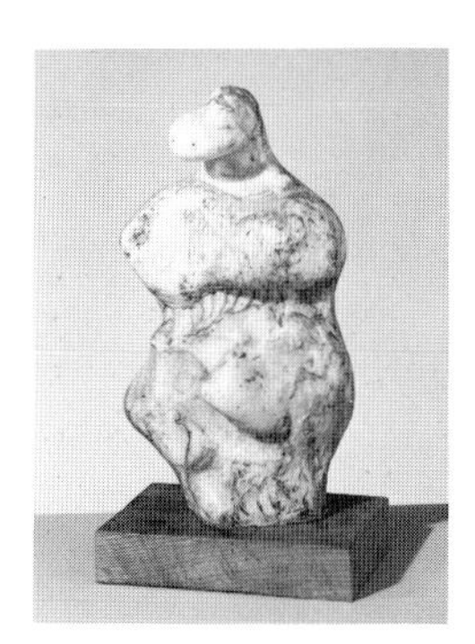

T.2288 **Three-Quarter Figure** 1961

Not inscribed
Plaster, 15⅜ × 9⅛ × 5⅛ (39.1 × 23.3 × 13.1)
Presented by the artist 1978

Exh: *Henry Moore*, Musée Rodin, Paris, 1971 (41, repr.); *Henry Moore Sculptures et Dessins*, Orangerie des Tuileries, Paris, May–August 1977 (98, repr.); *Henry Moore 80th Birthday Exhibition*, Bradford Art Galleries and Museums, April–June 1978 (34, repr.); *The Henry Moore Gift*, Tate Gallery, June–August 1978, repr. p.47

Lit: John Russell, *Henry Moore*, 1968, p.159 (bronze repr. pl.170); John Hedgecoe and Henry Moore, *Henry Moore*, 1968, p.366 (bronze repr. pp.366, 7)

This is the original plaster for L.H.487, which was cast in an edition of nine bronzes. Moore compared the piece to 'a hippopotamus'; it also reminded him, he wrote, 'of some white plaster casts of seated figures dating from the Neolithic period in the British Museum.' (Hedgecoe, op. cit.)

In conversation with the compiler (12 December 1980) the artist mentioned as having been particularly impressed by the Venus of Willendorf and other such effigies, with their strong and very real sense of the fullness, the quintessence of woman.

T.2289 **Three Piece Reclining Figure No. 1** 1961–2

Inscribed 'Moore 0/7' on back of figure b.l. and stamped with foundry mark 'GUSS: H. NOACK BERLIN' on back of figure b.l.
Bronze, $66\frac{5}{8} \times 110\frac{1}{4} \times 58\frac{3}{4}$ including base (169.3 × 280.1 × 136.6)
Presented by the artist 1978

Exh: *Henry Moore*, Arts Council, Tate Gallery, July–September 1968 (122, repr.); *Henry Moore Bronzes 1961–1970*, Marlborough Gallery, New York, April–May 1970 (3, repr. in colour); *Henry Moore Sculptures et Dessins*, Orangerie des Tuileries, Paris, May–August 1977 (100, repr.); *Henry Moore 80th Birthday Exhibition*, Bradford Art Galleries and Museums, April–June 1978 (10, repr. in colour); *The Henry Moore Gift*, Tate Gallery, June–August 1978, repr. p.47

Lit: Extracts from a BBC radio interview with David Sylvester, reproduced in *Henry Moore: Recent Work*, Marlborough Fine Art, July–August 1963, n.p. (13, repr. in colour); Herbert Read, *Henry Moore*, 1965, pp.229–32 (repr. pl.218); John Russell, *Henry Moore*, 1968, p.187 (repr. pl.196); David Sylvester, catalogue of *Henry Moore*, Tate Gallery, 1968, pp.93–4 (repr. pl.40, 41); Alan G. Wilkinson, catalogue of *The Drawings of Henry Moore*, Art Gallery of Ontario, Toronto, and Tate Gallery, 1977, p.133, no.228 (repr. fig.62); Alan G. Wilkinson, *The Moore Collection in the Art Gallery of Ontario*, Toronto, 1979, p.178 (original plaster repr. pl.158)

Repr: Alan Bowness (ed.), *Henry Moore Sculpture 1955–64*, 1965, pl.141–8

This sculpture is the first of the two three-piece reclining figures which Moore made between 1961 and 1963; the other is T.2292 below. This work is L.H. 500; there are in all eight bronzes including the artist's (the Tate's cast) and the original plaster is in the Moore Collection, Art Gallery of Ontario.

The principal source of information for the three-piece figures is Moore's 1963 interview with David Sylvester. In the course of the interview the artist discusses the origins of the sculptures in found objects such as bones (Moore had by this time stopped working from drawings) which might sometimes be incorporated unchanged into hand-size plaster maquettes or sketch-models. In T.2289 the middle piece was suggested by a vertebra which, Moore said, he found in his garden: '... the connection of one piece through to the other is the kind of connection that a backbone will have with one section through to the next section. But they've been separated. It's as though you've left the slipped disc out of them, but it's there.' (Sylvester–Moore, op. cit.)

Asked about the difference between the two- and three-piece reclining figures, Moore explained: 'The two-piece sculptures pose a problem like the kind of relationship between two people. And it's very different once you divide a thing into three: then you have two ends and a middle. In the two-piece you have just the head end and the body end or the head end and the leg end, but once you get the three-piece you have the middle and the two ends, and this became something that I wanted to do, having done the two-piece. I tried several little ideas before this one and what led me to this solution was finding a little piece of bone that was the middle of a vertebra, and I realised then that perhaps the connection through, of one piece to another, could have gone on and made a four- or five-piece, like a snake with its vertebrae right through from one end to the other. But three is enough to make the difference from two. That is what one tried to make: it is a connecting-piece carrying through from one end to the other like you might have with a snake. In a way, the more pieces you make, the easier it is. If you made a figure of ten pieces, then this dividing up would become a formula. The problem probably is more difficult when you're dividing into two only than if you divide it into three. Certainly it would be easier in four or five, so that there comes a certain stage where the problem has its maximum exhilaration for you to solve, and I think probably a three-piece is as much as one would want to attempt.' (ibid.)

Wilkinson (op. cit., 1979) finds the landscape elements of 'Three Piece Reclining Figure No. 1' 'so strong and dominant as almost completely to overpower the minimal figurative references.' In the interview with Sylvester, Moore said that the landscapes which had most influenced his work were those of his childhood – in particular, the slag heaps of Castleford and Adel Rock outside Leeds.

T.2290 **Large Slow Form: Tortoise** 1968

Inscribed 'Moore 0/9' on foot
Bronze, $16\frac{1}{2} \times 30\frac{1}{4} \times 16\frac{5}{8}$ ($42 \times 76.6 \times 42.3$)
Presented by the artist 1978

Exh: *Henry Moore*, University of York Visual Arts Society, Heslington Hall, March 1969 (32); *Henry Moore Drawings and Sculpture*, Arts Council, Supplementary Works lent by Henry Moore, Gordon Maynard Gallery, Welwyn Garden City, July 1969 (HM6); *Henry Moore Bronzes 1961–1970*, Marlborough Gallery, New York, April–May 1970 (5, repr. in colour); *Henry Moore*, Musée Rodin, Paris, 1971 (42, repr.); *Henry Moore 1961–1971*, Staatsgalerie Moderner Kunst, Munich, October–November 1971 (3, repr.); *Henry Moore: Sculpture, Drawings, Graphics*, Turnpike Gallery, Leigh, Lancs., November–December 1971 (30, repr.); *Henry Moore*, Playhouse Gallery, Harlow, March–April 1972 (6); *Mostra di Henry Moore*, Forte di Belvedere, Florence, May–September 1972 (122, repr.); *The Henry Moore Gift*, Tate Gallery, June–August 1978, repr. p.49

Lit: John Hedgecoe and Henry Moore, *Henry Moore*, 1968, p.365 (repr.); Alan G. Wilkinson, *The Moore Collection in the Art Gallery of Ontario*, Toronto, 1979, p.179

Repr: Alan Bowness (ed.), *Henry Moore Sculpture 1964–73*, 1977, no. 502a (addendum to catalogue 1955–64)

This work is L.H. 502a. There are ten bronzes in all, including the Tate's cast which was the artist's own. The $7\frac{1}{2}$ inch long plaster maquette (L.H. 502), in the Moore Collection, Art Gallery of Ontario, was made in 1962. It was not enlarged to its present size until 1968.

Moore wrote about the idea behind the work as follows: 'It is one right-angled form, repeated five times, and arranged together to make an organic composition. This repeated slow right-angle reminded me of the action of a tortoise.' (Hedgecoe, op. cit.) He also thought he would 'pursue the idea of using a repetitive unit in some future works.' (ibid.) See, for example T.2293 and T.2303 below.

T.2291 **Helmet Head No. 4: Interior-Exterior** 1963

Inscribed 'Moore' on side of base
Bronze, $21\frac{3}{4} \times 13\frac{5}{8} \times 15\frac{3}{8}$ including base ($55 \times 34.5 \times 39$)
Presented by the artist 1978

Exh: *Henry Moore*, Art Gallery of Ontario, Toronto, October–November 1967 and tour to Charlottetown (Prince Edward Island) and St Johns (Newfoundland), ending up at the National Gallery of Canada, Ottawa, June–September 1968 (18, repr.); *Henry Moore*, Rijksmuseum Kröller-Müller, Otterlo, May–July 1968, Museum Boymans-Van Beuningen, Rotterdam, September–November 1968 and Mathildenhöhe, Darmstadt, Spring 1969 (114, repr.); *Henry Moore Bronzes 1961–1970*, Marlborough Gallery, New York, April–May 1970 (13, repr. in colour); *Henry Moore*, Musée Rodin, Paris, 1971 (45, repr.); *Henry Moore: Sculpture, Drawings, Graphics*, Turnpike Gallery, Leigh, Lancs., November–December 1971 (14); *Henry Moore*, Playhouse Gallery, Harlow, March–April 1972 (5); *The Henry Moore Gift*, Tate Gallery, June–August 1978, repr. p.50

Lit: Herbert Read, *Henry Moore*, 1965, pp.238–40 (repr. p.239); John Russell, *Henry Moore*, 1968, p.193 (repr. pl.203)

Repr: Alan Bowness (ed.), *Henry Moore Sculpture 1955–64*, 1965, pl.155; Giulio Carlo Argan, *Henry Moore*, Milan, 1971, pl.180 in colour

This sculpture is L.H. 508; it was cast in an edition of six bronzes. The artist told the compiler (12 December 1980) that the smaller form hidden inside the larger and protected from the light lent an air of mystery to the work. For Moore's remarks on sculpture based on the idea of one form protected by another, see the note on T.2272 above, and especially the artist's reference to the helmets of 1939.

T.2292 **Three Piece Reclining Figure No. 2: Bridge Prop** 1963

Inscribed 'Moore 0/6' and 'H. NOACK BERLIN' on central foot
Bronze, $41\frac{1}{2} \times 95\frac{1}{8} \times 43\frac{3}{8}$ (104.9 × 241.7 × 110.3)
Presented by the artist 1978

Exh: *Henry Moore*, Art Gallery of Ontario, Toronto, October–November 1967 and tour to Charlottetown (Prince Edward Island) and St Johns (Newfoundland), ending up at the National Gallery of Canada, Ottowa, June–September 1968 (20, repr.); *Henry Moore Exhibition in Japan*, National Museum of Modern Art, Tokyo, August–October, 1969 (58, repr.); *Henry Moore 1961–1971*, Staatsgalerie Moderner Kunst, Munich, October–November 1971 (5, repr.); *Mostra di Henry Moore*, Forte di Belvedere, Florence, May–September 1972 (127, repr.); *Henry Moore – Fem Decennier Skulptur, teckning, grafik 1923–1975*, Heni Onstad Kunstsenter, Oslo, June–July 1975 and tour to Stockholm and Ålborg (67); *Henry Moore*, Expo Zürich, Zürcher Forum, Zurich, June–August 1976 (73, repr.); *Henry Moore Sculptures et Dessins*, Orangerie des Tuileries, Paris, May–August 1977, (102, repr.); *The Henry Moore Gift*, Tate Gallery, June–August 1978, repr. in colour p.51

Lit: Herbert Read, *Henry Moore*, 1965, pp.232–4 (repr. in colour pl.219 and on dustjacket); John Russell, *Henry Moore*, 1968, pp.187–191 (repr. pl.195); John Hedgecoe and Henry Moore, *Henry Moore*, 1968, p.404 (repr.); David Sylvester, catalogue of *Henry Moore*, Tate Gallery, 1968, p.141 (repr. pl.132); Alan G. Wilkinson, *The Moore Collection in the Art Gallery of Ontario*, Toronto, 1979, p.180 (original plaster repr. pl.162)

Repr: Alan Bowness (ed.), *Henry Moore Sculpture and Drawings 1955–64*, 1965, pl.163–6

L.H. 513. There are six casts plus one, the artist's, which is now the Tate's. The original plaster is in the Moore Collection, Art Gallery of Ontario. Wilkinson notes that the 'landscape images' of earlier two and three-piece reclining figures have given way, in T.2292, to 'the functional forms of engineering' (op. cit.), though an analogy with bone forms would be just as appropriate. Moore said that he was reminded of the view under Waterloo Bridge when working on the sculpture: 'The arches, seen from the Embankment, are strong' (Hedgecoe, op. cit.). See also the note on T.2289 above for Moore's remarks on the three-piece reclining figure.

T.2293 **Locking Piece** 1963–4

Inscribed 'Moore' and stamped with foundry mark 'H. NOACK BERLIN'
Bronze, height 115½ (293.4)
Presented by the artist 1978

Exh: *The Henry Moore Gift*, Tate Gallery, June–August 1978, repr. p.52

Lit: Herbert Read, *Henry Moore*, 1965, p.246 (repr. pl.236); Philip James (ed.), *Henry Moore on Sculpture*, 1966, pp.25, 144; John Hedgecoe and Henry Moore, *Henry Moore*, 1968, pp.455–6 (repr. pp.454–5); David Sylvester, catalogue of *Henry Moore*, Tate Gallery, 1968, p.141 (original plaster repr. pl.131 and details pl.127, 134); Paul Waldo Schwartz, *The Hand and Eye of the Sculptor*, 1969, pp.211–12 (original plaster repr. pp.213–18); Alan Bowness, Introduction to *Henry Moore Sculpture 1964–73*, 1977, pp.8–11, 17; Alan G. Wilkinson, *The Moore Collection in the Art Gallery of Ontario*, Toronto, 1979, p.183

Repr: Alan Bowness (ed.), *Henry Moore Sculpture and Drawings 1955–64*, 1965, pl.173, 174 and 175, 176 (details)

This is no.515 in the Lund Humphries catalogue of Moore's sculpture; there are three bronze casts. The Tate's bronze was previously on loan to Westminster City Council who placed it on its present site, outside Riverwalk House on the Embankment, in 1968.

Moore has explained how the idea for 'Locking Piece' 'came about from two pebbles which I was playing with and which seemed to fit each other and lock together, and this gave me the idea of making a two-piece sculpture – not that the forms weren't separate, but that they knitted together. I did several plaster maquettes, and eventually one nearest to what the shape of this big one is now, pleased me the most and then I began making the big one.' (James, op. cit., p.144.) The 'big one' referred to here is the 'Working Model for Locking Piece' 1962 (L.H. 514), the original plaster of which is in the Moore Collection, Art Gallery of Ontario. However, Moore later gave a slightly different account of the genesis of the sculpture when he said that 'the germ of the idea originated from a sawn fragment of bone with a socket and joint which was found in the garden.' (Hedgecoe, op. cit., p.456). He also said that the work was 'the largest and perhaps the most successful of my "fitting-together" sculptures. In fact the two pieces interlock in such a way that they can only be separated if the top piece is lifted and turned at the same time' (ibid., p.455). Alan Bowness has identified Moore's preoccupation with locking forms as being 'one general characteristic of the late style.' (op. cit., 1977, p.9).

Bowness calls 'Locking Piece' 'the first large compact sculpture', a product of the years 1959 to 1962 in Moore's works which were 'rich in new sculptural thinking.' (ibid., p.8). Other sculptures with compact forms in the Tate's collection are T.2296, T.2298 and T.2299 below, all three working models for monumental pieces. Bowness has written that these large-scale works 'display a freedom of scale that Moore has only recently achieved, now that he no longer attempts to enlarge beyond life-size the human figure.' (ibid.)

T.2294 **Two Piece Reclining Figure No. 5** 1963–4

Inscribed 'Moore 3/3' and stamped with foundry mark 'H. NOACK BERLIN' on back of figure at base
Bronze, 93½ × 145 × 78¼ (237.5 × 368.4 × 198.8)
Presented by the artist 1978

Exh: *Sculpture in the Open Air*, Battersea Park, May–September 1966 (28, repr.); *The Henry Moore Gift*, Tate Gallery, June–August 1978, repr. p.54

Lit: Herbert Read, Henry Moore, 1965, p.235 (repr. pl.222)

Repr.: Philip James (ed.), *Henry Moore on Sculpture*, 1966, pl.15; Alan Bowness (ed.), *Henry Moore Sculpture 1964–73*, 1977, pl.6, 7

L.H. 517, cast in an edition of three bronzes plus one, the artist's own (now the Tate's cast). This sculpture and T.2295 below, both double life-size reclining figures, were worked on for the commission Moore undertook in 1962 to provide a sculpture for the new Lincoln Center for the Performing Arts in New York. In the event Moore decided to go ahead and enlarge T.2295.

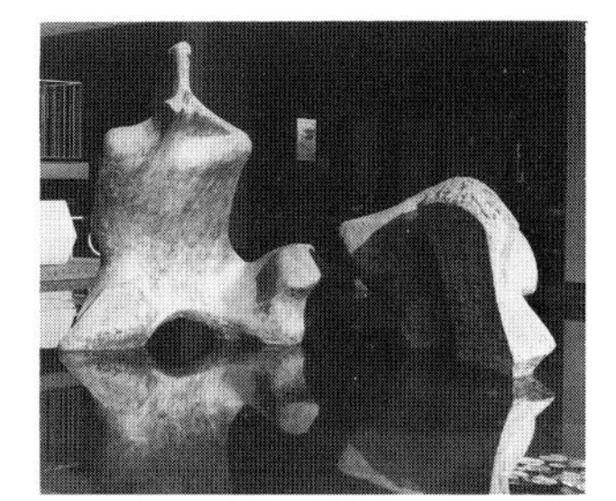

T.2295 **Working Model for Reclining Figure (Lincoln Center)** 1963–5

Inscribed 'Moore' and stamped with foundry mark 'GUSS: H. NOACK BERLIN' on back of figure bottom right
Bronze, $92\frac{1}{2} \times 146\frac{1}{2} \times 65$ ($235 \times 372.3 \times 165.2$)
Presented by the artist 1978

Exh: *Henry Moore*, Arts Council, Tate Gallery, July–September 1968 (89, repr.); *Mostra di Henry Moore*, Forte di Belvedere, Florence, May–September 1972 (128, repr.); *The Henry Moore Gift*, Tate Gallery, June–August 1978, repr. in colour p.55

Lit: Herbert Read, *Henry Moore*, 1965, p.250 (repr. pls.239, 240); Donald Hall, *Henry Moore: The Life and Work of a Great Sculptor*, 1966, pp.161–73; John Russell, *Henry Moore*, 1968, pp.193–4; John Hedgecoe and Henry Moore, *Henry Moore*, 1968, pp.345, 407–8; David Sylvester, catalogue of *Henry Moore*, Tate Gallery, 1968, p.93 (repr. pl.89); Paul Waldo Schwartz, *The Hand and Eye of the Sculptor*, 1969, pp.203–4 (repr.), 205–6; Alan G. Wilkinson, *The Moore Collection in the Art Gallery of Ontario*, Toronto, 1979, pp.184–5 (original plaster repr. pl.164)

Repr: Alan Bowness (ed.), *Henry Moore Sculpture 1964–73*, 1977, pls.8–11; John Read, *Portrait of an Artist: Henry Moore*, 1979, p.95 (repr. in colour)

L.H.518; the edition is limited to two bronzes. The original plaster is in the Moore Collection, Art Gallery of Ontario.

There is a large body of literature dealing with Moore's commission for the Lincoln Center, New York, much of it summarised by Bowness (op. cit., p.9) and Wilkinson. Both authors regard the final sculpture and its earlier, half-size working model (T.2295) as the climax to the series of two- and three-piece reclining figures in which Moore explored the implications of the figure/landscape analogy. Moore himself saw the origin of the arched leg part of the Lincoln Center figure in the earlier 'Two Piece Reclining Figure No. 2' (T.395), whose leg end reminded him of Monet's painting 'Cliff at Etretat': 'I kept thinking of this arch as if it were coming out of the sea.' (Hedgecoe, op. cit., p.345). It was intended that the Lincoln Centre sculpture should stand in a pool of water fourteen inches deep and the artist therefore took considerable care to work out the sculpture's reflection.

Moore's work on the Lincoln Center commission has prompted him to talk about the technical difficulties of enlarging sculpture to monumental size: ... 'A completely different perspective is physically involved. For example, the working model of the Lincoln Center sculpture was ... just over seven feet high, while the finished sculpture was nearly fifteen feet high.

'When I was working on the finished sculpture I found the perspective made the neck look shorter and the head look smaller. So I had to alter it to produce the same effect that I had achieved in the half-size working model.' (ibid., pp.407–8)

T.2296 **Atom Piece (Working Model for Nuclear Energy)** 1964–5

Inscribed 'Moore 0/6' and stamped with foundry mark 'H. NOACK BERLIN' on foot
Bronze, $46\frac{1}{2}$ × 36 × 36 including base (118.2 × 91.5 × 91.5)
Presented by the artist 1978

Exh: *Henry Moore*, British Council, Salla Dalles, Bucharest, February–March 1966 and tour to Bratislava, Prague and Jerusalem, ending up at the Tel-Aviv Museum, November–December 1966 (31, repr.); *Henry Moore,* Art Gallery of Ontario, Toronto, October–November 1967 and tour to Charlottestown (Prince Edward Island) and St Johns (Newfoundland), ending up at the National Gallery of Canada, Ottowa, June–September 1968 (22, repr.); *Henry Moore Exhibition in Japan*, National Museum of Modern Art, Tokyo, August–October 1969 (60, repr.); *Henry Moore Bronzes 1961–1970*, Marlborough Gallery, New York, April–May 1970 (14, repr. in colour); *Henry Moore – Fem Decennier Skulptur, teckning, grafik 1923–1975*, Henie Onstad Kunstsenter, Oslo, June–July 1975 and tour to Stockholm and Ålborg (70, repr.); *Henry Moore* Expo Zürich, Zürcher Forum, Zurich, June–August 1976 (78, repr.); *Henry Moore Sculptures et Dessins*, Orangerie des Tuileries, Paris, May–August 1977 (106, repr.); *Henry Moore 8oth Birthday Exhibition*, Bradford Art Galleries and Museums, April–June 1978 (13, repr.); *The Henry Moore Gift*, Tate Gallery, June–August 1978, repr. p.53

Lit: Herbert Read, *Henry Moore*, 1965, pp.246–8 (repr. pls.237, 8); John Russell, *Henry Moore*, 1968, pp.194–5 (repr. pl.197); Paul Waldo Schwartz, *The Hand and Eye of the Sculptor*, 1969, pp.201–6 (repr. pp.196, 7); Alan G. Wilkinson, *The Moore Collection in the Art Gallery of Ontario*, Toronto, 1979, pp.188–90 (original plaster repr. pl.168)

Repr: Giulio Carlo Argan, *Henry Moore*, Milan, 1971, pl.194 in colour; Alan Bowness, ed., *Henry Moore Sculpture 1964–73*, 1977, pl.16–18

This work is L.H.525; there is an edition of six bronzes plus the artist's cast, now the Tate's, and the original plaster is in the Moore Collection, Art Gallery of Ontario. The final, twelve-foot high version ('Nuclear Energy' 1964–6, L.H. 526), a unique bronze cast, is at the University of Chicago who commissioned it to mark the twenty-fifth anniversary of the first controlled generation of nuclear power by Enrico Fermi.

The story of the commission is told by Wilkinson, op. cit. Despite its resemblance to an atomic mushroom cloud, the idea for the sculpture came from a maquette (the plaster of which is in the Moore Collection, Art Gallery of Ontario) which Moore had made a few weeks *before* the commission was proposed; its relationship to the earlier series of 'Helmet Heads' is self-evident. 'In this way', Moore later told Paul Waldo Schwartz, '... you produce better work – through its being a natural development in your own direction – than if you try to stop and think of something special.' (op. cit., p.204). Maquettes as opposed to drawings have almost invariably been the starting-point for Moore's sculptures since the late 1950s. The artist usually produces several maquettes, each small enough to hold in the hand, which can be turned round and worked on, giving him a sense of overall shape, and which, when held up against a blank wall or the sky, he can envisage on a larger scale – life-size or monument-size. Eventually one of these maquettes will be selected for the final enlarged version.

In the case of monumental pieces, Moore will make an intermediary working model such as T.2296. In both the working model and its larger version alterations may take place: '... always one is prepared and ready to alter and make changes as one carries a thing on.' (ibid., p.206).

Alan Bowness has drawn attention to the 'smooth and polished bronze surfaces' which Moore began to introduce in his sculptures after about 1963, sometimes as a contrast to rougher passages, 'as in the polished cranium of the "Atom Piece".' (op. cit., p.12). Moore sometimes works on the bronze after it returns from the foundry, polishing or using chemicals to give it a patina. On the problems of working in plaster for bronze he has written: 'If I am not absolutely sure of what is going to happen when the white plaster model is cast into bronze, I paint it to make it look like bronze...'

'When working in plaster for bronze I need to visualise it as a bronze, because on white plaster the light and shade acts quite differently, throwing back a reflected light on itself and making the forms softer, less powerful ... even weightless.' (John Hedgecoe and Henry Moore, *Henry Moore*, 1968, pp.349, 386).

T.2297 **Moon Head** 1964

Inscribed 'Moore 0/9' on base
Bronze, $22\frac{3}{4} \times 17\frac{3}{8} \times 10$ including base ($57.8 \times 44.2 \times 25.5$)
Presented by the artist 1978

Exh: *Henry Moore Sculptures and Drawings*, New Metropole Arts Centre, Folkestone, April–May 1966 and City Art Gallery, Plymouth, June–July 1966 (10); *Henry Moore*, Arts Council, Tate Gallery, July–September 1968 (132, repr.); *Henry Moore*, University of York Visual Arts Society, Heslington Hall, March 1969 (35); *Henry Moore 1961–1971*, Staatsgalerie Moderner Kunst, Munich, October–November 1971 (7, repr.); *Mostra di Henry Moore*, Forte di Belvedere, Florence, May–September 1972 (130, repr.); *Henry Moore – Fem Decennier Skulptur, teckning, grafik 1923–1975*, Henie Onstad Kunstsenter, Oslo, June–July 1975 and tour to Stockholm and Ålborg (69); *Henry Moore*, Expo Zürich, Zürcher Forum, Zurich, June–August 1976 (76); *Henry Moore 80th Birthday Exhibition*, Bradford Art Galleries and Museums, April–June 1978 (37, repr.); *The Henry Moore Gift*, Tate Gallery, June–August 1978, repr. p.56

Lit: Herbert Read, *Henry Moore*, 1965, p.244 (repr. in colour pl.234); John Russell, *Henry Moore*, 1968, p.209 (repr. pls.218, 19); John Hedgecoe and Henry Moore, *Henry Moore*, 1968, pp.466–7 (repr., and in colour p.443); David Sylvester in catalogue of *Henry Moore*, Tate Gallery, 1968, p.119 (repr. pls.108, 9); Alan G. Wilkinson, *The Moore Collection in the Art Gallery of Ontario*, Toronto, 1979, p.186 (original plaster repr. pl.166)

Repr: Elda Fezzi, *Henry Moore*, Florence, 1971, pl.41 (repr. in colour); Alan Bowness, ed., *Henry Moore Sculpture 1964–73*, 1977, pls.14, 15

L.H.521. There is an edition of nine bronzes plus the artist's cast, now the Tate's, and the original plaster is in the Moore Collection, Art Gallery of Ontario. A smaller version in porcelain exists (L.H.522)

Of this work Moore has written: 'The small version of this piece was originally called "Head in Hand", the hand being the piece at the back. [See catalogue to *The Moore Collection in the Art Gallery of Ontario*, op. cit., no.165] When I came to make it in full size, about eighteen inches high, I gave it a pale gold patina so that each piece reflected a strange, almost ghostly, light at the other. This happened quite by accident. It was because the whole effect reminded me so strongly of the light and shape of the full moon that I have since called it "Moon Head".' (Hedgecoe, op. cit.)

David Sylvester, op. cit., relates T.2297 to Moore's preoccupation with thin, flat, sharp-edged forms, and especially to the 'knife-edge' sculptures – for instance, 'Knife-Edge Two Piece' 1962, later enlarged. Compare also with 'Divided Head' 1963 (L.H.506) and 'Thin Head' 1964 (L.H.523).

T.2298 **Working Model for Three Way Piece No.1: Points** 1964

Inscribed 'Moore 0/7' on base and stamped with foundry mark 'H. NOACK BERLIN' on foot
Bronze, $25\frac{5}{8} \times 28 \times 29\frac{1}{4}$ (65.2 × 71.2 × 74.3)
Presented by the artist 1978

Exh: *Henry Moore*, University of York Visual Arts Society, Heslington Hall, March 1969 (36); *Henry Moore Drawings and Sculpture*, Arts Council, Supplementary Works lent by Henry Moore, Gordon Maynard Gallery, Welwyn Garden City, July 1969 (H.M.7); *Henry Moore*, Musée Rodin, Paris, 1971 (47, repr.); *Henry Moore Sculpture Drawings Graphics*, Turnpike Gallery, Leigh, Lancs., November–December 1971 (16); *Mostra di Henry Moore*, Forte di Belvedere, Florence, May–September 1972 (132, repr.); *Henry Moore – Fem Decennier Skulptur, teckning, grafik 1923–1975* Henie Onstad Kunstsenter, Oslo, June–July 1975 and tour to Stockholm and Ålborg (71, repr.); *Henry Moore*, Expo Zürich, Zürcher Forum, Zurich, June–August 1976 (79); *Henry Moore 80th Birthday Exhibition*, Bradford Art Galleries and Museums, April–June 1978 (38, repr.); *The Henry Moore Gift*, Tate Gallery, June–August 1978, repr. p. 56

Lit: John Russell, *Henry Moore*, 1968, pp.204–9 (repr. pl.215, 16); John Hedgecoe and Henry Moore, *Henry Moore*, 1968, p.501; Alan G. Wilkinson, *The Moore Collection in the Art Gallery of Ontario*, Toronto, 1979, pp.192–3 (original plaster repr. fig.152)

Repr: Alan Bowness, (ed), *Henry Moore Sculpture 1964–73*, 1977, repr. pls.24, 25

This work is no.532 in Lund Humphries; an edition of seven bronzes was made, plus the artist's cast, now the Tate's. The original plaster is in the Moore Collection, Art Gallery of Ontario, but was irreparably damaged in 1974. T.2298 was based on a maquette (L.H.531) and was itself enlarged to over six feet high and nearly eight feet long. There are three casts of this final bronze (L.H.533), including one at Columbia University, New York.

Wilkinson, following David Sylvester (in the 1968 Tate Gallery exhibition catalogue), traces the source of the work to a flintstone with three points touching the ground. In Hedgecoe Moore wrote that the sculpture 'was an attempt to show one work from below as well as from on top and from the side. My idea was to make a new kind of sculpture, less dependent on gravity, which could be seen in at least three positions and be effective in all of them; a sculpture which you could understand more completely because you know it better. This worked in the maquette, but I made the finished bronze sculpture too large and heavy to be turned over by one person.' Wilkinson notes that the maquette can be placed in at least seven different positions.

Alan Bowness (op. cit., p.11) stresses the 'remarkable three-dimensional variety' of the two 'Three Way Pieces' – 'Points' and 'Archer' (T.2299 below) – both of which include a pointing motif.

T.2299 **Working Model for Three Way Piece No.2: Archer** 1964

Inscribed 'Moore 0/7' on side of base and stamped with foundry mark 'H. NOACK BERLIN' on foot
Bronze, $30\frac{1}{2} \times 31 \times 25\frac{5}{8}$ (77.6 × 78.8 × 65.2)
Presented by the artist 1978

Exh: *Henry Moore*, British Council, Salla Dalles, Bucharest, February–March 1966 and tour to Bratislava, Prague and Jerusalem, ending up at Tel-Aviv Museum, November–December 1966 (32, repr.); *Henry Moore Exhibition in Japan*, National Museum of Modern Art, Tokyo, August–October 1969 (59, repr.); *Mostra di Henry Moore*, Forte di Belvedere, Florence, May–September 1972 (133, repr.); *Henry Moore – Fem Decennier Skulptur, teckning, grafik 1923–1975*, Henie-Onstad Kunstsenter, Oslo, June–July 1975 and tour to Stockholm and Ålborg (72, repr.); *Henry Moore*, Expo Zürich, Zürcher Forum, Zurich, June–August 1976 (80); *Henry Moore 80th Birthday Exhibition*, Bradford Art Galleries and Museums, April–June 1978 (39, repr. in colour); *The Henry Moore Gift*, Tate Gallery, June–August 1978, repr. p.57

Lit: Herbert Read, *Henry Moore*, 1965, p.235 (repr. pl.227; plaster in progressive stages of modelling repr. pls.223–6); John Russell, *Henry Moore*, 1968, pp.204–9; Paul Waldo Schwartz, *The Hand and Eye of the Sculptor*, 1969, pp.199–200; Alan G. Wilkinson, *The Moore Collection in the Art Gallery of Ontario*, Toronto, 1979, pp.190–3 (original plaster repr. pl.170)

Repr: Alan Bowness (ed.), *Henry Moore Sculpture 1964–73*, 1977, no.534

Lund Humphries 534. There are eight bronze casts (including the artist's, now the Tate's); another is in the Hirshhorn Museum, Washington. The original plaster is in the Moore Collection, Art Gallery of Ontario. The large version of this sculpture (L.H.535) was unveiled in 1966 in Nathan Phillips Square, Toronto, in front of Toronto City Hall. A second cast is in the National Gallery, Berlin.

The history of Toronto's commission and the subsequent gift by Moore to the city of a large number of his sculptures and drawings can be found in Wilkinson, op. cit., who compares 'Archer' to the immediately preceding work 'Three Way Piece No.1: Points' (T.2298) and concludes that both 'attest to Moore's interest in full, three-dimensional realisation in sculpture.' (p.192). As Wilkinson notes, both sculptures were probably meant to be seen in more than one position. For Moore's interest in making sculpture which can be turned and shown from different angles, see the note on T.2281 above.

As with 'Pipe' (T.2300 below), the sub-titles 'Archer' and 'Points' were given after the pieces were made as a means of identification. The word 'Archer' is particularly appropriate, however, since the forms of the sculpture suggest tension and that quality of 'pent-up energy' which Moore as early as 1934 (in his famous declaration 'The Sculptor's Aims' published in *Unit One*) had announced as being of fundamental importance to his work.

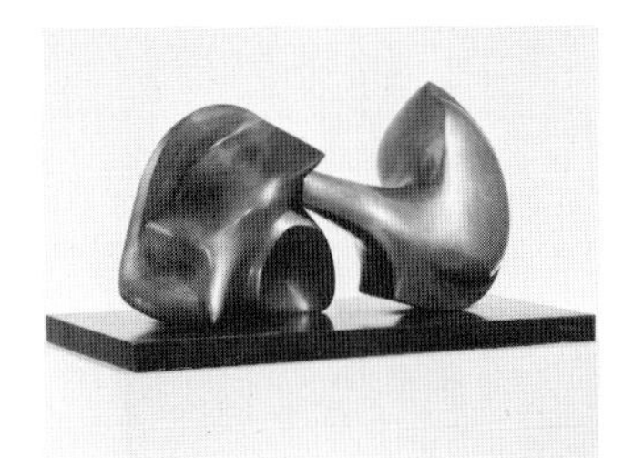

T.2300 **Two Piece Sculpture No.7: Pipe** 1966

Inscribed 'Moore 0/0' on base
Bronze, $17 \times 33 \times 12\frac{3}{8}$ (43.2 × 83.9 × 31.5)
Presented by the artist 1978

Exh: *Henry Moore*, Rijksmuseum Kröller-Müller, Otterlo, May–July 1968, Museum Boymans-Van Beuningen, Rotterdam, September–November 1968 and Mathildenhöhe, Darmstadt, Spring 1969 (118, repr.); *Henry Moore*, Arts Council, Tate Gallery, July–September 1968 (136, repr.);

Henry Moore, University of York Visual Arts Society, Heslington Hall, March 1969 (39); *Henry Moore Drawings and Sculpture*, Arts Council, Supplementary Works lent by Henry Moore, Gordon Maynard Gallery, Welwyn Garden City, July 1969 (H.M.8); *Henry Moore Bronzes 1961–1970*, Marlborough Gallery, New York, April–May 1970 (25, repr. in colour); *Henry Moore*, Musée Rodin, Paris, 1971 (49, repr.); *Mostra di Henry Moore*, Forte di Belvedere, Florence, May–September 1972 (141, repr.); *Henry Moore*, Expo Zürich, Zürcher Forum, Zurich, June–August 1976 (82); *The Henry Moore Gift*, Tate Gallery, June–August 1978, repr. p.58

Lit: John Russell, *Henry Moore*, 1968, p.193 (repr. pl.198); John Hedgecoe and Henry Moore, *Henry Moore*, 1968, p.504 (repr. and in colour p.442); David Sylvester in catalogue of *Henry Moore*, Tate Gallery, 1968, pp.38, 141 (repr. pls.29, 133); Alan G. Wilkinson, *The Moore Collection in the Art Gallery of Ontario*, Toronto, 1979, p.195 (original plaster repr. pl.171)

Repr: Giulio Carlo Argan, *Henry Moore*, Milan 1971, pl.197 in colour; Alan Bowness (ed.), *Henry Moore Sculpture 1964–73*, 1977, pls.38, 39

This is no.543 in Lund Humphries. There is an edition of nine bronzes and the original plaster is in the Moore Collection, Art Gallery of Ontario. The Tate's cast was the artist's own, making ten in all.

As with the two 'Three Way Piece' sculptures (T.2298 and T.2299 above), 'Pipe' is, in Moore's own words, 'an attempt to make a sculpture which is varied in all its views and forms.' (Hedgecoe, op. cit.). The main difference is that 'Pipe' is a work in two pieces, the seventh in the series which began in 1959 with 'Two Piece Reclining Figure No.1', and as such it offers, in common with all Moore's broken figures, an even greater variety of viewpoints. In 'Pipe', however, Moore has omitted the descriptive term 'reclining figure' from the title. The figurative references are kept to a minimum, although commentators have recognised a sexual element in the way the pipe stem seems to penetrate the second 'female' form. The two pieces actually touch and the sense of fitting together is strong.

Alan Bowness observes that the figure/landscape analogy in such works as T.2300, with their highly polished bronze surfaces, is less explicit and that 'the obvious metaphor is between figure and bone.' (op. cit., p.9).

T.2301 **Two Piece Reclining Figure No.9** 1968

Inscribed 'Moore' on base and stamped with foundry mark 'H. NOACK BERLIN' on side of base
Bronze, $56\frac{1}{2} \times 96 \times 53\frac{1}{8}$ including base (143.5 × 243.8 × 135)
Presented by the artist 1978

Exh: *Henry Moore*, Rijksmuseum Kröller-Müller, Otterlo, May–July 1968, Museum Boymans-Van Beuningen, Rotterdam, September–November 1968 and Mathildenhöhe, Darmstadt, Spring 1969 (124, repr.); *Henry Moore Bronzes 1961–1970*, Marlborough Gallery, New York, April–May 1970 (28, repr. in colour); *Henry Moore 1961–1971*, Staatsgalerie Moderner Kunst, Munich, October–November 1971 (25, repr.); *The Henry Moore Gift*, Tate Gallery, June–August 1978, repr. in colour p. 60

Lit: Alan G. Wilkinson, *The Moore Collection in the Art Gallery of Ontario*, Toronto, 1979, p.201 (original plaster repr. pl.179)

Repr: Alan Bowness (ed.), *Henry Moore Sculpture 1964–73*, 1977, pl.82–5

L.H.576; there is an edition of seven bronzes and the original plaster is in the Moore Collection, Art Gallery of Ontario.

Alan Bowness has commented that in his recent two-piece reclining figures Moore is primarily interested in 'the relationship between the two parts' and that 'the coming together of two or more parts of a sculpture is perhaps the essence of Moore's later work, both in form and subject.' (op. cit., p.9). 'Two-Piece Reclining Figure No.9' is typical of Moore's later, more abstract style with its fairly generalised references to the human figure. It is also an example of his interest in forms which touch, interlock or rest one upon the other. (See the notes on T.2300 above and T.2303 below). T.2301 relates to earlier two-piece reclining figures such as 'Two Piece No.2' 1960 (L.H.458), a cast of which is in the Tate (T.395), and the Lincoln Center sculpture of 1963–5 (T.2295 above), where the contrast between the upright torso section of the work and the horizontal leg part is clearly defined. In T.2301 the top leg projects over the lower leg, which contributes to the suggestion of a dynamic, thrusting force.

T.2302 **Large Totem Head** 1968

Inscribed 'Moore' on base and stamped with foundry mark 'GUSS: H. NOACK BERLIN' on side of base
Bronze, $96\frac{3}{4} \times 52\frac{3}{4} \times 49\frac{1}{2}$ including base (245.8 × 134.1 × 125.8)
Presented by the artist 1978

Exh: *Henry Moore*, Rijksmuseum Kröller-Müller, Otterlo, May–July 1968, Museum Boymans-Van Beuningen, Rotterdam, September–November 1968 and Mathildenhöhe, Darmstadt, Spring 1969 (123, plaster repr.); *Henry Moore Bronzes 1961–1970*, Marlborough Gallery, New York, April–May 1970 (30, repr.); *Henry Moore*, Expo Zürich, Zürcher Forum, Zurich, June–August 1976 (87); *The Henry Moore Gift*, Tate Gallery, June–August 1978, repr. in colour p.61

Lit: Alan Bowness (ed.), *Henry Moore Sculpture 1964–73*, 1977, p.11 (repr. pls.86, 87)

'Large Totem Head' is no.577 in Lund Humphries; there is an edition of eight bronzes.

The sculpture was developed from a small maquette-size work of 1963 called 'Boat Form' in which the same shape is tilted on its side. Moore suggested to the compiler (12 December 1980) that when enlarged and standing vertically the sculpture has a quite different presence, evoking a huge impassive face with eyes.

T.2303 **Working Model for Three Piece No.3: Vertebrae** 1968

Inscribed 'Moore 0/8' and 'H. NOACK BERLIN' on base
Bronze, 37 × 93 × 48 including base (94 × 236.3 × 122)
Presented by the artist 1978

Exh: *Henry Moore*, Tate Gallery, July–September 1968 (142); *Henry Moore Bronzes 1961–1970*, Marlborough Gallery, New York, April–May 1970 (31, repr. in colour); *Henry Moore 1961–1971*, Staatsgalerie Moderner Kunst, Munich, October–November 1971 (24, repr.); *Henry Moore – Fem Decennier Skulptur, teckning, grafik 1923–1975*, Henie-Onstand Kunstsenter, Oslo, June–July 1975 and tour to Stockholm and Ålborg (77, repr.); *Henry Moore*, Expo Zürich, Zürcher Forum, Zurich, June–August 1976 (88); *Henry Moore 80th Birthday Exhibition*, Bradford Art Galleries and Museums, April–June 1978 (14, repr.); *The Henry Moore Gift*, Tate Gallery, June–August 1978, repr. p.62

Lit: David Sylvester in catalogue of *Henry Moore*, Tate Gallery, 1968, p.141 (sketch-model repr. pl.140); Alan G. Wilkinson, *The Moore Collection in the Art Gallery of Ontario*, Toronto, 1979, p.202 (another cast repr. pl.180)

Repr: Alan Bowness (ed.), *Henry Moore Sculpture 1964–73*, 1977, pls.88–91

L.H.579. There are nine bronze casts including the artist's, now the Tate's; another is in the Moore Collection, Art Gallery of Ontario.

The sculpture was based on a hand-size maquette (L.H.578) and was itself enlarged to make a work over twenty-four feet long (L.H.580), of which there are three casts, in Seattle, Jerusalem and Düsseldorf. This large version can be arranged with the three pieces placed well apart from one another, in a roughly triangular format, so that the intervening spaces can be 'inhabited' or walked through. The 'Working Model', however, does not possess this environmental dimension.

Moore told the compiler (12 December 1980) that each form resembled the joins between vertebrae. What interested him was the idea of a series or progression of similar forms. The note on T.2289 above contains a more detailed explanation by Moore of this idea and its implication for multi-part sculpture in general.

Ben Nicholson, O.M. b.1894

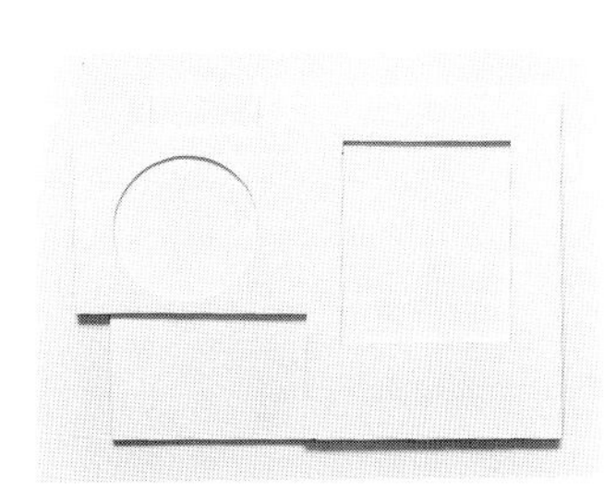

T.2314 **relief 1934** 1934

Inscribed 'Ben Nicholson' and 'title: relief 1934' on back
Oil on carved mahogany panel, $28\frac{1}{4} \times 38 \times 1\frac{1}{2}$ (71.8 × 96.5 × 3.8)
Purchased from the artist (Grant-in-Aid) 1978
Exh: (?) *Work by Members of the Artists International Association*, Brighton Art Gallery, August 1939 (71)

Ben Nicholson made his first completed relief in Paris in December 1933. This and the other reliefs made in the next month or two were usually painted in greys and browns. The first relief painted completely in white was executed in March 1934, the month in which he exhibited a white relief '2 circles' at the 7&5 Society exhibition at the Leicester Galleries. In most of the white reliefs the excavated areas were bounded by circles; a rectangular excavated area as in the right-hand side of T.2314 is unusual.

The artist told the compiler in April 1979 that he could not recall exactly when he made T.2314. Seven reliefs dating from 1934 were included in Nicholson's exhibition at the Lefevre Gallery in September 1935 and one dating from 1934 was included in his exhibition there in May 1947, but it is impossible to say whether this particular work was among them. The remains of an Artists International Association label on the back makes it almost certain, however, that it was included in the *Exhibition of Work by Members of the Artists International Association* at Brighton Art Gallery in August 1939.

T.2337–42 **Mulchelney**

6 reliefs (details as below), enclosed in glass-fronted case, $43 \times 48\frac{5}{8} \times 8\frac{3}{4}$ (109.2 × 123.3 × 22.2)

T.2337 **Jan 14–65 (Capraia) – Project for Free-Standing Relief Wall** 1965

Inscribed on reverse 'Jan 14–65 (Capraia) Ben Nicholson project for free standing relief wall'
Oil on millboard, $13\frac{3}{4} \times 10\frac{1}{4} \times \frac{1}{4}$ (35 × 26.1 × 6)
Presented by the artist 1979
Exh: *Ben Nicholson: Recent Work*, Galerie Gimpel & Hanover, Zurich, June–July 1966 (not in catalogue); *Ben Nicholson*, Tate Gallery, June–July 1969 (116)

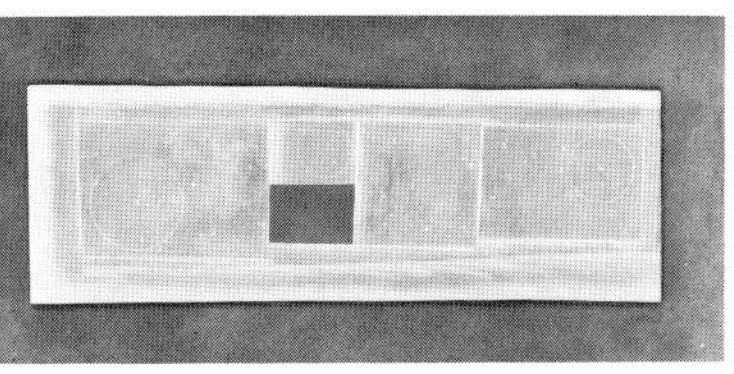

T.2338 Wall Project 62–75 1962–75

Inscribed on reverse 'wall project Nicholson 62–75'
Oil on millboard, $10\frac{3}{4} \times 24\frac{1}{8} \times \frac{1}{4}$ (27.3 × 61.2 × 6)
Presented by the artist 1979
Exh: *Ben Nicholson*, Tate Gallery, June–July 1969 (107) as 'December 1962 (galaxy project for a free-standing wall)'

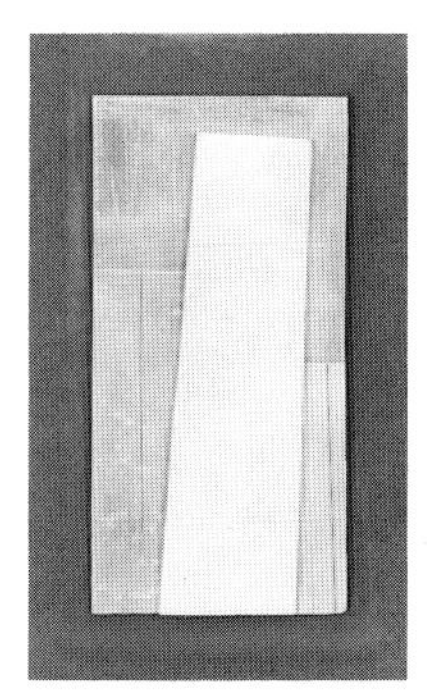

T.2339 Feb 65 (Cascais) Project for Wall with Trees & Water or Rolling Countryside Trees & Sea 1965

Inscribed on reverse 'Ben Nicholson Feb 65 (Cascais)/project for wall with trees & water or rolling countryside trees & sea'
Oil on millboard, $17\frac{5}{8} \times 10\frac{7}{8} \times \frac{3}{8}$ (45.2 × 27.7 × 9)
Presented by the artist 1979
Exh: *Ben Nicholson*, Tate Gallery, June–July 1969 (117)
Repr: John Russell, *Ben Nicholson drawings paintings and reliefs 1911–68*, 1969, p.40

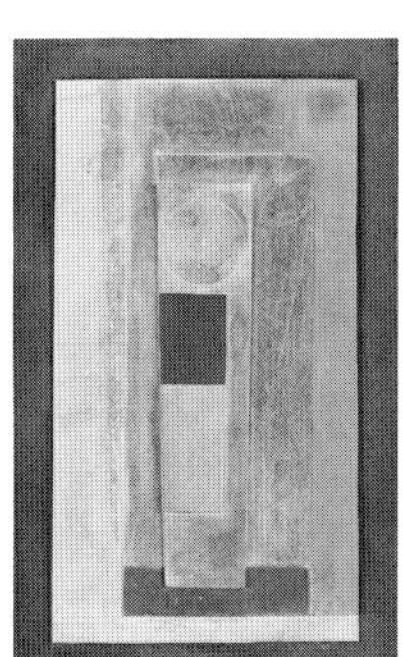

T.2340 Vertical Wall 66 1966

Inscribed on reverse 'Nicholson 66/vertical wall 66' 'do not change screwed on frame or its texture or its kind BN'
Oil on millboard, $17 \times 10\frac{1}{2} \times \frac{3}{8}$ (43.2 × 26.2 × 9)
Presented by the artist 1979
Exh: *Ben Nicholson*, Tate Gallery, June–July 1969 (118) as 'March 1965'

T.2341 (Forms) Nov 78 1978

Inscribed on reverse 'NICHOLSON (forms) Nov 78'
Bodycolour on paper on millboard, $9\frac{1}{8} \times 7\frac{1}{4}$ (23.2 × 19.1)
Presented by the artist 1979

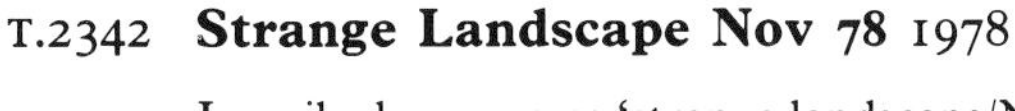

T.2342 Strange Landscape Nov 78 1978

Inscribed on reverse 'strange landscape/Nicholson/(probably) Nov 78'
Bodycolour on paper mounted on millboard, $5\frac{5}{8} \times 6\frac{1}{2}$ (14.2 × 16.5)
Presented by the artist 1979
Lit: Charles Harrison, in catalogue of *Ben Nicholson*, Tate Gallery, June–July 1969, p.116 for a general discussion of the reliefs

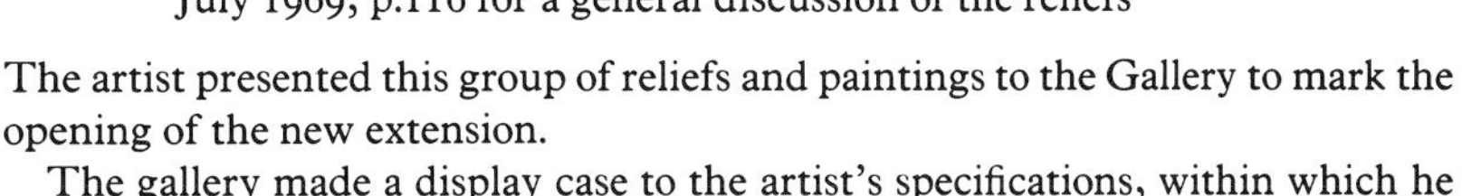

The artist presented this group of reliefs and paintings to the Gallery to mark the opening of the new extension.

The gallery made a display case to the artist's specifications, within which he positioned each work exactly. Having done so he considered the group as a whole, in this arrangement, to constitute a serendipity and gave it the title 'Mulchelney' (Mulchelney, a village in Somerset, contains the remains of a medieval abbey). Nicholson wrote to the compiler in April 1981 that 'The "place" virtually does not exist but the POETIC idea does exist mentally. I suppose a piece of "visual poetry"?'

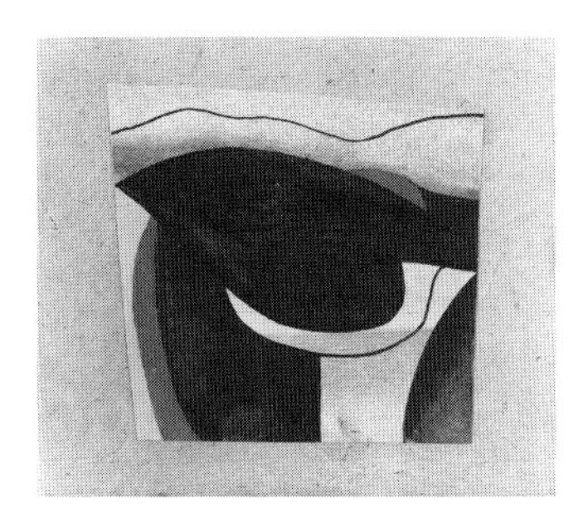

In an earlier letter he wrote 'So that I took a good deal of very considerable trouble to make it as one whole and it is not merely works enclosed in (a) glass case ... There are a number of works in the Tate very small and each enclosed in a glass case for protection but ... that is a different solution and mine is not intended in that way, *it came about* and has the incidental effect of being a protection.'

Several of the works were shown in the Tate Gallery retrospective exhibition of 1969. These works are all projects for wall sculptures, never built.

The only one of Nicholson's wall reliefs to be constructed to architectural scale was that shown at *Documenta III* in Kassel in 1964. It was subsequently demolished.

The most recent works contain references to the jugs and mugs that have been a subject of Nicholson's art for more than seventy years.

Nicholson has written to the compiler concerning the title of the works: 'I think the titles as pencilled in are a continuation of the works in question. One does not, I feel, require any rational explanation of them but merely records them as written by this (artist): in fact there is no logical explanation necessary – after all it is not the museum's responsibility but the artists . . . The details of title and dates of Mulchelney were deliberate and I suppose all of this is a strange kind of "poem".'

Quotations are taken from letters to the compiler of 28 October 1980 and 14 April 1981.

Roderic O'Conor 1860–1940

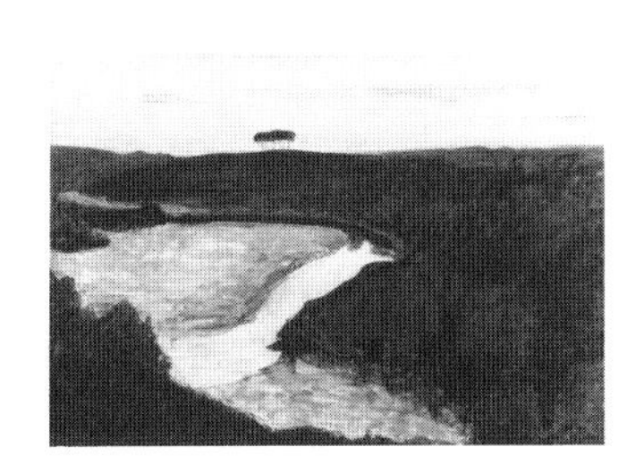

T.2328 **Landscape with a River** *c.*1900–14

Not inscribed
Oil on canvas, $26\frac{3}{4} \times 36\frac{3}{8}$ (68 × 92.5)
Presented by Mr and Mrs Barnett Shine 1978

Prov: Atelier O'Conor; Crane Kalman Gallery (purchased at a Paris auction, about 1966); Barnett Shine, 1967

Exh: Crane Kalman Gallery, Summer 1966 (no catalogue)

There are few dated landscapes by O'Conor between 1900 and 1914, but the thin paint and blurred shapes of T.2328 may be compared to a Provençal landscape 'The Balustrade' which is dated 1913 (repr. in colour in *Apollo*, XCIII, June 1971, advertisements). The Crane Kalman Gallery sold the painting as 'Landscape in Brittany', but the location of the landscape is not known.

Gordon Onslow Ford b.1912

T.2391 **A Present for the Past** 1942

Inscribed '14.8.42' bottom right and 'A present for the past/Erongarícuaro 1942/G. Onslow-Ford' on back of canvas
Oil on canvas, $39\frac{5}{8} \times 47\frac{1}{2}$ (100.8 × 120.7)
Bequeathed by Mrs Jacqueline Marie Onslow Ford 1979

Exh: *Gordon Onslow-Ford*, Nierendorf Gallery, New York, January–February 1946 (2); *Paintings by Gordon Onslow-Ford*, San Francisco Museum of Art, November–December 1948 (no catalogue); *California: 5 Footnotes to Modern Art History*, Los Angeles County Museum, January–April 1977 (Dynaton Revisited 4, repr.)

Repr: *Towards a New Subject in Painting: Gordon Onslow-Ford*, San Francisco Museum of Art 1948, p.43; *Art News*, LXXVI, January 1977, p.73

The artist provided the following note on this work in August 1979: 'When this painting was made, I was haunted by what went on beyond dreams in the psyche. I had no pre-existing model from which to work. My approach to the unknown was through numerous automatic drawings that were distilled on to canvas. The painting began with lines and blank space, the lines were then integrated with space, by giving off light on one side and by being dark on the other. From this base, the painting slowly grew out of itself. Each part was an invention that did not become clear until it was down on the canvas. I had the impression that, in venturing into the inner worlds, nothing was lost. All was there, but seen in a new way, a merging and interlacing of sky, mountains, plants and creatures.

'In writing of the inner-worlds, words say too much in that they have associations with the known, words say too little in that they are inadequate to express a new kind of reality.

'The painting took about six months of continuous work. Two versions were kept going at the same time, a clarification in one version led to a further clarification in the other. In their final state the two paintings were far from identical. The other version belonged to Wolfgang Paalen. He informed me a few months before his tragic death in 1959, that it had perished in a disaster about which he had not the heart to talk.

'This painting is a sequel to "The Circuit of the Light Knight through the Dark Queen", 1942. Here, the Queen has a halo-crowned head and a glowing crater, her body extends to form a landscape embellished with jewels and objects. The Knight has moved from being a questing Knight to being accepted as the Queen's Knight. As before, he is seen in different places and assumes different forms in the painting.

'The pair accommodate each other in a courtly way. There are chequer-board lines bent by space and time, some squares are filled in, some are empty, suggesting that a game or a quest is taking place. The whole is oriented towards a central egg form, as if in deference to a primordial parent. When this painting was made, my preoccupations, as I recall them, were mostly in terms of forms and colours. Forms and colours came to the pioneer painter first, words follow, perhaps years later, if at all.

'When this painting was finished, I saw that it did not succeed in expressing all the qualities that I had sought, for example: I felt that the realm of the Dark Queen should be transparent, but the world as painted gave the impression of being solid. I knew, that other ways of expression had to be found. In looking back, it can be seen that aspects of the landscape of the Queen had grown from Cezanne and Cubism, and the Light Knight was a distant relative of de Chirico's manikins. I called this painting "A Present for the Past", in the hope that it would add lustre to those paintings that had marked my way, and also to give me courage to venture further'.

There is a photograph of Onslow Ford's studio at Erongarícuaro in Mexico, where the picture was painted, which shows part of the other version and which confirms that the other picture was very similar but not identical in composition, and much darker in tone.

Wolfgang Paalen 1905 or '7–59

T.2392 **Le Messager** (The Messenger) 1941

Inscribed 'W/P41' bottom right
Oil on canvas, $78\frac{1}{4} \times 30\frac{1}{4}$ (198.8 × 76.7)
Bequeathed by Mrs Jacqueline Marie Onslow Ford 1979

Prov: Mr and Mrs Gordon Onslow Ford, Erongarícuaro, Mexico, and Inverness, California (purchased from the artist *c.*1941)

Exh: *Homenaje a Wolfgang Paalen el Precursor*, Museo de Arte Moderno, Bosque de Chapultepec, Mexico, September–October 1967 (8)

Lit: Gordon Onslow-Ford, 'Paalen the Messenger' in *Hommage to Wolfgang Paalen*, Museo de Arte Moderno, Bosque de Chapultepec, Mexico, 1967, pp.25–6, repr. n.p. in colour

Gordon Onslow Ford wrote of this work in a note of August 1979: ' "The

Messenger'' is one of the first paintings that Wolfgang Paalen made at his home at San Angel Inn, on the outskirts of Mexico City. This painting was an abrupt change from his previous work in Europe. As a member of the Surrealist Group he invented the automatic technique of *Fumage* (painting with smoke from a lighted candle into a ground of wet paint). *Fumage* was a means to evoke images of dream, wish and myth on the canvas that might otherwise have remained dormant. In Mexico, Paalen's preoccupations turned away from the romantic and towards pragmatic philosophies of the USA, Modern Science and Amerindian Art.

'While ''The Messenger'' was being painted, the first number of Paalen's magazine *DYN* was in preparation with a leading article entitled: ''Farewell to Surrealism'', which, when it came out in 1942, took the Surrealists in New York City completely by surprise.

'Paalen's studio was built around a Tlingit masterpiece that he had acquired in the Pacific North West. It was a wooden totem screen, 15′ × 9′, from a community house. The screen represented a brown bear (it is now in the Denver Art Museum). The bear had eyes and faces staring from the joints, paws and head and there was a hole in the body through which in certain ceremonies the chief and initiates emerged (being born). This Earth-Mother Bear was a powerful influence in the studio and may have engendered the leap of awareness that occurred in Paalen's painting.

' ''The Messenger'' is an apparition from deep space. He is made of the same stuff as space. Like most ghosts from the past or, in this case, from the future, he is silent; his message must be sought in the guise in which he appears. The painting is structured with rapid curved lines that have colours between them, playing hot and cold to accentuate an endless, undulating surface with occasional protrusions.

' ''The Messenger'' flies-floats in his ocean of space-matter; his world goes with him as he goes. He stops those who SEE him in their tracks, and once seen, he can never be forgotten. The white egg shaped face has an air of concentration. He is dedicated to his mission. The eyes are paraboloid. They touch the lips and are focused far away as if they are receiving and transmitting. Their lines of sight extend on each side of the observer; who is drawn in and ignored at the same time.

'The painting is a presage of man's first walk in space, 28 years later. This painting was titled ''Le Messager'' (masculine), but the apparition could be seen as being androgynous. It might be of interest to note that the Androgyne appears on Tarot card number 21 of the original Marseilles pack. If the major arcana numbered 1 to 22 symbolise the stages of awareness along the way to enlightenment, then the Androgyne is the final stage before union with the divine or, from another point of view, the root of Being in the Mind.

' ''The Messenger'' shows us his space-body and may be reminding us that our bodies too are made up of cosmic material, and that, if only we could realise it, we are, in our flesh and bones, already in relation to the heavens.

'Paalen's Messenger comes to awaken us to the urgent need for a quest in space both inner and outer'.

Paalen's other paintings of this period and type have titles such as 'Space Unbound', 'Aerogyl Prismatic' and 'The Cosmogons', and there is an etching of 1941 which is very similar to the present work and has the same title.

John Quinton Pringle 1864–1925

T.2329 **The Window** 1924

Not inscribed
Oil on canvas, 22 × 18 (55.8 × 45.7)

Presented by James Meldrum 1979

Prov: Given by the artist to William Meldrum, by whom bequeathed in 1942 to his son James Meldrum, the donor

Exh: *John Q. Pringle 1964–1925: A Centenary Exhibition*, Glasgow Art Gallery and Museum, summer 1964 (85) and subsequent Scottish Arts Council tour in 1968 of a selection of the 1964 exhibition; *Eighty Ninth Exhibition*, Paisley Art Institute March–April 1973 (59); *John Quinton Pringle 1864–1925*, City of Edinburgh Art Centre, October 1973 (no catalogue)

J. Q. Pringle did not paint in oils between 1911 and 1921. In the latter year he visited Whalsay, an island on the eastern part of Shetland Islands at the invitation of a friend, Dr W. G. Wilson, a physician, with whom he stayed, and painted three oils and a number of watercolours. Pringle sold his optical and repair business in 1923 in order that he could paint fulltime. The following year Pringle visited Whalsay again staying with Dr Wilson from June until August. In a letter to the donor dated 8 August 1924 Pringle wrote: 'I have been working on 4 small W.C. most of the time here and just feel at times I have not kept them simple enough . . . I have kept to the shore in all I have been doing in chalk or brush. I have only 1 oil with the weather we have here.' The oil referred to is not 'The Window' but 'Girl in White, Whalsay' (Glasgow Art Gallery), a view of a rocky sea shore to which he probably later added the figure of a girl.

'The Window' was also painted during this visit to Whalsay; Pringle told the donor that is was executed in his bedroom because for much of his stay the weather was cold and wet preventing painting out of doors. Like 'The Window', 'The Grandfather Clock' (Glasgow Art Gallery) an unfinished oil painting by Pringle dating from about 1924, also consists compositionally mainly of rectilinear forms.

This catalogue entry has been compiled largely from information supplied by Mr James Meldrum.

Bernard Reder 1897–1963

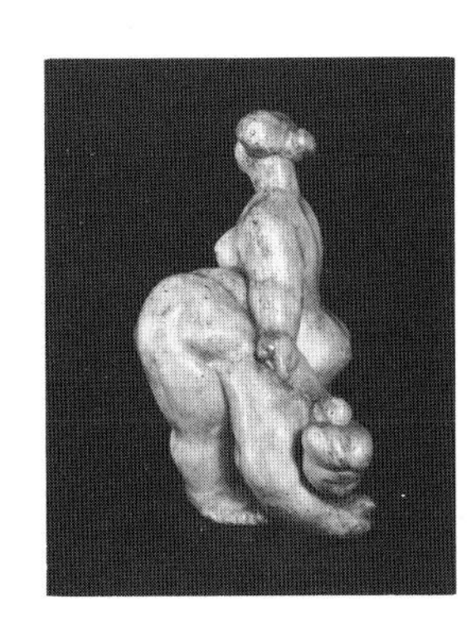

T.2320 **Two Bathers** 1934

Not inscribed
Plaster cast, $10\frac{5}{8} \times 10\frac{1}{4} \times 7\frac{1}{4}$ (27 × 26 × 18.6)
Presented by Eugene Rosenberg 1978

Prov: Eugene Rosenberg, Prague and London (purchased from the artist 1936)

Lit: John I. H. Baur in exh. catalogue *Bernard Reder*, Whitney Museum, New York, September–November 1961 and tour, pp.14–15, pewter cast repr. as cat. no.29

Executed in Prague, where Reder lived from 1930 to 1937 and where he established his mature style. His dominant theme at this time was the female nude and he worked mainly at stone carving. However this particular work appears to be one of several small sculptures modelled for bronze casting, which have a more sensuous quality than the stones. A cast in pewter then in the collection of Mr and Mrs Joseph D. Isaacson was included in his retrospective exhibition at the Whitney Museum, New York, in 1961 and is reproduced in the catalogue with the title and date 'Two Bathers' 1934. This plaster cast was bought from the artist in Prague by Eugene Rosenberg, who had a bronze cast made from it in England just after the war which is still in his possession. As far as is known, there are no versions on a larger scale.

The rounded, full forms and compact grouping accord with Reder's preoccupation with the importance of volume and 'all-sidedness'. 'Objects in nature are volumetric, all-sided,' he wrote; 'therefore axiomatic, not theoretical. All views of volumetric sculpture and all approaches to it – from around, above, below – are of the same importance. They have the axiomatic value of the sphere and require no theoretical explanations. In the volumetric approach to sculpture, none of its views can escape the control of the sculptor, the observance of the spectator.' (From a statement published in the Whitney Museum catalogue, p.7).

Oliffe Richmond 1919–77

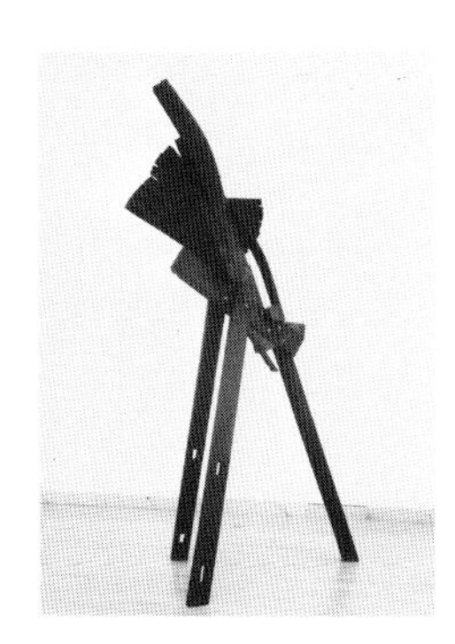

T.2405 **Tripod IV** 1973

Not inscribed
Oakwood secured with steel bolts and nuts, 123¼ × 65⅜ × 46 (311.3 × 166 × 177)
Purchased from the artist's widow (Grant-in-Aid) 1979
Exh: *Oliffe Richmond*, Commonwealth Institute Art Gallery, January–February 1976 (one of 14 works in wood, nos. 1–14, not individually titled)

Born in Tasmania, Oliffe Richmond studied sculpture at the East Sydney Technical College. Following the award of a New South Wales Travelling Scholarship in 1948 he moved to England, working as an assistant to Henry Moore in 1949–50. In the 1950s and part of the 1960s Richmond's work, in bronze, was concerned mainly with the human figure, either singly or in groups. Towards the end of the 1960s he started to make abstract sculpture, both in bronze and aluminium often suggesting the human figure. From 1970 until his death he often worked in wood; some of his works in this medium were 10 feet (*c.* 3 metres) or more high, as is 'Tripod IV' 1973, in which barrel staves were used in the construction.

Gerhard Richter b.1932

T.2348 **Abstract Painting No.439** 1978

Inscribed on back of canvas '439' top left, and 'Richter, 1978' top right
Oil on canvas, 78¾ × 118$\frac{3}{16}$ (200 × 300)
Purchased from the artist through the Whitechapel Art Gallery (Grant-in-Aid) 1979
Exh: *Gerhard Richter: Abstract Paintings*, Van Abbemuseum, Eindhoven, October–November 1978 (works not numbered, listed as 'No.439' and repr. in colour); Whitechapel Art Gallery, March–April 1979 (works not numbered, listed as 'No.439' and repr. in colour)
Repr: *Tate Gallery 1978–80*, p.56 in colour

The works in the Eindhoven–Whitechapel Art Gallery exhibition consisted mainly of a series of very large abstract paintings based on small tachiste oil sketches, the sketch used for this one being T.2380.

The artist writes (letter of 10 August 1980): 'I do not paint the oil sketches with the intention of using them for the big smooth pictures, but I subsequently use some of the sketches as patterns for the big pictures. The oil sketches look as though they had been painted quickly, but often take longer than the big paintings as they are altered from time to time to look as heterogeneous as possible. When I want to use an oil sketch for a larger picture, I make photographs or slides of it, which I then project onto the canvas in order to draw the outlines with charcoal. The painting in colours is then done with brushes in the classical manner

(Primamalerei), more or less freely after the pattern (a quite traditional method as with the "Old Masters"). I never use air-brushes as they are too cumbersome and imprecise. The smoothness is achieved in the course of the painting process, starting with small brushes and ending with large, approximately 10 cm wide soft brushes which efface all traces of the handwriting and create the sfumato-effect and the illusion of photograph-like smoothness.

'I should say that the fantasy-landscape, the science-fiction like effect appears of its own accord, without my consciously planning it'.

The paintings are executed with commercial oil paint made by the firm Schmincke of Düsseldorf, which he thins a little with lindseed oil with an addition of clove oil, and the numbers 439, 432/11 and so on refer to the serial numbering of his work catalogue.

T.2380 **Oil Sketch No.432/11** 1977

Inscribed on back of canvas '432/11' top left and 'Richter, 77' top right
Oil on canvas, $20\frac{5}{8} \times 30\frac{13}{16}$ (52.4 × 78.2)
Purchased from the artist through the Whitechapel Art Gallery (Grant-in-Aid) 1979

Exh: *Gerhard Richter: 17 Pictures*, Anna Leonowens Gallery, Nova Scotia College of Art and Design, Halifax, July 1978 (no catalogue); *Gerhard Richter: Abstract Paintings*, Van Abbemuseum, Eindhoven, October–November 1978 (not listed); Whitechapel Art Gallery, March–April 1979 (not listed)

The artist confirms that he used this oil sketch as a study for T.2348 and that it is unrelated to any other picture.

Manuel Rivera b.1927

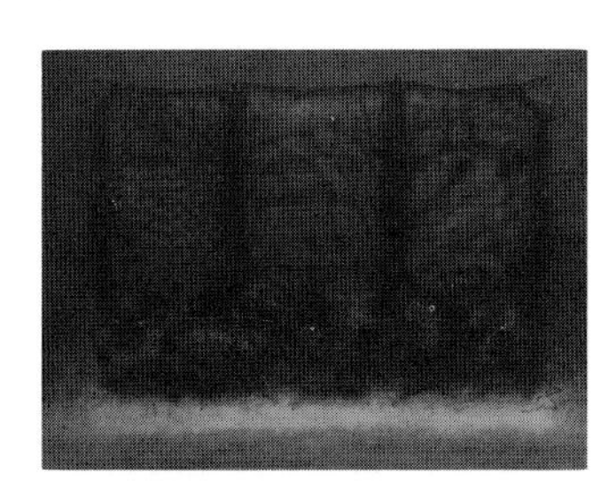

T.2384 **Metamorphosis (Three Mirrors)** 1963

Inscribed '–M.Rivera–' bottom right and on the back 'MANUEL RIVERA – "METAMORFOSIS" (TRES ESPEJOS) 1963/–M. RIVERA–', together with an arrow pointing downwards and the word 'BASE'
Painted wire, metal gauze and metal rod relief-construction on a wooden board, $35\frac{1}{4} \times 47\frac{1}{4} \times 4\frac{3}{4}$ (89.5 × 120 × 30.5)
Presented by Sir George Labouchere through the Friends of the Tate Gallery 1979

Prov: Sir George Labouchere, Madrid and Bridgnorth (purchased from the artist through the Galería Juana Mordó, Madrid, 1963)

Exh: *Colección del Excmo. Sr. George Labouchere*, Museo Nacional Arte Contemporánea, Madrid, June 1965 (17)

Repr: *The Friends of the Tate Gallery: Annual Report 1st May 1979–30th April 1980*, 1980, p.15

After making a series of works from 1958 onwards with web-like configurations of wire mesh stretched across an open frame (such as the Tate's 'Metamorphosis (Self-Portrait)' of 1961), Rivera began to work with painted wooden backgrounds and to introduce volume by building the forms forward from the background plane. The wire screens were used to create moiré patterns that attract the eye and create changing, shimmering surfaces, hence the subtitle 'Mirror' which he has given to these works.

William Roberts 1895–1980

T.2346 **Playground (The Gutter)** 1935

Inscribed 'Roberts. 36' bottom right
Oil on canvas, $56\frac{3}{8} \times 62\frac{3}{4}$ (143.2 × 159.4)
Purchased from Ernest Cooper (Grant-in-Aid) 1979

Prov: Ernest Cooper, Findon (purchased from the artist)

Exh: ('The Gutter') *William Roberts*, Lefevre Gallery, March 1938 (7) as 'The Gutter'; *International Exhibition*, Carnegie Institute, Pittsburgh, October–November 1938 (147, repr.); *Contemporary British Art*, New York World's Fair, April–October 1939 (British pavilion 110); *Contemporary British Art*, British Council tour to Canadian and US museums, December 1939–September 1940 (110); *Contemporary British Art*, Toledo Museum of Art, October 1942 (76, repr.); ('The Playground') *William Roberts ARA: Retrospective Exhibition*, Tate Gallery, November–December 1965 (53, 'The Gutter' repr.); Laing Art Gallery, Newcastle, January 1966 (53, 'The Gutter' repr.); Whitworth Art Gallery, Manchester, January–February 1966 (53, 'The Gutter' repr.); *Paintings and Drawings by William Roberts, RA from the Ernest Cooper Collection*, Worthing Art Gallery, April–June 1972 (21) as 'The Gutter I'

Repr: ('The Gutter') William Roberts, *Paintings 1917–1958*, 1960, p.41 as 'The Playground' 1934–5; *Tate Gallery 1978–80*, p.57 in colour

This was originally the left-hand part of a larger picture 'The Gutter', of which T.2347 was the right-hand section. The canvas was divided into two after its return from the USA at the end of the war as it had been slightly damaged and also because Roberts decided that it would not sell on such a scale. A strip about a foot wide between the two sections was partly folded back behind the stretcher and partly cut away, and there was a little overpainting along the divisions. The section removed showed three boys, one behind another, all playing with tops and whips; the one in the foreground was in a kneeling position.

William Roberts said that he made this exceptionally large picture because he had heard that artists were being commissioned to paint pictures for a new Cunard or P & O liner (probably the *Queen Mary*, for which various artists made decorations in 1935) and that representatives of the shipping company were visiting artists' studios to look at their work. His original intention had been to paint a picture more or less the same size and composition as 'The Playground'. The picture was painted at Haverstock Hill, NW3, which he left in 1935, and signed and incorrectly dated 1936 when divided years later.

T.2347 **Skipping (The Gutter)** 1935

Inscribed 'Roberts. 1936' bottom right
Oil on canvas, $56\frac{7}{8} \times 27\frac{3}{4}$ (144.5 × 70.5)
Purchased from Ernest Cooper (Grant-in-Aid) 1979

Prov: Ernest Cooper, Findon (purchased from the artist)

Exh: ('The Gutter') as for T.2346; ('Skipping') *William Roberts ARA: Retrospective Exhibition*, Tate Gallery, November–December 1965 (54, 'The Gutter' repr.); Laing Art Gallery, Newcastle, January 1966 (54, 'The Gutter' repr.); Whitworth Art Gallery, Manchester, January–February 1966 (54, 'The Gutter' repr.); *Paintings and Drawings by William Roberts, RA from the Ernest Cooper Collection*, Worthing Art Gallery, April–June 1972 (22) as 'The Gutter II'

Repr: as for T.2346

This was originally the right-hand section of 'The Gutter', of which the left-hand part is T.2346. The signature and incorrect date 1936 were added when the picture was divided.

Claude Rogers 1907–79

T.2326 The Paraplegic 1970–1

Inscribed 'C. Rogers' top left
Oil on hardboard, $19\frac{1}{8} \times 19$ (48.6×48.3)
Presented by the Trustees of the Chantrey Bequest 1978

Prov: Purchased by the Chantrey Trustees from the artist through Fischer Fine Art 1978

Exh: *Claude Rogers Paintings and Drawings 1927–1973*, Whitechapel Art Gallery, April 1973, Birmingham City Art Gallery, May–June 1973, Reading Museum and Art Gallery, June–July 1973, Southampton City Art Gallery, August–September 1973, Bradford City Art Gallery, September–October 1973, Mappin Art Gallery, Sheffield, November 1973 (73, repr.); *Claude Rogers Recent Paintings*, Fischer Fine Art, January–February 1978 (3); RA, May–September 1979 (15)

Lit: Andrew Forge, catalogue introduction *Claude Rogers Paintings and Drawings 1927–1973*, (op. cit., n.p.)

Repr: *The Connoisseur*, CLXXXIII, 1973, p.157; *RA Illustrated*, 1979, p.2

The woman being supported by two nurses in this painting is the artist's wife, the painter Elsie Few who died in December 1980. Following a stroke, in March 1970, she was admitted to the National Temperance Hospital, Hampstead Road, London, where she stayed for nearly three months. She believed that this hospital may have been chosen because it is a branch of University College Hospital and Claude Rogers was a fellow of University College.

While in The National Temperance Hospital, Mrs Rogers was under the care of Dr P. J. D. Heaf who wrote (letter 15 December 1980) that T.2326 shows one end of Ward 2 in the Insull Wing; a ward consisting of single rooms each opening off one side of a corridor.

In an earlier letter (2 December 1980) Dr Heaf said that he had tried to trace some of the nurses who might have been working on the ward at that time but that they had all left University College Hospital by now. The three he had contacted had been unable to identify those in T.2326. He pointed out that as the National Temperance Hospital is part of University College Hospital, all staff are interchangeable.

The artist visited his wife frequently during her stay in hospital and, shortly before she died, she told the compiler that she remembered that he made a great many drawings during these visits, including a series of preliminary sketches for T.2326. Mrs Rogers had in her possession two pencil drawings showing her in a hospital bed, one dated 7 April 1970, and a further drawing (undated) of the hospital ward taken from the angle at which it appears in 'The Paraplegic', but was unable to trace the whereabouts of the other drawings, although she thought it unlikely that her husband would have destroyed them. Professor Bruce Laughton who wrote the catalogue foreword for the exhibition at Fischer Fine Art in 1978 told the compiler that shortly after Claude Rogers' death, Mrs Rogers gave a number of his drawings to his friends and it could be that these included studies for T.2326. As no record was kept of the people to whom the drawings went, it would be difficult to trace their current locations.

Dr Igor Anrep, a neighbour of the Rogers' in Highgate, in whose house the artist sometimes worked during his wife's illness, thinks that while he made drawings in situ, Rogers did not start painting 'The Paraplegic' until some time after his wife was discharged from hospital. Dr Anrep remembers that the artist obtained nurses uniforms so that he could recreate the hospital scene using models, and believes that T.2326 was painted in the studio which Rogers then had in Tasker Road, Hampstead. Bruce Laughton recollects that when he visited the artist's studio in December 1977, shortly before the exhibition at Fischer's, he saw a nurse's uniform hanging there.

From the 1950's onwards Claude Rogers made a number of paintings of hospital scenes, often as a result of time he himself spent in hospital (e.g. 'The Patient Opposite' 1952, Tate Gallery 6217) but 'The Paraplegic' is unusual in that during the early 'seventies he was chiefly occupied with landscapes and a series of aircraft pictures.

Mrs Rogers was unable to remember during which month in 1970 T.2326 was started but wrote (letter 20 October 1980) that the artist thought of it as one of his best pictures.

Colin Self b. 1941

T.2398 **Garden (All May 66)** 1966

Not inscribed
Pencil on paper, $20\frac{1}{8} \times 13\frac{3}{4}$ (51 × 34.1)
Presented by the artist 1979

Exh: Bristow's Bookshop, Norwich, 1968; *11 englische Zeichner*, Kunsthalle, Baden-Baden, May–June 1973 and tour to Kunsthalle, Bremen, July–August (Self 10, repr.); *Recente Britse Tekenkunst*, Koninklijk Museum voor Schone Kunsten, Antwerp, September–October 1973 (Self 10)

Repr: Cover of *About the House*, the magazine of the Friends of Covent Garden, March 1967 (detail, showing the majority of the drawing, not quite finished); *Eastern Daily Press*, Norwich, 5 December 1979; *Tate Gallery 1978–80*, p.58 (the triptych)

T.2399 **Gardens with Green Garden Sculpture** 1966–9

Inscribed on reverse 'The Gardens from Imagination/with green garden sculpture./Colin Self/1966 – Finished 30th March/1969'
Pencil on paper, $10\frac{1}{8} \times 11\frac{1}{4}$ (25.7 × 28.6)
Presented by the artist 1979

Exh: *11 englische Zeichner*, Kunsthalle, Baden-Baden, May–June 1973 and tour to Kunsthalle, Bremen, July–August (Self 18, as 'Gardens with green garden sculpt'); *Recente Britse Tekenkunst*, Koninklijk Museum voor Schone Kunsten, Antwerp, September–October 1973 (Self 18, as 'Gardens with green garden sculpt')

T.2400 **The Gardens – with Four Eagles** 1972

Inscribed on reverse 'COLIN SELF./THE GARDENS – WITH FOUR EAGLES. 1972.'
Pencil on board, $7\frac{3}{8} \times 13\frac{3}{4}$ (18.8 × 35.1)
Presented by the artist 1979

Exh: *11 englische Zeichner*, Kunsthalle, Baden-Baden, May–June 1973 and tour to Kunsthalle, Bremen, July–August (Self 18); *Recente Britse Tekenkunst*, Koninklijk Museum voor Schone Kunsten, Antwerp, September–October 1973 (Self 18)

The following notes, which have been approved by the artist, are based on several conversations with and dated letters from him during 1980–1.

The theme of gardens was prominent in Self's work and thoughts throughout the period 1966–73. T.2398, a drawing of Waterloo Park, Norwich, made in May 1966, was his first drawing on the theme and T.2400, dated 1972, almost the last. His very last gardens drawing (now stolen) was based on a drawing by a mental patient reproduced in Norman I. Mackenzie, *Dreams & Dreaming*, London 1965, p.143. Influential on the series as a whole was Josiah Conder, *Landscape Gardening in Japan*, Yokohama 1893.

'The Gardens [series] was perhaps born on a Bank Holiday visit to Waterloo Park, Norwich in Spring (end of April – beginning May '66). The weather was fine – like Seurat's "Bathers" atmosphere. Playing with our baby daughter Jackie. A release – as happens when Spring arrives. But like most ideas of freedom it is relative, so the gardens are at once of freedom and imprisonment, the stalemate (check/checkmate), of some kind'.

Self's gardens phase ended with the inclusion of the present three drawings and others on this theme in the Baden-Baden exhibition cited above. Since then much of his work has been concerned with more extensive landscape views, sculpture and ceramics.

He conceived his gardens series of drawings as embodying a wide range of types of garden and of human experiences. It was to be 'a world series', comparable in this sense (though not in motif or technique) with his completed series of spray drawings *1,000 Temporary Objects of Our Time*, which was exactly contemporary with the gardens series. It is not known how many gardens drawings Self made, but the number is large. As with the Tate's group of three, some were drawn from nature, some from the imagination, and some were part-real and part-imaginary. An unknown number (and ownerships) of drawings are versions of the three in the Tate's triptych. A drawing closely related to T.2399 was reproduced on the back cover of the issue of *About the House* cited above; Self inscribed his copy 'This drawing repeated plus tall column of water as at Chatsworth'. Also closely related to T.2399 is the Arts Council's drawing 'Gardens No.3' 1966, which Self adapted as the three-colour cover for *The Paris Review* No.39, Fall 1966. A drawing still in his possession and of which the Tate owns a photograph combines the foreground eagles of T.2400 (reversed) with the extreme central vista between ranks of hedges among which tall trees rise, seen in T.2399. In all these versions except T.2399, the central vista is spanned by an arch. Self sees a connection between this and the female pelvic arch, the terraces at either side being analogous to legs and the tall trees being consciously phallic: there are also lines radiating from a central point, suggesting speed and directness.

Within the gardens series, the present three drawings were conceived independently, and each is a complete work in its own right. They are mounted in a single frame in a triptych format with T.2398 in the centre flanked by T.2400 at the left and T.2399 at the right. To offer them to the Tate, Self selected them from a larger number of gardens drawings in order to make a triptych which was put together by the Tate in a precise arrangement of heights and intervals determined by him. His aim in creating this arrangement was to give the group of drawings a weight or presence equal to that of a painting. 'On seeing the three framed ... I felt that ... they were catalising each other quite powerfully and I felt extra energy being created by the triptych format'.

The densely worked, almost relief, pencil technique of T.2398 is apparent in the detail reproduced in *About the House* cited above, which was photographed in raking light. All three drawings were made in Norwich, the outer two (as well as the last week of work on T.2398) being done in his home. The time required was so great that he could keep going only with the aid of music, which fed him creatively as he worked. He remembers in particular music by the Los Angeles group Love, and by the Doors, the Beatles, the Mothers of Invention, the Rolling Stones, Bob Dylan, and Captain Beefheart.

The central drawing, T.2398, represents details of Waterloo Park, Norwich. To draw the hedge required three weeks' work on the spot; Self omitted the wire netting of a tennis court which lay beyond it. In the fourth week of May 1966 he added, at home, the yew tree and the lawn. The yew was based on one seen elsewhere in Waterloo Park. Taken as a whole the scene is thus in one sense invented.

The right-hand drawing, T.2399, was completed in March 1969 by which date Self had already drawn the large garden sculpture in the foreground. However in that month he bought his present house in Thorpe, Norwich, and in its garden he found a green glass ashtray. Sad that this de facto garden object was only an ashtray, he was curious to know what it would look like enlarged. From then on he conceived the foreground sculpture in T.2399 as being made of green glass, solid all the way through. (In other gardens drawings he projected solid glass sculptures in other colours). He conceived the conical and ovoid forms in this drawing as being topiary, in cupressus or yew. Topiary interested him as being a living fusion of art and nature, the two working together in a way he found strangely analogous to Giacometti's long drawn out process of putting on and taking off clay. The giant avenues of hedges rising to a point, which are at right angles to the central vista, reminded Self of cathedrals. He imagined that one could walk between them in a dank green light. The tapering trees were partly inspired by the scene in a topiary garden in Resnais's film *L'Année Dernière à Marienbad* 1961, in which Self was struck by the absence (repeated here) of any shadows thrown by the trees. However, despite the considerable artifice implied by the topiary, Self envisaged T.2399 as representing a lost garden left by an earlier generation (a theme expanded below). He felt satisfaction at the way in which the natural processes of growth would take over in such a garden, so that it would then develop without any of the sense of urgency of which he was aware in much of the art and the art world of the late 1960s.

Of the two pairs of eagles in the left-hand drawing, T.2400, one is in the foreground and the other, which is dark, is on the parapet which runs horizontally across the picture. Self first drew these eagles in December 1971 from those on the entrance gates of the Wells Taxi Co., Chapelfield, Norwich. Birds of various kinds appear frequently in his art, from the peacocks in some of his gardens drawings (and which appear in his 'Power and Beauty' series) to his mobile sculptures of Birds of Fate, to recent drawings of parrots. The motif of the half-circle arch in T.2400 is inspired partly by a large one in Maidstone, partly by Self's interest in the problem of doing a drawing within that format, and more by the painting 'Two Chained Monkeys' by Peter Brueghel the Elder (State Museum, Berlin) which was reproduced in a book – his first on art – which Self's father had given him at fourteen or fifteen. In this painting the monkeys are chained within a half-round window, through which galleons can be seen beyond. Its theme of imprisonment combined with the implication, in the wide space beyond, of escape, is central to the two outer drawings in this triptych. Self draws attention to 'the contrasts of situations ... Two monkeys chained, the two flying ducks "free as a bird". The harbour, with its relevance for mariners. The sweet horizon and those chains. The oppressive arch bearing down and the escape "through" to serenity. re my left panel in the triptych. "Escapes" "freedoms" oppression, barriers physical and mental, release.' He is now at work on a three-part sculpture of which one section, involving a stuffed monkey chained to a rubber tyre on a garden swing, is inspired by the same Brueghel picture.

The drawings in this triptych cannot fully be understood by a description of their imagery. They spring directly from Self's experience of life and also involve the subconscious, relating in detail to his attitude, as someone born and bred in Norwich and as an artist, to both Norwich and London, society in general and its sub-group the art world. They are one result of his experiences of being rejected in various ways, while himself simultaneously rejecting many of the values of the world around him. Both rejection experiences led to his adumbrating in the series of gardens drawings a world of inner experience signifying a high moral, religious and imaginative reality.

For Self, the period of the gardens drawings was one of change after a hectic burst of work in *c.* 1962–65, done largely in London where he enjoyed a certain worldly success. During these years he visited the United States twice and his themes reflect the artificiality of modern city life and the threat of nuclear holocaust, 'fearful, bitter, comic and real'. His work had a certain connection with Pop art but he felt, albeit relaxedly, that its frequent classification as Pop was wrong at least insofar as it implied a celebration of modern mass culture. 'I always felt more akin to George Grosz'. For his work of *c.* 1962–5 had a central theme of warning and of grim realism, deriving in part from his religious, social and anarchist convictions. Although he enjoyed living in London and his return to Norwich in 1965 was an accident, by the mid 1960s he felt he had to withdraw from the metropolitan world and art world, both in order to reaffirm his regional identity and, more, to evade the temptations of public and worldly success. Circumstances of marriage also meant leaving London. Such withdrawal was also the only way to avoid giving both tacit assent and financial support to a system of which he disapproved on both social, political, environmental and aesthetic grounds. Of these, the last included the belief among artists that big was beautiful, and the growing response to abstract art of an increasingly reductive character. He felt that in order to make an effective statement about the world an artist must not only point out what is bad but more importantly evoke what is good. It seemed to him that Picasso, because he did this, was a better artist than Bacon. Much of his own recent work had been concerned with the threat of war; in persuading mankind away from this course it was equally necessary to evoke the beauty of peace.

The gardens drawings are evidence that his deliberate choice of a more restricted environment really involved an opening out, a journey of discovery of both visually and spiritually new lands and places. It was an inward journey of self-discovery. Confirmed in the Church of England, he felt himself open to the teachings of Christ. At the same time his reaction against the large scale of the metropolitan art of the period and his rediscovery of the satisfaction he had had in childhood in working on a really small scale, involving long hours of concentration in one room, meant that he was almost literally following the injunction in Matthew 6:6 which (correctly in its essentials) Self remembered as 'Go to a room by yourself and the Lord will come to you'. In the gardens drawings Self tried to rediscover his lost innocence. The gardens formed an inner world into which he could withdraw from the grim contemporary realities of his recent work. His work could now reflect his original nature, which was one of tenderness. (His work in the Gardens years was not exclusively on peaceful themes, but 'Fallout Shelters, bombers, guard dogs, etc. were put aside'. 'My art has always swung . . . from the bizarre . . . to New Edens').

He felt that a garden was one of the best and most civilised things to which man could apply his mind. He was struck by the selflessness involved in the work of those who lay out gardens with a view to long-term effects they cannot live to enjoy. He had in mind that Voltaire, when old and in disgrace, could get joy only from a garden. Some years later he bought a cushion at a jumble sale and was surprised then to find inside it a tea towel with the legend 'When the world wearies and society ceases to satisfy, there is always the garden'. He felt this unexpected occurrence to be a confirmation of his views.

Self's concentration from 1966 on the theme of gardens was influenced by imagery that had impressed him greatly in childhood. His father, a signwriter, had given paints to local Italian prisoners of the Second World War who in turn gave the Self family examples of the pictures they had painted with them. One by Alfonso Fortunato, which hung in their front room, represented an English garden. Self came to feel that its mood and composition reflected the oppression of being a prisoner; it thus directly foreshadowed his own gardens drawings, as explained below. His mother worked in a local sweet factory, from which coloured silver toffee papers were obtained to make images of crinolined ladies in stylised gardens. After an image had been stuck on glass, black shellac was painted behind it, making it stand out like something timeless. Because he was a child, Self believed in the existence of these places, as he also did in the garden scenes in Lewis Carroll's *Alice in Wonderland* (in which white roses were painted red) which he read at his grandmother's. He considers Carroll's 'Surrealism' as a whole a definite source for his gardens drawings, although by no means as powerful as the personal influences.

Later, when adult, Self 'had a most beautiful experience of discovering a huge country house, topiary gardens (of eight gardens contained within yew hedges), a private broad (lake), woods, watergardens and acres of marshes at How Hill, near Ludham, Norfolk. This had been empty and untouched for a year. I never knew of its existence and stumbled upon it, on a hot summer's day. Later the T. S. Eliot programme was on T.V. and it was just like this and something like my drawings'. Self saw this programme on Eliot (probably "The Mysterious Mr Eliot", a full-length feature film in the 'Omnibus' series, on BBC Television on 3 January 1971) after he had conceived the Tate drawing which relates to it most closely, T.2399. But through the programme he at once felt a close affinity between certain aspects of his gardens drawings and part of 'Burnt Norton' from Eliot's *Four Quartets*, '... relating to time and experience. Memory and possibility and actuality. Burnt Norton and my Gardens are harmonious works in different media. Neither illustrates the other because neither knew of the other when they were created, but as it happens, in the best sense, they go together well in parts'. The whole of the first forty-six lines (i.e. Section I) of 'Burnt Norton' relate in this way, the lines which do so most of all being:

> 'To look down into the drained pool.
> Dry the pool, dry concrete, brown edged,
> And the pool was filled with water out of sunlight,
> And the lotus rose, quietly, quietly,
> The surface glittered out of heart of light,
> And they were behind us, reflected in the pool'.

Self describes this as 'a sort of image of metamorphosis'. After seeing the programme on Eliot, Self made one garden drawing which this part of 'Burnt Norton' inspired directly.

Although the period of these drawings was one of escape from the metropolitan world, their evocation of a secret inner world must also be understood as an escape from Self's immediate personal and local circumstances. 'Being "in and out of love" did make me (perhaps) seek a solid world (ART) which was beyond what happened in everyday events. Which is also (part) of the level on which religion works, or word from God comes. Divine inspiration, creative inspiration ...Some of the insecurities posed by my first love affair (which was good but innocent in an old world). Some of this most definitely tints or taints the outlook of much of my work of this period ... Perhaps I am seeking "a perfect place" somewhere, away from the trials and tribulations of the world? in the Gardens.'

Self also identifies 'hurt pride' as one impulse underlying his work of *c.*1962–72, giving as one example 'the loss of a "perfect" "idealised" love', and quoting the lines

> 'My woman she done me wrong –
> She stayed out all night long ...'

His pride was hurt in another way by rejection and/or lack of appreciation of his ability as an artist, starting with his parents when he was three and continuing through the art schools he attended in Norwich and London. This rejection was specifically of his ability in drawing. His reaction (which he illustrates by the story of Rocco in Visconti's film *Rocco and His Brothers* (1960), who 'was motivated into becoming a champion boxer by some terrible events he had to witness through his loved one') was to develop this art with still greater intensity of both subject and technique. He felt that all artists were using drawing with some separate end in view, as a servile medium. By contrast, he was determined to give drawing greater status in its own right. He began to do this some years before at the Slade, but the period of the Gardens series was arguably that of his greatest concentration on and refinement of drawing. Since that period his range of media has again greatly diversified. At the height of his drawing phase he worked with a battery of pencils, from 12B through to 10H, all in his hand as he worked, rather like a painter with his palette.

When Self began the Gardens series, he was living in a concrete flat without a garden. He felt that such an environment suppressed important sides of human experience and that energies which are suppressed will always come out in some form. For many flat dwellers that form is the protest/self expression of aerosol graffiti. For him it was perhaps the expression of an inner imaginative world specifically having the imagery of gardens, of which he was deprived. Another aspect of Self that was suppressed by the move away from London was regular contact with sympathetic fellow artists sharing a wider view of life and art than was available in Norwich. 'My London friends are still my best friends'. In addition he found the extreme conventionality of local social attitudes restrictive. The two outer drawings in the Tate's triptych are enclosed in borders. It was only after this device was well-established that Self realised their autobiographical significance, when Robert Fraser pointed out that the same mannerism appears in the art of prisoners. For on many levels, Self, too, felt trapped, and in the imaginary drawings he correspondingly visualised an enclosed situation. But, able in the world of imagination to be more free, he indicated also the way out of it, which in each of the Tate's outer drawings can be seen down through the long vista. He was very much aware as he worked on these drawings of the parallel with Piranesi's also fantastic prints and drawings of prisons, in which, as in his own work, many elements in the scene recall the weight, for the prisoner, of the present, yet part of the scene (in Piranesi's case, the steps which lead in every direction) offers the hope of escape.

In Self's case, the way out lay, symbolically, straight through the middle. He saw this avenue as 'The Way' which, as in Bunyan's *Pilgrim's Progress*, the individual had to take, passing whatever temptations or frights might come at him from left or right. In the Tate's left hand drawing, he had to pass between two sets of eagles. The drawings symbolised that life is full of tests and challenges and that if one meets these with determination all will be well. Self compared this idea with his interpretation of J. S. Cotman's paintings (such as *Mountain Pass in the Tyrol*, and the versions of *The Waterfall* 1808 in Norwich Castle Museum) in which a tiny bridge spans a plunging chasm. The challenge of crossing the bridge without falling is akin to what Self sees as 'the ego, security, risk, the void, collapse, safety'. He sees the link with Cotman, like that with Eliot, as one not of influence but of deep affinity, 'which is something much better, much richer ... My works come before I discover their works. I realise then, we are in the same carriage, travelling the same route'. The link with Cotman is with 'the spirit of his vision and his expression of his insecurity. In my "Gardens from Imagination" I use all his abstract ideas to achieve the same ends that he does. Regarding insecurity, yearning for infinity, cutting off or obscuring the "pathway of life" by middle ground (sculpture, eagles with me – forest, hills with him)'. The parallel is so close that 'I could superimpose some of my "gardens from imagination" over some of his landscapes' (this refers to the ones cited above). This sense of tension and challenge is heightened in his drawings by the intensification of the sense of distance by means of deep vanishing points and radiating lines. Though not himself schizophrenic, Self consciously took these devices from the art of schizophrenics in order, through his own art, both to explain himself and to release his own great energy. (He was particularly impressed by the most extreme, elaborated – and essentially symmetrical – images made, when schizophrenic, by the cat painter Louis Wain. He points out the influence of one such drawing (repr. in Rodney Dale, *Louis Wain: The Man Who Drew Cats*, 1968, the right hand drawing on p.181) on the structure of some of his own 'Gardens from Imagination'. 'Seeing the work of Louis Wain, I saw I could take all my work a step (a large one) beyond my previous limits. Stretch things to the limits of insanity and put round it all a repressive oppressive border').

A further influence again relating to the theme of tests was Kafka's *The Castle* and *The Trial*. These novels are concerned also with the constant puzzle confronting the hero as to what is real and what unreal. In Self's view this is a problem continually posed in real life, in which the media lie to us all the time. Moreover he strongly opposes the view that what happened in history was inevitable and what we are told is what actually happened. There were many equal possibilities, of which the way things worked out was only one. On the level of historical possibility a hypothetical world is therefore just as real as the one we experience. Furthermore paintings which show us how the past actually was also show us, if we use our imaginations, how life *could* be today. (Related ideas are also touched on by Eliot in 'Burnt Norton', and Self's own *Fact and Fiction* series of collages of the early 1960s approaches the idea from another angle). Self therefore regards the scenes shown in his imaginary drawings as being in a sense just as real as in those drawn from life. In introducing the eagles from the taxi company's gates into T.2400 and related drawings, he was conscious of a connection with van Gogh, whose letters he read a great deal when at the Slade. For the same eagles guard the entrance to a mental home at Little Plumstead, Norfolk, and in the drawing their presence therefore gives an intentional sense of foreboding. It is as if they are guarding a domain in which distinctions between the real and the unreal, the sane and the insane, are confused, as they were for Van Gogh, who nevertheless sought, as does Self, to tell the truth about the contemporary world.

The drawings are assertions of Self's insistence that human beings must be free; that they cannot be restricted imaginatively; that source material of any kind is valid, there being no hierarchy of subject matter; that the mental environment must not be spoiled by departures from truth, or the physical either by impersonal architecture or (more fundamentally) by nuclear warfare. They are also a protest against the snobberies that restrict human life – the fashions and slavish imitations dominating the London art scene, and the narrowness of outlook of Norwich, from both of which Self was escaping into an inner world combining the innocence of a lost paradise with stern reminders of the need to keep to the path of truth and freedom.

The forces of snobbery and restriction are symbolised in the green glass garden sculpture which occupies the foreground of the right hand drawing but can be by-passed to reach the way which stretches beyond it. Self was angered that aspects of past art had been suppressed because of later generations' belief that some art forms were superior to others. He wished to be able to use photography and fine art techniques on equal terms, and could not accept that 'folk' art was 'low' and 'fine' art 'high'. He regarded as snobbery any approach to art which held that one kind of art was superior to all others. He points out that at the time he began the gardens drawings, a form of contemporary art which he regarded as by definition limited – abstraction – was being proposed by influential voices (even political ones) as *the* form which art must take. Experience in technical drawing had convinced him that beautiful form was not enough, and now the widespread zeal for purist abstraction seemed to him a new snobbism. To limit oneself to abstraction was to speak as if with a gag over one's mouth. 'Art which doesn't contemplate the world or universe as the mind perceives it through the eye ignores what is man's most highly developed organ . . . and as such can never utilise . . . the full range of impulses . . . and can by comparison only stand the chance of being very minor, or insignificant, art. For humans to turn their backs on *how things look* is to turn your back on possibility itself. For a spell working from concept and to ignore the look of the world may be useful in co-ordinating one's senses but to blindfold oneself from there onwards and be a one trick pony [is] quite perverted. It is not the way of nature, the seasons or man, or anything'.

Self had observed that the appearance of conventional garden sculptures such as gnomes improved when they became overgrown. For his imaginary garden he wanted to create an analogous modern garden sculpture. His aim was to take an example of what he considered the boring contemporary art of abstraction and, by placing it in a garden, creating a wonderful setting for it and allowing it to be overgrown, turn it into something human, even into 'high nature art'. The inclusion by this means of an abstract sculpture in T.2399 was the only way Self could find of justifying to himself, or appreciating, abstract art, 'as with World War II pill boxes and concrete blocks – time healing improving – inventing a situation in which even abstract art will look interesting'.

The gardens series was a demonstration of Self's wish 'to remain English or more importantly European and not sell out, by way of dialect, outlook, my culture Norfolk (peasant Anglo-Saxon), not become London trendy or sell out to this American cultural molehill when belonging to this European artistic Mt. Everest.' Nevertheless his subsequent experience of Norfolk was of misunderstanding or rejection of his work, of obstacles to recognition or employment, and of harassment of various kinds. Against this background, his presence by invitation at the ceremony and reception at which on 24 May 1979 the Queen opened the extension to the Tate Gallery (which had bought two of his works) struck him as 'a very necessary and overdue interlude of civilisation'. It was in direct response to this experience that he presented this triptych to the Gallery.

Richard Smith b. 1931

T.3060 **Cartouche II–10** 1979

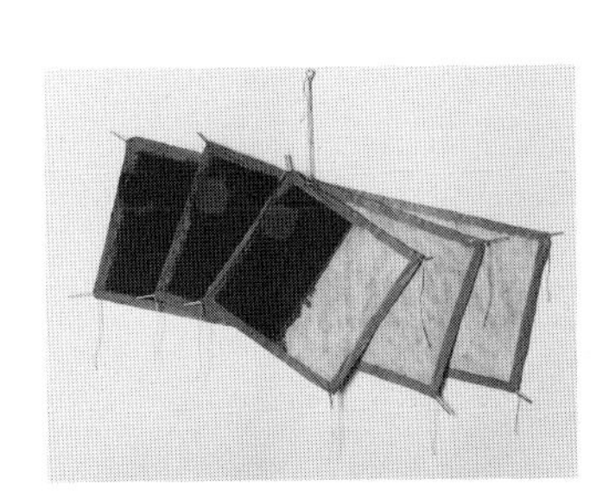

Inscribed 'R. Smith 79' b.r. on front panel
3 panels of cotton handmade paper and cloth suspended on aluminium tubes with cotton twine threaded through brass eyelets
Dimensions of panels, $19\frac{1}{4} \times 19\frac{1}{4}$ (48.89 × 48.89); $19\frac{1}{2} \times 36$ (49.53 × 91.44); $19\frac{1}{2} \times 52\frac{1}{2}$ (49.53 × 133.35); overall dimensions including twine, $45\frac{3}{4} \times 60 \times 2\frac{5}{8}$ (116.2 × 152.4 × 5.9)
Purchased from the Knoedier Gallery (Grant-in-Aid) 1980
Exh: *Richard Smith New Paper Works,* Knoedler Gallery, February–March 1980 (no catalogue)

This is one of a series of fifty-five original pulp paper works Richard Smith made between June 1979 and January 1980. It was the first time he had worked in this medium and the pieces were made in collaboration with Kenneth Tyler, Lindsay Green and Steve Reeves at the Tyler Graphics paper mill in Bedford, New York. Kenneth Tyler, previously founding partner and master printer of the Gemini Press in Los Angeles, founded Tyler Graphics in 1973 and his research into and

T.3036

T.3037

T.3038

T.3039

knowledge of the paper making process has led to collaborations with such artists as Kenneth Noland, Ellsworth Kelly and David Hockney, all of whom have made pulp paper works at the Tyler workshop.

Richard Smith chose 'Cartouche' as the generic title for the series because, when the works were first assembled, they reminded him of those heroic reliefs incorporating, for example, flags or scrolls of poetry and he remembered that 'cartouche' was the architectural term used to describe such ornamentation: the term was doubly appropriate because it derives from the Latin, *carta*, or paper.

The 'Cartouche' series is divided into five categories according to the number of panels used and the format in which they are designed to be suspended. Each category is denoted by a Roman Numeral and the works within each category are marked sequentially by an arabic number. 'Cartouche I' and 'Cartouche II' each comprise fifteen sets of three overlapping panels of approximately the same dimensions as those in T.3060, designed to be suspended vertically in category I and horizontally in category II. 'Cartouche III', comprising a set of eight two-panel works, each panel measuring 53 × 16 inches, is hung in a cross configuration and 'Cartouche V' comprises thirteen two-panel works hung diagonally, each panel measuring 53 × 17 inches. The fourth category contains four three-panel works, arranged vertically, each panel measuring 53 × 19½ inches.

Forty of the fifty-five works in the series were first seen publicly in three exhibitions held in the first quarter of 1980. The Knoedler Gallery, exhibited 'Cartouche I—10', 14; II-5, 10, 12; III-4, 7; IV-1; V-4, 10 (February 4–March 3); the Norman Mackenzie Art Gallery, University of Regina, Saskatchewan, Canada, 'Cartouche I-1,' 6, 7, 8, 9, 15; II-2, 6, 7, 9, 11, 14, 15; III-3, 5; IV-3, 4; V-1, 2, 12 (February 8–March 19) and the Bernard Jacobson Gallery, New York, 'Cartouche I-11', 13; II-1, 4, 13; III-3, 8; IV-2; V-3, 11 (March 4–April 22).

The catalogue for the exhibition at the Norman Mackenzie Art Gallery contains a foreword by Smith and a description of how the works were made, by Kenneth Tyler. In his foreword the artist stated (p.5), 'I had thought that the process of making paper would match my formal vocabulary very closely. The making of stencils or screens in squares and rectangles, in shapes and proportions that we familiarly accept in paper are the shapes I use in my paintings. The thinness of the paper is consistent with the thinness of the unsupported canvas in the paintings which do not have the implied objectness of canvas tacked to wooden stretcher bars. The pouring of pulp on the paper mould screens was a very natural process, something I found direct and right and not a substitute for a brush. The results hold the intentions. The way the pulp is poured gives direction and pulse to the paper in an equivalent of a painted surface and contrasts with the perfection of paper as it is pulled from the vat.' To make the 'Cartouche' series, Smith and his assistants used a selection of colour pulps, made from cotton fibres and *Kozo*, a fibre harvested from the bark of a small tree indigenous to the Far East. The bark is chemically treated, cleaned and softened by soaking, then mixed with water to form a pulp. The artist described (loc. cit.) the unpressed pulp as resembling a thin layer of snow, which, after pressing, formed a varied, though homogeneous surface.

Each panel was made in the following way. A newly formed sheet of white paper was transferred from its mould by pressure onto a sheet of felt, this process being referred to as *couching* in papermaking. Next, a wet piece of dyed cotton fabric was stretched over the base sheet and a further sheet of paper was couched onto the fabric. Afterwards, smaller shaped papers were added and the artist applied colour pulps and dyes by hand. In some cases, the fabric layer was dyed and dried so that the dye remained fast when the fabric was applied to paper; in others, the dyed fabric was applied wet so that the colour penetrated through subsequent layers of paper. When the multi-layered sheets had been hydraulically pressed, dried and trimmed, Smith punched a metal eyelet through the four

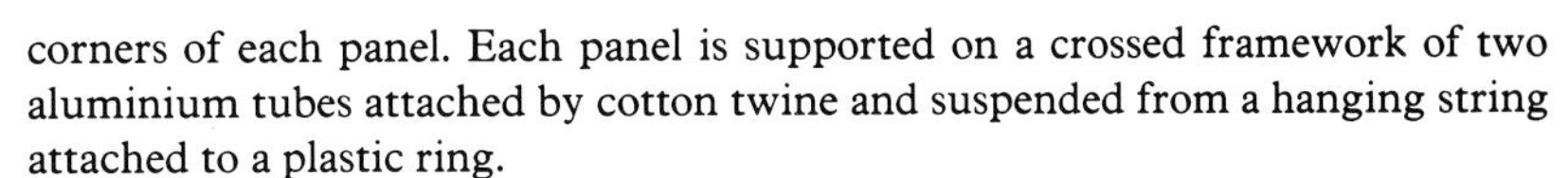
corners of each panel. Each panel is supported on a crossed framework of two aluminium tubes attached by cotton twine and suspended from a hanging string attached to a plastic ring.

Since 1972 Smith has concentrated his investigation of the relationship between illusionistic painted space and three-dimensional architectural space in banner-like works which deliberately advertise their fragility and materiality, laying emphasis on the way in which the painted surfaces are joined to their supports or suspended. The 'Cartouche' series with their simple motifs, overlapping rectangular or circular shapes in bright saturated reds, purples, pinks, blues or greens, arranged in deliberately "casual" configurations, can be seen as the direct successors of such large multipart canvas works as 'Five Finger Exercise' (1976) and 'Working Week' (1979).

This entry has been read and approved by the artist.

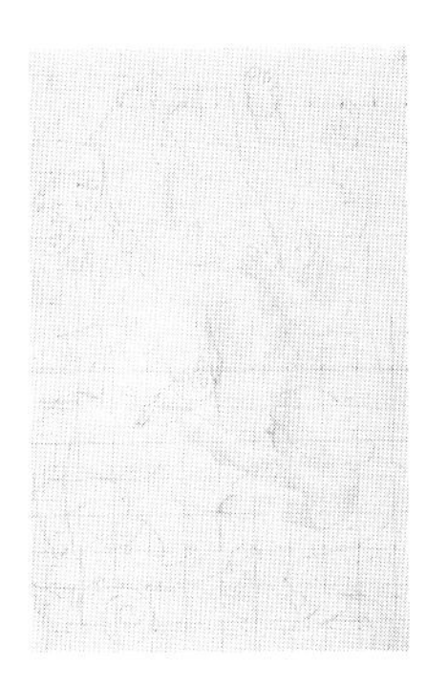
T.3040

Sir Stanley Spencer 1891–1959

T.3036–50, T.3061 and T.3062 **Drawings from a Sketch Book** *c.* mid 1940s

Pencil, each $15\frac{7}{8} \times 10\frac{7}{8}$ (40.4 × 27.6) with the exception of T.3044 which is $10\frac{7}{8} \times 15\frac{7}{8}$ (27.6 × 40.4). All are inscribed on the verso with densely packed writing in Spencer's hand

Purchased from Mrs J. M. Fothergill-Smith (Grant-in-Aid) 1979

Prov: Purchased by Mrs Fothergill-Smith at various times between 1955 and 1959 from the artist through Messrs Tooth with the exception of T.3043 and T.3048 which were purchased directly from the artist in 1955

Lit: R. H. Wilenski, *Stanley Spencer Resurrection Pictures (1945–1950)* with notes by the artist, 1951; Keith Bell in catalogue of exhibition *Stanley Spencer RA*, RA, 1980, pp.196–208

T.3041

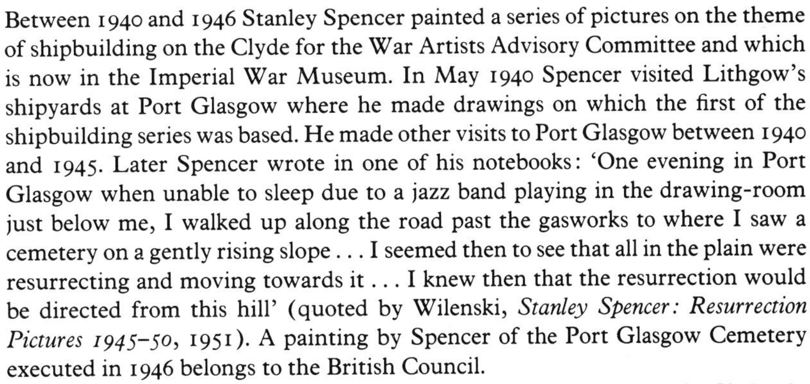
Between 1940 and 1946 Stanley Spencer painted a series of pictures on the theme of shipbuilding on the Clyde for the War Artists Advisory Committee and which is now in the Imperial War Museum. In May 1940 Spencer visited Lithgow's shipyards at Port Glasgow where he made drawings on which the first of the shipbuilding series was based. He made other visits to Port Glasgow between 1940 and 1945. Later Spencer wrote in one of his notebooks: 'One evening in Port Glasgow when unable to sleep due to a jazz band playing in the drawing-room just below me, I walked up along the road past the gasworks to where I saw a cemetery on a gently rising slope . . . I seemed then to see that all in the plain were resurrecting and moving towards it . . . I knew then that the resurrection would be directed from this hill' (quoted by Wilenski, *Stanley Spencer: Resurrection Pictures 1945–50*, 1951). A painting by Spencer of the Port Glasgow Cemetery executed in 1946 belongs to the British Council.

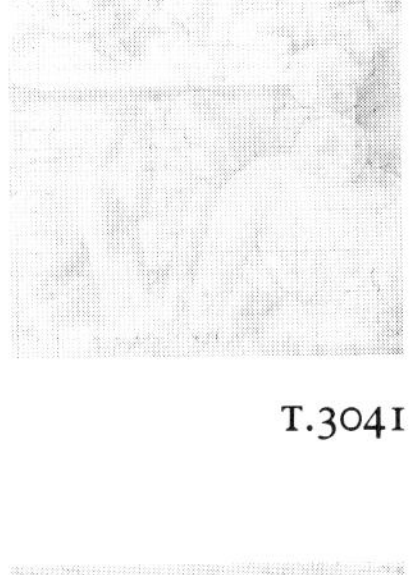
T.3042

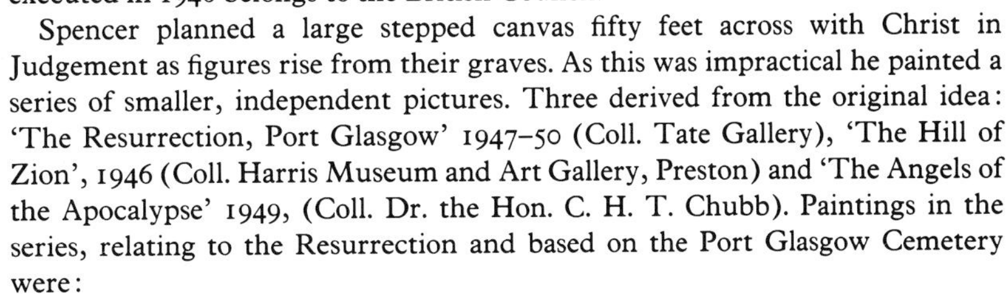
Spencer planned a large stepped canvas fifty feet across with Christ in Judgement as figures rise from their graves. As this was impractical he painted a series of smaller, independent pictures. Three derived from the original idea: 'The Resurrection, Port Glasgow' 1947–50 (Coll. Tate Gallery), 'The Hill of Zion', 1946 (Coll. Harris Museum and Art Gallery, Preston) and 'The Angels of the Apocalypse' 1949, (Coll. Dr. the Hon. C. H. T. Chubb). Paintings in the series, relating to the Resurrection and based on the Port Glasgow Cemetery were:

1. 'The Resurrection: Waking Up' 1945 (Coll. The Nevill Gallery, Canterbury and Bath)
2. 'The Resurrection: Tidying' 1945 (Coll. Birmingham City Art Gallery)
3. 'The Resurrection: Reunion of Families' 1945 (Coll. Dundee Art Gallery)

T.3043

T.3044

4. 'The Resurrection: Reunion' 1945 (Coll. Aberdeen Art Gallery and Museum)
5. 'The Resurrection: Rejoicing' 1947 (Coll. The Beaverbrook Art Gallery, Fredericton, New Brunswick)

A further painting 'The Resurrection with the Raising of Jairus's Daughter', 1947, was conceived originally in 1939 while Spencer was staying at Leonard Stanley in Gloucestershire and was not based on the Port Glasgow Cemetery.

Spencer made drawings for the Port Glasgow Resurrection series in one or more 'Derwent' scrapbooks bought from the stationer in Leonard Stanley in 1939. Nos. T.3036–3050 and T.3061 all relate to paintings in the Port Glasgow Resurrection series; no painting is known which relates to T.3062.

T.3045

T.3036 **Drawing for left-hand section of 'Resurrection: Rejoicing'**

Inscribed t.r. '29' and '31' in pencil and '61' in red crayon

This squared-up drawing is close to the painting in composition.

T.3037 **Drawing for centre section of 'Resurrection: Rejoicing'**

Inscribed t.r. '40' and '58' (crossed out) in pencil and '79' in red crayon

This squared-up drawing is close to the painting, in which the arm of the figure on the left is lowered.

T.3038 **Drawing for right-hand section of 'Resurrection: Rejoicing'** 1945

Inscribed t.r. '20' or '28' in pencil and '53' in red crayon and b.r. '1945' in pencil

Exh: *Stanley Spencer RA*, RA, September–December 1980 (245, repr.)

This drawing is close to the painting with the exception that the angel's wing in the top left of the drawing has been replaced by four children in the painting.

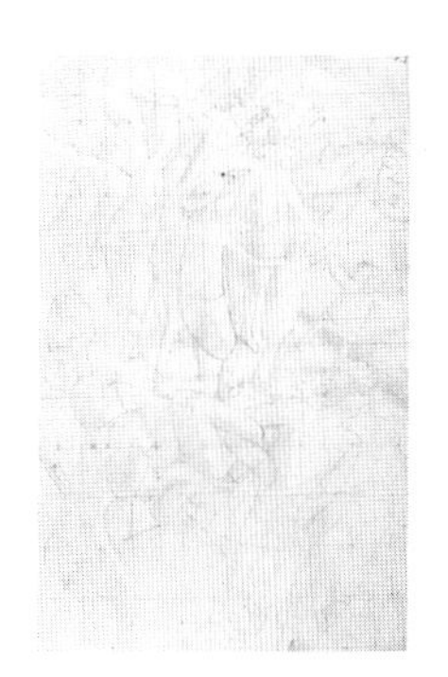

T.3046

T.3039 **Drawing for part of the right-hand section of 'Resurrection: Port Glasgow'**

Inscribed t.r. '21' and b.r. '34' in pencil and t.r. '48' in red crayon

This squared-up drawing differs considerably from the painted version in which only the figures in the top third of the drawing are retained.

T.3040 **Drawing for the left-hand section of 'Resurrection: Port Glasgow'**

Inscribed t.r. '54' in pencil and '107' in red crayon

This squared-up drawing is close in composition to the painting.

T.3047

T.3041 **Drawing for the centre section of 'Resurrection: Port Glasgow'**

Inscribed t.r. '30' in pencil and '63' in red crayon and b.l. '5ft 8ft' in pencil

This squared-up drawing is close in composition to the painting.

T.3042 **Drawing for right-hand section of 'Resurrection: Port Glasgow'**

Inscribed t.r. '45' and '4(?)3' in pencil and '89' in red crayon; b.l. of centre '5ft' and '4ft' in pencil

T.3048

This squared-up drawing is close in composition to the painting in which the figure on the right has his foot on a spade, unlike in the drawing.

T.3043 Drawing for the left-hand section of 'Resurrection: Waking up' 1944

Inscribed t.r. '12' and b.r. 'Stanley Spencer Sept Oct 1944' in pencil and '35' t.r. in red crayon

Exh: *Drawings by Stanley Spencer*, Museum and Art Gallery, Brighouse, January–February 1954 and subsequent tour to Chapel Barr Art Gallery, Nottinghamshire, Luton, Plymouth, Bristol and Bedford Art Galleries (55, repr. as 'People Yawning'); *Drawings by Stanley Spencer*, Arts Council Gallery, November–December 1955 (55, repr. as 'People Yawning'); *Stanley Spencer RA*, RA September–December 1980 (244, repr.)

T.3049

This squared-up drawing is close to the painting in which the woman lying on the tomb at the top is omitted.

T.3044 Drawing for the right-hand section of 'Resurrection: Waking up'

Inscribed b.r. '20' in pencil and '34' or '39' in red crayon

This squared-up drawing is close to the painting in which the alarm clocks are omitted.

T.3050

T.3045 Drawing for the left-hand section of 'Resurrection: Reunion'

Inscribed t.r. '26' in pencil and '54' or '58' in red crayon

Exh: *Stanley Spencer RA*, RA, September–December 1980 (249, repr.)

This squared-up drawing is close to the painting in which the figure in the centre right is clothed but naked in the drawing.

T.3046 Drawing for the centre section of 'Resurrection: Reunion'

Inscribed t.r. '27' in pencil and '53' in red crayon

The figures in the top half of the squared-up drawing are included, but those in the bottom half excluded, in the painting.

T.3061

T.3047 Drawing for the right-hand section of 'Resurrection: Reunion' 1944

Inscribed t.r. '25' in pencil and '49' in red crayon and b.r. '1944' in pencil

Exh: *Stanley Spencer RA*, RA, September–December 1980 (248, repr.)

This squared-up drawing is close in composition to the painting.

T.3048 Drawing for left-hand panel of 'Resurrection: Tidying'

Inscribed t.r. '22' in pencil and '43' or '45' in red crayon and b.r. 'Stanley Spencer' and (?) 'Sept 5'

Exh: *Drawings by Stanley Spencer*, Museum and Art Gallery, Brighouse, January–February 1954 and subsequent tour to Chapel Barr Art Gallery, Nottinghamshire, Luton, Plymouth, Bristol and Bedford Art Galleries (54); *Drawings by Stanley Spencer*, Arts Council Gallery, November–

T.3062

December 1955 (54); *Stanley Spencer RA*, RA, September–December 1980 (247, repr.)

This drawing is close to the painting in composition.

T.3049 Drawing for the right-hand section of 'Resurrection: Tidying'

Inscribed t.r. '23' in pencil and '4(?)5' in red crayon
Exh: *Stanley Spencer RA*, RA, September–December 1980 (246, repr.)

This drawing is close to the painting in composition.

T.3050 Drawing for the left-hand section of 'Resurrection: Reunion of Families'

Inscribed t.r. '24' in pencil and '47' in red crayon and b.r. in pencil 'Stanley Spencer'

This drawing is close in composition to the painting.

T.3061 Figures on either side of a window

Inscribed t.r. in pencil '39' and underneath '77' in red crayon

No painting is known which incorporates the composition of this squared-up drawing.

T.3062 Trumpet Player with Other Figures

Inscribed t.r. '35' in pencil and underneath '69' in red crayon

No painting is known which relates to this squared-up drawing.

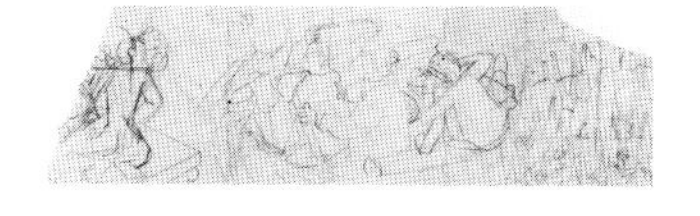

T.3035

T.3035 Preliminary Sketch for 'Resurrection: Rejoicing'

Not inscribed
Pencil $4\frac{3}{4} \times 16\frac{1}{4}$ (12.1 × 41.3)

The part of the drawing relating to 'Resurrection: Rejoicing' is squared up. The other part of the sheet in which figures appear to be looking at their tombstones does not relate to any known painting of Spencer.

Frank Stella b. 1936

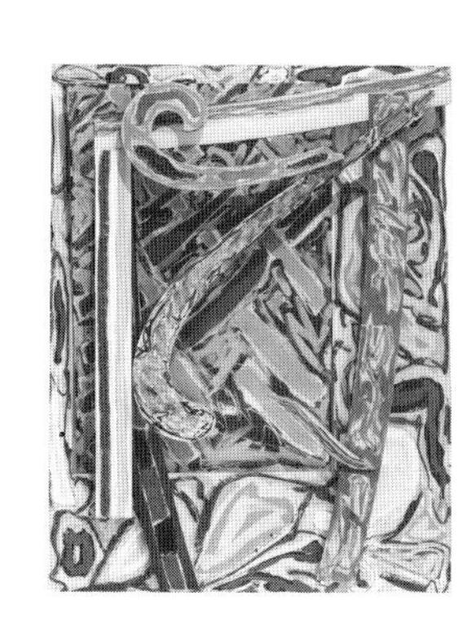

T.3058 Guadalupe Island caracara 1979

Not inscribed
Synthetic paints, lacquers and other materials on honeycomb aluminium, $93\frac{3}{4} \times 121 \times 18$ (238 × 307.5 × 45.5)
Purchased from the Knoedler Gallery (Grant-in-Aid) 1980
Repr: *The Artist*, xcv, September 1980, on cover (detail); *Tate Gallery 1978–80*, p.59 in colour

Stella regards this work as part of the 'completion' of the series of works named after exotic birds which he began in 1976. The caracara is a South American falcon family and Polyborus Lutosus, a now extinct species, was found only on Guadalupe Island, approximately 150 miles off the coast of Southern California in the Pacific. There does not seem to be any specific link between the birds and the forms in this work.

Stella made drawings for the works of this series on semi-transparent paper with instruments normally used by marine architects and railway engineers. These were converted into a foam-board maquette of the same size, which indicated the thickness of the final version, and then passed to an independent metal fabricator to make at 3 and 5.5 times the original size. The Tate's version is the larger.

The fabricator used standard building or packaging materials – aluminium sheets sandwiched around honeycombs made from paper or metal or expanded foam. The differing thicknesses are for structural rather than aesthetic reasons.

The work was delivered to the artist unpainted; he used a large variety of media to obtain his effects, notably silkscreen inks, acrylic colours, ground glass, aluminium glitter, reflective beads and lithographic crayons.

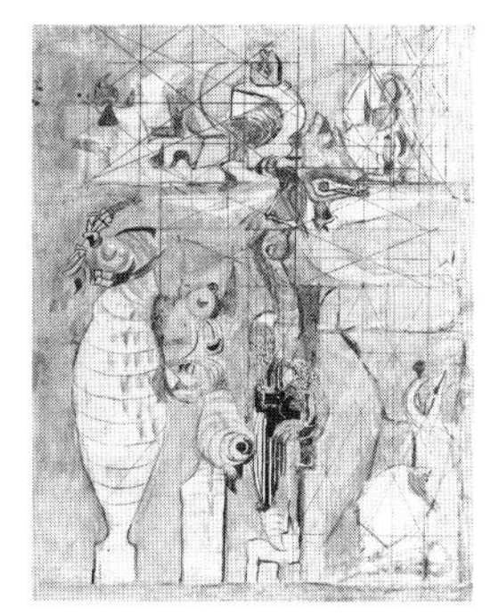

Graham Sutherland, O.M. 1903–80

T.2381 Working Drawing for 'The Origins of the Land' 1951

Inscribed 'to my friends K & Jane/with affection aug. 19 1951' b.l.
Pencil, ink, crayon, tempera and oil paint on paper, 25 × 19$\frac{7}{8}$ (63.5 × 50.6)
Presented by Lord Clark of Saltwood 1979

Prov: Presented by the artist to Sir Kenneth and Lady Clark 1951

Exh: *Graham Sutherland; Keith Vaughan; Contemporary French and English Lithographs*, Redfern Gallery, November–December 1952 (308 as 'Study No. 8'); *Drawings for Pictures*, Arts Council Gallery, February–March 1953 and subsequent tour to the Ferens Gallery, Hull, College of Art, Liverpool, Whitworth Art Gallery, Manchester, and Plymouth Art Gallery (25); *Graham Sutherland*, Akademie der bildenden Künste, Vienna, and Ferdinandeum, Innsbruck, 1954 (40); *Thirty Contemporary Paintings*, Arts Council exhibition, Gerrards Cross Memorial Centre, September 1954 and subsequent tour to Bootle Art Gallery and Brighton Art Gallery (28); *Some 20th Century Watercolours*, Arts Council exhibition, Lewes Art Gallery, April 1955 and subsequent tour to Scarborough Art Gallery and Gerrards Cross Memorial Centre (36); *Some Twentieth Century Watercolours: 2nd Selection*, Arts Council exhibition, Carlisle Art Gallery, January 1956 and subsequent tour to Brighouse Art Gallery, Turner Gallery, Penarth, The Mining Centre, St Helens, Royal Albert Museum and Art Gallery, Exeter, and the Edinburgh Office (41)

Repr: Douglas Cooper, *Graham Sutherland*, 1961, pl.114a

'The Origins of the Land' (oil on canvas 167$\frac{1}{2}$ × 129 in, collection Tate Gallery No. 6085) was commissioned by the Festival of Britain Office on 6 April 1950 for exhibition in 'The Land of Britain Pavilion' at the Festival of Britain, and was painted in the Tate Gallery between September 1950 and the middle of March 1951. Sutherland began by making a large number of studies, which show many variations and a gradual development towards the final composition. An exhibition at the Redfern Gallery in November–December 1952 of oils, gouaches and drawings for 'The Origins of the Land' included no less than eight works described as 'large size', including T.2381, fourteen 'medium size' and thirty-one 'small size'.

While working on the final picture the artist trimmed about an eighth off the top of the canvas and compressed the upper third of the composition. The composition as a whole underwent several changes as shown in photographs taken during the course of its execution (see pls.113c, 113d and 115 in Douglas Cooper's *Graham Sutherland*, 1961). The present study T.2381, which is extensively squared up, especially in the upper part and to the right, appears to have been the last of the studies, executed while the painting itself was already at a fairly advanced stage, as the more or less final working out of the upper section.

However the finished painting does not correspond exactly, as the shapes at the top left are more angular and have more straight lines, and the crescent shape at the bottom right is reversed and nearer the bottom.

John Tunnard 1900–71

T.2327 **Fulcrum** 1939

Inscribed 'John Tunnard 39' b.r.
Oil and graphite pencil on hardboard, 17½ × 32 (44.5 × 81.3)
Presented by the Trustees of the Chantrey Bequest 1978

Prov: Bequeathed by the artist to Peter Tunnard from whom bought by the Chantrey Trustees 1978

Exh: *John Tunnard*, Guggenheim Jeune, March–April 1939 (22, price 30 guineas); *British Surrealist and Abstract Painting*, Northampton Art Gallery, July–August 1939 (10, price 14 guineas); *British Art and the Modern Movement 1930–40*, Arts Council exhibition, National Museum of Wales, Cardiff, October–November 1962 (57); *Art in Britain 1930–40 centred around Axis, Circle and Unit One*, Marlborough Fine Art, March–April 1965 (162, repr.); *John Tunnard*, Hartnoll and Eyre, April 1971 (7, repr.); *John Tunnard 1900–1971*, Arts Council exhibition, RA Diploma Gallery, March–April 1977 (18, repr.) and subsequent tour to Kettles Yard Cambridge, Kettering Art Gallery, Manchester City Art Gallery, Laing Art Gallery, Newcastle and Newlyn Art Gallery; *Dada and Surrealism Reviewed*, Hayward Gallery, January–March 1978 (14.52, repr.)

Lit: Mark Glazebrook, catalogue of 1977 Arts Council Exhibition *John Tunnard 1900–1971*, p.25

Repr: *London Bulletin*, No. 18–20, June 1940, p.27

According to Mark Glazebrook (*op. cit.*) the first extant 'nonrepresentational' work by John Tunnard, a watercolour 'Two birds, one pebble, one boulder' suggesting abstraction from natural forms, dates from 1935. A watercolour of 1937 (Mark Glazebrook *op. cit.* p.24) has suggestions of natural and man-made objects joined by wires. In 'Fulcrum' objects appear to be man-made rather than natural and the wires are taut. Glazebrook quotes a reviewer of the exhibition at Guggenheim Jeune in 1939, where 'Fulcrum' was shown, as referring to Tunnard as 'the Heath Robinson of the Constructivist movement.'

The exhibition of Tunnard's work at Hartnoll and Eyre in 1971 included the Tate picture as well as another work entitled 'Fulcrum' (17 × 33 inches) dating from 1960.

Leon Underwood 1890–1975

T.2323 **Casement to Infinity** 1930

Inscribed 'Leon U 30' b.r.
Oil on canvas, 30 × 25 (76.2 × 63.5)
Presented by Garth Underwood 1978

Exh: *The Neo Society*, Godfrey Phillips Galleries, May–June 1930 (55, as 'Casement of Infinity', repr.); *Leon Underwood*, Archer Gallery, June–July 1971 (46); *Leon Underwood and 12 Girdlers Road*, New Art Centre, November–December 1976 (12, dated 1929)

Lit: Christopher Neve, *Leon Underwood*, 1974, p.131 and repr. fig.94

'Casement to Infinity' is one of six paintings exhibited by the artist in the first and

only exhibition of 'The Neo Society', at the Godfrey Phillips Gallery in May 1930. The artist's collection of newspaper cuttings (in the Courtauld Institute Library) includes a favourable review from R. H. Wilenski (*Evening Standard*, May 10, 1930), referring to Underwood's paintings as 'symbols of metaphysical ideas', but also a report (*Daily Sketch*, May 17, 1930) that the artist had removed all his works from the exhibition after he had been told that one of them, 'At the Feet of the Gods', 'was not fit for reproduction in a newspaper'. The objection was that the still life in the painting included an enema, but the artist defended the work as 'a mystical symbolism of modern civilisation as I see it'. Underwood was one of ten artists in this exhibition, but the only one whose work is now represented in the Tate Gallery collection.

Underwood's career is marked by abrupt changes of style, deliberately undertaken whenever he considered his message could most appropriately be expressed in a certain way. The six paintings shown in 'The Neo Society' exhibition were one such use of a certain style for a short time, in this case symbolical still lifes. Following a visit to Mexico in 1928 a number of Underwood's paintings were of subjects from Mexican history. Three of these – 'Coast of Yucatan', 'The Fates' and 'Chac Mool's Destiny' (all of 1929) – are a departure in his painting and a move towards the style of 'Casement to Infinity' of the next year, in that they are designed around a steep, theatrical perspective and combine unrelated objects as if in a narrative. It is likely that he borrowed this from the paintings of Giorgio de Chirico, which had been exhibited at Tooth's in October–November 1928, after Underwood's return from Mexico. De Chirico's paintings of sculptures of gladiators and classical horses in interiors resemble Underwood's 'Chac Mool's Destiny' particularly, and correspond with his interest in extending the meaning of sculpture. The paintings of 1930 were still lifes of contemporary objects, and a further source for Underwood was undoubtedly the marine still lifes of Edward Wadsworth. These had most recently been exhibited in Tooth's in May–June 1929, and typically featured shells, a distant view of the sea and a sharp separation of foreground and background, all also present in T.2323.

Underwood's message in these paintings is not explained directly by the titles, but was discussed by him in 1972–3 with Christopher Neve, who writes of the subject: 'the accumulation of still-life objects has paradoxically to do exclusively with the passage of time and contemplation: growth, in the roots, in the egg and in the spider busy spinning on the gnomon of the sundial; the single fallen wing to suggest arrested flight, and, instead of the traditional metaphysical symbol of decay – the fly on the skull – Underwood has put a butterfly: a thing of great beauty given poignancy by the extreme shortness of its survival' (op. cit. p.131). The painting was not exhibited by the artist after 1930, and from this time he was more concerned with sculpture than painting.

The wooden frame was carved by the artist. The signature, which was originally in brown, was repainted over the varnish before the painting was acquired, and in older photographs is not visible.

T.2324 **Torso** *c.* 1923–30

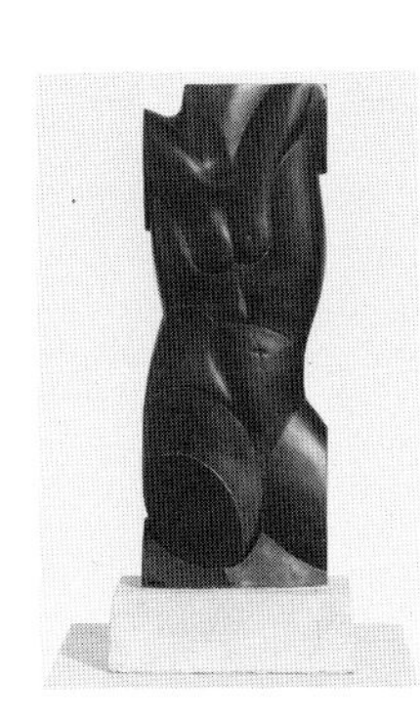

Inscribed 'Leon U 30' on reverse at base of figure
Slate, $16\frac{1}{8} \times 6\frac{1}{8} \times 2\frac{1}{4}$ ($41 \times 15.5 \times 5.8$) attached to a rectangular marble block $2\frac{1}{2}$ (6.4) high
Presented by Garth Underwood 1978
Exh: *Sculpture by Leon Underwood*, Kaplan Gallery, March 1961 (61, as 'Torso – Black slate 1923')
Lit: Christopher Neve, *Leon Underwood*, 1974, p.84, repr. pl.51

This sculpture is inscribed 1930, but the artist told Christopher Neve in 1972–3 that it was carved in 1923, at the same time that he was working on the large

Mansfield sandstone 'Torso' (repr. Neve, op. cit., pl.49). The latter was first exhibited in May 1924 in Underwood's exhibition at the Alpine Club, but T.2324 is not listed in the catalogue, which suggests that it was not completed by then. Underwood's early sculpture is difficult to date accurately, as he worked on some pieces over a number of years, or altered them at a later date, and he sometimes exhibited pieces for the first time many years after they were made. This particular work was exhibited for the first time in 1961 (at the Kaplan Gallery), when it was dated in the catalogue 1923. However some of the dates in this catalogue are not reliable, since the wood carving 'The Cathedral' is listed there as 1924 but was actually made in about 1930.

Although there is a superficial resemblance between T.2324 and the two early relief carvings 'Hunter and Dog' and 'Female Figure' (repr. Neve, pls.46–7) dated by Neve 1921–2, the carving of the Tate's 'Torso' is more skilful than either of these. A third 'Torso' in Ancaster stone (repr. Neve, op. cit., pl.124), though carved in the round instead of in relief, is closer in appearance to T.2324 in the complex curves of its surface and the unusual outlines of the breasts. This 'Torso' is dated 1925 by Neve, but a photograph of it from the artist's collection (Conway Library, Courtauld Institute) is dated both 1931 and 1932.

The material of T.2324 was identified by the artist as 'Tournai Slate'. At least three bronzes of T.2324 were cast during the 1960's.

Georges Vantongerloo 1886–1965

T.2306 **Rapport des Volumes** (Interrelation of Volumes) 1919

Inscribed 'VTL' in monogram on base plane
Sandstone, $8\frac{7}{8} \times 5\frac{3}{8} \times 5\frac{3}{8}$ (22.5 × 13.5 × 13.5)
Purchased at Christie's (Grant-in-Aid) 1978

Prov: Prof. and Mrs. Philip Sandblom, Lund and Lausanne (purchased from the artist); sold by them at Christie's, London, 4 April 1978, lot 44, repr. in colour

Exh: *Exposition Internationale d'Art Moderne*, Bâtiment électoral, Geneva, December 1920–January 1921 (Belgium 127 or 128, both entitled 'Construction des Rapports des Volumes'); *Internationell Utställning av Post-Kubistisk Konst*, Parkrestauranten, Stockholm, August–September 1930 (87) as 'Skulptur VIII. Rapport des Volumes. Sandsten'; *Samling S*, Moderna Museet, Stockholm, June–July 1967 (86, repr.)

Lit: Gunnar Hellman, 'Vart tog tavlorna vägen? – Många gåtor alltjämt olösta i konkretisfiaskot 1930', *Aftonbladet*, 13 June 1957, p.3; *Dagens Nyheter*, 15 October 1957, p.1 repr.

Repr: *De Stijl*, III, No.2, December 1919, facing p.23 (the right-hand plate) as one of two sculptures of 1919 by Vantongerloo; Georges Vantongerloo, *Paintings, Sculpture, Reflections*, New York 1948, fig.6; *Tate Gallery 1978–80*, p.60

This sculpture is No. 13 in Vantongerloo's manuscript oeuvre-catalogue, now in the possession of his executor Max Bill, and is recorded under the title 'Rapport des Volumes' with a note that it was made in Brussels in 1919.

It was included in an exhibition *Internationell Utställning av Post-Kubistisk Konst* in Stockholm in 1930 arranged by the painter Otto G. Carlsund, devoted to 'Cubism, Post-Cubism, Purism, Constructivism, Neo-Plasticism, Surrealism and Sur-Impressionism'. Unfortunately this exhibition, which contained many fine works, proved to be too far in advance of its time and was a financial and organisational disaster. When the exhibition closed people who were owed money by Carlsund came and carried off paintings and sculptures, even if they still belonged to the artists. Vantongerloo managed to recover his two paintings in 1934, but both sculptures lent by him were lost for twenty-five years until they were found by chance amongst rubbish in a cupboard in a framer's shop in Stockholm on 16 December 1955. After being the subject of a law suit in October 1957, they were returned to the artist. This piece was afterwards bought by Professor Philip Sandblom from his studio in Paris in 1959, and Vantongerloo said that he would use the proceeds for a trip to the far north to see the Aurora Borealis, in which he was greatly interested at the time.

Although he published a schematic compositional analysis of a sculpture by Archipenko 'The Gondolier' in *De Stijl*, I, as early as September 1918, his early references to sculpture are mostly in terms of an interrelationship of volumes and voids. It seems unlikely therefore that this sculpture is based on any geometrical system of proportions, whereas this is characteristic of his later sculptures of the same type and is indicated by their titles. For example, the similar sculpture of 1924 in the Peggy Guggenheim Foundation in Venice is known as 'Construction in an Inscribed and a Circumscribed Square of a Circle'.

Carel Visser b. 1928

T.2313 **Fish Spine** 1954

Not inscribed
Welded sheet metal, 46⅜ × 10¼ × 2⅛ (117.8 × 26 × 5.4)
Purchased from Mrs. Margareet Visser through the Whitechapel Art Gallery (Grant-in-Aid) 1978

Coll: The artist's wife, Mrs Margareet Visser

Exh: *Carel Visser*, Whitechapel Art Gallery, January–February 1978, and tour to Arnolfini Gallery, Bristol (March–April) and Third Eye Centre, Glasgow (May–June) (7, the work's Dutch title incorrectly spelt with an 'n' in place of the final 'a')

The following entry which is based on Carel Visser's replies in an interview on 21 August 1978, has been approved by him.

The work's Dutch title, 'Ruggegraat', does not imply any reference to fish in particular. It simply means spine or backbone (of a being, species not specified). However, Visser does not regard any title he gives as an exact indication of what he is trying to express in the corresponding work, but rather as a foothold or way in for the spectator, from which the spectator can develop his own ideas.

One of the things that appeals to Visser about the title 'Ruggegraat' is its sound. Roughly this is 'roocherchrart', if each 'ch' is pronounced as in 'loch'. In considering what title this work should have in English, he felt that 'spine' by itself was too compact a word, and also that it might tend to give the work a specifically human connotation in the spectator's mind, thus restricting its meaning more than Visser intended. Thus the choice of the title 'Fish Spine' was influenced not only by Visser's long-standing interest in fish but also by the fact that the idea of fish makes the spectator think of the horizontal, thus suggesting more general readings for this sculpture than the simple title 'Spine' might seem to imply when given to an upright form.

Some years before 1954, Visser visited the studios of Brancusi and of Giacometti. Brancusi's concern with the repetition of one given element in a single upright sculpture influenced him strongly. He was greatly shocked by Giacometti's 'Woman with her Throat Cut' 1932, in which vertebrae are exposed. This led to his experimenting with loose bones laid on a base. These themes, of repetition and of vertebrae, are combined in 'Fish Spine'.

Visser had been interested in the common concern of Brancusi and Giacometti with gravity, a basic property of sculpture which he felt they acknowledged by seeking solutions to the problem of relating a sculpture to the ground in a natural way. He considered that gravity in this sense was not of central importance to Picasso and Gonzalez as sculptors, and their sculpture thus interested him less. An interesting aspect of Brancusi's concern with gravity in sculpture was his use, paradoxically, of motifs based on creatures which in their living form move as though no laws of gravity exist, namely fish and birds. These subjects recurred in Visser's own work of the early 1950s, both overtly and in the expressive character of various works which might at first appear unrelated, such as 'Luchtschip' ('Airship') 1954, which in Visser's mind is a hollow fish.

In 'Fish Spine' and other works of this period (e.g., 'Rietstengel' ('Reed') 1954), Visser's intention was to make a flat sculpture, in conscious reaction against the three-dimensional complication of, for example, Gonzalez, in whose work it seemed to him that the spectator had, to a degree, to struggle to find the structure. He aimed to make sculpture that should be equally effective while using fewer variables. An influence on Visser's concern with flatness was those sculptures of Arp in which a flat outline is projected in depth to make a three-dimensional form. In his determination to throw out many available properties of sculpture in a wish to find the basic ones, Visser was influenced by all three sculptors, Brancusi, Arp and Giacometti.

One of Visser's central concerns was with revealing structure. This preoccupation underlay his interest in such things as bones, bicycles, insects, lobsters and crabs – all of them things in which the spectator can easily grasp how they are built up and put together. The same characteristic was one of the things that interested him most in Brancusi's sculpture. The 'Endless Column', in particular, was a direct influence on 'Fish Spine'. The same interest led him to natural history museums to study and draw underlying structures, including spines. Among the sculptures which resulted directly from Visser's museum studies of vertebrae were 'Over' ('Crossing') 1953 (coll: Rijksmuseum Kröller-Müller, Otterlo), which was followed by 'Werwels' ('Vertebrae') 1954 (coll: Gemeentemuseum, The Hague; repr., with closely-related drawing, in J. L. Locher, *Carel Visser*, 1972, p.22; another version seen at extreme left in installation photograph repr. in catalogue of Whitechapel Gallery exhibition, 1978, cited above, p.10), and then the Tate's sculpture. 'Fish Spine', which Visser saw as a vertical development from 'Werwels', was the last of his sculptures to be developed directly from studies made in natural history museums. The catalogue of Visser's exhibition at the Stedelijk Museum, Amsterdam, May–June 1960, reproduces (n.p.) a drawing which Visser thinks he made shortly before the Tate's sculpture, which is a semi-invented variation on the spine motif, developed from the drawings of real spines which he had made in museums.

A further source of inspiration was 'primitive' art, which at this period Visser often discussed with the Dutch architect Aldo van Eyck. The Tate's sculpture had a specific source in a Dogon mask, consisting of the 'face' element surmounted by tall vertical members crossed, ladder-like, by horizontal bars, which Visser had studied in the Musée de l'Homme in Paris. Brought up in the countryside, Visser also had a strong interest in the structures and shapes of farm implements. These were an influence on 'Fish Spine' and works like it. One implement, a hay rake known in Dutch as a rekel, has a close formal connection with the Tate's sculpture.

The Tate's is the only version of the 'Ruggegraat' motif in Visser's work in either sculpture or drawings, but Visser sees a close connection between it and those of his wood engravings in which a single horizontal ('horizon') line is crossed by vertical bars of different lengths, each of which it bisects. However, around 1954 Visser made a number of vertical stacked sculptures, a division of his work into which 'Fish Spine' falls – for example 'Jacobsladder' and 'Vier

Elementen', both of 1954 (repr. Locher, op. cit., p.28). Two of these were exceptionally slender, viz, a column made of three or four standing human figures stacked directly one above another (this preceded 'Fish Spine'), and 'Rietstengel' ('Reed') 1954 (repr. Locher, ibid.), which came after 'Fish Spine'.

'Fish Spine' consists of the repetition eleven times of a unit consisting of a closed, vertical cylinder, to which are welded two horizontal spikes pointing in opposite directions. Both the cylinders (formed from flat sheets of steel) and the spikes were made by Visser specially for this sculpture. None of the variations in sharpness or thickness is deliberate; Visser simply stacked the different repeating elements in the sequence in which they happened to come. When the structure was complete but the work was still warm, he dipped it into oil to give it a surface. Although he has provided elementary maintenance instructions, he accepts natural changes in the work's surface, through atmosphere and time, as being part of its nature, an acknowledgement that in life everything decays.

The cast concrete base ($7\frac{5}{8} \times 11\frac{7}{8} \times 3\frac{5}{8}$ (19.4 × 30.2 × 9.3)), made in 1954, is not part of the work, but is Visser's preferred form of presentation of it, no additional pedestal being necessary between it and the ground. Visser finds that the work is often displayed to best advantage when placed some 10 to 15 cms from a wall, but a fully free-standing position is perfectly acceptable to him.

T.2349 **Auschwitz** 1957–58

Not inscribed
Welded mild steel, $23\frac{7}{8} \times 33\frac{1}{2} \times 32$ (60.5 × 85 × 81)
Presented by the artist 1979
Exh: *Carel Visser*, Whitechapel Art Gallery, January–February 1978 (15, repr. three times), as 'Auschwitz II', and tour to Arnolfini Gallery, Bristol and Third Eye Centre, Glasgow, to June 1978

Auschwitz is the German name of the Polish town of Oswiecim, where in 1940 Nazi Germany established the Auschwitz-Birkenau concentration camp. In this camp, during the Second World War, between one and five million people were murdered (*Encyclopaedia Britannica*, 15th edition). Except where stated otherwise, the remainder of this entry (which has been approved by the artist), is based on an interview with Carel Visser and his wife Margareet on 18 November 1980.

During most of the Second World War, the Netherlands was under German occupation. While the Dutch people as a whole, especially those in the cities, suffered many deprivations, Jewish citizens were first singled out for even harsher treatment and then deported to concentration camps. However Visser, though living in the Netherlands, was relatively protected from these experiences, since his family lived in the country, which meant that they did not starve. Moreover Visser himself either saw no Jews (who were forced, before being deported, to wear distinctive yellow stars) or, if he did, suppressed the memory.

However, very soon after the Liberation, the Vissers took into their family two Jewish children who had been freed from a concentration camp (not Auschwitz), and who arrived with shaved heads. Visser and his brothers and sisters were at first incredulous and then aghast when, through observing these children acting out in play their own experience of life, they realised for the first time what had really happened in the concentration camps. Almost at the same time, Visser learned through the media (and sought further to inform himself) about the camps. He also digested allegations that places like Auschwitz had been able to continue because the West had in practice tolerated them; and that compared with other occupied countries the Netherlands had provided an unusually large number of Nazi collaborators and of recruits to the S.S. Thus throughout the period 1945–57 Visser, as a Dutchman and one whose war experience had been mild, had deep-seated feelings of guilt on the subject of the concentration camps.

During these years, his reading was much concerned with ethical problems, and included Augustine and other early Church fathers, Pascal, Kierkegaard, Kafka, Bonhoeffer and the eighteenth century German mystic Jakob Boehme.

In the mid 1950s an international competition was announced for the design of a monument to the victims of Auschwitz, of which the winning design would be erected on a large scale on the site of the camp's demolished barracks. The participation of Dutch artists in this competition was co-ordinated by Willem Sandberg, Director of the Stedelijk Museum, Amsterdam. As a competitor Visser was invited to visit Auschwitz but felt unable to face the experience. However Sandberg arranged for the Dutch competitors a special showing of Alain Resnais's film about the Nazi extermination camps, *Night and Fog* 1955. The section of this film devoted to Auschwitz provided the direct inspiration for Visser's concept. The commentary explained that while the camp buildings had been allowed to deteriorate since the war, the chimneys, some or all of which had been used for the crematoria, had been retained as a kind of memorial. This was the source of the motif of intermittent vertical members in Visser's design. Visser was specially struck by the single railway track along which the trains entered the camp bearing new victims who unknown to themselves would never leave; and by the legend over the entrance, 'Arbeit macht Frei' (Work Makes You Free), which in the circumstances seemed to him quite intolerably false. This railway track gave the motif of the sculpture's longest, lowest bar, which, starting from the sculpture's outermost point, penetrates its centre. Visser was also very impressed by the film's title. In the years just after they were made he titled the Auschwitz sculptures 'Nacht und Nebel' (the German for 'Night and Fog'), when exhibited. He explained in a letter of 18 December 1980 that this title was 'a kind of . . . understatement because in that time I was a bit scared to use the word Auschwitz. Now I prefer just: Auschwitz'.

Visser found in the experience of making this sculpture a tremendous sense of release from the feelings of guilt he had had since 1945. To work through these feelings was much more important to him than whether he would win a prize or get the commission (neither of which he did). Yet although the sense of release was so strong, he found the negative sensations produced by concentrating on so terrible a subject almost overpowering. These included not only sorrow but also near-despair. For the degree and extent of the aggression at Auschwitz seemed both to indicate a relentless escalation in the level of aggression in the world and to imply the moral and physical end of mankind ('if this thing could happen, anything was possible'.) Auschwitz seemed to him almost to represent an act of suicide by the human race. In his letter of 18 December 1980, Visser explained that the Auschwitz sculptures mark the beginning of a new phase in his work, because they 'are the first with a strong emotion', even though 'to me it is and has been always a problem to put emotion in a sculpture'. At the time he made the Auschwitz sculptures, gestural art in which strong emotion was overt was widespread (e.g. COBRA, Pollock). Visser's work was criticised as being by contrast purely graphic, formal and unemotional. But for him the opposite was really the case. It was precisely because he was experiencing such intense emotions that he found it necessary both to control and to concentrate these by formal means.

Visser's attitude to his Auschwitz structure as it developed was one almost of fear (at what it expressed). The long, low 'railway line' element embodied the sculpture's partial theme of the suicide of mankind in more than one way. Visser had in mind the analogy with a Mexican custom of placing a scorpion inside a circle of petrol which is then set alight round its whole circumference. When the scorpion realises that it has no avenue of escape it commits suicide by stabbing itself. It does this by curving its tail right round so as to implant the sting in itself. At Auschwitz a victim, once inside, could not escape either. Visser expressed this notion of the evil of Auschwitz as a symbolic suicide of mankind by giving his sculpture, as viewed in plan, the form of a continuous line (body) which finally turns back and pierces itself ('final coming back with a deadly weapon'). The theme made Visser feel ill. With this sculpture, alone of all those he has made, he experienced stabbing pains as he worked.

All the versions of Visser's Auschwitz sculpture were made at his studio in Amsterdam. Photographs of one of them with earth and distant cityscape backgrounds were taken by Jan Versnel, in consultation with Visser, to give an impression of how the work would appear if executed full-scale. On the scale Visser intended, the tallest vertical element would have been thirty metres high. Visitors would have been able to ascend the monument (perhaps by spiral staircases) up the wholly enclosed vertical elements. The horizontal elements, though appearing from the ground to be enclosed also, would have been open along their top side, forming walkways with edges low enough for people to be able to see over. The monument would have been in natural-coloured concrete. Although Visser was aware of the international competition in 1953 for a monument to The Unknown Political Prisoner, neither this theme nor any of the designs created for it had any conscious influence on his Auschwitz work.

Visser made at least eight Auschwitz sculptures with the same configuration. The first made (collection Geertjan Visser) measures 40 × 57 × 52 cms., and was exhibited in Visser's 1978 Whitechapel Gallery retrospective as 'Auschwitz I'. Visser then made a copy of this, in the same material; this was the maquette sent to Poland as his submission to the competition. It was later returned to him and destroyed. In ascending order of size, the versions that have been traced are:

- a version approx. 12 cms. in its widest dimension (private collection, Germany). This is the only version with a white patina, which was produced by Visser firing it in wood and applying chalk to the surface
- a version approx. 20 cms. wide (private collection, Amsterdam)
- a version measuring 20 × 28.5 × 26 cms. belonging to the artist's wife
- the original version mentioned above (coll. Geertjan Visser)
- the version of similar dimensions reproduced in J. L. Locher, *Carel Visser*, 1972, plate 34 (coll. C. Kuijlman)
- the Tate's version, which was given the title 'Auschwitz II' only for the 1978 Whitechapel show and tour
- the Stedelijk Museum, Amsterdam's 'Auschwitz' (accession no. ba 535, acquired 1962), iron, 81 × 103 × 113 cms
- the Rijksmuseum Kröller-Müller's 'Grote Auschwitz' 1967, iron, 220 × 300 × 300 cms.

The four smallest versions are in solid steel, while the Tate's and those larger than it are hollow. Visser darkened the surface of the Tate's version at the time it was made, by dipping it into motor oil while hot. The vertical elements in the Tate's version were sawn off at the bottom to prevent wobbling. There survive on this version marks of various joins with additional elements which in the end Visser decided not to retain. This indicates that it is one of the earlier versions made. One of the problems in establishing the Auschwitz image was how far to continue each horizontal and vertical element and at which point to stop adding more. This implicit element of improvisation is echoed by the fact that in some versions the sculpture turns back on itself to the left and in others to the right.

Though set in train by the competition, Visser's Auschwitz sculptures were produced as works in their own right. Their forerunners in his work include destroyed sculptures of 1952–53 in which concrete blocks of various heights rise from a base. In 1956 he started making the 'Notenbalken' (Musical Staves) sculptures, in which the building of a work by steadily adding bars, each set at ninety degrees to the next, is carried upwards into space rather than along the ground. There followed the 'Equilibrium' sculptures of 1958. 'Pen en Gat' (the Dutch term for a mortise and tenon joint in woodwork) is one title of a sculpture of 1958 in which Visser's Auschwitz structure is employed twice, one beside the other like a mirror image (cf. his 'Dubbelvorm' sculptures of 1957–58, and his drawing 'Eiland' (Island) 1957, all repr. J. L. Locher, op. cit., Nos.39 and 45–50). This effect is achieved by welding a 'left-turning' to a 'right-turning' version of 'Auschwitz' (see end of previous paragraph), the welds being at all those points which in normal versions of 'Auschwitz' rest on the ground. However, in 'Pen en Gat' the two 'mirror' versions, welded together, are also turned on their sides so as to rise into the air. The element nearest the ground is a horizontal bar formed out of the two 'mirror-paired' examples of the taller of the two terminal uprights of 'Auschwitz'. This is attached to a metal base plate. 'Abstract Composition' c. 1958 (Museum Boymans van Beuningen, Rotterdam), an iron sculpture which Visser calls 'Romeo and Juliet', brings together the formal language of the 'Notenbalken' with bars as in 'Auschwitz' and the double-image idea – here differently arranged – of 'Pen en Gat'.

Although Visser believes he made no drawings or woodcuts explicitly on the Auschwitz image, an unspecified number of woodcuts of the period – all of them black and white – are very close to it formally.

About three years before making 'Auschwitz', Visser had begun to make sculptures without bases. The abandonment of the base had psychological as well as formal significance for him. It reflected the fact that in a world where things as horrific as Auschwitz could be done by man to man, he could no longer feel certain of the absolutes in which as a child he had been taught to believe. The experience of concentrating on the tragedy of Auschwitz confirmed this move away from solidity and certainty (implied by bases) towards a mode of presentation more reflective of the vulnerability of mankind. Up to that time the question had been whether he should use a base or not. From now onwards he did not do so. (A related effect on Visser's work was produced by the Vietnam war, during which the stability of the sculpture itself was called in question, by the use of non-rigid materials). Ideally the Tate's version of 'Auschwitz' is shown direct on the floor. If a base of any kind is used, this should be a very low platform much wider all round than the work itself.

Drawings by Visser of his Auschwitz image are reproduced in the catalogues of his one-man exhibitions in the Dutch pavilion at the Venice Biennale 1968, the Palais des Beaux-Arts, Brussels, October–November 1972, and the Lucy Milton Gallery, London, May–June 1973. The Tate Gallery Archive owns a collage by Visser made in 1979 by drawing the 'Auschwitz' image on a colour photograph of an amaryllis bloom, then cutting out this image and collaging it onto an identical colour photograph in approximately the same position. A sinister image is thus integrated (almost invisibly) into one of beauty; one of steel, rectilinear, into one which is fragile and organic.

Carel Weight b. 1908

T.2325 **Clapham Junction** 1978

Inscribed 'Carel Weight' b.r.
Oil on canvas, $27\frac{7}{8} \times 35\frac{3}{4}$ (70.8 × 90.8)
Presented by the Trustees of the Chantrey Bequest 1978
Exh: RA, May–September 1978 (471)

In a letter to the compiler (1 October 1979) the artist wrote: 'The picture was painted early in 1978. The setting is the original entrance [to] Clapham Junction railway station (now about to be demolished). I pass it almost every day on the way to my studio and have always been fascinated by the switch-back aspect of the composition which suggested violent movement. The rather eerie architecture supports this feeling. It is a district where violence is a frequent feature and where robbery is commonplace. It is of course also the setting for "Up the Junction".' [Nell Dunn's novel of working-class life in South London].

Asked whether the scene depicted was suggested by, or recorded an actual incident, he replied that the picture was an effort to create a mood rather than a record of a real event.

Weight added in a further letter (4 October 1979) that he tends to develop his pictures using the minimum of sketches or photographic data and relies principally on memory and invention. In the case of T.2325, two or three drawings and a photograph were sufficient to get the work started because he passed the setting frequently and could memorize it clearly. He likened his compositional procedure when relating the figures to the setting to that of solving a mathematical problem where one is given certain information (in this case the setting) and required to find X (the relation of the figures to the landscape), but stressed that this constitutes only one aspect of the problems he encounters when making a painting; he is also concerned with resolving the mood of the picture, psychological issues, conveying an illusion of movement, the function of colour etc. He wrote that his paintings are always about people and that he invents his characters rather as a novelist does; 'Dickens used to say he invented his characters and they ran away with him. I feel this, they assert themselves often making me depart from my plan and taking over. This is one of the exciting elements of picture making.'

T.2325 shows the original high-level entrance to Clapham Junction station, looking east towards Lavender Hill. The central building is the old booking office, closed in 1967. British Rail confirmed (31.10.80) that the site is scheduled for redevelopment but, as yet, no date has been set for the demolition of the existing building. To its right, across the road, can be seen the clock tower of Arding and Hobbs, a large South London department store.

In 'Clapham Junction', where a group of youths are seen being chased by two policemen, Weight heightens the atmosphere of panic and suspense by emphasising oblique angles in the composition, by the lines of force which accentuate the movement of the running figures and by the way the figure in the foreground is truncated so that he appears to be in the process of bursting out of the picture plane. Other works where the artist has employed the same compositional devices, using sombre yet commonplace urban settings as the backdrop for incidents both enigmatic and violent are 'Cops and Robbers' (1956) (see exhibition catalogue, *Carel Weight*, Reading Museum and Art Gallery, September–October 1970) and 'Fury' (1961) (coll. Herbert Art Gallery and Museum, Coventry). This entry has been read and approved by the artist.

Ethelbert White 1891–1972

T.2390 Study for 'Under the Hills' 1923

Not inscribed
Black conté crayon on paper, $7\frac{11}{16} \times 9\frac{7}{8}$ (19.5 × 25.2)
Presented by the heirs of the Ethelbert White Estate 1979

This drawing is almost identical to the Tate's watercolour of the same subject No. 3848, which was painted in September 1923. The drawing does not show as much of the subject at the right hand edge and lacks the figure.